Praise for *Work PAUSE Thrive*

"Ask yourself two questions: Do you want women to make as much impact as they can on society? Do you want men to fully engage as fathers? If your answer is yes to either or both questions, then read this book. And buy a copy for your daughters and your sons."

—Guy Kawasaki, chief evangelist of Canva and former chief evangelist of Apple

"Lisen Stromberg takes the prevailing cultural narrative that anything other than working all out, all the time in our punishing American work culture is a career killer, particularly for women and mothers, and turns it soundly on its head. With illuminating original survey data, the compelling stories of hundreds of women, and research-backed practical advice, *Work PAUSE Thrive* is essential reading for all people, not just women, who want full lives at work and at home, and for the policymakers and business leaders who have the power to make that happen. Stromberg makes a powerful case for why we all stand to benefit as a result."

—Brigid Schulte, award-winning journalist,*New York Times* bestselling author of *Overwhelmed: Work, Love & Play When No One Has the Time*, and director of The Better Life Lab at New America

"A secret treasure map for the next generation that wants children as well as careers. Lisen Stromberg mines jewels of advice from hundreds of working parents who, despite a cultural bias to overwork, insisted on having great family lives as well as great careers. Take heart, somewhere in these pages is a brave example that will work for YOU—as well as a call to arms to change employment policies that will strengthen the American economy by helping all kinds of American families."

—Lisa Stone, start-up advisor and cofounder of BlogHer

"For millions of women looking to pause their careers without sacrificing long-term professional success, *Work PAUSE Thrive* is essential. Combining a powerful personal story, new research, and a journalistic commitment to accuracy, Lisen Stromberg captures the great challenges and offers pragmatic steps forward. She also understands that today's fathers are and must be a critical part of the solution as we all work together to build work–life structures that allow a level playing field."

—Josh Levs, author of All In: How Our Work-First Culture Fails Dads, Families, and Businesses—And How We Can Fix It Together

"*Work PAUSE Thrive* is a landmark. It's the must-read manual for working women who don't want to look back with regret on either career or family choices. Beyond the passionate rallying cry to blow up the male, 'straight up the ladder' career model in favor of a better journey featuring guilt-free pauses, *Work PAUSE Thrive* offers blueprints for how to do it. Filled with insights and ideas built on rock-solid data and inspiring examples from women from a wide spectrum of the working world, this is the book I'm putting on my daughter's shelf—and wish I'd had myself. Stromberg reaches out generously and thoughtfully to empower every woman torn by seemingly impossible choices, and in turn, challenges the newly enlightened reader to pay it forward. Count me in."

—Nancy Vonk, cofounder of Swim and author of *Darling You Can't Do Both (And Other Noise to Ignore on Your Way Up)*

"*Work PAUSE Thrive* represents! It details how inflexible workplace structures, public policy failures, and cultural stigmas against parents in the workplace hold women AND men back from living lives of authenticity and meaning. This is a must read!"

—Jennifer Siebel Newsom, founder and CEO of The Representation Project

"Forget climbing some corporate ladder, you want a career with twists and turns and adventure, but how? In *Work PAUSE Thrive*, author Lisen Stromberg shows how trailblazing women have crafted a big life on their terms and how you can too."

—Ann Shoket, author of *The Big Life* and former editor-in-chief of *Seventeen*

"Our lives are not straight lines, so not surprisingly neither are our careers. Yet when they inevitably take an unexpected turn we worry that we have fallen off the career track. Lisen Stromberg, in *Work PAUSE Thrive*, is here to tell you that there is no 'track,' there is just the path you and your family create for your own fulfilling lives."

—Lisa Heffernan, *New York Times* bestselling author of
Goldman Sachs and the Culture of Success
and cofounder of the "Grown and Flown" blog

"*Work Pause Thrive: How to Pause for Parenthood Without Killing Your Career* doesn't just offer tactical solutions for integrating kids with careers, it also is a call to action so individual companies and our country as a whole will finally focus on providing meaningful solutions for all parents."

—Joan Blades, cofounder of MoveOn.org and MomsRising.Org

"Former advertising exec and veteran journalist Lisen Stromberg offers stats, anecdotes, and advice in her deep analysis on how to navigate the career journey that includes a 'pause.' Learn from her wise and thoughtful approach to managing the nontraditional career path."

—Carol Fishman Cohen, CEO of iRelaunch

"Lisen Stromberg explodes the false dichotomy faced by generations of career-minded women—either be an engaged mother or stay on track in a career. *Work PAUSE Thrive* delivers a fresh alternative that millennial women (and men) are craving in their quest to thrive as parents with careers; for many women, the zig-zagging career path is the perfect fit! This is a must-read for women in every profession, for the partners and mentors who care about them, and for any leader serious about talent management!"

—W. Brad Johnson, PhD and David Smith, PhD, authors of
Athena Rising: How and Why Men Should Mentor Women

"A refreshing new take on the work–life conversation! *Work PAUSE Thrive* 'disrupts' the all-in model of career success and maps innovative paths to professional and personal fulfillment. A must-read for next generation employees and the companies that hire them!"

—Samantha Walravens, editor of *TORN: True Stories of Kids,*
Career & the Conflict of Modern Motherhood and coauthor of
Geek Girl Rising: Inside the Sisterhood Shaking Up Tech

"Lisen Stromberg isn't just an author—she's a whistleblower. The alarm she's sounding is music to my ears: that the obstacle course of working motherhood is doable. With stats and stories, Stromberg reveals an alternate path for working parents . . . all while urging society to step up to better meet the needs of American families."

—Kat Gordon, CEO and founder of The 3% Movement

WORK
PAUSE
THRIVE

WORK

PAUSE

THRIVE

How to Pause for Parenthood
Without Killing Your Career

LISEN STROMBERG

BenBella Books, Inc.
Dallas, TX

BenBella Books, Inc.
10440 N. Central Expressway
Suite 800
Dallas, TX 75231
www.benbellabooks.com
Send feedback to feedback@benbellabooks.com

Printed in the United States of America
10 9 8 7 6 5 4 3 2 1

Library of Congress Cataloging-in-Publication Data
Names: Stromberg, Lisen, author.
Title: Work pause thrive : how to pause for parenthood without killing your career / Lisen Stromberg.
Description: Dallas, TX : BenBella Books, Inc., [2017] | Includes bibliographical references and index.
Identifiers: LCCN 2016034628 (print) | LCCN 2016047697 (ebook) | ISBN 9781942952732 (trade cloth : alk. paper) | ISBN 9781942952749 (electronic)
Subjects: LCSH: Working mothers. | Work and family. | Work-life balance. | Career development. | Women—Vocational guidance.
Classification: LCC HQ759.48 .S776 2017 (print) | LCC HQ759.48 (ebook) | DDC 306.3/6—dc23
LC record available at https://lccn.loc.gov/2016034628

Editing by Leah Wilson
Copyediting by Elizabeth Degenhard
Proofreading by Greg Teague and Kristin Vorce Duran
Indexing by Amy Murphy Indexing & Editorial
Text design and composition by Aaron Edmiston
Cover by Allison Gellner and Sarah Dombrowsky
Printed by Lake Book Manufacturing

Distributed by Perseus Distribution
www.perseusdistribution.com
To place orders through Perseus Distribution:
Tel: (800) 343-4499
Fax: (800) 351-5073
E-mail: orderentry@perseusbooks.com

To my mother, father, sister, and brother,
for believing in me.

To Nora,
for bearing witness.

To William, Maret, and Soren,
for lighting the way by choosing me to be your mother.

To Bill,
for staying the course,
always.

And to mothers and fathers everywhere.
May you, too, have the support you need to nurture the next generation.

CONTENTS

INTRODUCTION

The Best-Laid Plans

Picture this: I'm thirty thousand feet in the air, flying from San Francisco to Chicago. I've just been promoted to vice president at Foote, Cone & Belding, one the largest advertising agencies in the country, and I'm off to an important meeting with a new client. I'm nervous as hell. I'm also thirty-three years old and twenty-four weeks pregnant with my second child.

The plane is rollicking through choppy air. Passengers grip the arm rests. I see, perhaps only imagine, small beads of sweat break out on the upper lip of the man who sits next to me. He told me he hates to fly. I've told him I used to hate to fly too, but then my two-year-old taught me to love it.

My son, William, loves to fly. Whenever we travel and the plane hits turbulence, he bursts out laughing and squeals, "Better than a merry-round!" The other passengers will laugh along with him, at least until the plane takes another big dip. William doesn't know he's supposed to be afraid. He doesn't understand the risks; he just revels in the moment. His infectious enthusiasm has taught me to try to enjoy the ride, as unsettling as it might seem.

And I am trying—to enjoy it, that is. But this shuddering sardine can is challenging my resolve. Suddenly I feel a familiar tightening across my belly. Then another. And another.

It doesn't take long for me to realize these aren't the mild, normal Braxton Hicks contractions that are part of nearly every woman's pregnancy. No, this is the real deal. I'm in pre-term labor.

If I was scared before, I'm terrified now. And I have reason to be. I've been down this path and, let me tell you, bumpy plane rides have nothing on premature birth.

I was five months pregnant with William when I woke one morning in a pool of blood. Convinced I was having a miscarriage, my husband, Bill, and I raced to the emergency room. After much testing and analysis, we learned I wasn't miscarrying. Turns out, I have a uterine anomaly that puts my pregnancies at risk for early delivery.

"I advise rest and a reduction of stress," my doctor said.

Rest? Reduction of stress? I didn't have time to rest and, frankly, I didn't want to. Why would I? My career was on fire!

I'd worked almost non-stop since I was fourteen years old, when I talked my way into a job scooping ice cream at the local parlor in my hometown of Mill Valley, California. After that, I worked at a jewelry store piercing the ears of girls, women, and the occasional man. I managed a clothing store my senior year in high school and then waitressed throughout most of college. Put simply, from an early age work defined me.

In college, I majored in government, thinking I might become a lawyer like my father, but I soon discovered an interest in marketing and went to business school instead. After getting my MBA, I landed a coveted job on the brand management track at the Nestlé Corporation. Back in the day, if you wanted a career in marketing, this was about as prestigious as it could get. My future glittered, and, as far as I was concerned, nothing was going to get in the way of my rise to the top.

When I was coming of age in the 1980s, opportunities for women seemed wide open. The pill, which was introduced in 1960 and became ubiquitous in the 1970s, provided women with the first reliable and relatively affordable birth control. That meant my generation was the first to grow up knowing we would be able to choose when to have children, or if we were going to have them at all. Then, major legislation between 1970 and 1978 changed what it meant to be a woman in our society. For the first time, we were assured equality in the classroom and on the sports field (Title IX), access to family planning (Title X), the ability to get our own credit without our husband's approval (the Equal Credit Opportunity

Act), and the security to know if we did get pregnant, we couldn't be fired (the Pregnancy Discrimination Act). Add to that the legalization of birth control (1972) and the landmark *Roe v. Wade* case allowing abortions for unwanted pregnancies (1973), and you can well see why my generation of women thought we could do anything.

As at most colleges across the country in the mid-1980s, my graduating class was the first to have gender parity: 50 percent women and 50 percent men. With degrees in hand, we women stormed the corporate world, law offices, academia, and so much more. The glass ceiling was above us, but we believed we would be the ones to shatter it. Certainly our mothers told us we would. Nothing would stop us.

And then we had babies.

Unexpectedly, women like me began leaving the workforce in droves. We became the proverbial "canaries in the coal mine"[1] of workplaces that hindered our abilities to be both the professionals we had worked so hard to become and the mothers we wanted to be. Our decision to seemingly abandon our careers confounded employers and the women before us who had fought so hard to give us the equality they were denied.

The truth is, our choices confounded even ourselves. Dani Klein Modisett, a close friend from college, had always been single-minded in her ambition. An actress, she landed a few Broadway tours and a handful of TV jobs, but she found her calling as a stand-up comic. Eventually she married, and although being a mother wasn't at the top of her list, Dani told me she was concerned she "might die and regret not having been one." And then she became pregnant.

Dani was thirty-nine weeks along when she got a call about hosting a talk show—a professional dream come true. But when the female executive saw how pregnant Dani was, she pushed her resume back across the desk and said, "I think you're going to want time with your new baby." Dani was offended, but one week later when she was holding her newborn son, she realized, "That woman was right." So Dani paused, but not for long. She went on to become an author and host of a hilarious stage show called Afterbirth. But Dani didn't know this was ahead of her when she held her baby for the first time. She just knew that, at that moment, nothing was more important.

I understand what she means now, but I didn't then. I knew many women who wanted a child more than anything, women who cherished their pregnancies, who couldn't wait to be a mother. But that wasn't me. I wasn't sure I wanted to have children and, if I did, I couldn't imagine how I was going to be a mother and have the career I had worked so hard to build.

Plus, wasn't being a mother a hindrance to women's achievements? Certainly that was what I had read in my college women's studies classes, what I had heard from the media, and what I saw from successful women themselves. The vast majority of female leaders I knew didn't have children or, if they did, seemed to rarely spend time with them.

It was also what my mother taught me, not directly but in oh-so-many other ways. She was born and raised in Norway, the daughter of a successful canning entrepreneur. She married my American father when she was nineteen, had me at twenty, and had my brother, Chet, two years later. At thirty, when my brother and I were both busy with school, our mother could have gone on to get her college degree and find a career she loved. Instead, she got pregnant with my sister, Kirsten.

She told me years later she decided her destiny was to follow in her own mother's footsteps and be the devoted wife of a successful man. That may have been her path, but my mother was determined nothing would hold back her daughters. Though she stayed home to care for us, our mother made damn sure we had every opportunity to lead independent, productive lives. My sister and I knew it was up to us to get the college degrees and have the careers our mother was denied. Being mothers ourselves? We never discussed it.

The lessons I learned from my own family and the world around me was that mothering was inconvenient at best, an unrelenting burden at worst. Joy and deep meaning weren't part of the experience. If I was going to have children at all, they were going to have to fit into my carefully laid career plans. So when I became pregnant with William, I expected to have a fast, easy pregnancy, take the requisite six weeks of maternity leave, and rush back to work to continue my determined climb up the corporate ladder.

After that first miscarriage scare, I decided "rest and a reduction of stress" meant pulling back to fifty hours from the sixty I'd been putting in. Sure, I had an hour commute from our home in Menlo Park to the company's offices in San Francisco, but at least I was sitting. The bumper-to-bumper traffic couldn't be too stressful, could it?

When I was thirty-two weeks pregnant with our son, my water broke and I went into preterm labor. That trusty pregnancy bible, *What to Expect*

When You're Expecting, told me my baby was almost four pounds, the size of a jicama, and about nineteen inches long. His digestive tract was developed and his skin was becoming opaque, hiding the veins and arteries beneath. He had nails and some peach fuzz that would eventually be his hair. Most babies born at this phase survive, although their quality of life is in question. William could be born blind and intellectually challenged. He would likely suffer learning differences and be required to enroll in special needs classes. What lay ahead threatened to be more challenging than anything I had ever experienced, certainly more challenging than all the work I had put in to building my career.

Somehow the doctors proved themselves to be miracle workers and managed to stop the labor. With no amniotic fluid to protect my yet-to-be-born baby, I was forced to lie on my back in the hospital, tethered to an IV, praying I would stay pregnant for as long as possible. William wasn't due for eight weeks, but because the amniotic sac had been ruptured, I was at major risk for infection. If that happened, the doctors would be forced to induce labor. So the waiting game began.

Bill spent his days working and his nights at my bedside. My mother and friends came to give him a break, even though he hated to leave. It was a grueling schedule for my husband and a tedious one for me, but we would have happily continued our vigil. However, it wasn't meant to be. Two weeks later infection set in and the doctors were forced to bring our premature son into the world.

William was born squinty-eyed and big-nosed, looking like Mr. Magoo, one of those old cartoon characters my brother, Chet, and I used to watch together on Saturday mornings when we were kids. He weighed 5 pounds, 5 ounces, huge for a baby with a gestational period of only thirty-four weeks. In the delivery room, as the neonatal specialists checked and prodded our disturbingly quiet son, the doctor tried to relieve the tension by joking, "Well, he may be funny-looking now, but a preemie baby that size is sure to be a future football player like his dad." We tried to laugh, but we were too scared.

Then William found his voice and began to cry—not loudly, but enough to give him Apgar scores (the measure of how healthy a baby is upon birth) that gave us hope. Before I was able to cuddle or nurse him, the specialists raced our newborn son off to the ICU to ensure he had everything he needed to make it through those first few critical days. I thank God that he did.

For the next few weeks, I spent every waking hour by William's side, talking to him, singing to him, and finally holding him when the doctors said he was strong enough. Because he was too premature to have developed the proper muscles to suckle, they taught me to feed him my pumped breast milk through a tube down his throat. I tried to make William comfortable and to keep him calm, but it was hard. The ICU beeped and squawked with various machines that monitored my son and the other highly vulnerable premature babies. Each day was a lesson in life and death as some of those little souls survived and some of them didn't.

Eventually, William came home. He may have been premature, but darn if that kid wasn't a fighter. I spent four months with him, the longest maternity leave Nestlé had given someone at my level. Within the first two months, it was clear my preemie baby was going to be fine. By the third month, he'd nearly caught up to his peers. When it was time to go back to work, I returned confident that William would not only survive, but thrive.

Crisis averted. Hello ladder, here I come!

Now, here I am, two years later, on a plane far from home. I've changed jobs and been promoted, eager to prove myself. I missed William's first word, his first step, the first time he heard *Goodnight Moon*. But it's been worth it, hasn't it?

The contractions are coming six minutes, five minutes, four minutes apart. I'm doing everything I can to keep from panicking. Breathe in. Breathe out. In. Out. I drink water. And I pray.

"Please God," I whisper into the void, "I will do anything you ask. I'll slow down and stop this crazy work schedule. I promise my family will come first. Just give me one thing. Well, one more thing. Please give me one more healthy baby."

Four agonizing months later, the vast majority of which I spent lying flat on my back in bed, our daughter, Maret, arrived. She was everything I prayed for, pink-cheeked and bawling. As I held her safe and healthy in my arms, I knew I would never ever be the same.

During the months between that fateful plane ride and her birth, something in me changed. I had tried to keep working from my bed, but the pressure from client calls and work crises sent me racing to the emergency room with stress-induced contractions. Meanwhile, I found unexpected pleasure teaching William new words (knife, elephant, Rapunzel), memorizing the names of his favorite construction equipment (digger, excavator, bulldozer, backhoe), and watching yet another episode of *Thomas the Tank Engine* together from my bed. He begged me to take him to the park, but I couldn't get up, the risks were too great, so we imagined what we would do when I could.

After sixteen weeks of bed rest, my career, the very thing that had defined me, simply was not what defined me anymore. Yes, I had skills and abilities I wanted to put to good use in the world, but right here, right now, this new baby, her older brother, and my husband mattered more than my job.

Don't misunderstand me—we needed my paycheck. Beyond the unexpected medical bills, we still owed tens of thousands of dollars in student debt, had a hefty mortgage on our new home, and were desperate for a second car. We both had long commutes (of course, in opposite directions), but Bill generously patched together carpools and took public transportation while I drove our old, beat-up Honda Civic to work each day. It wasn't fair to him and it was hard on me when he arrived home late and exhausted every night.

"Just think," I said when I broached the subject of quitting my job, "your commute will get so much easier because I won't need the car every day."

Bill laughed at the thought, but not heartily. He'd told me one of the things he found appealing about me was my commitment to my career. "I knew we'd always be partners, sharing equal weight at work and in the home," he'd said. And we had, until now.

I promised him I'd find some way to cover my share of our bills, but going back to a job that required me to commute an hour each way, to work well past our children's bedtime, to travel frequently, and to forgo weekends at the whim of my clients simply wasn't something I was willing to do. At least not for the time being. Bill, who had always supported me, reluctantly agreed. Then I called my boss and told her I was quitting.

"Are you sure?" she asked. "It'll be hard to get back on track if you leave."

I knew she was probably right. The messaging in the media and the stories from older, more experienced professional women said leaving the workforce was career suicide. I wanted to keep my job, but there was no option for part-time work and telecommuting didn't exist at the time.

Plus, our advertising clients needed me when they needed me, not when I was available. What I needed was to pull back. Not forever, but for now.

And so, I did something I never imagined I would do: I paused.

Fifteen years later I'm at the Journalism and Women Symposium's annual conference. Female journalists from around the country are gathering to gain skills, network, and learn about the latest exciting, and sometimes concerning, changes in our industry. I'm pinching myself. Thrilled to be here amongst so many heroes in my new field.

After I left my big job at the advertising agency, I changed careers—twice. First, I became a social entrepreneur and launched a nonprofit focused on meeting the needs of boys in the classroom. Now, I'm an independent journalist reporting on women in the workplace, life in Silicon Valley, and the ongoing challenges facing American families. For the Journalism and Women Symposium, I have been asked to co-develop a panel on women, caregiving, and careers in journalism. I have much to say on the topic of work and life and that elusive thing called balance. So do the panelists, each of whom is highly successful with careers to envy.

Our moderator, Lauren Whaley, a rising multimedia journalist and new bride at thirty-one years old, wants answers. She tells me she's excited to moderate the panel if for no other reason than to learn from those who've gone before her.

In front of a standing-room-only crowd, Lauren asks the panelists, "How can women be both committed professionals and committed mothers?"

"They can't," one panelist, a divorced mother of two, answers.

"Very difficultly" answers another, also a mother of two. She's doing research for a book on how our over-scheduled lives are impacting our health and well-being.

"I didn't even try," says a third. This panelist shared how she had chosen to not have children at all because she knew she couldn't be the kind of mother she wanted to be *and* have a successful career.

"I am so depressed," Lauren tells me later. "I want children and I want a career. I love my work, but hearing what we did today tells me you can't do both. At least not well. I thought these issues were on their way to being solved, but it seems it's not any better now than it was for the previous generation."

As Lauren and I talked, I wondered, is it true? Could it be that all these years have passed and nothing has changed for mothers in the workplace? Given what we'd heard from the panelists, it certainly seemed so. In that moment, Lauren may have been depressed, but I was furious. Is this what my daughter, soon entering college, would be facing as she embarked on adulthood? How could this be? What happened? Or more importantly, what hadn't?

We had initiated the panel because the topic of women's careers, the lack of women in leadership, and the issue we all face around work–life balance had become part of the collective consciousness, again. First, Anne-Marie Slaughter, a Princeton professor of politics and CEO of the New America Foundation, wrote an essay for *The Atlantic* magazine entitled "Why Women Still Can't Have It All." She addressed the challenges she experienced trying to integrate work with her family and, in doing so, put to words what so many women had been feeling.

And then Sheryl Sandberg, chief operating officer of Facebook, published her seminal book, *Lean In: Women, Work, and the Will to Lead.* In it, she urged young women to forget the naysayers and commit to their careers. Her goal was to increase the number of women in leadership, but little mention was given to the challenges women face in the workplace once they become mothers.

Together these two women unleashed a hurricane of controversy, discussion, and debate about women, their careers, and the lack of female leadership across our country. "Yes it's hard, but don't give up!" was the underlying message to ambitious young women. Answers for how to actually navigate the slippery slope of work and mothering weren't part of the conversation.

Meanwhile, women *and* men continue to try to understand how it is that so little has been gained in the last twenty years in terms of advancing women in the workplace. My generation was supposed to be the one that broke down that seemingly impenetrable glass ceiling. But in the decades since I had graduated from college, very few of us have broken on through. The subtext? We failed.

Sandberg's book, in particular, hit hard at the hearts of many women who had downshifted their careers to focus on claimed. Already vulnerable to the accusations of having "opted out," they felt her book was an indictment of their choices—choices that many claimed were not choices at all. Journalist, author, and former lawyer Joanne Bamberger said it best when she wrote, "I leaned in so hard I fell on my face."

When Anne-Marie Slaughter, who had leaned in to her professional life to seemingly great success, admitted even she couldn't "have it all," women across America began to ask, "Why bother?" It appeared that no matter our path, we were destined to fail.

Standing with Lauren in the conference hall after our panel, it was hard not to be angry and discouraged. Then she turned to me and said, "Looks like you made it work. How'd you do it?"

Me? Made it work? Ha! I wanted to laugh and then to cry. I realized that to Lauren, my career—my life overall—looked like one long series of successes, but hidden below my seemingly impressive LinkedIn profile were hard realities.

How could I explain the circuitous path that had me fumbling and failing and pivoting and launching and relaunching and, eventually, accomplishing much—just not any of the things that were part of my original plan? I'd given up the corner office, the big paycheck, the prestige that comes from the fancy title. Instead, I'd spent days trying to string together consulting jobs, nights writing freelance articles that barely covered our monthly food bill. My office was filled with books, not people. If I was lonely, I had to commute to my other office, the local Starbucks. But I got to write on issues that mattered to me, I got to consult on projects with fascinating people who inspired me, and I got to pick my children up from school nearly every day.

Oh no, I hadn't made it work, at least not by the standards I was told defined success. And yet, despite a lack of role models and systemic support, despite messaging that said my choices reflected some sort of failure, I did manage to carve out a professional and personal life that allowed me to achieve my own, altered definition of success. Somehow I had found a way that worked for me and my family. A way that allowed me to place as much value on my role as a mother as it did on my role as a career woman.

And I knew I wasn't alone. Many of the women in my extended network and many of the women I interviewed for my work as a freelance journalist had pulled back from their professional lives and, eventually, managed to power forward to great success. Like me, they too had careers that, though not always part of their original plans, enabled them to thrive. How did they do it? Were they the exception? Was I?

I wanted to find answers—for myself, for the men and women of Lauren's generation, and for my own two sons and daughter. I started by reading every book on the subject I could find. I spoke to CEOs, heads of human resources, sociologists, economists, and experts on social policy and the law. And I interviewed women themselves, nearly 200 in all, to understand their choices, their satisfactions, and their regrets.

I looked for quantitative data and was astounded to discover little contemporary research has been done on women's non-linear career trajectories, particularly those of women who have paused their careers and re-entered the workforce. So I launched the *Women on the Rise* survey and nearly 1,500 women across the country shared their experiences as they tried—and continue to try—to "balance" family and work.

This book is what I learned.

Work PAUSE Thrive is what I wish I had when I was embarking on my journey as a woman, a professional, and a mother. It is not a panacea but rather an alternative view for how to manage the challenges we face as mothers (and fathers) in a culture that doesn't value that which is most important to us: our families.

The book is divided into three sections. Part I provides readers with insight into what some women have done to create, as one *Women on the Rise* survey respondent wrote, "lives well lived rather than lived in lives." It tells the hidden stories of successful women who disrupted the traditional paradigm of being all-in, all-of-the-time, by creating non-linear careers that enabled them to achieve their professional and personal goals. It reveals the three paths of career innovation that allowed them to pull back for a period of time to put their family first and then empowered them to recommit to their professional goals. These trailblazers are models that prove pausing does not have to be career limiting.

Part II offers insight into how and why it remains deeply challenging to integrate kids and careers. It looks at the failed public policies that divide us, reinforcing and fomenting class dynamics that ensure some of us get more than others and leave many far behind. It argues that overcoming caregiver bias is the last frontier of true workplace inclusion and is at the heart of so much that is ailing American families. It addresses the significant shifts in attitudes by men who want a richer, more engaging personal life. Finally, it considers workforce dynamics that are opening up new ways to be a significant contributor without sacrificing one's passions and ability to meet one's personal commitments.

In Part III, the book offers strategies and tactics to help readers develop their own personal plans for integrating caregiving with careers. The goal? Enabling them to lean in not just to their careers, but to the full bloom of their lives. It challenges readers to consider the risks and consequences of a career break and then offers them solutions if they feel that break is a family necessity. The book concludes with targeted solutions for individuals, companies, and our country as a whole.

Work PAUSE Thrive is not an anthem for the "opt out" movement. To be clear, my agenda is not to convince women to leave the workforce. On the contrary, I wish women didn't have to put their careers on the back burner so they could give their families the care needed. But the reality is we have a culture that does not place caregiving as a priority and so women remain forced to find alternative solutions. Until we see real changes in our public policies and workplace cultures that support families, women *and* men will need solutions. This book offers some.

Also, it must be stated that the advice in this book is not for all women, or men, for that matter. It doesn't try to solve the seemingly intractable problem of mothers in poverty or mothers barely holding on to the middle class or men who want to be more than just the "ideal worker." Not because they don't deserve to be supported or empowered to find solutions to their work–life issues, but because I can't speak for their journeys. I can only speak for mine.

Not long ago, my daughter asked me how I had planned my career so that I could be the mother I am. I told her I hadn't. I told her I have spent much of my time on the defense, zigging and zagging in response to the things life put in my way. I told her I had regrets and ongoing self-doubt that still nags me to this day. I told her of the financial challenges and the compromises and the "woulda, coulda, shouldas" that are the reality of having pulled back and paused my career. And then I told her what the women I interviewed told me: I don't regret a thing.

The deeper truth is that I had limited options. With one premature baby and a second who required I spend months on bed rest, my family had to come first—not forever, but for a while. When I became a new mother, there was no clear path for those of us who wanted to be deeply engaged with our families and still have rewarding careers. The workplace was unforgiving and unyielding to women like me. Sadly, I've learned my experience is still the norm.

But my path is not my daughter's path. She, like her brothers, will have to find a way to navigate the world in which they live. I want them to be better prepared than I was to face the realities of trying to have a career and a family. I want them to be empowered by self-knowledge, as well as by clarity about the cultural zeitgeist and institutional structures that impact their opportunities and choices.

I don't want her (or her brothers, for that matter) to face the same unrelenting challenges I did. At the heart of it, I want the workplace to be more supportive of families. I want national policies that support caregiving. I want the deep meaning and reward that comes with being a parent to be honored and valued. But sadly, society won't change fast enough for my children or for any of the other tens of millions of Millennials who will become parents in the next decade or so.

At the end of the first chapter of her book *Lean In*, Sheryl Sandberg asks, "What would you do if you weren't afraid?"

Here's my answer: If I weren't afraid, I would have believed in myself enough to know I could integrate a pause for my family into the arc of my career trajectory. I would have understood that women like me are disrupting the outmoded models of what a successful career looks like. I would recognize my actions were not a sign of failure but a sign of innovation and reflected a willingness to take risk that many didn't have the courage to do. I would refuse to believe men aren't as passionate about their families and would support them to be publicly and actively engaged fathers, husbands, and sons. I would fight the work-first culture boldly and directly by revealing caregiver bias at its root. And, I would work to change our national policies so that mothers and fathers have the basic support they need to not only survive, but thrive.

I can't go back and tell myself to not worry, to let go of self-doubt, to have confidence that I was on the right path and that it would all work out, not as planned, but in a way that would meet my needs and the needs of my family.

But I can tell you.

I can share with you the stories of trailblazing women who disrupted the conventional career narrative that tells us there is only one way to achieve success. I can show you how they pulled back, paused, pivoted, and prospered. I can highlight the hidden truths that keep women from following their heartfelt desires and keep men from participating fully in the home. I can introduce you to companies and organizations that are trying to get it right and reveal new and exciting trends in the workplace that mean things just might be different for my daughter and sons.

When Lauren, and then later my daughter, asked me how I managed to integrate kids with my career, I wasn't sure what to tell them. I wanted answers. I think I found some.

Work PAUSE Thrive is a journey of discovery, a blueprint for the next generation, and a call for change so that women *and* men will be able to engage in work they love while living the life they choose.

Part I

TRAILBLAZERS IN ACTION

CHAPTER 1

Disrupting the Paradigm

Successful Women Pause

"The path to success is never quite what you imagine it to be."
—*Women on the Rise* survey respondent

Bowls of pasta, platters of chicken, and salads of all sorts were laid out atop the long dining table at my friend Sue's house. Wine glasses were filled high and emptied quickly. Around the table women shared stories about their children's senior proms, upcoming high school graduation activities, and plans for the future. We were having a reunion of the New Mothers Support Group and we twelve proud women had much to celebrate.

Tibi's daughter was going to Georgetown to study engineering; Lisa's son was headed to University of Colorado. Grace's daughter would be attending college in Texas. My daughter was heading across the country to attend her dream school, Wesleyan University. Just the thought of her leaving could bring me to tears, so I tried not to think about it. Tonight it was hard not to.

These women, these other not-so-new mothers and I, had been gathering since the spring of 1996 when we had all given birth at Stanford Hospital. We originally met at the New Mother Training Class recommended to us by our doctors. Once a week, we sat in a circle sharing our concerns as a nurse educator led the discussion. It was like those consciousness-raising sessions from the 1960s, but unlike our mothers who had gathered to secure their place in the professional world, we gathered to figure out how to be mothers in spite of it.

We were a part of the sandwich generation that came of age after Betty Friedan, author of *The Feminine Mystique*, gave voice to the frustrations of millions of women by identifying "the problem that has no name," and well before Sheryl Sandberg told us to "lean in." Most of us had graduate degrees and we all had careers we'd worked damn hard to succeed in. Now we had children.

That wouldn't be a problem, would it?

Exhausted and confused, we huddled together during our New Mother class, looking for some measure of control. At the very least, we could get answers to the issues at hand: "How do I establish a regular feeding schedule?" "What do I do about diaper rash?" And, the most pressing: "How do I get my baby to sleep?"

In the weeks that followed, we slowly developed confidence in our new roles. We shared tips on burping techniques, recommended breastfeeding routines, and marveled at first smiles. We celebrated when one of us managed to get a full night's sleep and commiserated when colic had another of us up every two hours. After we graduated from the eight-week New Mother class, we decided to keep meeting. On Monday nights, we gathered, drank wine, and talked about our babies. One by one, as our maternity leaves ended, we went back to work.

After a brief leave, Grace Zales returned full-time to her litigation consulting job. Chrissie Kremer decided to pursue her dream of becoming an entrepreneur and managed to secure $2 million in venture funding for her Internet company. Monica Johnson, who had been promoted to chief financial officer at her start-up while she was on maternity leave, came to our Monday gatherings breathless from some new office excitements. After a distressingly brief two-week maternity leave, Lisa Stone raced back to her job as a TV producer for CNN.

Others of us took a more leisurely path back to the paid work world. Tibi McCann enjoyed six months of maternity leave from her job heading a quality assurance team at a tech company before she went back to work full-time. Patricia Nakache managed to negotiate a part-time schedule at her prestigious consulting firm. Inspired by Patricia, cancer researcher

Lisa McPherson arranged to work a reduced schedule at her Stanford laboratory. Laurie Gadre decided to stay home with her daughter, as did Ruth-Anne Siegel, Nancy Rosenthal, and, eventually, our dinner hostess, Sue Tachna. Each of us made a personal choice that was right for her and, collectively, we supported those choices.

In the years that followed, I watched as my friends developed their own personal work–life solution. Some remained out of the paid workforce continuing to focus on their families and contributing to their communities through active volunteerism, but the majority of us returned to paid work struggling to find some measure of balance, as if there is such a thing.

It wasn't easy, and yet, we thrived: Now, eighteen years later, our group includes one of the few female venture capitalists in Silicon Valley, the CEO of a digital media company, a division head who leads a team of computer programmers, and a repeat CFO who has helped build a number of groundbreaking Silicon Valley start-ups. We have a scientist, an elementary school math teacher, a corporate litigation consultant, and an award-winning journalist (yep, that would be me).

Oh yes, we leaned in, but on our terms.

The LinkedIn profiles of most of the Not-So-New Mothers Group look like a direct trajectory to the top of our professions, but buried deep within our résumés are twists and turns, pull backs and pauses. You wouldn't know that Patricia worked part-time for four years, first at McKinsey & Company, then at Trinity Ventures, one of Silicon Valley's leading venture capital firms. Or that a few years before Lisa co-founded the hugely successful media company BlogHer, she left her television producer job and took a nine-month career pause to focus on the needs of her young son while she figured out her next professional move. Tibi, who runs the computer programming department for the city of Santa Cruz, has worked a condensed four-day work schedule for years. Earlier in her career, she worked part-time and, at one point, took a full stop for nearly seven months. And yet she has, to all outward appearances, always been a "working" mom.

I've had two brief pauses, each of which inspired career pivots. After I left my job as a vice president at Foote, Cone & Belding, I became a "single shingle" marketing and strategy consultant to keep money coming and help plan my next move. Eventually, I became a social entrepreneur, co-founding a nonprofit called Supporting Our Sons in partnership with Dr. William Pollack, a clinical psychologist, associate professor at Harvard Medical School, and author of *Real Boys: Rescuing Our Sons from the Myths of Boyhood.* I ran that organization for five years. When our funding sources dried up, I paused and then pivoted again.

I loved writing. In fact, my dream job had always been to be a writer. It became clear that pursuing that dream was a now-or-never proposition, so I returned to school to get my master's of fine arts with a concentration in prose. Since then, I've become an independent journalist covering issues facing women, families, the workplace, the tech industry, and life in Silicon Valley. My work has appeared in such influential media outlets as *The New York Times*, *Fortune*, *Newsweek*, *Salon*, and others.

Over the years, young women have reached out to me for career advice. They start by asking the usual questions about mentors or pay negotiation or working with challenging bosses, and then the conversation shifts. What they really want is insight on how to integrate work and home. I realized what's needed isn't more career advice, but life advice. The young, driven women I have spoken to had clarity about their professional goals; they just couldn't square their ambition with their deep desire to be mothers.

The sad truth is Millennial women are facing the same dilemmas, same work-first culture, same unyielding demands that I, and other college-educated, professional women of my generation, faced. Despite all of our well-intentioned women's initiatives and leadership training programs, nothing has changed for mothers in the workplace.

And yet, looking back now, I see that my friends and I somehow managed to weave our careers in with our families and our families in with our careers. While that weaving didn't happen at the same time, over the course of decades we found, not balance per se, but integration. It wasn't easy, it wasn't obvious, and our paths went against what we were told to do, but we did it anyway. We pulled back, we paused, and we managed to have careers that by most accounts would be considered successful.

Were we the exception?

I began interviewing professional women about their work–life strategies. I started with women whose careers looked from the outside as if they were role models for the "lean in" movement. Like many of us in the Not-So-New Mothers Group, most of the women I interviewed had paused, although few identified those pull backs in their careers as actual "pauses." One senior vice president of a highly successful Silicon Valley start-up emphatically told me she had never paused. "I'm a working mom!" she insisted. When I pointed out that the year she took a career break to move to Hawaii with her then-husband and their two young sons looked a lot like a pause to me, she said, "I never thought of it that way and yet, you're right. I did pause when my sons were babies. And then, I re-entered and never looked back!"

I also spoke to women who had taken significant career breaks. Their experiences resembled the more traditional "opt-out" model, but unlike the stories we keep hearing in the news about "opting out" as a form of career suicide, they too had eventually re-entered, and never looked back. In all, I interviewed 186 women, and a handful of men, who had worked, paused, and thrived. I also conducted an extensive survey that resulted in 1,476 women sharing their career journeys (see the appendix for details on the compelling results of our *Women on the Rise* survey).

The message I heard again and again is that, despite the narrative that pausing would kill their professional aspirations, the women I spoke to have privately and quietly found work–life solutions that have allowed them to have successful careers *and* fulfilling family lives. That wasn't the national narrative about how careers are built when I was a new mother, and it isn't the narrative today. The message then as now is that women who aren't all-in, all-of-the-time, won't amount to much. But many women who have enviable careers have paused.

It's just that, well, we don't talk about it. As one woman said to me, "Why draw attention to something that is only likely to hurt you professionally?"

There's a reason career pauses are buried in the résumés of successful women. They aren't necessarily trying to be deceitful; in most cases, they aren't trying to hide their choices. They are simply responding to the constraints imposed by the world in which they live.

The message then as now is that women who aren't all-in, all-of-the-time, won't amount to much. But many women who have enviable careers have paused.

In a society that values paid work and devalues the power and importance of caregiving, ambitious women are forced to suppress their commitments to their families. They gloss over their stints at home and reduced work schedules and they don't list their PTA participation or anything that screams "mommy" because they fear, rightly, those choices are not valued. So, to the outside world, it looks as though they have been all-in, all-of-the-time. Even if, over the course of their careers, they actually haven't.

Sadly, hiding our stories does a disservice to our children and to the estimated 64 million Americans[2] who are about to embark on the rewards and challenges of parenthood. Like us, they are being taught to believe work and life can't integrate, that women can't put family first for any period of time and still be successful, and that men can't be as deeply engaged in the home as they are in the workplace. As a result, they are reporting the same anxiety, self-doubt, and sense of failure (at work, at home, in the community, and in society at large) that my generation has felt these past twenty years.

Take Anne Freeman. She is the proud mother of two young children and an accomplished litigator focusing on high-stakes venture capital and private equity cases. She is also deeply torn between her dual priorities. Like many of us, she loves her work, but the needs of her family and her own desire to spend more time with them causes heartache each and every day.

When I sat down with her to discuss my research and share the message that one can pause and still, over the course of her lifetime, have a successful career, Anne was shocked to hear the stories of women who have done it and done it well.

"You mean you can actually step off track for a while and it won't ruin your career? Why don't we know this?" she said, her lips trembling as though she were struggling to hold back tears.

Anne does not want to be a stay-at-home mom, but the either/or dichotomy of work and life has her twisted and torn. What if she knew her career wouldn't be ruined if she decided to pull back for a period of time? What if she didn't feel squeezed by the warring "working" mom/"stay-at-home" mom camps who collectively tell women their choices aren't valid? What if she was able to find a way to support her desire to nurture and still meet her drive to succeed?

What if?

PAUSE: A DEFINITION

First, let's define what exactly a pause means. In brief, I would argue that a pause is a temporary reframing of one's priorities to place the personal before the professional. For some, like my friend Patricia Nakache, a pause isn't a full stop from the paid workforce; it's more of a downshifting that often includes part-time or flexible work. For others, like my other friend Tibi McCann, a pause can mean leaving the paid workforce fully and then returning after a brief period of time. For still others, pausing resembles the "opt-out" model in which they leave the workforce for years. A pause is not a dead end. Unlike the narrative that says you can't get back into a paid job and re-ignite your career, my research shows women can and do.

Consider Diane Flynn. She could be the face on the wanted sign of those who revile highly qualified women with pristine educational pedigrees who "opt out" of their careers to focus on family. But for those who have elected to put their careers on the back burner and then, when the time is right, dream of re-igniting their professional ambitions, she is a role model.

Diane graduated from Stanford University with a degree in economics and joined the prestigious Boston Consulting Group. There she worked with, and was mentored by, Indra Nooyi, the current CEO of PepsiCo. After Diane graduated from Harvard Business School, she accepted a marketing job working in the burgeoning educational software industry at a company called Electronic Arts. She proved herself and was quickly promoted up the ladder. Diane stayed at the company for more than ten years, rising to become vice president of sales and business development. During her tour of duty at EA, she had two daughters. It wasn't easy being a "working" mom, but she loved her job and, because she had a husband who shared in the home duties, Diane managed to make it all work. That is, until it didn't anymore. Underlying health issues and infertility finally convinced her to take a break.

"I never imagined I would leave my career, but it seemed like the only solution," Diane told me. "I agonized over the decision. I felt as if my identity was wiped out and I doubted I would ever have a successful career again. Of course, that was exactly what the media and the work world were telling me. But my body was telling me I needed to step back and regroup. In the end, there was no other option. I had to make a decision that was right for me."

So Diane paused.

Her son was born a few years later. He had a cleft palate that required extensive surgeries, and this experience inspired her to volunteer time and talent to the hospital where he had received care. Soon the hospital found she was indispensable and hired Diane as a part-time marketing and strategy consultant. Her career, which had been on the back burner for nearly a decade, started to percolate. It didn't take long for Diane to realize she was ready for full-time work, but she was unsure how to make it happen given the wide gap in her résumé.

If we froze Diane's career story right here, we'd see everything so many have told us about "opting out." If only Diane had stayed the course, hadn't left her career to focus on her family, she could have been leading a company, driving change, and modeling for the next generation of women who aspire to great heights. Instead, she was struggling to figure out how to get back in.

But Diane's career didn't end there. She used her network to find a consulting job in marketing at GSVlabs, a start-up incubator in Silicon Valley. Within six months, she was hired full-time to become their chief marketing officer. And, to help women like her, she co-founded ReBoot Accelerator, a skills training program for re-entering moms. Like so many of the women I interviewed for this book, Diane worked, paused, and thrived. Despite her extended career break, she is now a model of female leadership.

Diane told me, "Everything I've done has led to where I am today. I have no regrets now, but I spent years filled with self-doubt. It wasn't easy, but it was all worth it."

We don't often read about successful women like Diane Flynn. Why? Because pulling back on one's career to put family first is anathema to our work-first culture. One of the most telling passages in Sheryl Sandberg's game-changing book is where she recounts what Judith Rodin, the first woman to serve as president of an Ivy League university and currently president of the Rockefeller Foundation, said to a group of mid-career women: "My generation fought so hard to give all of you choices. We believe in choices. But choosing to leave the workforce was not the choice we thought so many of you would make."[3]

Because a successful career has traditionally been defined as one in which the individual subsumes everything to rise to the top of their profession and does so as quickly as possible, the idea that someone can have a career that is less linear, takes longer, and allows for priorities other than one's job is hard for many of us to accept. Pausing flies in the face of what those before us have defined as success. To some, like Rodin, leaving the workplace is tantamount to giving up. But "leaving" the workforce—that is to say, pausing—is not abandoning ambition.

Pausing takes the long view on one's career and honors the reality that sometimes we must reframe our priorities to meet the immediate needs of our family. Doing so doesn't have to end a woman's career. In fact, it can lead to even greater success than if she had stayed on the traditional career ladder. For many successful women pausing was essential to their path to the top.

Pausing takes the long view on one's career and honors the reality that sometimes we must reframe our priorities to meet the immediate needs of our family.

THE A LIST

There are any number of prominent business women who have paused their careers. Consider Linda Zecher, past CEO and president of Houghton Mifflin Harcourt, and Brenda Barnes, past CEO of Sara Lee.

Linda started her career as a geophysicist. She managed to move into business by taking a job at Bank of America when she and her husband moved from Denver to San Francisco. Soon, she caught the start-up bug and joined PeopleSoft as their ninth employee. Eventually, they went public and Linda retired to spend more time with her family. But after a three-year career break, she was back in the paid work world as a senior vice president at Oracle. A few more major career moves and she was running a company with more than 3,500 employees. Not bad for an "opt-out" mom.

In 1998, when Brenda Barnes was CEO of PepsiCo North America, she decided to take a career break to focus on her three children. Her decision made national headlines and was called a giant step back for women's advancement. In 2004, she went back to full-time work as COO of Sara Lee; a year later, she became CEO. Brenda followed her own path and emerged at the top of her industry. That certainly isn't what we've been told about pausing, now is it?

Business women aren't the only ones who've taken career breaks. Leading media personalities including Meredith Vieira; actresses such as Michelle Pfeiffer, Annette Bening, and Meg Ryan; and even cultural icons such as singer, songwriter, poet, author, and iconoclast Patti Smith have paused to focus on their families.

Did you know retired Supreme Court Justice Sandra Day O'Connor was a pauser? She left her law practice for five years to care for her young sons and then returned to launch her public service career. World tennis champion Kim Clijsters paused her career for two years after the birth of her daughter. In 2011, she returned to tennis and won the Australian Open.

The luminous Tory Burch credits her career pause with the inspiration for starting her eponymous fashion company currently valued at $3 billion. After college, Tory worked her way up in the fashion industry and eventually was offered the presidency of Loewe, a Spanish luxury brand, but she turned it down to spend time with her three young sons. During her four-year career break, she realized there was a business opportunity in the fashion market.

As Tory recounted in her 2014 commencement speech on entrepreneurship at Babson College, "It was during that time that I began developing the concept for my company. It all started when I noticed a void in my own closet for beautifully designed, classic pieces that didn't cost a fortune. It wasn't just a void in my closet; it turned out to be a white space in the market."[4] The rest, as they say, is *her*story.

The list of successful women who have temporarily elected to reframe their priorities to spend time with their families goes on. These women, and the millions of other women like them, aren't the exceptions. In fact, despite the national narrative about professional women and their career choices, they may be closer to the norm than most of us realize.

WHO PAUSES?

You've probably heard the statistic that 70 percent of U.S. mothers with children under the age of eighteen work.[5] But what's the real story? Turns out these statistics include full-time *and* part-time work. In fact, according to the most recent Bureau of Labor Statistics report, only 48 percent of mothers with children under the age of eighteen work full-time, 16 percent work part-time, and 6 percent are unemployed and looking for work.[6] The remaining 30 percent are stay-at-home mothers.

The numbers also vary by age of child. Of American mothers with children under the age of six, 36 percent are completely out of the paid workforce. Many of them go back to work once the children are in school, leaving 25 percent of moms still home full-time when the children are between the ages of six and seventeen.

Who are these stay-at-home mothers? According to Pew Research Center, two-thirds live in traditional arrangements with husbands who work while they stay home to care for the children—you know, the households that once represented the typical middle-class American family.[7]

The remaining one-third of stay-at-home moms are single. Most of them are unemployed and, sadly, most live in poverty. They typically lack a college degree and do not have the resources necessary to find child care. They may want to work, but our system does not provide them with the necessary supports such as paid sick leave and subsidized day care so they can.

The above statistics cover American moms overall, but what about the 39 percent of American women who are college-educated?[8] What happens when they become moms? These are the women Betty Friedan spoke to all those years ago when she talked about the frustrations of not having a career and urged them to get into the workforce. They are the same ones Sheryl Sandberg is urging to lean in today. They are the ones we all hoped and continue to hope will fill the huge leadership gap between women and men at the top of every sector of our economy.

According to research compiled by the U.S. Department of Labor and economists at the Federal Reserve, and corroborated by iRelaunch, a company dedicated to helping women return to work, a significant subset of college-educated mothers pause their careers. In fact, on average around 23 percent take a significant (more than one year) career break.[9]

That's approximately 2.3 million highly qualified women who are out of the paid workforce focusing on their families right now.

And that doesn't include women like my friends scientist Lisa McPherson or venture capitalist Patricia Nakache who manage to negotiate a part-time solution for themselves, their employers, and their families. A 2013 study by Professor Joni Hersch of Vanderbilt University Law School found that college-educated married women with children were 20 percentage points less likely to work full-time than those without.[10]

That study also unveiled other significant insights about college-educated American moms, particularly when it comes to college selectivity. Professor Hersch wrote,

> Although elite graduates are more likely to earn advanced degrees, marry at later ages, and have higher expected earnings, there is little difference in labor market activity by college selectivity among women without children and women who are not married. But the presence of children is associated with far lower labor market activity among married elite graduates.

She reported that when it comes to women who have graduated from the most selective universities, such as Stanford University and others that are typically highest on the college-ranking scales, only 43 percent of these alumnae work full-time after they have children. Let me say that another way: *57 percent of women who have attended the most elite schools in this country either downshift their careers or leave the paid workforce completely after they have children.*[11] That's a lot of well-educated talent not being used to help boost our economy.

And for graduates like me with business school degrees, Professor Hersch found on average 65 percent (!) of graduates from elite colleges who go on to get an MBA and then become mothers no longer work at all.[12] Consider the 2015 Harvard Business School survey of alumni that revealed 43 percent of Gen X Harvard Business School graduates did in fact interrupt their careers for kids and a surprisingly high 56 percent of Baby Boomers did as well.[13] In other words, despite all of their best-laid plans, a significant portion of the "best and brightest" paused. Hard to change the leadership gap when the very women we might expect to be leading Corporate America have left the workforce.

However, pausing isn't limited to elite college graduates, and it isn't the sole province of the upper and upper-middle classes. There is truth to the fact that women who attended elite schools, or who married men who did, are more likely to have greater financial resources and so may have confidence that a career break will not significantly impact their family's financial well-being. But, the 23 percent of college-educated women who pause their careers each year to stay at home with their children can't *all* have attended, or be married to men who attended, the Ivy League.

A 2014 Pew Research Center report stated, "Although they are often in the media spotlight, relatively few married stay-at-home mothers (with working husbands) would qualify as highly educated and affluent . . . In 2012, nearly 370,000 U.S. married stay-at-home mothers (with working husbands) had at least a master's degree and family income exceeding $75,000. This group accounted for [*only*] 5% of married stay-at-home mothers with working husbands."[14] The argument that pausing is only for rich women doesn't hold up to the facts.

What is true is that the ability to *consider* a career break, at least as I have defined it for this book, is a privilege. Women at the lower end of the socio-economic spectrum don't have the luxury to downshift their work. They are living day to day. That said, there is a growing segment of women at the bottom end of the socioeconomic spectrum who are moving out of the workforce to care for children. Why? Because the high cost and limited availability of quality child care and the lack of paid sick leave means they have few options. In essence, they are forced to leave their jobs whether they want to or not.

The argument that pausing is only for rich women doesn't hold up to the facts.

Meanwhile, as noted above, the data reveals a significant portion of middle-class American mothers are pausing for a period of time to focus on family. For them money is tight, but their actions speak volumes about their values. They care so deeply about being their own children's primary caregivers that they are willing to make significant lifestyle compromises to do so.

Take Jennifer Tamborski. When she graduated from college in St. Louis in 1998 with a degree in environmental science, the economy was in a mild recession and she couldn't find a job. She worked as a health care administrator, a receptionist, and as an assistant to a real estate broker. Eventually, she married and became a mother. Jennifer wanted to be able to stay home with her children. By refusing to eat out, cutting coupons, eliminating travel, and doing anything else they could to keep costs low, she was able to pause for a few years. Eventually, Jennifer found work as a virtual assistant. Now she has a thriving business serving clients from all over the country. She works while her children are in school and still has time to be the mom she wants to be. As Jennifer told me, "I'm solidly middle class and I still worked, paused, and thrived."

So what will the next generation do? If you want the career of your dreams, some would argue, "Don't become a mother." A longitudinal study from the Wharton School of Business at the University of Pennsylvania revealed that in 1992 78 percent of Generation X female graduates planned to have children, but by 2012, only 42 percent of female graduates (all of whom are Millennials) planned to have kids.[15] Deciding not to be a parent is one way to reduce the stress of work–life balance, but for the 90 percent of Americans who do want children, that isn't really a solution.[16]

As of 2015, there are 22 million Millennial parents in the United States and about 9,000 new babies are born to them each and every day. These new mothers (and fathers) are just beginning to grapple with the issue of how to integrate work and family. Despite the well-intentioned efforts of companies and those committed to getting more women to the top of every industry, I believe we are going to see a growing number of the next generation of women *and* men temporarily shifting their priorities to focus on family. The data supports this.

A 2013 study of generational attitudes about parenting by *Working Mother* magazine revealed that 60 percent of Millennials believe that one parent should stay home to raise the children. Generation X? Only 50 percent of respondents in that age group believed kids needed one parent at home.[17] And a 2016 study by the ManpowerGroup revealed that 61 percent of Millennial women anticipate taking a break in their careers once they have children.[18] It's already happening. A concerning 2015 study of white-collar Millennials by Ernst & Young revealed that 59 percent reported their spouse was "forced" to quit to care for the kids.[19]

As Katy Steinmetz wrote in her *Time* magazine article, "Help! My Parents Are Millennials," "the pressure among millennials to be great parents is fierce."[20] She reports that, in February 2015, parenting site Baby Center conducted a survey of 2,700 U.S. mothers between the ages of eighteen and forty-four. They found that 80 percent of Millennial moms said it is important to be the "perfect mom." But those of us who have been there can tell you, it is hard to deliver on that scorecard and also be all-in, all-of-the-time when it comes to your career.

Whether middle class or part of the One Percent, Millennials are more likely to pause than their predecessors. Remember that 2015 Harvard Business School survey of alumni?[21] Not only did it reveal that their Gen X and Baby Boomer alumnae did, in fact, pause, it also revealed that 37 percent of Millennial alumnae *plan* to interrupt their careers to care for their children. This is a dramatic change from their predecessors. Only 28 percent of Gen X and 17 percent of Baby Boomer women who secured their MBAs from Harvard expected to do the same. Of course, their reality proved quite different. For these women, who had every opportunity available, pausing was likely the only option. Why? Certainly not because they lacked ambition. What they lacked was a system that supported mothers in the workplace.

> Whether middle class or part of the One Percent, Millennials are more likely to pause than their predecessors.

It should be noted that career pauses don't just happen when children are young. Many women wait until their children are older to pause. Consider Monica Johnson, my friend from the Not-So-New Mothers Group: She continued working full-time as a start-up CFO until her kids were in high school. Then, their busy athletic schedules and a series of related sports injuries, coupled with the fact that her children would soon be leaving the nest, finally convinced Monica to downshift her career.

"I knew they would be heading off to college soon and I wanted to be able to spend as much quality time with them as I could before they left," she told me. Today, Monica works as a part-time CFO on a consulting basis for a number of early-stage companies. When her youngest heads off to college, she plans to fully reengage in the workforce.

Another subgroup of women who pause are those with elderly parents. Women who never considered pausing when their children were young are now being forced to as their parents are getting older. As a result, a later-in-life career break is becoming more and more of a reality for working daughters.

In truth, pausing is likely to become the norm for more and more working women. The classic career ladder paradigm—you know, the one that says you've got to climb one rung after the other until you finally reach the top—doesn't work for those of us with caregiving responsibilities. As a result, women are disrupting the paradigm and fashioning non-linear careers that allow them to integrate their personal and professional goals.

Sadly, almost every single woman I spoke to shared that she had suffered deep self-doubt, regret, and insecurity while she reframed her focus away from her career to her children. When they tried to reengage professionally, some felt they faced significant roadblocks. Sexism, ageism, and a perception that their time away from the paid workforce meant they did not keep their skills fresh and relevant left them feeling resentful and angry.

Despite it all, the vast majority reported they wouldn't change a thing. And they are not alone. The Pew Research Center reports that 87 percent of those who have quit their job to care for a family member are glad they did, as are 94 percent of those who have reduced their hours and 88 percent who turned down a promotion.[22] Putting the needs of one's family ahead of one's career can be hard, but for the vast majority of those who choose to do so, it is exactly the right decision. It is time we come to recognize that those who place the personal before the professional aren't failures; they are career innovators who have the courage and grit to risk it all for that which matters most to them.

We need a new narrative that recognizes the realities of women's (and men's) lives. We need to understand that, for most, pausing isn't a choice, it's a last-resort solution. We need to support those who pause to care for family. *And,* we need to help them keep their pauses brief so they can bring their full talents back to the workforce as soon as possible.

> It is time we come to recognize that those who place the personal before the professional aren't failures; they are career innovators who have the courage and grit to risk it all for that which matters most to them.

If we don't make these changes, another twenty years will fly by and the next generation of highly skilled, well-educated talent will do what my generation has done. They'll hunker down and find private solutions that may work for their families but don't do anything to change the system for all.

CHAPTER 2

Innovating the Path

Work PAUSE Thrive Non-Linear Careers

"Pick your path, make it work for you, and let go of regret."
—Debbie Lovich,
partner and managing director, Boston Consulting Group

We used to call it the suit of armor. Red blazer, matching skirt, padded shoulders, and an off-white blouse with a soft, floppy bow like two long dog ears that sat below our chins and rested safely above our breasts. The media told us this was the "power woman's outfit" and so my friends and I donned it, or something like it, every day to our post-college jobs.

It was the 1980s. Ronald Reagan was in office; Donald Trump's book, *The Art of the Deal*, was on every aspiring capitalist's bedside table; and Gordon Gekko, the tycoon from the original *Wall Street* movie, was extolling the message "Greed is Good." Getting money, gaining power, and storming the gates of Corporate America was on the ambitious woman's to-do list.

There was a path, a clear one, or so we were told. Get an entry-level job at a big company, work for two or three years, go to business school (or law school or medical school or . . .), then move to the next big job, progressing steadily up the ladder (no stopping!), and eventually you'll rise to the top. Success can be yours *if* you follow the rules. But if you pivot or pull back or (God forbid) pause, you'll be forever off track. No brass ring for you.

It's like that old board game called Life. There are many paths one can take. The wrong one and you end up with nothing; the right one and, well, you win! And we wanted to be winners, so my generation followed what we were told was *the* path to success. We worked and worked and worked . . .

And then we had children.

That didn't stop us. Well, at least not at first. We continued to work, and while we did so we missed our children's first words, first steps, sometimes even first smiles. Many of us managed to make it through baby number two, sometimes even baby number three, but, eventually, we raised the white flag. We admitted we weren't up to the task, and then we did something we never envisioned we would do: We stepped off the track, fell off the ladder, and went home. We were supposed to be the generation to break through that glass ceiling, but all we managed to break was our belief in ourselves and our confidence in a system that promised us so much.

Then Lisa Belkin published her iconic 2003 *New York Times* article, "The Opt-Out Revolution." Thoughtful and troubling in equal measure, Lisa's article was a sucker punch to any professional woman who had stepped away from her career.[23] In it she recounted story after story of highly educated women who had "given it all up" to focus on the needs of their families. Lisa wrote,

> Wander into any Starbucks in any Starbucks kind of neighborhood in the hours after the commuters are gone. See all those mothers drinking coffee and watching over toddlers at play? If you look past the Lycra gym clothes and the Internet-access cellphones, the scene could be the 50's, but for the fact that the coffee is more expensive and the mothers have M.B.A.s.
>
> We've gotten so used to the sight that we've lost track of the fact that this was not the way it was supposed to be. Women—specifically, educated professional women—were supposed to achieve like men. Once the barriers came down, once the playing field was leveled, they were supposed to march toward the future and take rightful ownership of the universe, or at the very least, ownership of their half.

Not only were these women failing feminism by throwing away all the work of the women before them, Lisa cautioned they were also setting themselves up for a rude awakening. When quoting one "opt-out" mom who claimed, "My degree is my insurance policy," Lisa queried,

> But is it enough insurance? Not only in the event that she needs to go back to work, but also when the time comes, that she wants to. Because at the moment, it is unclear what women like these will be able to go back to.

The overall message was loud and clear: If you "opt out" you're committing career suicide. Sure, it may be easy to leave, but how the hell are you going to get back in?

A decade later, in 2013, Judith Warner, author of *Perfect Madness: Motherhood in the Age of Anxiety*,[24] wrote the seemingly definitive follow-up article for *The New York Times* called "The Opt-Out Generation Wants Back In."[25] Judith detailed how and why getting back in was, as Lisa Belkin had predicted, a seeming impossibility. And if a woman did manage to do it, well, her second career was a mere shadow of her first, tinged with second-rate options and second-rate results. Financial ruin, professional regrets, and wasted talent were the key themes of her piece.

Given these bookend articles and the firestorm about work, life, motherhood, and female ambition they wrought, it's no wonder modern women believe pausing is a career killer. But that hasn't been the case for the members of my Not-So-New Mothers Group. And it isn't true for the many successful women I interviewed for the articles I have written in my career as an independent journalist.

In 2012, I profiled the BOMs (Business Owner Moms), a group of inspiring entrepreneurs who meet monthly to support each other as they work in careers intentionally created to allow them to integrate their personal and professional goals. BOM-er Julie Ligon, a mother of three, left her marketing position at The Gap to open one of the first franchise studios of the Dailey Method, an exercise program. Kriste Michelini left her lucrative job in sales at Intuit and eventually became an award-winning and highly sought-after interior designer. Jennifer Chaney left her job in magazine publishing to become an in-demand portrait photographer.

The BOMs had each taken career pauses and then launched second careers in which they were making as much money, if not more, than they had previously in their big corporate jobs. By making the choice they did, these women didn't break any glass ceilings, but they haven't faced financial ruin, and their talents certainly aren't being wasted. Most important, they each told me they have no regrets.

In 2014, I wrote about the tech industry and exciting entrepreneurs such as Mary Page Platerink, CEO of First Aid Shot Therapy. She left a vibrant career at Coca-Cola to care for her children and then raised $3.3 million in venture capital funding for her clinical beverage company. I also profiled Umaimah Mendhro, a rising star at West, one of Silicon Valley's most highly regarded tech innovation agencies. After an extended maternity leave, she managed to raise more than $1 million in angel funding and launch her online shopping company, Vida. These women and so many others I know in Silicon Valley worked, paused, and thrived.

But perhaps they, too, were the exception. So I began reaching out to friends and friends of friends and even to complete strangers who were willing to share their stories. In all, I interviewed 186 women and, as I expected, their experiences debunked the notion you can't pull back for a period of time and then, eventually, successfully power forward in your career.[26] They proved it isn't easy to go your own way, but it certainly can be done.

While my research and reporting validated what I had personally experienced, I still craved more data. Rather than anecdotal, qualitative evidence, I wanted contemporary quantitative research on women's careers to prove what I was seeing and hearing. I was surprised to learn there wasn't any.

Pamela Stone is a professor of sociology at Hunter College and the leading academic focused on women who have paused their careers. In 2004, she interviewed fifty-four women about their "choice" to leave the paid work world. She published her findings in *Opting Out? Why Women Really Quit Careers and Head Home.*[27] Her research revealed a much more nuanced and complex look at "opt-out" moms than the narrative the media had previously presented. Professor Stone had found that, like me, these women didn't necessarily *want* to leave their careers but were forced out by a system that punished the realities of their lives.

However, Professor Stone's original research is more than a decade old. So is other compelling data from Sylvia Ann Hewlett, a workplace innovation expert and author of numerous books on women's career choices. In 2004, Hewlett and her team from the Hidden Brain Drain Task Force studied 2,443 "highly qualified" women who had taken a voluntary career break. She published their findings in *Off-Ramps and On-Ramps: Keeping Talented Women on the Road to Success.* Like Professor Stone, Sylvia Ann Hewlett found a cohort of women who left their careers but were eager (like the vast majority of unemployed people) to get back into the paid workforce. Her research showed that 93 percent of respondents wanted to return to their careers. But, as she made clear, only 74 percent of those who wanted to rejoin actually managed to do so and when they did they often worked part-time or for lower pay. She wrote, "Off-ramps are around every curve in the road, but once a woman has taken one, on-ramps are few and far between—and extremely costly."[28]

Talk about a yield sign.

And yet, given the incredible workplace changes that have happened in the last ten years (technology alone has changed not only *how* one works but *where* one works), I wanted more recent data on the 2.3 million college-educated women who pause their careers to care for their families every year. In particular, I wondered about those women who pulled back and then dreamed of powering forward. Were they able to get back in? How did they navigate their re-entry? What worked for them? What would they do differently if they could go back in time to their younger selves? Would they do it again? Did they have regrets?

I wanted answers, so I reached out to Erin St. Onge-Carpenter, CEO of TWTW Companies, a direct-to-client research service, to help me craft a quantitative study of the modern woman's career path. I had met Erin, a mother of four, when I interviewed her for this book. She told me about her non-linear career including two pauses, a corporate rise up to a vice presidency, and a launch into entrepreneurship with her own market research firm. For many years, she has been the primary breadwinner in her family and her pauses haven't hindered her career. Erin understood exactly what I wanted to achieve with our research because she lives it each and every day.

With the guidance of Professor Stone and Carol Fishman Cohen, founder and CEO of iRelaunch, a company dedicated to helping women re-enter the paid workforce after a career break, Erin and I conducted a comprehensive quantitative analysis similar to the *Off-Ramps and On-Ramps* survey completed a decade before. Our goal was to detail the career paths of well-educated, high-potential women.[29] In all, 1,476 respondents shared

WOMEN ON THE RISE

A Quantitative Survey of 1,476 Highly Qualified Women

Who They Were: Predominately white, married, highly educated Gen X mothers

What They Did: Worked, paused, and thrived

Have you ever taken a voluntary career pause?

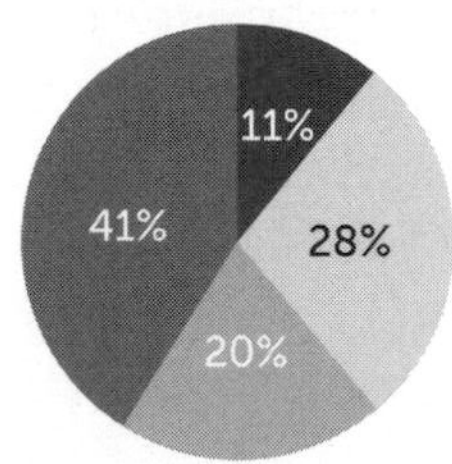

How long was your pause?

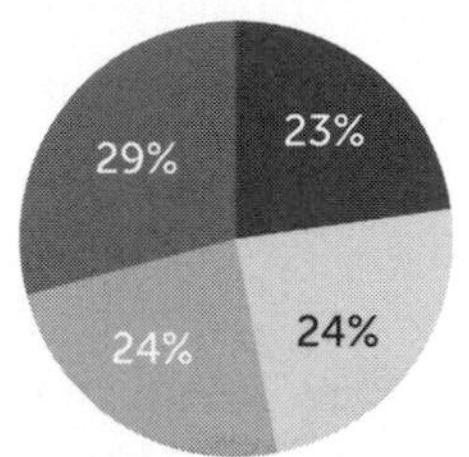

Paused/Re-entered
Downshifted/Worked Part-time
Never Paused
Currently Pausing

Less than 2 Years
2–5 Years
6–10 Years
11 or More Years

Of those who had paused and relaunched their careers...
78% had NO regrets at all.

Women on the Rewards of Pausing and Re-Igniting Their Careers

See the appendix for details on the study and deeper insight into the results.

Note: Survey of 1,476 highly qualified women conducted via SurveyMonkey in the fall of 2015

with us their feelings, ideas, thoughts, and experiences as they worked to integrate their personal and professional goals. We called it the *Women on the Rise* survey because that is what they told us they were.

WOMEN ON THE RISE SURVEY

The vast majority of respondents were college-educated (99 percent), married (88 percent), between the ages of thirty-five and fifty-four (68 percent), with children under the age of eighteen at home (69 percent). They were right in the center of the busy child-rearing years and fully experienced with the work–life integration challenges we read about and many of us live with every day. Given that 61 percent had graduate degrees, it can safely be said the respondents to our *Women on the Rise* survey were the very women who we would have expected to see lean in to their careers. They didn't. At least not continuously.

While 28 percent of respondents told us they never paused, 72 percent reported they downshifted their careers by either working part-time (20 percent of total respondents) or leaving the workforce altogether (52 percent of total respondents) for a period of time. Forty-one percent of respondents left the paid workforce completely and have since relaunched their careers, while 11 percent are still pausing. Of those currently out of the paid workforce, 83 percent expect to return in some capacity.

The headline news? Of those women who had left the paid workforce and then later re-entered, the vast majority reported they had no regrets. In fact, 78 percent reported they had no regrets AT ALL. Remarkably, 79 percent agreed their career pause enabled them to gain better work–life balance, with 31 percent reporting their lives were *very* balanced and a further 50 percent reporting feeling *moderately* balanced as a result of their pause, even though they were now back in the paid workforce. As one respondent said, "I discovered I could have it all, just not all at once."

The headline news? Of those women who had left the paid workforce and then later re-entered, the vast majority reported they had no regrets.

One of the most exciting and surprising results from the *Women on the Rise* survey was that so many women who had paused still managed to move into senior leadership positions. While 35 percent of the women who had never paused their career reported being senior managers or above, 30 percent of women who had paused and relaunched also reported being senior managers or above. In other words, not only did pausing not kill their careers, they still became the leaders society expected them to be.

Sharon Meers is a perfect example. She is the co-author of *Getting to 50/50: How Working Parents Can Have It All.* Sharon was a highly successful investment banker. She joined Goldman Sachs in 1988 and rose to be a managing director. She finally left in 2005 in part to spend more time with her children but also because she was eager to try something new. She spent the next five years researching and writing her book. After it was published, she pivoted her career to become the head of Strategic Partnerships at eBay and a board member of Sheryl Sandberg's LeanIn.org. Sharon left one big job and downshifted while her children were young, keeping her skills sharp, her contacts alive, and résumé current by writing a book. Then, she launched a new and exciting professional adventure. She leaned in to be the leader she is today by working, pausing, and thriving.

See the appendix for a deep dive into the results of the *Women on the Rise* survey.

HOW DID SHE DO IT?

As exciting as the results from the survey are, the question is, of course, *how* did these trailblazers manage to integrate a pause into their careers? Interview fifty women and it isn't obvious; interview 186 and survey 1,476 more and you begin to see patterns that have previously been hidden.

Taken together, my qualitative and quantitative research showed women who had paused weren't failures—they were career innovators.

Theirs were not the traditional stay-in-the-game, one-foot-in-front-of-the-other, march-up-the-ladder careers we were told would ensure our success. Their careers zigged and zagged, paused and pivoted. The actions of these trailblazers reflected agility, grit, and clarity of purpose. Despite the narrative that says women who put their families first lack ambition, the paths these women took required hard work, tenacity, and resilience. While they may have been filled with self-doubt and anxiety about their unconventional courses of action, these pioneers blazed a self-defined route that enabled them to integrate their personal and professional goals.

> Taken together, my qualitative and quantitative research showed women who had paused weren't failures—they were career innovators.

However, blazing new territory when it comes to one's career requires courage and much more. In my qualitative and quantitative research, I discovered that these trailblazers had a collection of personal traits that enabled them to break free from tradition and follow their own path. These innovators were imbued with an intrinsic motivation. Their choices and actions were driven by a very clear sense of who they were and what they wanted out of life.

Most of the women I spoke to thought they were the exception, that their path was unusual, that what they had done was unique. While it is true each woman's trajectory was specific to her individual circumstances, together their innovative solutions reveal a set of blueprints for creating a non-linear career, one that can enable you to work, pause, and thrive.

The three *Work PAUSE Thrive* career innovators are as follows:

- **Cruisers** are those women who stayed in the paid workforce but who pulled back from the fast track by electing to work part-time or on a reduced schedule and then reengaged full-time when their children were older.
- **Boomerangers** are the women who left the paid workforce completely and then returned in full force to their previous industry and careers. In some cases, they even returned to their same companies and same jobs.

THE 8 TRAITS OF *WOMEN ON THE RISE*

- They have clarity about what is truly most important to them.
- They take a long-term view on their careers.
- They are willing to make trade-offs in the short term to achieve their long-term goals.
- They know their value.
- They aren't afraid to ask for what they want.
- They leave if they aren't thriving.
- They are willing to fail, adapt, and adjust.
- They are committed to continuous self-improvement.

- **Pivoters** are the ones who stepped back, evaluated their personal goals and priorities, and then transitioned to new careers that were more in line with their skills, abilities, and interests. Some found new professions while others became entrepreneurs and/or social change agents.

Cruisers: Taking the Scenic Route

You'll recognize the Cruisers. They work in Corporate America, big law firms, prestigious consulting companies, powerhouse financial services firms, and other large and mid-sized institutions. They bang their heads against the glass ceiling every day, and every day they do their best to lean in and lean in hard. But rather than let the corporate structure impede them, they harness it to meet their own goals and needs.

Karen Catlin is a classic Cruiser. She graduated from college with a degree in computer science and became a software engineer working for a Silicon Valley start-up. She was soon recruited to work for a more established company called Macromedia. There Karen quickly moved into a management position. Eventually she managed to rise to a vice presidency. When you look at Karen's résumé, it presents like a straight shot to senior management. You wouldn't know that for nearly eleven years, Karen worked a reduced schedule to spend Fridays with her two children.

In a guest blog for *Global Tech Women*, Karen wrote about her experience:

> I remember the day I told my boss that I was pregnant with my first child. We were having a one-on-one meeting, and my manager, Joe, presented me with an exciting opportunity: a promotion to director of quality assurance. There was a caveat: one of my main responsibilities would be to break up the department within three months, decentralizing the quality teams to report directly into the software development teams. It wasn't going to be easy, and I'd have to trust that there would be more responsibility for me to pick up after reorganizing the department. I remember smiling, saying yes to the promotion, and then explaining that I was pregnant and wanted to work part-time when I returned after my maternity leave. His response? "Cool!"

> With that promotion, I began a new phase of my career. I worked a reduced schedule (75%) for the next ten years, during which I had two children, learned how to be a parent in tandem with developing my leadership style, and grew my responsibilities. I was even promoted to vice president while working part-time.[30]

When I queried Karen on how she managed to be a Cruiser in the tech industry, a place notorious for work environments that are unfriendly to women, she said, "It's quite simple. I had a boss who understood the value proposition of a committed employee and I had the courage to ask for what I wanted. It was a win for everyone."

When Macromedia was purchased by Adobe, Karen was offered the opportunity to work in a bigger, even more mission-critical job. The key requirement was that Karen had to be "all in," no more reduced schedule. This was her "lean in" moment and Karen was ready.

"I had spent the early years of my children's lives placing them front and center. Now, it was time to recommit to my career," she explained during our interview.

Karen took the big job and proved herself yet again. She was promoted and continued to gain more responsibility and experience. Karen ended up staying at Adobe for seven years. She credits her career success to her original manager, who was willing to work with her when she first got pregnant. If he hadn't, Karen told me she likely would have ended up like the majority of other women in tech who leave their jobs when they have children.

"I'm grateful I had the opportunity to pull back on my career when I did. It allowed me to stay in the game and also meant that when the company truly needed me, I had the energy and loyalty to be there for them," Karen said.

Karen's story spotlights how smart companies can keep talented women engaged through the early years of child rearing by offering flexible schedules and partnering with the women themselves to find a mutually beneficial career path. For most Cruisers, I learned it was an enlightened boss, not progressive company policies, that afforded them these opportunities. As a result, many Cruisers found they had to leave and create a new solution when corporate leadership changed and the commitment to flexibility waned.

Lawyer Lauren Gage Segal was on the partner track at Orrick, Herrington & Sutcliffe, a San Francisco–based law firm. Then, her primary client, Oracle, approached Lauren, asking her to join the company as an in-house counsel.

"It was a tough decision, but I loved the general counsel at Oracle and knew I could build a great career under her, so I took the risk," Lauren told me. The risk paid off. She thrived at Oracle. After her first child was born, Lauren negotiated a reduced workweek, 75 percent time, with Fridays off. Lauren continued this for four more years, through the birth of her second child. And, like Karen, she was promoted while on her reduced schedule.

"It was the perfect situation for me," Lauren said. "I was able to focus completely when I was in the office and still have time one day a week to be the mother I wanted to be."

Then a new general counsel came in and decided flexible schedules were no longer "in the company's best interest"—so Lauren left. Otherwise, she believes she would still be at Oracle today. Since then, she has parlayed her experience to serve as in-house counsel at a number of technology companies and is currently working as an interim general counsel for a publicly traded company called Phoenix Technologies. The one thing that hasn't changed for Lauren is her commitment to a flexible work schedule.

"I am very clear on my goals. I value time as much as prestige and money. So I make sure to include that when I negotiate my employment contracts," Lauren explained. "I've managed to continue to work in a way that allows me to have time with my family and still be committed to my job and career. I like to say I've leaned in, but on my terms."

What makes Cruisers so impressive is the absolute clarity they have in their own value proposition. They understand their skills and talents are worthwhile to employers and yet they are also very clear that their families are their number one priority. If the company won't work with them, they move on. Rather than operate from fear and fall prey to the narrative that says "everyone's replaceable," they have a deep confidence they are employable and are not afraid to ask for what they want.

As one Cruiser told me, "When I was able to take the emotion out of it and realize that the goal was to match what I needed with what the company needed, I was then able to negotiate with confidence. If we couldn't find common ground, I knew I could find another job where the needs and values of the company were more aligned with my own."

The hallmark of the Cruiser path is their decision to downshift for a period of time while committing to not leaving the paid workforce completely. Interestingly, for a number of the women I interviewed, that downshift didn't happen until later, as their children entered their teen years.

Take Debbie Lovich. She worked hard for the first twenty years of her career and became one of the fastest people to make partner at the Boston Consulting Group. As a partner, she traveled extensively and was often out of the house before her four children awoke and home well after they were in bed. Unlike many highly successful women, she didn't have a spouse who could serve as lead parent. Her husband, Mark, was equally committed to his career as a physician/scientist. Tough as it was, the two of them made it work. That is, until their daughters hit middle school. Then it became clear to Debbie she needed to be more available to her children.

"I realized I couldn't outsource the support my girls needed during those challenging middle school years, so I downshifted my career by taking an administrative role at the firm," Debbie told me. "I was able to be in at nine o'clock and leave by five o'clock. I was always home for dinner and never worked on weekends. It was the perfect solution for me and my family."

Now that her daughters are older, Debbie has reengaged and is back working as a partner at BCG. "I never fully left the workforce, but stepping off track as I did felt like a huge pause in my career. It was a tough decision, but I had achieved everything I needed professionally. I realized though there was more I needed to do with my kids and my community. Now I am back on track and am excited about what is ahead. That said, I have no doubt pausing was the right choice for me," she said.

Temporarily pulling back on one's career (rather than quitting completely) may be the right solution for some, but it should be noted a number of the respondents to the *Women on the Rise* survey who had taken "the scenic route" said the cruising model wasn't perfect either.

A woman I interviewed who had negotiated a reduced workweek said, "I had a great situation. In fact, the dream schedule for most moms in the workplace. But when I pulled my foot off the pedal of my career, it took a lot of effort to not be jealous of my friends as they passed me by. I had

WORK PAUSE THRIVE PATH 1: CRUISERS

Pros	Cons
"Staying in the game" professionally	Being sidelined professionally
Keeping skills current	Working full-time on a reduced salary
Maintaining some income source	Dealing with the financial hit as a result of reduced salary
Having greater control of your time frame	Being assigned work that is less challenging and/or less high profile
Having an easier time re-igniting your career	Facing unconscious caregiver bias and the assumption that you are not committed to your career
Being able to hide the pause on a résumé more easily	Being dependent on a boss who is supportive and risking the reality that if s/he leaves, the opportunity to work a reduced schedule may go away
Being able to more easily maintain your professional networks	Struggling to develop and maintain new contacts
Having the opportunity to expand skills even if working on a part-time basis	Dealing with frustration and envy as those who have not paused get promoted faster

to remind myself that what I was doing was as important. In the end, I missed being in the thick of it and that inspired me to reengage full-time."

Beyond struggling to make peace with the slower pace of their careers, another issue Cruisers faced was the challenges of managing the workload. One *Women on the Rise* respondent wrote, "I worked part-time, but found I was working full-time on a half-time salary."

Cathy Benko, vice chairman (and previous head of talent) at Deloitte, says she sees this all of the time. "Women negotiate a part-time schedule and then find themselves working full-time. The challenge is we women are pleasers and find it really difficult to say no. But if you are truly committed to your choice to pull back, you need to be clear that you truly do mean it. Otherwise, the work will creep into your time with your family, which defeats the goal in the first place."

Of course, to take the scenic route of a Cruiser requires the opportunity to do so. The sad truth is negotiating a reduced schedule or securing part-time work can be challenging if you don't have a boss and/or a company that supports you. I would have relished the chance to work a flexible schedule for a period of time after my daughter was born. Having that opportunity would have kept me in the game and would have meant I wasn't forced to leave my job at the advertising agency—a loss for them and for me.

Becoming a Cruiser can be the right path for women who want flexibility and yet want to "stay in the game" professionally. Doing so takes a supportive boss, clarity of purpose, boundaries about workflow, and the willingness to watch your colleagues pass you by. Importantly, as the stories of Karen Catlin and Debbie Lovich show, it can also put you in the best position to re-ignite your career when you are ready to be fully back in.

Boomerangs: Work, Pause, Repeat

While Cruisers never fully leave the workforce, Boomerangs leave the workplace completely and then recommit to their careers by returning to their previous industry, previous company, and even, occasionally, their previous jobs. These women have career paths that often look like they are "opt-out" moms, but like Diane Flynn, their careers don't end with kids. Rather, they re-ignite their professional lives when the time is right for them and their families. We rarely hear about their second acts, and so this path is not an obvious one for most women. As one Boomerang told me, "The story about our career paths isn't what makes the headlines, but the truth is, we rock it."

I had the pleasure of meeting four Boomerangs when I moderated a panel on return-to-work internships at the 2015 iRelaunch conference. The four women each left illustrious careers in the financial services industry, took significant pauses, and then relaunched to great success.

Panelist Raeshma Patel took five years off while her children were young and is now an associate at Goldman Sachs. She shared, "The power of my returnship was that it allowed me to test the waters and see what working full-time again would be like. Now that my children are older, I found I was able to be the fully engaged professional I wanted to be—something I didn't feel I could do when they were younger."

Panelist Andrea Chermayeff was out of the paid workforce for fifteen years and is now vice president of asset management at JPMorgan Chase & Co. When I asked how her colleagues viewed her extended break, Andrea laughed. "It's funny. I don't think most of them even know I was out of the workforce at all, let alone for a decade and a half."

Each of the iRelaunch panelists I interviewed had benefited by participating in a return-to-work internship offered by their respective companies. These short-term internships are targeted to mid-career professionals who want to onramp after a career pause. While not promised a job, many who participate in these programs are offered a full-time position after the end of the "returnship." While these programs are a fantastic way for companies to fast track talent, the vast majority of returners don't have the opportunity to participate in some forward-thinking company's innovative return-to-work program. So most Boomerangs figure it out themselves through grit and determination.

Consider mother of four Susannah Albright, who worked in Silicon Valley for over a decade in high-tech product management with a focus on telecommunications. After her second child, Susannah managed to negotiate a part-time schedule at her company. She stayed working in that capacity through the birth of her third child. It wasn't until after her fourth child was born that Susannah finally left the workforce completely, but she did so only because her company was downsizing and she was officially laid off.

For seven years Susannah was, in her words, an Uber Mommy. She carpooled, coached the kids' sports teams, and volunteered at their schools. Then her husband was offered a great job in Jacksonville, Florida, so they decided to move and start fresh. This gave Susannah a chance to relaunch.

It took time to find a house, settle her children into their new schools, and begin building a new life in their new town, but eventually Susannah was ready to return to the paid workforce. Using her college network, she met the CEO of a fast-growing software company who needed marketing help. She started working for him on a contract basis but was quickly pulled in to work for the company full-time. Susannah has since been promoted to vice president of marketing and is responsible for about 25 percent of the company's head count.

"I'm making more money than I've ever made and have more responsibility than I had at the height of my career before my kids," Susannah told me. "I have no doubt the years I focused on raising my children taught me how to be a better manager and leader. It wasn't the career path I thought I would have, but I wouldn't change a thing."

Rosine Matthews, senior vice president for Wells Fargo, is another sterling example of the Boomerang path. She relaunched her career in the banking industry thanks to "luck, connections, and the support of other women."

Rosine grew up in Texas and is a proud graduate of Texas A&M, where she studied finance. With the encouragement of her professors, she decided to secure a master's degree in finance and then went into banking, working for a regional bank in Houston after graduation.

In the years that followed, Rosine's life flourished. She worked hard and then married. Just as the Houston economy began to suffer in the wake of the savings and loan crisis, she gave birth to her first child. While she was on maternity leave, Rosine's bank, First City, was acquired by JPMorgan and she found herself working for a new, "less than supportive" boss. She asked if she could on-ramp slowly after her six-week maternity leave by working part-time for six months. Her new boss told her to either be "all in or not in at all." Though she had never previously before thought of quitting and staying home, when her husband got a job offer in Melbourne, Australia, they decided to take the risk and relocate.

During the three years they lived abroad, Rosine didn't work outside the home. She gave birth to a second child, a daughter, and took up crafting hobbies, including quilting and baking elaborately decorated cakes. While they loved living abroad, Rosine and her husband missed being around family and so decided to move back to the United States. Her husband found a job quickly, but Rosine struggled to get back into the workforce. She took on part-time consulting jobs to help pay the bills while she looked for full-time work. A female banking colleague's referral and recommendation to an analyst job at the Bank of Nova Scotia was the break Rosine needed.

"It was a step backward professionally," Rosine told me, "but the pay was good and I really liked the woman who hired me." Within four months that woman left and Rosine was promoted into her job as vice president of client relations.

"I don't know for sure, but I believe my boss knew she was leaving and wanted to give me the chance to get my feet wet as she prepared to move on," Rosine said. "Thanks to her, I was back on track." Not long after, she was recruited to another bank and finally ended up at Wells Fargo where she has made her career ever since.

"I have no regrets when it comes to my career pause. It allowed me a chance to explore a different side of myself. Heck, who knew I had an inner Martha Stewart?!" Rosine said, laughing as we talked. "But, in the end, I knew I was committed to my career and I was determined that being home with my children for a few years was not going to be the end of it."

Rosine believes she was able to re-ignite her career thanks to the two women who advocated for her. "I was lucky they were willing to 'help a sister out' and I've tried to do that for other women as well," Rosine said.

"Sisters helping sisters" was a consistent theme in the stories of the women I interviewed, but particularly for Boomerangs. Grace Zales, a friend from my Not-So-New Mothers Group and an executive at Cornerstone Research, a litigation consultancy, said it was her old boss who helped her get back on track after nearly a decade at home.

"Together, we crafted a job that worked for the company and for me," Grace said. "Without her willingness to help me, it would have been so much harder to get back in."

Interestingly, 68 percent of respondents to the *Women on the Rise* survey reported that they believe women who are in the workforce have a responsibility to help those who are trying to re-enter. Over half of the

WORK PAUSE THRIVE PATH 2: BOOMERANGS

Pros	Cons
Being fully focused and immersed in caregiving role	Finding relaunching to be more challenging than you expected
Reducing stress on family	Facing others' perceptions of you as not ambitious or career-committed
Spending more time on community engagement/ volunteerism	Confronting bias against unpaid volunteer work
Exploring other careers/ hobbies/interests	Requiring additional financial resources to implement
Expanding your network beyond your original profession or industry	Losing your professional network by not staying in touch
Building new skills	Needing re-training if your skills have lapsed
Feeling empowered and modeling self-determination	Feeling self-doubt, regret, and a sense of failure
Re-igniting one's previous career	Dealing with résumé gaps
Finding some measure of work–life balance	Confronting caregiver bias and age bias when trying to re-enter paid workforce
Modeling for others that putting family first does not have to be a career killer	Dealing with the potentially negative consequences to your family's financial well-being given you have been out of the paid workforce

respondents who paused and re-entered reported they have actively helped other returning professionals find jobs. However, only 35 percent of those who never left the paid workforce reported they helped another woman get back in after a career break. This may be because they don't know anyone in their network who has been a stay-at-home parent or it may also be partly a result of an unconscious bias against that alternative path.

If there is a key ingredient to the recipe for solving the Mommy Wars, helping unemployed "sisters" find jobs is certainly one of them.

If there is a key ingredient to the recipe for solving the Mommy Wars, helping unemployed "sisters" find jobs is certainly one of them.

Boomerangs look like "opt-out" moms until they don't anymore. The narrative on their career path is that after leaving the workplace, they won't be able to get back in. My research says otherwise: 66 percent of the *Women on the Rise* respondents who quit work and then re-entered at a later time reported they found their first position within six months. Sixty-nine percent of relaunchers reported they felt "back on track" within one year.

While the chance to step back and focus on one's family can be incredibly validating, the challenges of re-entry are manifold. Between bias against those with caregiving responsibilities, bias against those who have experienced long-term unemployment, and the flawed belief that women who pause their careers lose their professional skills and abilities, it can be hard to relaunch. Add to that the ageism that a number of Boomerangs who had taken extended pauses felt they faced and you can imagine why this path can be risky. But, for those who made it work, their life satisfaction was incredibly high.

As one woman told me, "It wasn't easy, but I figured it out and now I have the job of my dreams. My break gave me a chance to be the mom I wanted to be and now I am completely recommitted to my career. For me, it was the perfect work–life balance solution."

Pivoters: Getting It Right, the Second Time Around

The choice to return to one's previous profession might seem the most obvious and easiest path to re-entry, but for many women that wasn't an option either for personal or professional reasons. Instead, they pivoted.

Some found the re-entry to their old careers too challenging. As one respondent to the *Women on the Rise* survey who had pivoted her career wrote, "I could not find a job in 2009 and being 50 years old [made it even harder]. So I moved, got my real estate license, and went to work for a builder. Now, I run all aspects of the construction business. It's a career I never dreamed of, but one that uses all of my skills and abilities."

Other *Women on the Rise* respondents found that stepping away from the paid workforce gave them a chance to reevaluate. They came to realize they had been in the wrong profession and used this opportunity to move to a new one.

Pivoting to a new profession after a career pause requires more than smarts; it requires vision, tenacity, and the help of inspired employers who are willing to take a risk on you.

My friend from the Not-So-New Mothers Group, Patricia Nakache, was lucky enough to have just that kind of support. Before she became a mother, she worked her way up the ladder at McKinsey & Company as a management consultant. After her son, Robbie, was born, Patricia worked three days a week for McKinsey. She also wrote a number of articles for *Fortune* magazine about the business climate in Silicon Valley. In that role, she interviewed a variety of venture capitalists and found she loved what they did and dreamed of joining their ranks.

Luckily for her, one of the men she interviewed thought she had what it took to be a successful venture capitalist. He offered to bring her into his venture firm as a part-time contractor to try it out. Today, Patricia is a partner at Trinity Ventures, the very firm that took a risk on her. She credits much of her success to having bosses who were in it for the long haul. They gave her the flexibility she needed while her children were young, and then she rewarded them by being one of their top investors.

"I couldn't have moved to a new industry with young children and also ease my way back into full-time work without true allies who were committed to my long-term success," Patricia told me.

For interior designer Kriste Michelini it was her friends who empowered her to find her second career.[31] Before her pause, Kriste worked in software sales for technology company Intuit. She told me she enjoyed her job, had the flexibility she needed as a mother, and was making very good money, but a painful divorce caused her to reevaluate her choices. When Kriste remarried, she decided to devote herself to her new family. When she wasn't focused on her children, she spent her free time decorating the family's home and playing tennis. In other words, she looked like the classic "opt-out" mom. But Kriste knew she wanted to be back in the work world. She just didn't know how that would take shape.

"I knew I didn't want to go back into software sales, but I wasn't sure what my next career should be so I turned to my closest friends and asked them what I should do. To a woman, they encouraged me to pursue interior design. In fact, one even hired me to redo her house. That was the gift that allowed me to pivot careers," Kriste said.

Today, Kriste is a sought-after interior designer whose award-winning work can be found in the homes of some of the most discerning clients in and around the San Francisco Bay Area. In 2014 she was named one of *Traditional Home* magazine's "Top 10 Decorators to Watch." Her full-time staff of three can barely keep up with the demand for her talents.

Kriste told me, "I would never have been where I am today if I hadn't paused my career. I finally found my passion and now I have the career of my dreams *and* I am exactly the kind of mother I always wanted to be."

Moving to a completely different career can be challenging even if you haven't stepped back from the workforce. But for those who have paused, pivoting can be especially challenging. Often it means you have no network to assist you as you try to relaunch. With no one to turn to for guidance and advice and a much-needed introduction, breaking into your dream profession can feel like a near impossibility.

As a result, many Pivoters return to school to get new skills and, importantly, build new contacts. When I decided I wanted to pursue my dream of writing, I enrolled in an MFA program at Mills College. I loved being amongst a vibrant community of younger students, and I met my mentor, Professor Sarah Pollock. Her support and guidance gave me the confidence to believe that I, a forty-six-year-old mother of three, could pivot to become a journalist and writer.

Pivoter Sub-Group 1: Mom-preneurs

There were two distinct subgroups within the Pivoters I interviewed and surveyed. The first were those who became entrepreneurs. Kriste is emblematic of a Pivoter who, in using her pause to springboard into a new career trajectory, became an entrepreneur. And she is not alone. In fact, 27 percent of the *Women on the Rise* survey respondents who relaunched said they too had chosen to go it on their own.

For those Pivoters who became entrepreneurs, the sizes of the businesses they created varied widely. For many of these women, entrepreneurship meant a "single shingle"[32] or "cupcake" business that brought in just enough income to cover their expenses while allowing them to be active and engaged mothers. According to the U.S. Department of Labor, as of 2012, 89 percent of female-owned businesses have no other employees than the owner. As one *Women on the Rise* respondent shared, "Having my own company allows me to work around the kids' schedules. I love having something that is mine and independent from my kids' worlds and my world as mother."

Pivoter Kriste Michelini's interior design firm was a "cupcake" business at first. So was public relations whiz Lee Caraher's company. When she put out her "shingle" she never imagined how successful her agency would become. Today, Double Forte is one of the San Francisco Bay Area's leading public relations and marketing services firms, with over twenty-five employees on staff, in addition to a vast network of consultants who help out as needed. As you can imagine, Lee is a passionate supporter of entrepreneurship for women.

"The power and freedom that comes from running your own business cannot be underestimated," Lee told me. "It made all of the difference for me and I believe can unlock the path to true success for women overall."

Don't be fooled by these "cupcake" businesses. As Kriste and Lee experienced, these businesses often become hugely successful. According to a 2014 Majority Report of the U.S. Senate Committee on Small Business and Entrepreneurship, female-owned businesses account for nearly 30 percent of all business in the United States.[33] They created 23 million jobs, which accounts for 16 percent of all jobs in the United States. The growth of women-owned businesses outpaces all other privately held firms,[34] up

26 percent since 2007.[35] Women-led businesses brought in receipts of $1.3 trillion for their owners.[36] Not a bad payday, if you ask me.

Around Silicon Valley, women and entrepreneurship is a heated topic. A recent report by the Kauffman Foundation[37] notes that 97 percent of technology start-ups are founded by men and only 7 percent of venture-backed start-ups have a woman on the executive team. Meanwhile, ambitious female entrepreneurs have been frustrated for years by the lack of access to capital. Only 2.7 percent of venture-backed start-ups are led by women,[38] perhaps partly because only 4 percent of venture capitalists are women.

Women, money, and entrepreneurship are a good recipe for controversy. Add the word "mother" into the mix and, well, that's as close to a deal breaker as it can get. As one venture capitalist said to me only half-jokingly, "Mom-preneurs can't get no respect."

The term "Mom-preneurs" is the latest weapon being wielded in the "Mommy Wars." Ambitious women who envision building the next Facebook or Google often distance themselves from "cupcake" entrepreneurs for fear they will be considered too narrowly focused and lose out on significant investor funding. Unlike the small business owners who often become entrepreneurs because the workplace could not or would not accommodate their desires to integrate work and family, these female entrepreneurs have bold visions for their endeavors and would never want to have the word "mom" put in front of their title.

In her essay entitled "I Hate 'Mompreneurs,' But I Support Women in Business,"[39] business writer Lindsay Cross wrote,

> . . . the "mompreneur" title lets your customers and competitors know that your business is a side-job, instead of something you take seriously. Even worse, the name "mompreneur" is being used outside these part-time sales-party opportunities. It is being applied to every business that happens to be owned by a woman with children. And then we wonder why female start-ups aren't always taken seriously! We're allowing them to be lumped in with women who sell candles to their friends and family. Is it really so amazing that investors don't want to risk giving capital to "mompreneurs"?

In response, *Forbes* staff writer Meghan Casserly wrote an essay entitled "'Mompreneur': Own It, Ignore It or Prove It Wrong."[40] In it she said,

> In terms of the girl-on-girl hate of businesswomen (with children) who feel they have a "real" business towards businesswomen (with children) who feel they are "mompreneurs" and no doubt consider their businesses just as "real," I've had enough . . .
>
> Here's the thing. I support every woman who wants to start a business, whether she wants to create a cloth diaper company while on maternity leave to supplement her household income or she aims to build the next great social network. As far as I'm concerned, . . . they're [both] business women who happen to have children . . .
>
> When it comes to the term "mompreneur," you've got three choices: Own It, Ignore It or Prove It Wrong.

Jessica Herrin, who co-founded WeddingChannel.com and is now founder and CEO of social sales jewelry brand Stella & Dot, is all about owning it. Her business savvy has been written about in *Forbes*, *The Wall Street Journal*, and *The New York Times*, and she has been named by Ernst & Young and Inc. 500 as a "Top Entrepreneur." And, she is not afraid to be called a mom-preneur. She says, "When I became a mom, I decided I wanted to be a 'mom working,' not a 'working mom.' The mom part comes first."[41]

When she founded Stella & Dot, she had "moms who work" in mind. In a profile on NBC's *Today Show*, she said, "Too many women are sidelined by the lack of flexibility in traditional jobs, so by modernizing what flexible work-from-home opportunities look like, we are giving women the ability to take control of their lives."[42]

Jessica Herrin is a woman who's long-embraced the mom-preneur moniker. She has proven you can be a successful, scalable, and fundable serial entrepreneur who is also a mom. She's comfortable with the stereotype even as she proves it false.[43] Meanwhile, as we dither over what it means to be a "real" entrepreneur who is also a mother, many are arguing about the power and importance of supporting women and their entrepreneurial efforts.

In its 2014 report,[44] "Sources of Economic Hope: Women's Entrepreneurship," the Kauffman Foundation wrote,

> While short-term growth seems to have recovered to pre-recession rates, the permanent damage wrought by the Great Recession may have knocked the United States to lower potential GDP for a long time to come . . . One potential boost is a crucial economic area where women continue to be underrepresented: entrepreneurship, especially high-growth entrepreneurship.

In fact, mom-preneurship may well be the perfect solution for both the economy and the work–life integration issues mothers face. Now, if we can only get beyond our deep-seated motherhood bias to support them.

Pivoter Sub-Group 2: Warriors

The second subgroup of Pivoters my research uncovered were those women who dedicated their post-pause careers to becoming a Warrior for Good. Perhaps it's something about being able to step back and ponder the impact of one's life and work or perhaps it's the lessons one learns being fully responsible for another human being, but, whatever the inspiration, numerous women shared that once they had children they knew they could only do work that "made a difference." Jennifer Mazella is a classic Pivoter who became a Warrior for Good.

Jennifer graduated from the University of Nebraska and was busy building her career working in the juvenile justice system. She never planned on having children, but then she met her husband and the rest, as she said, "was history":

> Before I met my husband, I never imaged getting married or having children. Then, once I had children, I never imagined I would stop working, but my son was born two months early. It wasn't long before we learned he had developmental issues, specifically, autism. Once he hit school, there was no way I could go back to work given the amount of effort it took to get the support he needed. Being a Special Needs Mom is a full-time job! I realized I could share what I learned to make it easier for others.

At first, Jennifer donated her time to helping other families and then went back to school to get a formal coaching certificate. She launched a business coaching families through the special education process, but the demand was so great Jennifer knew she couldn't have the impact she wanted working one family at a time, so she launched an online training program. In addition to her online classes, Jennifer has written three books, and she tours the country speaking to organizations, parents, and schools about how they can become better advocates for children with special needs.

She was only half joking when she told me, "My goal is to become the Tony Robbins of Special Ed."

Becoming a Warrior for Good is a risky adventure. It takes courage and the unflagging support of a partner who is willing to underwrite your passion project. Jennifer and the women Warriors like her I interviewed are lucky to have husbands who are deeply invested in the social change their wives are making. As one woman shared, "You need a financial foundation if you want to make a difference."

That said, as Jennifer Mazella notes, making change can also be about making money. After years of being a stay-at home mother, she is proud to say she is now the primary breadwinner of the household, making six times what her husband brings in. He's still working, but now they're sharing the kid duty. Jennifer told me, "I was able to care for my kids, monetize my passion, and make a difference along the way. That to me is a sign of true success."

Not-So-New Mothers Group member Lisa Stone may well agree. As a journalist, she was often frustrated by the lack of women's voices, stories, and experiences in the media. She helped build a leading online site, Women.com,[45] and then was chosen as a Nieman Fellow at Harvard University, where she studied how to capitalize on the new online media trend. As a mother, she found journalism an unforgiving career, so she paused after the fellowship and freelanced while she tried to figure out how to integrate journalism with motherhood.

Then blogging became "a thing." Lisa saw it as a chance to empower women by giving them a platform to share their stories and helping them monetize the power of their networks. So, with two other forward-thinking women, Lisa co-founded BlogHer in 2005, just as blogging was taking off. As CEO, she helped give millions of women the chance to share their stories, connect online and in person, and make money along the way. Without a doubt, Lisa is a Warrior who worked, paused, and thrived.

WORK PAUSE THRIVE PATH 3: PIVOTERS

Pros	Cons
Living your life's dream	Needing new training, skills, and education to accomplish your pivot
Using your pause to reflect, reevaluate, and reset your personal and professional goals	Facing the challenge of switching careers at mid-life (Pivoters can face age bias in addition to motherhood bias)
Creating job that allows you to be in control of your time	Working full-time on reduced salary
Reinventing yourself	Not using skills and abilities developed in previous career, as they may not be applicable
Expanding your network beyond your previous profession and/or industry	Trying to build a new network and/or develop new contacts
Building new skills	Requiring training and/or a return to school
Feeling empowered and modeling positive self-determination	Requiring additional financial resources to implement (to attend school, to start a company, to become a social entrepreneur)
Leaving a legacy and making social change	Dealing with the potentially negative consequences to your family's financial well-being given you have been out of the paid workforce and your new career may require an additional investment in training/education

Many of the Warriors I interviewed told me they saw their new work as a way to make a difference but also as a way to model a new path for their children. As one *Women on the Rise* survey respondent shared about her post-pause career, "I joined the nonprofit world to ensure that I am working not only for myself but also for the greater good. It has helped open new doors and given me the opportunity to teach my daughter about the power of finding inner peace and satisfaction in your career choice."

UNFINISHED BUSINESS

Despite the outdated notion that careers are linear, the paths of the *Work PAUSE Thrive* career innovators show there are a number of ways to (re)make your way, each with its own opportunities and challenges. Despite the overarching narrative that says pausing will kill your career, the trailblazing women who integrated a pause into their careers prove it doesn't have to preclude one from achieving professional success. Whether they moved to new careers, became entrepreneurs, or started social movements, for all of the women who paused and then pivoted, it was the pause that empowered them.

As one *Women on the Rise* respondent shared, "My career break gave me the chance to step back and assess what really mattered to me. That became the fuel for all that I have done in my life both personally and professionally ever since. I wish every woman AND man had the chance to pause and find their purpose."

In the next decade, as more data points become available and more research is done on the topic of women's non-linear careers, I believe we are going to see a different "lean in" model for high-potential women. While many will follow the conventional career path of being all-in, all-of-the-time, a portion of them will do what Karen Catlin, Patricia Nakache, Jennifer Mazella, and so many of the other women I interviewed have done. They will work hard, rise up the ladder, pause or pull back to put their personal lives first, and then re-ignite their careers to great success. They are, and will continue to be, the very leaders Sheryl Sandberg and so many of us want to see at the tops of their fields. The only difference is they will have done it *their* way.

Forget what you've heard about how pauses are career limiting, about how those who pause lack ambition, about how what you do while you pause is irrelevant, that if you do pause you won't be able to re-enter the workforce. That's a flawed reality, part of a self-negating narrative that reflects a larger culture truth: We have a bias against caregiving in this country.

High-potential women (and men) who want lives that are more than just work, work, work, need to fully understand the ecosystem in which they are operating. They need to recognize their individual situations exist in a cultural, social, economic, and political environment that remains rooted in an outmoded reality.

Wendy Wallbridge, career coach to many high-powered women in Silicon Valley and author of the book *Spiraling Upward: The 5 Co-Creative Powers for Women on the Rise*, argues that life happens in, well, spirals.[46] We as individuals and as a culture cycle back to unresolved issues until we can move beyond them and up to the next turn of our evolution.

I thought of her message when I was flipping through a recent copy of *InStyle* magazine. Page after page showed models in the latest fashions for work. What were they wearing? Suits with padded shoulders and blouses with floppy bow ties. I couldn't help but laugh. It was the same attire I and my female colleagues donned back in the day. As I write this, Donald Trump is the Republican candidate for the presidency and the tech industry has become the new Wall Street where greed is (still) good. Blink your eyes and we're back in the '80s again.

A new generation of women is ready to take its place on the path to leadership and yet little has changed in the workplace for women in general and mothers in particular. As this next cohort of well-educated, high-potential women become parents, will they too feel forced to choose between work and family? Most likely. As I have shared before, I wish the workplace was structured so women (and men) are not forced to choose between their personal and professional goals. But it is. As Anne-Marie Slaughter wrote in *Unfinished Business*, "If we want to move forward for women and men, for our workplaces, and for our society as a whole . . . We have to ask ourselves why we are so certain of our oft-buried assumptions about the way things are."[47]

Part II of this book challenges how things are and addresses the unfinished business of how our country deals with mothers in the workforce. It looks at why pausing was a necessary reality for many women in my generation and why it is likely to continue to be so today. It gives you insights into the cultural, social, and economic environment in which we are operating, and it gives much-needed information to be empowered to make fully informed decisions about your life and your career. It provides the context I wish I had when I was embarking on parenthood and helps explain why it is so damn hard to integrate parenthood and careers.

> Forget what you've heard about how pauses are career limiting, about how those who pause lack ambition, about how what you do while you pause is irrelevant, that if you do pause you won't be able to re-enter the workforce. That's a flawed reality, part of a self-negating narrative that reflects a larger culture truth: We have a bias against caregiving in this country.

Part II

CANARIES IN THE COAL MINE

CHAPTER 3

Pausing and the Issue of "Choice"

"It's not a choice when women have limited options for integrating work with their family obligations."
—Pamela Stone,
professor of sociology, Hunter College

I remember the first time I saw Diane Keaton's 1987 movie, *Baby Boom*. It came out a few months after I had married my husband, Bill. He was in business school, and I was the primary breadwinner. I had a job working in marketing at Fidelity Investments and was struggling to support us on my modest salary. In the movie, hard-charging New York advertising executive J. C. Wiatt gets unexpectedly saddled with a relative's baby. It doesn't take long for her to realize she can't "do it all" and so she ends up leaving New York City for life on an upstate farm. Eventually, J. C. finds professional success as an entrepreneur and personal fulfillment as a mother to her adopted daughter. In other words, she was the harbinger of working, pausing, and thriving.

When I first saw that movie, I was deeply critical of J. C.'s "choice." Ironic, I know, given my own path. But at the time all I saw was that she'd abandoned her career. And for what? A baby?! To me, her "choice" represented failure. Only now, all these years later, do I see it for what it was: an innovative career solution that brought her even greater life satisfaction and success.

I also understand it for what it revealed: a deep failure of our system, in which those with caregiving responsibilities are forced to make compromises that may solve their problems as individuals but don't change the system for the benefit of all.

In 2004, when Professor Pamela Stone extensively interviewed fifty-four highly skilled women for her book, *Opting Out? Why Women Really Quit Careers and Head Home*, it became clear their decision to abandon their careers was not a "choice" per se, but a reaction to a punishing and unrelenting work structure. Rather than view them as failures, Professor Stone saw them as pioneers whose actions reflected a "silent strike" against an unforgiving workplace. She wrote,[48]

> They were not acquiescing to traditional gender roles by quitting, but voting with their feet against an outdated model of work . . .
>
> When women quit, not wanting to burn bridges, they cited family obligations as the reason, not their dissatisfaction with work, in accordance with social expectations. Their own explanations endorsed the prevalent idea that quitting to go home is a choice . . .
>
> These strategies and rhetoric, and the apparent invisibility of the choice gap, reveal how fully these high-achieving women internalized the double bind of the intensive mothering and ideal-worker models on which it rests. The downside, of course, is that they blamed themselves for failing to "have it all" rather than any actual structural constraints.

It wasn't until I read Professor Stone's book and dove headlong into her research that I realized how I had internalized so much of the cultural narrative around mothers in the workplace. I believed the system wasn't wrong; women who left it were. When I left, I thought I was the failure, not the workplace itself.

I had spent decades of my young life getting the best education possible and was deeply committed to being successful in my career, but, like J. C. Wiatt, I worked in advertising. It's a profession that values the cool, the hip, the cutting edge, and all that is "sexy." Motherhood? That's Norman Rockwell, apple pie, the 1950s, women baking cookies for their children who are outside playing on the tree swing. Lovely images, but certainly not sexy.

When I first joined Foote, Cone & Belding, a senior creative director invited me into his office for a get-to-know-you chat. Dressed in a black shirt and black Levi jeans (cutting-edge office wear for those suit-and-neck-tie days), this guy was the agency's rising star, an unspoken arbiter of all that was cool. At the end of our little talk, he said, "I knew you'd be OK; you know how to dress."

Image mattered (and still matters) in the agency world. Being a mother was simply not part of the successful persona. My boss was a mother, but she was the primary breadwinner and had a husband who stayed home to care for their son. Besides her, there was not a single woman at the top of the agency. As for "working" mothers, we were few and far between. The male leaders may have been fathers, but they never talked about their children. Fatherhood wasn't cool then either.

After I had my daughter and my maternity leave was at its end, I started having nightmares. I can't remember them now in detail, but I have a vague memory of one in which I was walking down the office hallway. I wasn't pregnant anymore, but I was wearing tent-like maternity clothes because I was still twenty pounds overweight and couldn't fit into my "cool" outfits. Large dark spots bloomed on my blouse where breast milk leaked through. At the end of the long hall stood the rising star, his arms crossed, his head shaking, his mouth twisted in disgust. I wanted, needed, to reach him but the hallway seemed to get longer and longer. I started to run. My engorged breasts hurt from the pounding, and I nearly tripped in my high-heeled shoes. I woke up crying, absolutely sure I'd never make it to the end.

I'd spent four harrowing months on bed rest, almost losing my daughter on numerous occasions. Then I spent three months on maternity leave trying to recover from it all. I needed help to regain my footing as a mother and a professional. But when I attempted to work part-time or work a reduced schedule, it wasn't an option. Not even a consideration. No one at the agency had any form of flexibility. Why should I be the exception? My agency wanted me to work all of the time, or not at all.

And then, as luck would have it, our au pair quit. Vicki was young, British, and loving with our son, William. She lived with us, which meant when I left the house at 7 AM (often before William awoke) and returned home around 8 PM (often after he was in bed), I had no doubt he was being well cared for by his beloved Vicki. But she was ready to move on with her life.

Vicki waited until our daughter came home from the hospital and then announced she was heading back to England. We couldn't afford a nanny who lived outside the home, and we struggled to find a new au pair. Vicki was hard to replace. We looked into day care, but we couldn't find one on such short notice with room for two children under the age of three. And anyway, the cost of day care was prohibitive. Nearly three-quarters of my salary would be going to pay for someone else to take care of our children. In that moment, it just didn't seem to make sense.

And so, as you know by now, I quit.

I thought it was my choice. Thought that I was exercising my freedom to live my life as I chose. I believed I was lucky to be able to downshift my career, consult from home, and give my children more of my time and attention. And I was lucky we had enough resources to give me options, which is something a large percentage of American women don't have. And yet, it is only now, all of these years later, I see it wasn't *really* a choice. There was no way for me to be successful in my chosen career and be confident my children were getting the care they needed. I couldn't be like my boss. I didn't have a stay-at-home husband.

My husband's job in the technology industry required long hours with extensive travel, and although I had the more senior title and managed a larger team than his, Bill's salary and bonus trumped mine by more than $75,000. If one of us had to pull back, there was no question it was going to be me.

Because I didn't understand the larger dynamics in which I was operating, my "choice" undermined my sense of self-worth. I faced deep doubts about my path and my future employability. Like the women Professor Stone interviewed for her book, I had convinced myself that I wasn't good enough to "have it all." It never dawned on me that I lived within a workplace construct that was stacked against me and all women, for that matter—first for being female, second for being mothers, and third for needing the flexibility to be an engaged caregiver to those we love.

The reigning narrative around my "choice" was that what I was doing was risky and would make me professionally irrelevant. And worse, I believed the underlying message that focusing on caregiving was not worthy of my human capital. All that education and you're spending it *on your children*? What a waste.

Enter one of my professional heroes: Ann Fudge.

An African-American woman and mother of two, Ann managed to rise to prominence in the packaged goods industry to become president of the beverage and desserts division of Kraft Foods (a $5 billion business). In 1998, Ann was named by *Fortune* magazine as one of the "50 Most Powerful Women in Business."

In 2001, all of those years of experience, commitment, talent, and results were thrown to the dogs when Ann announced she wanted to take a pause. She made it clear she had accomplished all she wanted at that phase of her career and needed time to reflect and make her family a priority. Although successful men have done this for years, Ann Fudge was roundly denounced in the media as yet another female professional who "opted out" because she just couldn't hack it.

Of course, she could hack it and more. Ann remained on various national corporate boards, volunteered her time to important causes, and stayed active with her professional network. A few years later she relaunched her career by becoming president of Young & Rubicam advertising agency. When I learned she had done this, I did a victory dance in my home office. See, it could be done! There was hope!

And yet, the announcement of her selection for the post was met with deep resistance. An article in *BusinessWeek*[49] challenged her appointment by writing,

> A surprising number doubt—quietly for now, anyway—that a woman who openly hugs fellow execs and values her life beyond the workplace can raise Y&R to new creative and financial heights. As one senior executive puts it: "I just don't know if someone who can spend months on a bicycle has the 24/7 drive we need" . . . Few high-level women dropouts have the opportunity to rejoin the corporate elite with their credibility intact.

"Dropouts"? "Credibility intact"? It's no wonder those who ponder whether they should pause are worried about their future careers. When women like Ann Fudge are skewered for creating their own paths, it reinforces the notion that there is only one acceptable way to manage a career and that's to toe the company line.

Given the resoundingly negative connotations about pausing, it's a wonder that women who have spent years on their education and then more years working to build a rewarding career would actually leave. The thing that's driving them out must be very powerful.

It sure is.

The following provides an overview of the dynamics I faced when I "opted out" and what women (and, in particular, professional women) still face today.

IDEAL WORKER BIAS

Hastings Law Professor Joan C. Williams has spent years researching how workplace culture and expectation affect both women *and* men. According to Joan, to succeed in the modern, professional workplace, an employee has to personify what she calls the "ideal worker."[50] He's the one who is available 24/7, can travel at a moment's notice, and is never, ever, away from email. Because he has no outside obligations that compete for his time and attention, he can be all-in, all-of-the-time. Family? Household obligations? Not to worry; he has someone at home taking care of all that.

Kind of reminds me of Don Draper from one of my favorite TV shows, *Mad Men*. It also reminds me of my own upbringing. My dad worked all of the time while my mom was at home baking cookies and making our Halloween costumes from scratch. To some it might seem idyllic . . . until you realize Dad was deeply exhausted by the burden of being the sole breadwinner and Mom was frustrated by having no outlet or reward beyond her three lovely children (her words, not mine).

As we all know, that dynamic rarely works today. To get by, most families need two incomes, and yet the workplace still assumes we are each able to be "ideal workers" and that each has someone at home caring for the needs of the family.

The problem isn't just with the workplace itself; our own attitudes toward our careers feed into the dynamic as well. If you go to college, you've likely worked hard to get there. Once there, you spend even more time and money to ensure you can have the career of your choice. Once in your career, you likely want to be successful, to validate the incredible amount of time and money you've invested to get there. How does one do that in the current system? Only by becoming an ideal worker. And how do we make peace with the sacrifices required of the ideal worker? We become what Mary Blair-Loy, associate professor at UC San Diego and founding director of the Center for Research on Gender in the Professions, calls "work devoted."

In her book *Competing Devotions: Career and Family Among Women Executives*, Mary wrote,[51] "Work devotion defines the career as a calling or vocation that deserves single-minded allegiance and gives meaning and purpose to life." In other words, we let what we DO define who we are. Our relationships? They are relegated to second place as our work becomes our life and our life becomes less and less important.

Mary Blair-Loy's research has shown that those who are work devoted personify the ideal worker: They are more likely to be promoted, more likely to become the boss, and more likely to expect work devotion from those below them. It's a perfect self-reinforcing system. To get to the top, you must be an ideal worker, and to be an ideal worker you need to be work devoted and to be able to place your family in someone else's care.

The truth is that this ideal worker construct and notion of work devotion is so embedded in our culture, our organizational practices, and our policies that most of us take it for granted. We don't even realize it exists, so we certainly don't question the underlying beliefs it's built on. It's like fish swimming in water. Do they even know the water is there?

If you are a parent and ambitious, you have two choices: You work all of the time and abandon your loved ones, or you don't work all of the time and watch as your career stalls. It's a classic Hobson's choice: You think you have options, but, really, you don't. To be successful, there is only one real choice, and that is to be an ideal worker who is work devoted.

This construct doesn't just penalize women; men suffer too. Because they are often the primary provider, they get locked into a life of all work and no fun. It's a lose/lose for everyone. But while men do face challenges, we know women face more of them in the workplace, starting with the conscious and unconscious bias that says they are "other."

CONSCIOUS AND UNCONSCIOUS BIAS

When it comes to what holds women back, it is hard not to start with the obvious: good old-fashioned sexism and sexual harassment. Even though

I've tried to explain that it is not uncommon for women to face sexual harassment in the workplace, most of my male friends and colleagues simply don't understand how pervasive it truly is.

I've shared personal stories to highlight what I and others have faced as we worked our way up the ladder. I tell them about the day I gave a major presentation to a group of male colleagues. I was twenty-five years old and had been recently promoted. It was my first time presenting to this group of managers. The room was freezing, and my light sweater wasn't enough to keep me warm. One of the executives announced he couldn't focus on what I was saying because my "headlights" were blinding him. I can still remember the shame I felt as the entire room burst into laughter.

Then there was the night that a team of managers and I went out for a celebratory dinner. We were in Atlanta at a sales meeting, and we'd had a long day of presentations, talks, and client negotiations. We were tired but excited by our success. We went out to enjoy a delicious meal and some very fine wine. After dinner, my boss's boss and I entered the elevator to go to our hotel rooms. He turned, cornered me, and stuck his sloppy tongue down my throat. I pushed him away. He did it again. When we arrived at my floor and the doors to the elevator opened, he held my arm and begged me to come up to his room. I yanked my arm away, raced to my own room, and spent the night wondering what I had done to invite his unwelcome advances. The fact that I was married seemed to be irrelevant to him.

These examples are just two of many I could list from my own life, and I am not unique. And yet, my male friends and colleagues argue that surely this kind of overt harassment is a thing of the past. Not so much. Consider what Trae Vassallo,[52] a former general partner at venture capital firm Kleiner, Perkins, Caufield and Byers, learned when she sent out a survey to her vast network of high-profile women in technology.

Trae had worked alongside Ellen Pao, who notoriously tried to sue KPCB for creating a hostile workplace rife with sexual harassment. Ellen lost her lawsuit, and the talk around Silicon Valley was that it wasn't a company or a systemic issue, just one cranky woman. Trae knew she had faced issues around sexual harassment and guessed other women had as well.

She decided to get data. In the fall of 2015, Trae partnered with researcher Michele Madanksy to create a survey called the "Elephant in the Valley."[53] She asked her network to respond anonymously and heard back from more than 200 women, most of whom had ten or more years of experience in tech. The results were astonishing:

- 60 percent reported experiencing unwanted sexual advances
- 65 percent said at least one of those advances came from a direct superior
- 66 percent said they were intentionally left out of important networking opportunities
- 84 percent had been told they were too ambitious

And those results aren't unique to the tech industry. I've worked in financial services, packaged goods, journalism, and advertising. I've researched the military, academia, and medicine. The data is consistent: Women face overt harassment and conscious bias in just about every industry.[54]

As one father said to me, "It's enough to want to make you lock your daughters in a tower."

Don't worry, dads; we're big girls. We can handle it. We have been for years. We, finally, have laws and systems in place to help us. And while these systems and laws are often flawed, they are far better than the nothing we had before. Most of us can deal with conscious bias. It's the unconscious bias that's so truly insidious.

Study after study has shown that when two candidates with similar skills and abilities are placed next to each other, the candidate with the male-sounding name (e.g., Jack versus Jill) is invariably offered the job, the promotion, the higher pay. One recent study showed that within just two short years of graduation, female MBAs are paid 20 percent less than their male peers who graduated with them from the *same* schools and entered the *same* careers and, sometimes, who even worked at the *same* companies.[55] Perhaps this is because, as some have suggested, the women weren't as good at negotiating their pay. Or, as others have suggested, perhaps it's because they were facing a system that is perfectly happy to pay them less.

The good news is that much attention is finally being given to unconscious bias. Companies are finally taking action to deal with it and how it leads to discrimination in the workplace. For example, in 2015 the CEO of Intel committed $300 million to eradicate bias in his workplace, with much of the money geared to efforts focused on unconscious bias.

Change is happening—but it will take years to see any real results. Meanwhile, for women, conscious and unconscious bias is simply the cost of doing business.

Sadly, it's what happens when we become mothers that crushes the professional dreams of so many bright, talented women.

MOTHERHOOD BIAS

In 2007, Stanford University Professor Shelley Correll set out to understand why women weren't advancing in their careers. She believed one powerful reason was motherhood, and so, with a team of professors from two other universities, Shelley conducted research about attitudes toward mothers in the workplace.

The research team presented 192 undergraduates with a series of potential job applicants for a marketing job at a telecommunications company. After controlling for race and gender, the key distinguisher was that one set of applicants included on their résumés that they had been a Parent-Teacher Association Coordinator and had two children. The other résumés made no mention of their roles as parents. The results were definitive:

- Non-mothers were recommended for the job 84 percent of the time, while mothers were recommended only 47 percent of the time
- The recommended starting salary for mothers was 7.4 percent less than non-mothers
- The mothers were rated as less promotable and were less likely to be recommended for management
- The mothers were also viewed as less competent and less committed

OK, this proves that undergraduates are biased against mothers, but they don't have significant work experience. Shelley Correll and her team wanted to know what happens to mothers when they try to get real jobs.

They sent similar résumés to open jobs listings for entry and mid-level marketing positions. Again, the only distinction between the sets of résumés was that one indicated participation in the PTA and the other did not. Same name, same skills, same background. Then they waited for callbacks. Non-mothers were called in for an interview 2.1 times more often than mothers. Lesson learned? Mamas, if you want to get a job, hide your truth.

More research by other academics have shown:

- Employed mothers face a 24 percent wage penalty for one child,[56] and 44 percent for two or more children independent of their work interruptions, part-time work, and job level
- The pay gap between mothers and non-mothers is larger than the pay gap between women and men
- Visibly pregnant managers are deemed to be less authoritative, less dependable, and more irrational

All of this research has finally given a name to what so many mothers in the workplace intuitively know they face each and every day: motherhood bias. And it cuts both ways because this bias often leads to what Joan C. Williams has called the "maternal wall."[57]

While the glass ceiling keeps women from rising to the top, the maternal wall keeps them locked in a professional box. It's fueled by the unconscious bias that underlies the belief that mothers must be the primary parent and as such can't be as committed to their jobs. Joan's research and those of others has shown that when women become mothers they are perceived as less competent, less committed, and less promotable. One study found that when women return from maternity leave their subsequent performance reviews plummet.[58] A 2004 landmark federal case validated this.

Elana Back, a school psychologist, claimed that after returning from a three-month parental leave, her female supervisors began making biased comments and remarks including asking how she was "planning on spacing [her] offspring," with one even suggesting Elana "not . . . get pregnant until I retire."[59] Elana claimed her supervisor expressed concern about her ability to work because she had "little ones" at home and it was "not possible for [her] to be a good mother and have this job."

In *Back v. Hastings-on-Hudson Union Free School District*, the federal court agreed[60] with Back and ruled that the use of motherhood stereotypes of female employees is gender discrimination under the Equal Protection

Clause of the Fourteenth Amendment, which prohibits discrimination on the basis of sex in public employment.

Fighting against the maternal wall is something all mothers face whether they want to pull back their careers or not. Carolyn Herzog, vice president of Symantec's Legal and Public Affairs department, can certainly attest to this. As the primary breadwinner in her family, she is willing and able to "lean in" but has found she often has to "help" her bosses overcome their misperception about her commitment.

I met Carolyn when she agreed to participate on a panel I was moderating about women's leadership for an event at LinkedIn. When I asked the panelists if they felt they had faced motherhood bias in their careers, Carolyn said, "Absolutely, but not as you might think."

She told the audience, "As I was preparing to go on maternity leave, my boss suggested I might want to ease back slowly. She even offered to let me work part-time at first." Carolyn went on to say, "You'd think that would be great for a new mother, but I didn't want or need that. I had a husband at home who was the primary parent, which allowed me to focus on my career. I was raring to go. My boss's preconceived idea of what a mother wants or needs could have held me back if I hadn't spoken up and been very clear about my professional goals and dreams."

The maternal wall presumes all women *want* to put their families first and also that all women *must* put their families first. But as we know, how each woman integrates her work and her family obligations is unique to her own set of circumstances. At the very least, we should be empowering women by giving them the opportunity to make self-directed choices, not forcing them into preconceived ideas of what it means to be a mother in the workplace.

For those mothers who do want or need to downshift temporarily, Professor Joan Williams has discovered they face yet another issue: an unrelenting stigma against flexibility.

FLEXIBILITY BIAS

In 2013, Joan C. Williams and a team of other researchers released a series of studies in the *Journal of Social Issues* addressing how the use of flexible work solutions impacts our careers.[61] The news is not good.

In the past decade, more and more employers have increased options to help their employees manage where and when they work. These employee "perks" can include part-time work, condensed workweeks, job sharing, and telecommuting. In fact, 79 percent of U.S. firms allow some of their employees, and 37 percent allow all or most, to periodically change starting or quitting times.[62] A 2014 National Study of Employers found that 38 percent of employers allow some of their employees to regularly work from home,[63] up from 23 percent in 2008. But while flexibility programs have become widespread, according to Joan C. Williams, their usage rates remain low: Only 11 percent of the full-time workforce has a formal agreement with their employer to vary their work hours, while another 18 percent have an informal agreement.

Why? Employees worry those who actually use these "benefits" will face career repercussions, a flexibility stigma that can have long-term implications for one's career.

"Many times these policies are on the books, but informally everyone knows you are penalized for using them," said Professor Williams.[64]

I can certainly relate. When I returned to work at the Nestlé Corporation after my first child was born, I negotiated a much-needed condensed workweek. My employer and I agreed that I would work Monday through Thursday and would be off on Friday. My title and salary would remain the same; I would simply be working longer hours to make up for the day I was not in the office. Sounds good on paper. I was grateful for the support my company gave me. That is, until my new manager started complaining.

He said I was never available when he needed me. He continually scheduled important meetings on Fridays and openly pondered my commitment to the job. At one point, he told me he thought children benefited from being raised by their mothers and asked me why I wasn't at home with my son.

"Isn't it hard leaving him home with a complete stranger every day?" he asked me not long after I had returned from maternity leave. I fantasized about saying something like, "Yes, you idiot, of course it is," but instead I decided to leave the company. It didn't take long for me to find a better job with more responsibility and a bigger salary. It's true I lost my free Friday, but at least I didn't have to work directly for a boss who believed I was neither fully committed to my career nor a good mother.

The flexibility stigma can derail a good career when companies and managers don't see flexibility as a retention tool. A number of respondents to the *Women on the Rise* survey found that working part-time kept them from key assignments and limited their ability to be promoted. As a result, many eventually quit working—yet more women's careers derailed because the workplace simply couldn't accommodate their short-term caregiving needs.

The ideal worker construct, motherhood bias, and flexibility stigma are the workplace dynamics that send women slinking toward the door, but there are also cultural dynamics that draw them home. The *Women on the Rise* survey revealed it wasn't just the challenges they faced in the office, it was the dynamics at home that, as one respondent said, "drove a nail into the coffin" of their careers.

"SECOND SHRIFT" BIAS

In 1989, Arlie Hochschild, professor of sociology at UC Berkeley, published her book *The Second Shift: Working Parents and the Revolution at Home*. In it, she argued that what was holding women back from having success in their careers was that they were forced to work two shifts. The first in the office and the second at home. Men, according to Arlie, weren't holding up their end when it came to caring for the children and the household.

She wrote, "One reason that half the lawyers, doctors, business people are not women is because men do not share the raising of their children and the caring of their homes."[65]

It's convenient to blame men, but much of this can be seen as a workplace issue. If, to succeed, someone needs to operate like an ideal worker, then someone else needs to be focused on the home front. Traditionally, as we know, it has been women bearing the weight of this burden. Add to this the reality that women are more likely to find their careers stalled once they have children and it's no wonder many women have ended up privileging their husband's careers by leaving the paid workforce to care for their families. In essence they are not only doing a second shift at home; they are short shifting their careers or giving those careers the "second shrift," as one woman I interviewed called it.

A majority (55 percent) of respondents to the *Women on the Rise* survey revealed that having a partner whose career was demanding was influential in their decision to pause. In the comments section, many cited their husbands' heavy travel and intense work requirements as the rationale for why they left.

We can argue that a woman who allows her husband's career to take precedence wasn't really committed to her own profession, but that ignores the reality that her husband was likely already making much more than she was. Many of the women I interviewed had met their husbands in college or graduate school. They expected to move ahead in equal measure both in terms of their professional advancement and their pay, but they were dismayed when they came to discover their husbands were consistently paid a higher salary and were being promoted faster *even before kids came into the picture.* But as we have seen, women (and mothers in particular) are paid less than their husbands. So, what's a smart woman to do when she is faced with the challenges of work and family?

I believe women who put their husbands' careers first for a period of time while they pause to care for the needs of the family aren't lacking ambition; they're being strategic. If the couple both agree that having one partner at home caring for the children while they are young is a priority, it makes sense to have the partner with lower lifetime earning potential be the one to downshift temporarily. The dream of the two-career power couple who are both all-in, all-of-the-time, remains elusive for most of us. If both partners are forced to operate like ideal workers to be successful, then who is there to care for the family? Sure, you can staff it out as some have chosen to do, but for many that is not an optimal solution. As a result, women often are forced to privilege their husbands' careers.

That was true in my case. Bill was making more money, loved his job, and was on a faster track to the top than I before we had kids. Once we had kids, he made even more money and was on an even faster track. Meanwhile, there were few two-career couples showing us the way. There are more today, but certainly not enough.

Getting men to co-own the home front duties is one answer, as Sharon Meers and Joanna Strober argued in their book *Getting to 50/50: How Working Parents Can Have It All.* They believe we'll see more women stay on track with their careers if more men engage at home. In their chapter entitled "Women Don't Quit Because They *Want* To," they wrote,

> As we watched our female peers leave the workforce, it rarely looked to us like they were choosing to quit. Yes, some were drawn by a desire to focus full time on kids, but more often, the women weren't leaving because of a deep desire to spend all day, every day with their children. Instead, these new moms were caught in a vise—between husbands who weren't doing their share at home and bosses who didn't give an inch at work. Overwhelmed and disillusioned, these women made the seemingly rational decision to stop working until the storm passed.[66]

I wish all of us could live lives in which we shared the responsibilities of the home front on a 50/50 basis. Like Sharon and Joanna, I truly believe both women and men would benefit by being able to be fully engaged at home and at work. Men benefit by having a more fulfilled partner who shares the financial burdens. Women benefit by being able to share the home burdens and being able to stay on track professionally.

Sounds great, but I believe that even if we try to share duties 50/50, the modern workplace won't allow for it. If we want to be successful, we need to be ideal workers, which means we aren't available to do our 50 percent of the caregiving and housework. As result, many couples unintentionally end up reinforcing traditional gender roles. No fun for men who carry the monetary burdens and are kept from having the time to be deeply engaged with their children. No fun for women who carry the household and parenting burdens and whose careers get "short shrifted" in the process.

IDEAL MOTHER BIAS

In a 2012 comprehensive study[67] of attitudes toward working mothers, only 16 percent of American men and women thought a mother should work full-time. Meanwhile, a full 30 percent believed a mother should not work at all. Why? Because they believe moms are best.

I'm sure I don't need to regale you with all of the studies that show children need committed, engaged caregivers to thrive, but there is little definitive data that says moms are the best caregivers of all. When it comes to helping children flourish, study after study has shown children actually do well, if not better, if their mothers work.

According to a 2015 article by *New York Times* journalist Claire Cain Miller, "In a new study of 50,000 adults in 25 countries, daughters of working mothers completed more years of education, were more likely to be employed and in supervisory roles and earned higher incomes. Having a working mother didn't influence the careers of sons, which researchers said was unsurprising because men were generally expected to work—but sons of working mothers did spend more time on child care and housework."[68]

And, a 2010 meta-analysis[69] that rounded up sixty-nine studies over fifty years confirmed that young children with working mothers went on to have no major learning, behavior, or social problems. In fact, they tended to be high achievers in school and have less depression and anxiety than those whose mothers didn't work outside the home.

And yet, we still convince ourselves that mothers (not fathers!) are best. Isn't the most insidious bias of all the one that reinforces the myth that children only thrive with a mother at home to care for them? If that truly is the case, how can a woman possibly justify having a career? What mother wouldn't be wracked with guilt every time her child got a cold, had a challenge in school, didn't get invited to that special playdate? It is this very thinking that sends so many bright, talented women racing for home.

It happened to Julie Ligon. She was a rising star working in marketing at The Gap when she became pregnant with her first child. Her female boss, who was a mom and a vice president, told Julie, "If you're doing your job well that means you're not being a good mom and if you are being a good mom, you're not doing your job well. It's a no-win situation."

Julie loved the fast pace and the dynamic group of people she worked with, but Julie had no idea how to prove her boss wrong and be both a good mother and good at her job. Before her child was born, she was already set up to feel like a failure. After she gave birth, she put her daughter into a small day care group where Julie knew her new baby was safe and well cared for. And then her daughter got sick.

"My baby got a fever and I was in meetings and unavailable all day. Good moms don't do that," Julie told me. She asked to work part-time, three days a week. No go. Then she asked if she could at least work from home a few days a week. Again, no go. So Julie quit.

Like so many women who leave the workforce, Julie loved her job, but she felt the pressure to be an "ideal" mom, one who is available to meet the needs of her children at all times. As Julie told me, "I always wanted to be a mom. So leaving wasn't that big of a deal."

Perhaps not. Julie has since become a franchisee of the Dailey Method and happily teaches classes around her children's schedules. But the truth is, she may well have stayed and become one of those women we all say we want at the top, if the flexibility she needed had been there for her. The intransigent workplace coupled with her own sense of the "ideal" mother meant the only solution for Julie was to leave the corporate world.

When I asked why her husband couldn't have taken care of their ill daughter, Julie said it never even occurred to her. Partly because his career in sales was so demanding, but also because she felt she was "the mom" and would take better care of their baby.

Therein lies yet another problem with the notion of the "ideal" mom: Fathers get second billing.

We are seeing a huge spike in the numbers of fathers who are taking the lead as primary parent and yet we still convince ourselves mothers are best. Not only does this keep mothers from being able to fully commit to their careers, it keeps fathers from being fully committed to their roles as engaged parents. As one stay-at-home dad told me, "It's so damn insulting when everyone assumes my children aren't getting the best care because my wife works and I'm the one at home."

I believe the ideal mother bias is a key reason most ambitious women leave their careers. Yes, the workplace can be intolerable, but many of us still tolerate it. It's the inability to make peace with our perception that we are the best caregivers for our children that holds most women back. I know it did me.

Good mothers, we were (and still are) told, put their children's needs first. Mothers who put their careers first were (are) selfish. Just as I had internalized the message that women needed to be all-in if they wanted a successful career, I had internalized the message that mothers need to be all-in if they wanted their children to thrive. I knew I couldn't do both, so something had to give. When it came to weighing what I was willing to sacrifice, I realized I was more willing to sacrifice my career than I was willing to sacrifice my sense of my children's well-being. I knew I couldn't live with the guilt if anything were to happen to them.

Can you even call that a choice?

If you want to make yourself crazy, read Judith Warner's book *Perfect Madness: Motherhood in the Age of Anxiety*. Judith crystallizes the world as I saw it when I became a mother when she wrote,[70]

> As the 1980s turned to the 1990s the word "guilt" was everywhere in the magazine stories on motherhood, and it wasn't about "not feeling guilty" anymore. It was guilt about working, guilt about *not being there* for the children. Working mothers were no longer heroines, symbols of the new and healthy freedoms won by Mothers' Lib. They were villains, selfish, and "unnatural."

The ideal mother and the attendant guilt are the final "nail in the coffin" of the careers of so many women. And once they go home, what's an ambitious woman to do?

Say hello to the Uber Mommy.

She's the one who has taken the notion of "perfect" parenting to a fever pitch and has become the standard bearer of modern motherhood. We've convinced ourselves babies need homemade organic food, cloth diapers, constant engagement to help build their IQs, Mommy and Me classes, entrance to the right preschool, which requires the right networking, and so on and so on. Then they get older and they need us to "help" with homework, manage the tutors, carpool to after-school activities, get them on the elite sports team that will ensure they get a scholarship to the best college, ghostwrite their college applications, send them off to college, before doing it all again for their little brother or sister.

Judith Warner details how the rising demands on parents and the birth of the Uber Mother has made mothering a competitive sport. She wrote,[71]

> We have taken it upon ourselves as super mothers to be everything to our children that society refuses to be: not just loving nurturers but educators, entertainers, guardians of environmental purity, protectors of a stable and prosperous future. This ultimately impotent control-freakishness is the form of learned helplessness acquired by a generation of women confronted by a world in which finding real solutions to improve family life seems impossible.

The truth is mothering hasn't just become who we are; it has become what we do—our new full-time job. The narrative that told us an ideal mother was all-in, all-of-the-time with their children and the concomitant guilt women faced when they weren't was alive and well when my children were young, and is alive and well today.

We want women to commit to their careers by "leaning in" so we can have more women in leadership, but we haven't changed our ideas about what it means to be a good mother. What's going to happen when all of today's amazing, well-educated women are faced with having to "choose" between an unrelenting workplace and ensuring their children's well-being?

I think you know the answer.

FAMILY: THE NEW FEMINIST FRONTIER

When Betty Friedan wrote her 1963 book *The Feminine Mystique*,[72] she gave voice to the deep malaise, frustration, and self-doubt many women in the 1950s and '60s felt in their roles as housewives. She called it "the problem that has no name" and inspired millions of women to join the fight for the opportunity to have careers outside of the home.

Well, now we have them. Yet, women still are only a fractional share of leaders of the vast majority of industries, professions, and careers in this country. Why?

Yes, sexism and unconscious bias in the workplace are part of the problem that holds women back, but I believe there is something deeper going on. I believe the reason more women are not in leadership positions is because they don't want to be. For many of us, the world as it is currently structured is not a world we women generally want to rule. A 2015 study out of Harvard Business School[73] of more than 4,000 highly educated, highly skilled adults revealed that "compared to men, women have higher life goals, associate more negative outcomes with high-power positions, perceive power as less desirable (though equally attainable), and are less likely to take advantage of opportunities for professional advancement."

In other words, we value more than the singular goal of being at the top. As the researchers concluded, "women may not assume high-level positions in organizations—at least in part—because they desire other things as well." It's not that we lack ambition; it is that we want more than what the current paradigm offers. We want to rule a different world, one that allows us to have professional impact AND have deep and meaningful relationships with our families, our friends, and our communities.

> We value more than the singular goal of being at the top.

Sure, there are some women who are willing to forgo their family and relationships and commitment to their communities to rise up within the current paradigm. But for many women, the sacrifices are simply not worth it.

The *Women on the Rise* survey laid bare this truth in rich and beautiful data. Of the 1,476 respondents, 60 percent considered themselves *very* ambitious and yet nearly three-quarters paused their careers at some point.

Why? No doubt it had to do with the workplace. The majority (68 percent) reported the excessive travel, long hours, unrelenting demands, unfair pay, limited options for promotion, and ongoing sense they would never achieve their professional goals were key reasons for why they left.

But, there was more to it than that.

The number one reason these very ambitious, well-educated, high-potential women paused their careers was because they wanted to be the primary caregiver of their children. Over 85 percent reported this as the biggest motivator for their decision to step off the well-trodden path and embark on a non-linear career.

As Friedan showed us, when women were stuck at home with limited options for professional rewards, many were deeply dissatisfied. They wanted to find their rightful place in the paid workforce. But now, after decades of being in the workplace doing our best to compete with and against men, we've come to understand that this is not enough, either.

The work-at-all-cost life doesn't bring us joy or meaning. It denies us the time we want and need to care for our loved ones. It denies us the chance to be our fully integrated, authentic selves. As a result, like so many men who have struggled for generations against the constraints of work, our hard-won professional opportunities often leave us exhausted, demoralized, and even ill.

> **The work-at-all-cost life doesn't bring us joy or meaning. It denies us the time we want and need to care for our loved ones. It denies us the chance to be our fully integrated, authentic selves.**

There is something missing from all of the talk about women's careers and the lack of female leaders and the challenges of work–life balance. What is missing is the acknowledgment of the deep meaning we humans derive from our roles as caregivers. What is missing is the power and importance of family. What is missing is our humanity. The women who "choose" to pause are the proverbial "canaries in the coal mines" giving notice that something is deeply wrong with the way we Americans have structured our lives.

The goal of the original women's empowerment movement was focused on getting women in the workplace. To do this, we were forced to play by men's rules. And we did. But now, more than fifty years since Friedan's book gave voice to our frustrations, we have a new problem with no name. While our grandmothers and mothers were kept from choosing to pursue their professional dreams, professional women today who want to place their families as a priority are discouraged from honoring their personal desires.

New mother Jessica Levy said it best in a 2015 op-ed she wrote for *The New York Times* entitled "I Wanted to Stay Home with My Son. So Why Would I Lie About It?"

> I'm 27 and Ivy League–educated; I was 26 when my son was born. I'm not supposed to be a mother yet, according to most of my peers, and certainly not a stay-at-home one. It's a message that was drilled into me by countless high-powered women who came to give keynote speeches during my university days, driven by the need to warn us about lessons that many of them had learned the hard way: You can't count on anyone but yourself. Lean in. Stay independent . . .

> I knew I wanted to stay home, at least for the near future, when my son was just a few days old. I just couldn't bear to leave him . . . [But] there was a lingering sense of shame that I couldn't shake when friends and family members asked when I was going back to work.[74]

Jessica's shame, her sense that the work she is doing is not worthy, is how The New Problem That Has No Name manifests for women of today. It isn't about a lack of ambition; it's about fighting against a system that doesn't honor or acknowledge the importance of caregiving. At its heart, it's about being denied our full authenticity as women or, more broadly, as humans.

This isn't just a woman's issue. Men have long craved the freedom to be more than their jobs. They, too, want to be with their families in ways that don't force them to sacrifice their careers. If women are locked into a no-win situation, men are bound and gagged.

In fact, a 2015 study by the Public Religion Research Institute,[75] a nonpartisan think tank, reports Millennials aren't worried about women working full-time. When asked what they consider the greatest threat to family life, they say they're worried about men working too much.

Have you heard about Friedan's follow-up book, *The Second Stage*? It was published in the early 1980s. In it, she wrote,

> I believe that feminism must, in fact, confront the family . . . if the movement is to fulfill its own revolutionary function in modern society. Otherwise it will abort or be put on history's shelf—its real promise and significance obscured, distorted, by its denial of life's reality for too many millions of women. Locked into reaction against women's role in the family of the past, we could blindly emulate an obsolete narrow male role in corporate bureaucracy which seems to have more power, not understanding that the power and the promise of the future lie in transcending that absolute separation of the sex roles, in work *and* family.[76]

Betty Friedan goes on to ponder why feminists who succeeded in passing laws that support women in school and in the workplace didn't put as much energy and passion into creating support for parents. With 80 percent of American women destined to become mothers, she argued that unless we create workplaces and national policies that support mothers so they can work, we would see women's advancement stalled.

She was right. As of this writing, it's been thirty-five years since she wrote her second book and the paltry numbers of women in leadership bear her out. It's no wonder Sheryl Sandberg has been driven to call on the next generation to "lean in." It's a much-needed and admirable goal, but unless we change how we treat workers with caregiving responsibilities, my guess is we'll find the movement still stalled thirty years from now.

I believe the conversation around caregiving is at the heart of the next feminist frontier. It's time we broadened our efforts as feminists from a laser-like focus on advancing women professionally to an expanded discussion of what it means to be an American with caregiving responsibilities. Professional women want it. Under-resourced women need it. And men are ready to join the fight for it.

We need to stop making the notion of caregiving an individual woman's "choice" and realize it is an economic and political issue. And how do we do that? By recognizing that the personal *is* political.

It's time we broadened our efforts as feminists from a laser-like focus on advancing women professionally to an expanded discussion of what it means to be an American with caregiving responsibilities.

CHAPTER 4

The Politics of Pausing

"Ultimately, there is no good or bad here, no right or wrong, feminist or anti-feminist. There are only our unique, complicated, and precious stories— may we learn to embrace each other's and our own."
—Michelle Obama

My friend Lee Caraher and I met for lunch at the Hayes Street Grill, a San Francisco institution that dates back, way back, to when both she and I were in high school. Lee is founder and CEO of Double Forte, a well-regarded public relations and digital communications agency with offices in Boston and San Francisco. She is also the author of *Millennials and Management: The Essential Guide to Making It Work at Work.* I wanted Lee's advice on writing a book. I also wanted to understand how my theme might resonate with successful women like her.

Here's what she said: "Sounds like it will be great for stay-at-home moms, but what about those of us who've worked like dogs all these years? We never got the chance to pause."

"Didn't you?" I asked.

Lee, who is the primary breadwinner in her family, had written in her book about how she left her senior-level job as an executive vice president at one of the largest public relations firms in the world to care for her dying mother. Lee didn't pause for parenthood, but she did pause for her mother. Lee spent months in limbo as her mother withered and finally passed away. During that time, to support herself, her husband, and her two young sons, Lee took on consulting projects that allowed her the flexibility she and her family needed.

After her mother died, Lee knew she couldn't return to work for a corporate structure that denied her the flexibility and support she needed to care for those she loved, so Lee decided to launch her own agency. Although Lee's pause was what gave birth to Double Forte, in her view, she had never paused.

Why? Because, as Lee explained to me, she was a "working mother." She never considered herself someone who had taken time out of her career to focus on family. And yet, she had for nearly a year.

Lee's story is not unique. I spoke to many women who emphatically told me they never paused to care for their families (be it for children or elderly relatives) and yet when we discussed their career trajectories, most had spent months, sometimes years, putting their loved ones first.

Take Karen Appleton. She was employee number eight at Box, the highly successful Silicon Valley start-up that is an innovator in online file sharing. Today, thanks to the company's IPO, she is a wealthy woman and a role model for many who aspire to the top of the technology industry.

Like Lee, Karen considers herself a "working" woman who never paused. "I wasn't a stay-at-home mother because I never had the chance to be," she told me when we spoke about her career path.

But Karen did pause. After the birth of her second son, she left her job in business development and moved with her then-husband to Hawaii. She may well have ended up staying at home for longer than the one year she was out of the paid workforce, but divorce led her to become a "mother of reinvention." She returned to Silicon Valley and, thanks to her strong network, eventually managed to land a job in business development at Box.

"I was the only woman there and I was a single mother. I can tell you this: It wasn't easy. But I made it work for my children, for my company, and for me," Karen said. "My sons only know me as a working mother and I'm proud of that."

It is those memories and that passionate commitment to an ideology of "working" motherhood that trumps her sense of herself as pausing, but Karen's career break meant that not only did her personal life change, so did her professional one. Like Lee, the long-term outcome of Karen's pause has meant she has been able to accomplish many things she might never have imagined. Her career break set her life on a new trajectory, *and still* she doesn't think of herself as someone who paused.

And why would she? When we think about pausing, we've been trained by the media to envision those "One Percent" yummy mummies who wear yoga pants while carpooling their kids to soccer practice. Pausing means you've abandoned your career, aren't ambitious, and can't really compete in today's "Most Powerful Women" world.

As a result, many highly accomplished women in the workforce distance themselves from their own truth. They, understandably, don't want to be associated with the idea of taking a break because they want others to view them as committed. In their own minds, they have been all-in, all-of-the-time and want to be perceived that way. The unintended consequence is that other women, who look to these leaders as the role models they are, have no idea "how she does it"—because how she has *really* done it isn't part of the successful woman's career narrative.

By not fully owning their non-linear career paths, successful women do not convey to the world the alternative ways one can rise to the top—that it is possible to pull back and still power forward. The result? Pausing is seen as a failure, not as a strategic move in the overall arc of a career.

More important, pausing becomes viewed as the "choice" of individual women, not a necessary response to the realities of the workplace. But collectively those "choices" have big consequences. Let's start with the leadership gap.

PAUSING AND THE LEADERSHIP GAP

In 1985, women started graduating from college at the same rate as men. In the decades that followed, men have fallen behind. By 2014, over 60 percent of college graduates were women[77] and nearly 40 percent of women in the United States had earned a college degree, compared to only 32 percent of men. Looking ahead, the predictions are that the ratio will never go back to 50/50. We women are outpacing men, at least when it comes to education.

When it comes to running the show, men still rule the world.

You've probably seen these statistics before, but here's a refresher on a few traditionally male-dominated professions. In 2015, men made up the following:[78]

- 96 percent of Fortune 500 CEOs
- 94 percent of firefighters
- 87 percent of police officers
- 83 percent of corporate board seats
- 80 percent of law partners
- 81 percent of members of Congress
- 74 percent of presidents of colleges and universities
- 74 percent of scientists
- 72 percent of full professors
- 66 percent of doctors

Those professions are all highly paid and are highly regarded by society as a whole. What professions do women dominate? Low-paid ones such as kindergarten teachers (97 percent), dental assistants (96 percent), nurse practitioners (91 percent), and so on.[79]

Given women are the majority of college graduates and have been for decades, how could this be? One rationale has been that we don't have enough women in the pipeline to the top of these male-dominated professions. But in most cases, that's a myth.

To give a few examples, women make up:[80]

- 52 percent of entry-level jobs in the financial services industry but only 22 percent of senior leadership
- 59 percent of entry-level jobs in health care and pharmaceuticals but only 23 percent of senior leadership
- 48 percent of entry-level jobs in logistics and transportation but only 15 percent of senior leadership
- 46 percent of entry-level jobs in retailing and consumer goods but only 13 percent of senior leadership
- 37 percent of entry-level jobs in technology but only 15 percent of senior leadership

The truth is we do have women in the pipeline. But it's a pipeline that's leaking. Women leave during the critical career-building years, which coincide with those critical child-bearing and child-rearing years. And when women leave, not only are there fewer female candidates for leadership positions, there also aren't enough women left to challenge the culture and make change for others. This is a powerful reason for the negative view of highly qualified women who pause their careers.

Professor Stone captured it best when she said, "Once they leave the corporate workplace, their ability to imbue workplace culture with their values is gone. They leave, and the door closes behind them, and everything stays the same."[81]

But does having more women at the top really change things for the women below them? It seems obvious that it would, but given there are so few women in leadership, the answer to this question has been elusive. There are more women at the top than there were when I graduated from college, and yet the workplace still looks exactly the same. Why is that?

Look closely at the women who are currently running major companies and other organizations in our country, women like Anne-Marie Slaughter.

Anne-Marie is president and CEO of New America Foundation and a professor of politics at Princeton University. She has a storied career, which she details in her book *Unfinished Business: Women Men Work Family.* In all of her writing and speaking on the subject, Anne-Marie has been very clear that she could do what she has done professionally only because her husband, Andrew Moravcsik, was willing to be the primary (or "lead," as he calls it) parent. And Anne-Marie's situation is not unique.

Not so long ago, she was at an invite-only event put on by the *Fortune* magazine "Most Powerful Women" team. The room was filled with female leaders from a variety of industries. Anne-Marie asked the mothers in the room how many had working husbands. Turns out, very few.

As Anne-Marie learned, the majority of women at the top of their fields who have children also have husbands who have put their own careers on the back burner and taken on the role of "lead" parent. In other words, today's female leaders didn't get to where they are with a partner whose job was equally demanding; they got where they are because they, like generations of male leaders before them, have someone at home caring for the needs of the family.

So, when it comes to rising to a leadership position, we've got the same dynamic, just opposite genders in the roles of primary breadwinner and primary parent. I passionately want to have more gender equality at the top, but is a gender role reversal of the same broken system really the goal?

And there's another issue: If the women who are currently in leadership positions followed the same paths that men have followed for years, how can they fully understand the demands on those mothers in the middle who might want to get to the top but don't have husbands who are willing or able to step back? The current batch of women in leadership succeeded despite the challenges that women face in the workplace, which means they figured out how to play it like a man. Given that the system worked for them, are they truly motivated to change it? Or, do they suffer a hidden "bootstrap" mentality that has them secretly harboring a resistance to changing the status quo? Do they think, "I figured it out. Why can't you?"

Even if these leaders want to make change, they are often the only women at their level. It is likely they truly are committed to changing the workplace to make it more family- and female-friendly, but because they are the lone voice in the room, their ideas and concerns aren't given full due.

We are finally beginning to see research that reveals that having women at the top does make the workplace more hospitable for the women below them. For example, a 2015 industry-wide study conducted by The 3% Movement,[82] a company dedicated to increasing the number of women in advertising, revealed that in agencies with more than 25 percent women in creative leadership, the mid-level and junior-level female creative talent had greater job satisfaction, higher pay, and less hostile working environments, and were assigned more exciting and rewarding creative work.

That's great news for women in general, but what about mothers in particular? Looking more closely at the data from The 3% Movement, it turns out only 38 percent of women who responded had children. That's a whopping 42 percent lower than the national average of American women who are mothers and 10 percent lower than the number of American mothers who work full-time. We don't know if having women in leadership actually helps mothers in the advertising industry, but we do know that the majority of women leave the agency world during those intense child-rearing and child-bearing years. Do they leave because the environment is hostile to mothers? Did the lack of female leaders who were also mothers convince women below them that it couldn't be done? It was true for me all those years ago, and my guess is that it is true for many women in the industry today.

We see the same issues in STEM (Science, Technology, Engineering, and Math) careers where over 60 percent of women leave the field during their thirties and early forties. We like to blame pay inequity, hostile work environments, conscious and unconscious bias, but it doesn't take much to put two and two together. Women in STEM (like women in many other male-dominated professions) are leaving right during those intense children-bearing and child-rearing years. Do they all really lack ambition?

Which brings us back to the original point. The leaky pipeline is a significant problem. When highly qualified women leave the workforce, we lose the very women who are motivated to make change for others because they understand how challenging it is to integrate work and family obligations.

So, let me be clear: Of course we want more women in leadership. But if it means the women who get there don't have the personal motivation or the institutional support to create inclusive cultures, then nothing will really change for working families. As Anne-Marie Slaughter wrote in her book,[83] "It's easier for employers to marginalize an issue if they label it a 'women's problem.' A women's problem is an individual issue, not a company-wide problem."

What we really need is the *right people* at the top. We need leaders who are committed to making the workplace work for families so that men who want to care for their children or women who want to care for their parents or mothers who want to (or have to) care for both have the flexibility to do so without risking their careers and their financial well-being.

PAUSING AND THE ECONOMY

Another powerful reason many have argued we must keep women engaged in the workforce has less to do with social politics and more to do with economics. If you've taken a basic economics course you know that an economy can't grow if there aren't enough workers to do the work.

After World War II, we had tons of young men returning to the workforce, but by the mid-1970s we'd tapped out on potential new workers. Sure, we could have relied on immigrants, as we had since this country was founded, but the recession in the early 1970s caused many Americans to fight against expanding our immigrant population (a fight that, as we know, continues today). So where was our country supposed to get new workers? Women!

There is no debate amongst economists that the single greatest benefit to our economy in the past thirty years has been the rise of women in the workforce. Since 1979, the proportion of working-age women with a full-time job has surged to 40.7 percent from 28.6 percent. A study by the Center for Economic and Policy Research[84] says that if, over the last thirty years, women hadn't been in the workforce in such great numbers, the economy would be about 11 percent smaller. And according to the World Economic Forum, if women's working patterns were more like men's (that is, with the majority working full-time rather than only 48 percent working full-time), our economy would increase by another 9 percent.[85] No wonder the notion of pausing is anathema to those who want to see the American economy thrive.

Sadly, female workforce participation in the United States has stagnated since the 1990s. According to the Organization for Economic Cooperation and Development (OECD), between 1991 and 2014 the rate of workforce participation for women has remained at 74 percent. It actually rose to 77 percent during the mid-1990s before then dropping back down to 74 percent where it has stayed since.[86] Meanwhile, as noted in chapter 1, we are seeing an ever-increasing rise in stay-at-home moms. Compare our female workforce participation trend with Norway (79 percent to 84 percent), Germany (72 percent to 82 percent), and Canada (76 percent to 82 percent) and you can sense that we are not moving ahead. Even Japan is outpacing us (65 percent to 75 percent). The average growth of women's workforce participation for industrialized nations went from 67 percent to 79 percent. Why is the United States lagging behind? The OECD blames our lack of family-friendly policies.[87]

We need bright, talented women in the workforce so much that there is actually a whole new field of study called Womenomics devoted to figuring out how to get more women working. But we already know one powerful solution: Solve the caregiving dilemma.

How do we do that? By developing systems and structures that support the needs of parents. High-quality universal day care, paid parental leave, paid sick leave, onsite after-school programs that don't require someone to chauffeur their children back and forth, flexible workplaces, bosses who value results and not "face time," and re-entry programs that support those who have stepped out to care for their families, are just a few of the ways we can support mothers so they can work. Sure, women will benefit, but the biggest winner of all will be our economy.

The sad truth is, it's unlikely we will see this anytime soon. Why? We have wrapped the notion of pausing under the cloak of "choice" and "privilege," fueling class wars that keep us from focusing on the real problem at hand: public policies that don't support families.

PAUSING AND THE ISSUE OF PRIVILEGE

One of my friends is a hard-working single mother of two. Ellen (as I'll call her) never went to college, but makes ends meet by working as an in-home care nurse. She is often one paycheck away from being booted from her rental apartment. She has never considered taking a pause because she has never had, as she calls it, the "luxury" to do so. Pausing, as she sees it, is the purview of wealthy women who married rich husbands.

She's not alone. When we think of women who pause, we think of "opt-out" moms like the Princeton-educated women Lisa Belkin profiled in 2004. There is no doubt there is some truth to this profile. These women graduated from prestigious schools, married husbands destined to be successful, and then left their careers when their babies were born because they had the resources to do so. As noted in chapter 1, nearly 60 percent of women who graduate from elite universities do step back from their careers for a period of time to care for their children. But, these elites make up only 5 percent of current stay-at-home mothers.

The reality is two-thirds of stay-at-home married moms are middle class. True, they are privileged to be married, but they, along with their husbands, are cobbling together suboptimal solutions to meet the demands of work and family. For many of them, it is often cheaper to stay home because they cannot find work that covers the cost of day care. Today, a year of day care costs more than a year of college in many states.[88]

And it's not just the outrageous cost of child care, but also the unyielding payload of school debt that is poised to impact mothers in the workplace.

Today, more and more middle-class families are sacrificing everything to send their children to college. Arguably, that's good news. More women with college degrees means there are more women contributing to the economy and, we would expect, more women in the pipeline to leadership. The bad news is that most of these newly minted college-educated women are burdened with mountains of school debt and/or have husbands—as I did—with mountains of debt. Juggling the high cost of day care with the immovable burden of school loans means couples have few options, and often one of them (typically, the woman) is *forced* to pause. There's no "luxury" in that.

Rising journalist Annamarya Scaccia is facing this issue right now. She unexpectedly got pregnant a few months after she started her master's program at CUNY Graduate School of Journalism. She and her partner, Richard, decided they could afford for her to finish her degree, but when she graduates, Annamarya won't be able to work full-time until their son starts kindergarten. The loans she has from both college and graduate school make paying for day care prohibitive.

"I am so eager and ready to work, but we can't afford it. We've decided I'll try to freelance as a journalist for the next few years while Richard provides the steady income," she said. "Hopefully by the time my son goes to school, the culture of work will have changed enough so that my career break won't mean career suicide."

More than 40 million Americans currently hold nearly $1.3 trillion in student load debt, averaging around $40,000 each.[89] Given that women make up over 60 percent of college graduates, it falls to reason that they share a majority of said debt. If women can't afford to work because we can't afford the twin burdens of child care and school debt, believing that women's workforce participation will increase is simply a fool's dream. How then is their pause a privilege?

And what about the 34 percent of women at the bottom of the economic ladder who are stay-at-home moms? For them, the "privilege" of pausing has nothing to do with luxury and everything to do with having no institutionalized support in place to help them get back into the workforce after they have children. They don't have paid leave, and few have access to subsidized day care. And, because they are often hourly workers, they are at the whim of companies who refuse to give them regular schedules.

Consider Jannette Navarro, single mother to four-year-old son, Gavin. She was profiled in a 2014 *New York Times* article by Jodi Kantor about the challenges low-income parents face when it comes to managing their jobs and families. Jodi wrote,

> Flexibility—an alluring word for white-collar workers, who may desire, say, working from home one day a week—can have a darker meaning for many low-income workers as a euphemism for unstable hours or paychecks.[90]

Jodi explained that Jannette was thrilled by her new job as a barista at Starbucks, but she couldn't handle the inconsistent schedule the company claimed allowed them to efficiently and economically meet customer demand. Jannette and her son had challenges finding a place to live, and Gavin's day care placement was at risk because of his mom's erratic schedule. Sure, she had a "flexible" job, but without consistent hours, Jannette couldn't create the stability she and her son needed.

Jannette is not yet, though she may soon become, one of the under-resourced, stay-at-home mothers who want to, but can't, work. While no one considers these women as "pausing" their careers, they too are not engaged in the paid workforce because of their caregiving needs. Their situations highlight even more strongly the problems with our system and give insight into why pausing—however it looks—becomes the solution of last resort.

At its core, pausing is about the lack of support structures we have in this country for caregiving. As long as we view pausing as a personal decision for women of means, we won't be forced to actually change our policies to help families at every economic level.

As E. J. Graff, a journalist and senior fellow at Brandeis University, has written,

> If women are happily choosing to stay home with their babies, that's a private decision. But it's a public policy issue if most women (and men) need to work to support their families, and if the economy needs women's

> skills to remain competitive. It's a public policy issue if schools, jobs, and other American institutions are structured in ways that make it frustratingly difficult, and sometimes impossible, for parents to manage both their jobs and family responsibilities.[91]

We need to look at when and how and why women leave the workforce through the caregiving lens. Wealthy women may leave because they can and under-resourced women may leave because they have to, but if we want more women in aggregate in the workforce we need to recognize that both of these groups are leaving for the same reason: The workplace punishes families.

> We have wrapped the notion of pausing under the cloak of "choice" and "privilege," fueling class wars that keep us from focusing on the real problem at hand: public policies that don't support families.

PAUSING AND THE ISSUE OF RACE

We all have our heroes, but for me, Michelle Obama is at the top of the list. Sure she's a fashion icon and has done wonders for childhood health and obesity, but it is how she has integrated her work and personal priorities that I find so deeply inspirational.

Before she became first lady, she was a lawyer, a public servant, and a vice president at the University of Chicago's Medical Center. She was also a mother to two young daughters and the primary breadwinner for the family. While Barack Obama was busy devoting himself to his work as a community organizer and rising politician, Michelle was "leaning in."

In 2008, when her husband was running for office, Michelle Obama was asked what she planned to do professionally if he won. Her answer? "My most important job will be Mom-in-Chief." It was a sucker punch to those who imagined Michelle and Barack as the ultimate power couple, she working on policy while he ran the country. Most were willing to overlook her statement as political posturing meant to calm more traditional voters and preferred to believe that once Barack was in office, she'd roll up her own sleeves and apply her many talents and skills in some significant way.

Instead, once in office, she focused on helping her daughters make the tough transition to Washington and on helping other children with her campaigns promoting healthy eating and exercise. When her husband decided to run for a second term, hopes were again raised that maybe now she would start doing something really important.

Then in 2012 at the Democratic National Convention, as she finished her speech introducing her husband, Michelle Obama said, "And I say all of this tonight not just as first lady, and not just as a wife. You see, at the end of the day, my most important title is still 'Mom-in-Chief.'"[92]

In other words, she meant it. She really meant it.

As you can imagine, her speech created a firestorm. Lilith Dornhuber wrote in a comment on Feministing.com, "Judging by Michelle Obama's speech, feminism is dead to the Democratic party."[93] She went on to accuse the first lady of "valorizing mid-20th-century gender roles." Jessica Valenti, a well-regarded Millennial feminist writer and leader wrote, "I long for the day when powerful women don't need to assure Americans that they're moms above all else."[94]

But Michelle Obama's choices go beyond feminist rhetoric. When she paused her career to become "Mom-in-Chief," she didn't just send a signal that highly qualified women can pause, she sent a signal that highly qualified *women of color* can pause.

For decades now, we have scrutinized unemployed women of color (and in particular, African American women) and questioned their actions. Sure white women might "choose" to pause their careers, but when women of color do it, they bump up against racist and classist notions related to welfare.

In 1976 when he was running for office and again in the 1980s when he actually was in office, Ronald Reagan said he would fight to prevent fraud and protect taxpayers' dollars from those who might "cheat" the system—the "those" here being primarily under-resourced mothers of color. The term "welfare queen" became code for black mothers in poverty who needed the support of welfare to survive. To this day, that term and the women it represents are paraded around by the far-right as a threat to our country.

In the past decade, we are seeing more and more women of color leave the workforce when they have children. Some of this is as a result of a system that provides no support to under-resourced women, and some of it has to do with family values.

According to Pew Research Center, only 23 percent of black children and 26 percent of white children are being raised by stay-at-home mothers, but 37 percent of Asian and 36 percent of Hispanic kids have moms at home.[95] Why are so many Asian and Hispanic moms staying home to care for their young children? For some it is economic, but for many it is about a belief system that values having mothers home raising children when they are young. With the growing diversity of our country and the continued influx of well-educated immigrants,[96] we are likely to see a further increase of highly qualified women of color who pause from the workforce when their children are young.

As a white woman, I can't presume to understand the subtle complexities of race and class Michelle Obama and other college-educated women of color face each and every day. But Kuae Mattox does. She's an African-American broadcast journalist who paused her career when her three children were young. Kuae was deeply conflicted about her choice and not just because she was a college-educated woman with a rising career, but also because she is a black woman whose cultural heritage of economic hardship meant that to "give it all up" was doubly challenging.

Kuae and I met in New York when I moderated a panel on women who have successfully relaunched their careers. She told me, "Historically, African American mothers have not had the opportunity to stay at home with their children. The heavy focus has always been on rising up economically. Financial success has always been the pinnacle. Staying at home was seen by many as something that white women did. But I remembered the few years my mother was able to be home with me and my siblings. I wanted to be there for mine as she was for us."

Kuae needed community support for her untraditional path, and so she joined Mocha Moms, a national organization for stay-at-home mothers of color, the vast majority of whom are college-educated. The group was founded in 1997 and now has more than 100 chapters across the country. It is, as Kuae told me, "growing like wildfire."

Kuae became so actively involved in Mocha Moms that she rose to be its national president. During that time, she was consistently dismayed by the misperception of women of color who had stepped away from the paid workforce.

"When I speak at conferences or with other groups, I often realize people have certain assumptions about our organization," she told me. "They wrongly perceive that we are single mothers on welfare. We are mostly married, college-educated professionals who have temporarily stepped away from the workforce to raise our kids. Mocha Moms is committed to setting the record straight. We are here to prove there are, in fact, professional couples of color who elect to have the mother stay home."

Kuae was out of the paid workforce for nearly fourteen years, but like so many of the women I interviewed, she eventually re-ignited her career. Her re-entry path wasn't easy, partly because she was out of the workforce for so long, partly because her industry changed, and also likely because she was a woman of color who had challenged expectations about working and the definition of success.

But despite her lengthy pause, Kuae did relaunch her career. She is now working as an editorial producer for CNN's top-rated morning show, *New Day*. Kuae Mattox is yet another model of how women can work, pause, and thrive, but her story is even more complex given the deeper issues of race and class.

Kuae said, "My generation of accomplished women of color are creating a new narrative around being a mother and a professional. We are going to see more and more women like me step back for a period of time to be with their children. I would argue that making the choice to stay at home is the new indicator of success."

If Kuae's prediction becomes the new reality for accomplished women of color, will we see a greater connection for college-educated mothers across the race divide? I can only hope so. At the very least, perhaps it will help reinforce what my hero Michelle Obama wrote in an article for *More* magazine entitled "What Women Owe One Another." In it, she said,

> The real story is what happens as we each struggle, agonize, compromise and make the best decision we can with the information and resources we have. And it's time that we all stepped back, took a deep breath, and started really listening to one another rather than viewing one another through the layers of our own judgment, insecurity, and anxiety. When

we do that, we can finally start to understand the challenges other women are facing and the doubts they're wrestling with. Only then can we respond appropriately: with compassion, support, and respect.[97]

PAUSING AND THE MOMMY WARS

In 1992 when her husband was running for office, Hillary Clinton was asked to defend why she didn't leave her career to care for her daughter. She said, "I suppose I could have stayed home and baked cookies and had teas, but what I decided to do was to fulfill my profession." Her words became a rallying cry for those on both sides of the debate about mothers and work. The notion of "staying home to bake cookies" was anathema to traditional feminists who were focused on advancing female economic empowerment. The notion of not putting your children first was equally offensive to those women who believed there was more at stake in life than just careers.

At the time, Hillary Clinton was fighting against the widely held belief that children are best cared for by a stay-at-home mother. In the 1990s, most Americans shared that belief,[98] but the Great Recession has had an indelible effect on our attitudes toward mothers in the paid workforce. Before 2009, 43 percent of adults said the ideal situation for a young child was to have a mother who doesn't work outside the home. Today, only 30 percent of adults report they believe that and most of those who do were born more than fifty years ago.

Looked at another way, according to Pew Research Center, before 2007, only 21 percent of mothers reported that their ideal situation would be to work full-time.[99] By 2014, that number had jumped to 37 percent. For mothers who say they "don't have enough to meet basic expenses," 47 percent say the ideal situation is full-time work. But for those mothers who are married, only 23 percent say their ideal situation would be to work full-time. In other words, under-resourced mothers (whether married or single) want full-time work, but married women with resources would rather work part-time.

What does this have to do with pausing and the Mommy Wars? Well, it shows that the Mommy Wars isn't really about being a stay-at-home mother versus being a "working" mother. And it definitely isn't about what's best for the kids. The Mommy Wars is about class and how we, as a country, don't support caregiving.

How do we know this? Because our definition of good mothering varies depending on class. For under-resourced women, being a good mother means working outside the home. We revile "welfare queens" and expect them to get out into the workplace so they can "get off the dole." These mothers, like men, are told that being a good parent is being a provider. When they leave the paid workforce, we don't want to support them, so we call them lazy and bad mothers.

> **The Mommy Wars is about class and how we, as a country, don't support caregiving.**

Meanwhile, women who have resources are told that a good mother is one who is primarily responsible for her children. In fact, a recent study revealed that we support mothers who "must" work in their role as "working" mothers, but we are deeply skeptical of mothers who have the financial resources and who choose to work.

How can it be that a poor mother is the best mother when she is working and a wealthy mother is the best mother when she is not?

Despite the reality that the vast majority of Americans need two full-time salaries to reach and maintain a position in the middle class, we still fantasize that working is a choice for women. It isn't. The way to solve the Mommy Wars is to realize that the question isn't whether a mother will work, it is whether our country will support her when she does.

The good news is most mothers believe in themselves. A 2015 Pew Research Center study revealed that across income groups, nearly identical shares of parents with incomes of $75,000 or higher (46 percent), $30,000 to $74,999 (44 percent), and less than $30,000 (46 percent) say they are doing a "very good" job as parents, and similar percentages say they are doing a "good" job.[100]

The bad news is we still don't support each other as we could and should.

Erin St. Onge-Carpenter, who worked with me on the *Women on the Rise* survey, has felt the sting of reprisal for being both a stay-at-home mother and a "working" mother. Like many, she's had a non-linear career path so she could meet the needs of her family. Erin has worked for pay full-time and part-time, not at all, and then full-time again. In each of these phases, she has been frustrated by the way in which women have criticized her choices. She believes the winnowing of women at the top of industry is a driving force in the Mommy Wars.

"It's like a big game of musical chairs where there's one pink chair and the rest are blue. If we're all fighting for that one pink chair, it makes sense that we'd fight against each other," Erin told me.

For college-educated women, the Mommy Wars is less about class and more about the politics of traditional feminism. When I was coming of age, the best "feminists" were considered those who didn't need a man. Like many of my friends, I had a poster in my college dorm room that said, "A woman needs a man like a fish needs a bicycle." I bought into it hook, line, and sinker.

I don't believe that anymore, but the vestiges of that outdated concept remain imbued in modern feminism, particularly when it comes to female economic empowerment. Because we, as a country, still do not believe that all women will, in fact must, work, we passionately cling to our side of the debate on what's "best" for our children. As a result, we conflate women's careers with women's roles as mothers.

If women of means and education (that is, those most likely to be able to activate real change because they have the time and the money) are too busy fighting amongst themselves to focus on fighting against a system that needs to change, no real change can happen for anyone. We need to reframe the fight. It's not about us or our "choices"; it's about family.

PAUSING AND THE VALUE OF UNPAID LABOR

In the 1930s, when we developed economic benchmarks that would eventually evolve into the Gross Domestic Product (used by economists to determine the health of a country's economy), the calculations only included the monetary value of goods and services that could be bought and sold. This meant that things like primary caregiving by an unpaid person (such as a stay-at-home mother) and volunteer work[101] (like active school involvement, which is more often done by women) was not included in the "scorecard of capitalism."[102]

By the 1950s, the entire world used our same statistical model to evaluate their own economies. This model completely kept what has been traditionally considered "women's work" out of the accounting for the cost of managing a family, a community, a country. However, by the 1990s, enlightened economists were starting to take issue with the way the GDP was calculated.[103] In many countries efforts were put in place to include the work of unpaid workers. Except, of course, in the United States.

To this day, we do not include the unpaid labor of caregivers in our economic policies, and the consequences can be financially devastating for women. Those who provide unpaid caregiving earn no Social Security credits for raising children. Ann Crittenden, in her brilliant book, *The Price of Motherhood: Why the Most Important Job in the World Is Still the Least Valued,* details how economists have systematically denied the value of caregiving in their calculations. She quotes economist Nancy Folbre, who focuses on non-labor market activity, and who said, "Economists have been profoundly uncomfortable—even resistant—to the notion that time devoted to children is economically important."[104]

Here's the rub: As our country has moved away from manufacturing toward a more service-based economy, the need for well-educated, highly skilled workers has become paramount. Based on our government's economic policies, those who provide the caregiving do something of little or no value. But, wait, aren't those children who are being cared for the very people we hope will one day become well-educated, highly skilled workers our economy needs? Seems like that caregiving should be considered one of the most valuable jobs of all.

As Ann Crittenden observes, "If our national prosperity reflects the productivity of our human capital, then the people who provide primary care to children are the single most important source of our most valuable economic assets."[105]

Given this truth, it's shocking we don't provide paid parental leave, paid sick leave, or national child care. Makes you wonder about our future as a great country if we refuse to invest in those who protect our most important asset, the next generation.

THE POLITICS OF PAUSING

PAUSING AND THE VALUE OF VOLUNTEERISM

I hear it again and again. A stay-at-home mom decides to volunteer at her kid's school and soon discovers that the other stay-at-home moms she's volunteering with have MBAs, PhDs, law degrees, and so on. One woman I spoke to said she was astonished to learn that one of her co-PTA volunteers worked at the White House, another had had a byline for *The New York Times*, and another worked for years on the bond-trading desk at Goldman Sachs. Yep, you don't have to go very far at your local PTA to discover a wealth of well-educated, unpaid talent.

In fact, 46 percent of mothers with children under the age of eighteen volunteer in school settings.[106] But their human capital is not counted when we consider the economic inputs that drive education in this country. In 2014 alone, women donated 4.5 billion hours of unpaid time to causes and issues they care about. How much was their unpaid effort worth? An estimated $103.8 billion.[107]

Would these hours have been donated if every woman worked all of the time? Of course not. We already struggle to "do it all." How could we possibly work full-time, care for our families, and still volunteer 4.5 billion hours each year? We don't like to admit it, but our schools and our communities rely on the unpaid human capital of stay-at-home moms.

No wonder these women bristle at the notion that their "work" is not worth anything. As one *Women on the Rise* respondent shared,

> Part of me laments that I am part of a cohort of highly educated women/moms who must engage in our schools and communities because society has de-funded education and de-funded social services for the poor, etc. How I WISH WISH WISH that society could see that the contributions women make in communities has a VALUE. Can you imagine men "giving away" their time like this on such a mass scale for years and years? It wouldn't happen!

While we argue that we need women to be in the workforce to increase our GDP, if we actually counted the totality of women's work, we may not be so eager to have them rush back in. We need women's labor in all its forms for our society to flourish. It's time to start counting that labor whether it's paid or not.

PAUSING AND WORKING DAUGHTERS

This book has focused on the demands mothers face in the workplace, but caregiving isn't just about children. A large segment of the *Women on the Rise* survey shared they could have handled working if children were the only issue, but when their parents became ill, they couldn't juggle the double burden.

Public relations executive Liz O'Donnell never paused to care for her children, but when her parents fell ill, she put her career on hold. In an article for *The Atlantic*, Liz wrote, "Working daughters often find they need to switch to a less demanding job, take time off, or quit work altogether in order to make time for their caregiving duties."[108] Sound familiar? "As a result," Liz said, "they suffer loss of wages and risk losing job-related benefits such as health insurance, retirement savings, and Social Security benefits."

According to Anne Tumlinson, a health care policy analyst and consultant who also runs a website called Daughterhood.org, "Eldercare requires a high amount of emotional engagement that only a family member can provide. It's not a situation where economically advantaged women are spared. I know lots of very accomplished women with lots of degrees who have dropped out."[109]

Sharon Marts has been forced to create a "patchwork quilt" career, as she calls it—she's been a data analyst, a supply chain manager, a hospice trainer, a marketing executive, and an author—because of the ongoing caregiving needs related to her parents. Both her mother and her father were diagnosed with Parkinson's. The compounding effect of trying to deal with the needs of her children and the needs of her parents meant she couldn't hold down a full-time job.

"It was too expensive to hire full-time help for my children and then different full-time help for my parents. So I ended up having to put my career on hold to care for them all," she said when I interviewed her.

It wasn't until they both passed away that she was able to get her career back on track. Today, she is the director of operations for

TeccSociety, an online platform and community of technology events managers.

"After so much professional chaos, I feel lucky to have found this. Now, I can finally focus on building my career. I just wish the workplace could understand the caregiving challenges women face. Kids are one thing, but with the aging population, my experience is going to become more and more common."

She's right. Ten thousand people turn sixty-five every day in this country. By 2030, the AARP predicts the United States will need between 5.7 and 6.6 million caregivers to support the sick and aging.[110] Who is going to do that work? Very likely, unpaid family caregivers—also known as women.

Consider the next two decades. We have a tsunami of Millennial women who are about to become parents and who have been very clear that work–life balance matters to them. A significant portion of them will leave the workforce either because they have too much school debt and can't afford child care or because they simply want and need to put family first for a period of time.

We also have a tsunami of Baby Boomers who are going to get old very quickly and need care. They are already leaving the workforce in droves. In fact, we are losing their talents and abilities at the rate of 10,000 workers per day. By 2026 nearly every Boomer is expected to have retired or died.[111]

What about the women who are currently overwhelmed with work and raising kids? If they aren't already, they'll soon likely be forced to take care of their aging parents too. What will happen to them? Like Sharon Marts and Liz O'Donnell, millions of them will probably be forced to leave the workforce. Is that what's best for them and for our country?

Given all of this, it makes you wonder how we got to our current situation. In other words, how did the greatest country in the world become a place that makes it so difficult for mothers (and fathers) to thrive? I went back to my mother's homeland, Norway, to find out.

CHAPTER 5

A Tale of Two Countries

"The American mantra is that we have choice, but we don't have the choices other people have in other countries."
—Joan Blades,
co-founder, MomsRising.org

My mother's earliest memory dates back to World War II in her childhood home in Kristiansand, Norway. Her older brother was huddled in the corner of the family's large basement. My three-year-old mother stood on a chair, peeking out a small window, ignoring her own mother's calls for her to step down and get away from the glass.

Outside the early morning air was green from the smoke of fire-bombs the Nazis had spent the night dropping across the city. Since the onslaught began the night before, my grandfather had been on the roof of the house, intent on brushing off any bombs that might make contact and harm his family. When they finally had the courage to leave their home that morning, my family would learn that whole sections of their town had been decimated, flattened to rubble, burnt beyond recognition.

Eventually, Norway recovered from the devastation of war. My grandfather prospered as his canning business thrived. He and my grandmother became pillars of society in their small but growing city. My mother remembers dinner parties with visiting dignitaries, and the night her parents were honored with the privilege of dining with the king and queen of Norway.

But it's another wartime experience that seems to have predestined the course of my mother's life: the arrival of the Americans who came to liberate her country. They brought food, clothing, wood, and nails. They also brought candy for the children and pantyhose for the women. They were handsome, young, conquering heroes. It's no wonder then that when she was sent to London to "finishing" school and met my American father, she fell in love not only with him but with the idea of living in the country where freedom and opportunity reigned.

In preparation to be married to the dashing American, my mother, at the insistence of my grandparents, attended housewifery classes where she learned the important art of killing a chicken by snapping its neck, how to properly set a table (salad fork farthest left, dessert fork due north), and embroidery. She spent the year of their engagement working on her trousseau, which included handmade tablecloths and linen pillow cases. My parents were married in December of 1960, and my young mother arrived in the United States prepared to be the perfect wife just as her new country was on the cusp of the tumultuous '60s.

Like the United States, Norway experienced significant advancements in the lives of women after World War II. In the 1970s, a series of laws and programs intended to break down workplace inequality were passed in both countries.[112] But it is how each country approached the idea of "working" mothers that speaks to the deep differences in our cultures and reflects our truest values.

Despite the rise of the feminist movement both in her home and in her adopted country, my mother remained a housewife, raising the children, hosting dinner parties, and being the ambitious executive's gracious "better half" as she had seen her own mother be. My mother, who never went beyond high school, would not start her own career as a clothing consultant for Doncaster until well after my siblings and I had left for college.

Meanwhile, my Norwegian aunt, Sidsel, who was born a few years after the war and came of age during the '60s, always assumed she would have a career. Although she didn't go to college, she attended vocational school and became an esthetician, a profession in Norway that is more akin to dermatology than being a facialist, as it often is in the United States. Eventually, my aunt built a company distributing beauty products across Europe. She was often a keynote speaker at industry conferences and created a magazine targeted to her profession. She also married, had two children, and was deeply proud she had created the career of her dreams and the family life she wanted. My aunt was a trailblazer and model of what women could achieve in the New Norway. And she did it before the country had enacted the family-friendly policies for which so many of us consider it the Promised Land. She never said it directly, but other things my Aunt Sidsel communicated led me to believe she felt sorry for my mother and her lack of career. I remember her telling me, "I did it. So can you."

MY GENERATION: HAVES AND HAVE-NOTS

My cousin-in-law, Kitty Eide, came of age after Norway had become a beacon of gender equality. She is a modern Norwegian success story. As chief of communications for Shell Oil, she is one of the most senior women in business in her country. She's been with Shell since 2002, working her way up the corporate ladder. She's well regarded in her field and at her company, but public relations is a second career for Kitty. She spent the first thirteen years of her professional life as a broadcast journalist and producer. Like me, Kitty is the mother of three children. Her youngest, Filip, was born just days before my youngest son, Soren.

While my mother and her sister represent the starkly different paths of the previous generation, Kitty's career path and my career path in many ways are emblematic of how each of our countries have handled having women, mothers in particular, in the workforce. While I have struggled to find personal solutions to integrate career and family, Kitty has been blessed with support at every step by her government, by her workplace, and by her society at large.

In the summer of 2015, Kitty and I saw each other during an extended family reunion. Over a hundred relatives gathered in Kristiansand to celebrate our shared connections and to drink and laugh under the midnight sun. The day after the festivities were over, Kitty and I had coffee to discuss life, family, and careers.

She and her husband, Johan, live in a house that is large by even American standards. While close to downtown and a mere fifteen minutes from her office, their home feels as though it is deep in the woods with a large tree-filled garden and views of Kristiansand's bay. Johan, with his deep belly laugh and mischievous smile, is a successful entrepreneur. He has his fingers in a variety of businesses. Kitty, with her round face, large blue eyes, and short dark brown hair, is still broadcast journalist beautiful and also one of the highest paid women in her hometown. They are the definition of a power couple.

When Kitty gave birth to her first child in 1995, Norway had already long been a trailblazer when it came to maternity leave. In 1956, it mandated that mothers receive twelve weeks' fully paid leave. Over the course of the next few decades, the parental leave policy in Norway was continually extended, and by 1995 mothers had the luxury of 100 percent paid leave for up to forty-nine weeks or 80 percent paid leave for up to fifty-nine weeks with the security of knowing their exact same job would be held for them while they cared for their babies.

In 1996, a year after her daughter was born, Kitty returned full-time to her job as a broadcast journalist. Her career wasn't hindered or held back by her professional pause. In fact, it wasn't even questioned by her coworkers or employer. She did exactly what was expected of her—to be both mother and professional.

As my cousin and I sipped our tea, I shared the story of William's premature birth, the pressure I felt to return to my job after only three months, the courage it took to ask for a fourth month, and the professional risk I took when I begged for a condensed, four-day workweek.

"My boss and his boss couldn't understand why I would want to be away from my baby and often asked me if I missed him," I told her. "They scheduled critical meetings on Fridays, the day I had set aside to be home with the very baby they wondered if I missed. It was as though they were trying to get me to quit."

Kitty shook her head in disbelief. "It's so cruel. How can a mother have a career in that environment?"

Yes, how can she?

You probably know how truly abysmal it is here in the United States, but let me give you a bit of history. While Norway was assuring mothers they could be home with their newborns for up to a year by offering them full pay and the confidence their job would be there when they returned, the U.S. Congress deigned to pass the Pregnancy Discrimination Act in 1978. This meant you couldn't *fire* a woman for being pregnant. But, neither companies nor the government were expected to *pay* a woman for taking time off after her child was born. That was her choice.

And hold her job for her? Ha! The argument then as now is that to stay competitive, companies needed their employees to be all-in, all-of-the-time. Holding a job for someone could hold the company back, placing limits on its productivity and profitability.

It wasn't until 1993, one year before my first child was born and thirty-seven years after Norway first offered its citizens maternity leave, that the United States finally put the Family and Medical Leave Act into law, ensuring mothers could take up to twelve weeks of *unpaid* leave and be confident they wouldn't lose their job. However, the law applies *only* to companies that have fifty or more employees, which means only 40 percent of the American workforce is covered.

Shockingly, 20 percent of employers who do fall within the scope of the law actually admit to not complying with the FMLA in the first place.[113] Makes you wonder how many aren't even admitting their lack of compliance. And when a woman is faced with a company that fires her for being a mother, the burden of proof is on the exhausted, financially challenged new mother, not the government or company itself.

In Norway, according to my cousin, the vast majority of mothers take the full year of paid maternity leave.[114] In the United States, the average length of leave is ten weeks.[115] One-quarter of new mothers take only two weeks because they have no other choice.[116] Unless you are working for a company that subsidizes the leave, you are forced to choose between earning money to pay for your expanding family or being home to care for your newborn. And today, according to MomsRising.org,[117] an advocacy group committed to creating better systemic support for parents, only 13 percent of workers have access to paid leave through their employers.

According to the United Nations, the United States is the ONLY industrialized nation that does not offer its citizens paid maternity leave. Of the 185 countries that are part of the UN, only two don't financially support new mothers (the other country is Papua New Guinea). How can we truly be a great country if we refuse to support the very well-being of our future citizens?

When Kitty's second child was born in 1997, she took the requisite year leave and, again, she returned to full-time work without missing a beat. It was only after Filip was born in 1999 that Kitty raised the white flag and said, "I need more time."

Kitty took the full year off as expected, but she decided to add another year of unpaid leave to allow her time to be with her three young children. She knew she could do this because Norway requires employers to hold positions for mothers for up to two years after the birth of a child.[118] When, two years after she paused her career, Kitty returned to work, she negotiated a 60 percent part-time schedule.

"Was it difficult to do this?" I asked. "Did your employer expect you to hide it from others as mine did when I got my four-day workweek?"

Kitty shook her head, a perplexed look on her face. "Difficult? Of course not. Why would they want me to hide it? Women often transition between part-time and full-time work." In other words, women in Norway move from the "mommy track" to the fast track without having their careers derailed in the process.

In 2002, when Filip was three years old, Kitty was recruited by Shell Oil to come work in their communications department. She explained she was working only part-time and they replied that wasn't a problem; she could work part-time with them as well. In Norway, 83 percent of mothers work, but 41 percent work part-time while their children are young. The norm with jobs in service industries such as teaching or nursing, this is standard in business and media as well, as Kitty's career reveals.

Kitty took herself off the "mommy track" a few years later because she was ready to commit full-time to her job. Her career has skyrocketed ever since. She has faced no repercussions for her pauses and pull backs. She's done exactly what Norwegians expect her to do: fully integrate her family and her professional life.

I told Kitty about my repeated attempts to find solutions to the seemingly competing desires to be an engaged mother and a committed professional. How I left my job at Nestlé to work in an advertising agency for an inspiring woman who was the primary breadwinner in her family but who had no will to find solutions to my request for a flexible workweek after I had spent months on bed rest with my second child. How I had turned to consulting to get the flexibility I needed, but how that consulting meant I had little safety net in terms of benefits or a consistent paycheck. How, after my third child was born, I eventually abandoned my business career altogether, realizing there was no way I could accomplish my personal and professional goals in that arena. I also told her about the challenges of finding good care for my children while I worked; the lack of child care centers, the high-cost nannies we were forced to hire, some of whom were excellent, but some of whom I realize now to have been not just neglectful but actually harmful to my children. And I told her I was one of the lucky ones blessed with enough resources and family support to eventually find solutions at all.

It's not pleasant to be on the receiving end of pity, but I felt it that day when I spoke with my cousin. I asked Kitty who cared for her three youngsters while she was rising up the ladder; she responded, "They were in day care, of course."

Today, a mix of state-run and private centers are at the heart of Norway's child care solution.[119] Whether private or public, these centers must meet extensive state-defined requirements to exist. That means every parent can feel confident their child will be cared for by well-trained professionals who have dedicated their careers to early childhood development.

Unlike the United States where a full 53 percent of children are cared for by a parent, a relative, or a nanny,[120] the vast majority of Norwegians use these child care centers for their young. Oslo-based marketing professional Else Marie Hasle explained in an interview for *Slate* that in Norway parents are very skeptical about nannies and rarely use them: "We feel that day care centers are the safest places for kids."[121]

In Norway you can't put a baby younger than eight months in day care because the state expects parents to be home with their children until that time AND pays them to do it. Let me repeat that: The country as a whole values the early bonding period so much that it both pays mothers to stay home and refuses to allow young babies in its state-regulated day care facilities. It's not that it expects women to work and cobble together alternative solutions during that time like we are forced to do in the United States. No, Norway wants babies home with their mothers because the country understands those young babies are the future of the country.

> In Norway you can't put a baby younger than eight months in day care because the state expects parents to be home with their children until that time AND pays them to do it.

For children under the age of two, Norway offers a cash-for-care program[122] of around $719 per month to help cover the cost of care. Parents are required to pay a set amount for that day care, above which the government funds the rest. The average annual cost to parents for day care in Norway runs around $3,000, or $290 a month.

We still don't have universal child care nor do we regulate on a national basis child care facilities and programs here in the United States. Yet nearly half of the children younger than five with a mother in the paid workforce are cared for in group settings, 32 percent are in child care centers, and 16 percent are in family child care homes, which typically consists of a mother bringing in other children to care while also caring for her own child or children. A 2012 report by Child Care Aware of America reveals that twenty-seven states didn't regulate small family child care providers unless they served at least four children, including their own.[123] Eight states didn't license until the providers cared for at least seven children, again including their own. And in South Dakota, licensing isn't required until the provider serves at least thirteen children.

The U.S. government reports that 3 million children are in multiple child care arrangements.[124] Millions of overworked parents are forced to piece together suboptimal care solutions, leaving both them and their children frazzled and exhausted.

As for the cost of child care in our country, as I mentioned before, one year of child care costs more than one year of college in twenty-four states. The average annual cost of full-time care for an infant in center-based care ranges from $5,496 in Mississippi to $16,549 in Massachusetts.[125] According to a report by the Economic Policy Institute, in a two-parent household with an infant and a four-year-old, child care costs range from 19.3 percent to 28.7 percent of a family's total budget.[126] The private sector does offer some reprieve, but not much. The reality is that only 7 percent of companies offer onsite day care and only 33 percent offer child care subsidies.[127]

As I spoke to Kitty, I wondered, how did we in the United States get so far off track when it comes to valuing how we care for the next generation?

THE POLITICS OF CARE

In her brilliant book, *Overwhelmed: How to Work, Love, and Play When No One Has the Time*, journalist Brigid Schulte details the moment we lost the fight for child care and, arguably, the fight to support mothers in the workforce. She explains that, in 1971, "a coalition of bipartisan lawmakers, early childhood educators, civil rights activist, feminists, and labor leaders came together to craft federal legislation to create a high-quality, universal child-care system for all Americans." Called the Comprehensive Child Development Act, the bill had broad public and bipartisan support. In fact, as Brigid recounts, Idaho's Orval Hansen, one of a number of Republican cosponsors in the House, said the good that the "landmark" bill could do could "have a more far-reaching impact than any of the other major education bills enacted during the past twenty years."[128]

The biggest stumbling block? Patrick Buchanan, a conservative political operative and advisor to then-President Richard Nixon. Patrick, who never had children himself, believed in the need to preserve traditional family structures with father as breadwinner and mother as housewife. The notion of providing universal child care violated his sense of the "natural" order of things. Corralling other conservative pundits and writers, he launched a juggernaut to kill the bill. Arguing that it was an effort to "Sovietize" the American family and that "there is no substitute for a mother's presence,"[129] Patrick easily convinced then-President Richard Nixon to veto the child care bill. In fact, Patrick Buchanan actually wrote the very veto itself. As Brigid recounts, "The child care centers, [Buchanan] wrote, would not only create an 'army of bureaucrats' but would also diminish 'both parental authority and parental involvement with children—particularly in those decisive early years when social attitudes and conscience are formed, and religious and moral principles are first inculcated.' The bill was, simply, un-American."

A quick history lesson: Did you know that during World War II, we had national child care paid for by the United States government? Why? Because we needed women to work in factories and other traditionally male jobs while the men were off fighting. When the men came back from war, the country ended its universal child care. The rationale? Women needed to return home to make room for men in the workplace. Advertising campaigns and television programs such as *Leave It to Beaver* and *Father Knows Best* extolled the virtues of being a housewife, so you can understand why those who came of age in the 1950s were terrified by the rise of working mothers. It literally flew in the face of what they were led to believe was "natural."

In researching her book, Brigid Schulte met with Patrick Buchanan to discuss his role in the vetoing of the bill. He told her, "What surprised me was the ease with which we won this battle." In one fell swoop, Patrick proudly told Brigid, "That sucker was gone . . . Gone forever."[130]

Patrick Buchanan was right. In the forty-five years since he managed to block access to universal child care for parents in this country, no new meaningful policies around this issue have been enacted. We have never regained the political will or momentum as a country to support mothers (or fathers, for that matter) in the workforce.

Now that's a legacy.

In recent years, President Obama tried to make child care more accessible. In 2013, the U.S. Department of Health and Human Services finally went around Congress and instituted regulations for those child care facilities that accept government subsidies for the very poor. These efforts were estimated to reach only 1.4 million children nationwide. However, to get the subsidy, a parent must fill out extensive forms and take off days from work to wait in interminable lines. It's the very definition of punishing.

In his January 2015 State of the Union address, President Obama proposed an $80 billion program that would dramatically expand the Child Care and Development Fund, a federal program that provides states with grants for child care assistance programs to help low- and middle-income families. President Obama said,

> In today's economy, when having both parents in the workforce is an economic necessity for many families, we need affordable, high-quality

> child care more than ever. It's not a nice-to-have—it's a must-have. So it's time we stop treating child care as a side issue, or as a women's issue, and treat it like the national economic priority that it is for all of us.[131]

His plan called for "expanding access to child care assistance for all eligible families with children under four years of age, within ten years." Ten years?! And these additional efforts will reach only a total of 2.6 million children. He also recommended offering a tax credit to middle-class families of up to $3,000 per child under the age of six, which would reach an additional 3.5 million children. There are currently 24 million children in our country between the ages of zero and five.[132] In a decade, the number is expected to jump at least a million more. President Obama's policies, as well intentioned as they are, would still only reach a quarter of all young children in this country.

We can hope that President Obama's policy agenda will be put into practice, but as the numbers reveal, it won't do a whole lot of good for the vast majority of mothers (or fathers) in our society. How is it Norway got it so right when it comes to supporting mothers working outside the home, and we got it so wrong?

IT'S THE ECONOMY, STUPID

In 1992, when Bill Clinton was running for president, Democratic strategist James Carville is said to have posted a sign outside the campaign "war room" that read: "It's the Economy, Stupid." He did this to remind Clinton and those working for him that how people are faring is at the heart of how we make decisions in this country.

James Carville could also have posted a sign that read, "He who frames the issue, wins the debate." In 1971 Pat Buchanan framed the debate against child care by claiming it was a fight against traditional "American" values. But it was also the economy that empowered President Nixon to veto the bill. Inflation was at an all-time high. Middle-class families were burdened with rising taxes and the increasing costs of daily living. As a result, women were "forced" to work outside the home to make ends meet. This meant an abandonment of what had become the post-war norm: breadwinning fathers, stay-at-home mothers. Paying more in taxes for programs such as child care that would help mothers work (and which conservatives argued would mean more mothers would *have to work* to cover the cost of the increased taxes) hit at the heart of the financial pain many Americans were experiencing. In the 1970s, American's didn't want women to work, they wanted to go back to the way it was in the 1950s. Patrick Buchanan may have been the snake in the grass, but it was the economy that doomed universal child care.

The '80s? They were one big disco party for America. I know, I was there. The economy was booming. Talent was in high demand and we women, who were for the first time in history graduating from college at the same rates as men, had much to offer. Worrying about who was going to care for the children and how was not on anyone's radar, including feminists. In the late 1970s through the 1980s, feminists continued to focus their activism on women's economic empowerment, putting their collective energy into the Equal Rights Amendment, an effort to change the constitution to ensure women have the same legal rights afforded to men. By 1982, the ERA finally died when supporters couldn't get enough state legislatures to approve it.

The women's empowerment movement then shifted its attention to reproductive freedom and control. Family matters such as paid parental leave, paid sick leave, or universal child care were not organizing principles, and with no cohesive group fighting on behalf of families, the needs of mothers in the workplace became the individual's problem to solve.

But something else was afoot during the '80s. Conservative think tanks and others with pro-capitalist agendas worried about the rise of the consumer advocacy groups such as Ralph Nader's Public Citizen. They were concerned that efforts to curtail corporate actions would undermine profitability. They began a subtle and interwoven campaign to link the notion of American individualism as a means to capitalist success to every aspect of our society.[133] They built off of our deeply rooted anti-government sentiment and resistance to taxation. They extolled the notion that bootstrap success was the only way to real success. Collectivism was akin to communism. National programs such as universal day care or universal preschool or universal parental leave paid for by taxpayers was sold to us as un-American.

Here's the problem: In all of their efforts to ensure capitalism would remain free from governmental intervention they didn't plan for the fact that economic growth relied on women (over 80 percent of whom become mothers) to do the work. The tidal wave of women entering the workforce in the 1980s became, a decade later, another tidal wave of women who were forced to leave once they became mothers. We women had invested time and money into our careers, and yet we couldn't raise our children and stay on track with those hard-won careers. We needed help, but anti-taxation sentiment was so high, there was no way our collective tax dollars would be used to underwrite supporting mothers in the workforce by giving us, at the very least, paid maternity leave or nationally subsidized day care.

By the 1980s and 1990s, as college-educated women entered the workforce in droves, the burden of caring for our young moved completely from society to the individual, where it has remained ever since.

That's why, in 1993, when President Clinton passed the Family and Medical Leave Act, he didn't ask taxpayers to cover the cost of maternity leave; he placed the burden on employers and employees. The employer pays by not having someone working during the twelve weeks of federally allowed leave. The employee pays by being forced to either go without her salary during said leave or by not taking leave at all. Some women are able to use paid sick or vacation leave or buy into disability insurance that covers some but not all of their salary while they are home caring for their newborns, but the vast majority of Americans don't have access to these offerings. By the 1980s and 1990s, as college-educated women entered the workforce in droves, the burden of caring for our young moved completely from society to the individual, where it has remained ever since.

It's interesting to note that in the early 1990s, the country was reeling again from a recession. In fact, in 1992, the percentage of stay-at-home mothers hit its lowest point in our history, bottoming out at 23 percent of all mothers.[134] Women were working not only because they wanted to, but because they had to. We may have still been fantasizing that women would just go back home when they became mothers, but we finally understood our economy needed women for it to grow. So, it wasn't the notion of gender equality that helped pass the anemic and arguably punishing FMLA; it was the economy.

Say what you will about his personal foibles, during President Clinton's reign, the United States experienced one of the largest economic expansions in history. When he was elected in 1992, 10 million Americans were unemployed, the country faced record deficits, and poverty and welfare rolls were growing. After he took office, the economy grew for 116 consecutive months, the longest period of economic expansion in history. Bill Clinton can claim more jobs were created in his eight years in office than under any other single administration, even more than when Franklin Delano Roosevelt used his New Deal to get the country out of the Depression.

But all that largesse did not result in sweeping benefits for mothers working outside the home. We didn't secure paid maternity leave. Our husbands didn't get paid paternity leave. Our children didn't get high-quality, universal day care. All that money, all that opportunity. There is something more than the economy that's keeping us from supporting families.

WE, THE PEOPLE

Many have claimed that the reason Norway has such generous benefits is because it's oil rich. In the late 1960s oil was discovered off the country's coast. Today, Norway is considered one of the largest producers of oil. Each day it produces 1.9 billion barrels of oil. The United States? We produce 13.9 billions of barrels of oil a day. Seems if oil is the measure, by comparison, we're rich too. According to the International Monetary Fund, Norway is the sixth wealthiest country per capita (per person) in the world. The United States? We're not far off at tenth. There are 322 million people in our country. There are 5 million people in Norway. We're sixty-four times larger and yet we are almost as rich as Norway on a per person basis.

In many ways, our two countries are aligned on how we spend our money. Norway spends 18 percent of its national budget on health. We spend 19 percent. Norway spends 16 percent on education; we spend 17 percent.[135] But here's the difference: We put significantly more of our money into building up our defense. In 2015, 19 percent of our $3.8 trillion budget went to the military. Norway? Just 4 percent of their $500 million budget goes to defense. As a result, we don't have "extra" money to invest on supporting families. We're too busy building bombs. Seems to me that old adage "how you spend your money reflects your values" applies here.

When Norway discovered it had significant oil deposits, rather than divide it up to private interests, the country declared the oil fields were state owned and that the state was to have a 50 percent interest in every production license.[136] That money, the country decided, would go to benefit the people. The majority of the revenue from Norway's oil fields has been deposited in the Government Pension Fund, which as of 2014 had more than $160,000 in reserve for every Norwegian. By contrast, each American actually owes $54,733 thanks to our national debt.[137] The rest of Norway's money didn't go to defend the country from external threats (for example, Russia is an ever-present and looming oppressor of Norway) or to protect its interests around the world. Instead, Norway focused on empowering its citizens to thrive, especially its mothers.

It isn't only Norway, with its rich oil deposits, that views supporting the next generation a public policy priority. Consider Italy, where my sister, Kirsten, lives. Following in our mother's footsteps, Kirsten has made her home in a country different from where she was born. She is a professor of art in Florence and a practicing artist. She and her Italian husband have two young boys.

When my nephews were born, Kirsten had twenty-two weeks of paid (at 80 percent) maternity leave and the confidence to know if she took more time off, her job remained secure. She and her entire family also have full medical care covered by the state. While there is no real support for child care (most Italians have a *nona*—a grandmother—who helps care for the kids), she only expects to pay around $4,000 for college tuition. Try as I might to convince her to move back home to the states, Kirsten says she doesn't want to raise her children in a country that doesn't provide support to families.

"I live in a society that places children at the top of its list of values," she told me. "This allows me to be the mother I want to be and still have a career I love. Why would I want to live in the United States where the values are placed on making money, not living a full and rich life?"

The other thing Norway and Italy and other enlightened countries do is to place leisure at a high premium. In these countries, the standard workweek is legally required to be fewer than forty hours. According to Kitty, the offices of Shell Oil in Norway clear out at 5 PM every day—not because the employees are slackers, but because they understand the importance of being home to enjoy time with their families. And their government backs them up with laws that reinforce this value system.

Ironically, Kitty shared that she has to explain to expats who come to Norway from the United States that employees who leave at 5 PM aren't being indolent. "Americans seem to think more hours means better work. But we have a different view of life. We believe we do our best work by being efficient in the office and having a fulfilling life outside of it," Kitty said.

Here in the United States, we are conflicted by notions of leisure. Work is what matters. Our standard workweek? For the typical American, only 40 percent who work full-time report they clock the "standard" forty hours a week.[138] Professionals *average* forty-nine hours per week, and nearly 20 percent report they work more than sixty hours each week.

And vacation? The United States is the only westernized country in the world that does not legally require any paid vacation days. Every single country in the European Union requires at least four weeks of paid vacation.[139] Ah, that's the life.

What's the net effect of our refusal to support leisure? Gallup has tracked employee engagement for years.[140] As of 2014, only 31 percent of American workers report being "engaged" in their jobs and Millennials report the least engagement of all. What does this mean for the economy? Around $350 billion in lost productivity.[141] But these losses are about more than money. They reflect our silent strike against a system that is not working for any of us.

According to Nobel Prize–winning economist Joseph Stiglitz, economic theory would lead one to believe that if our basic needs are met, then with our additional financial resources we would buy ourselves leisure. He wrote, "One might have assumed that reasonable people would have decided to enjoy both more goods and more leisure. That is what happened in Europe. But America took a different turn as women joined the labor force with less leisure per household and more and more goods."[142]

So we convinced ourselves we needed things, not leisure, and, because we needed workers to enable the economy to grow and make these things, we encouraged women to join the workforce. But we didn't provide them with the necessary supports they needed to put their family obligations aside and focus on work. The result? For the last thirty years, this country has built its success on the backs of women and at the expense of families. Why? Because we still have not reconciled to the reality that mothers actually work outside of the home.

"WORKING" MOTHERS?

We in the United States are deeply conflicted about having mothers in the workforce. Even today, 60 percent of Americans report they believe a mother should stay home when their children are young.[143] Despite the rhetoric extolling the benefits of working motherhood on children, the importance of having one's own career, and the need for more women in leadership, we do not provide systemic solutions to make it truly feasible for women to commit to their professions. The underlying belief reflected in our policies is that women should be home. As a result, we don't make it easy for them to work. We make it harder than nearly every other industrialized country for mothers to work. It's no wonder that for the last decade we have seen a rise in stay-at-home mothers.

Kitty says the notion of being a stay-at-home mother simply doesn't exist in Norway. When we spoke, she could think of only one woman she knew who did not work outside the home. "Why wouldn't women want to work?" she pondered.

For the last thirty years, this country has built its success on the backs of women and at the expense of families. Why? Because we still have not reconciled to the reality that mothers actually work outside of the home.

I explained to her that in the United States, we hear about the "luxury" and "privilege" of staying home. "Choosing" to do so has become a status symbol, equated with the wealthy "One Percent." Being able to "afford" to stay home is not a status symbol in Norway because women's workplace participation is not linked to her husband's income. In other words, women's workforce participation is not class based in Norway, nor is it an extension of her husband's ability to provide. There the assumption is that mothers will work, not because they have to, but because they want to—*and because the country needs them to.*

Sigbjørn Johnsen, the finance minister of Norway, says, "I strongly believe that female employment has brought about large economic benefits for Norway . . . Choosing workers from a pool of male and female workers, as opposed to choosing from a pool where half of the potential talent is excluded, leads to productivity gains."[144]

Basic economic theory says that when a country has more efficient and productive workers, the gross domestic product (GDP) increases. Essentially, the higher the GDP, the more productive the workers, the more the country is thriving.

Norway is ranked number one in the world for productivity, measured by GDP per total hours worked, according to the Organization for Economic Cooperation and Development.[145] The reason for their efficiency? As Johnsen argued, it's largely because they have figured out how to keep mothers like my cousin Kitty productively contributing to the workforce. We're third in productivity, but our relative happiness is significantly lower.[146]

In my deepest heart, I wish we lived in a country that actually valued family and caregiving, where the structures of work and governmental policy reinforced these essential values. But we don't. And as a result, we'll likely see even more women forced to leave the workforce to give those they love the care they need.

One way to solve this mass exodus? Men.

CHAPTER 6

Men Want a Place in the Home

"We cannot get to an equal world without men leaning in at home."
—Sheryl Sandberg,
chief operating officer, Facebook

I usually hate to talk on planes. The forced intimacy feels more than a little violating. Plus, how often does a mother get six hours alone by herself? But it was hard not to talk with Benn Eifert when I met him on a flight from New York City back home to San Francisco in the fall of 2015. Dashing and tall, Benn and his long legs seemed to barely fit into the middle seat he'd been assigned. What was most appealing about Benn was the brimming enthusiasm he expressed for his growing family. His wife, he told me, was expecting their first child in a few months. He said he couldn't wait to be a dad. And then he shared with me how frustrated and sad he was that his workplace was so unsupportive.

Benn, who traveled for business two to three weeks a month, wanted to slow down his frantic schedule. He wanted more time with his wife, Erin, and their child. At the very least, he wanted to take an extended paternity leave when the baby was born. No, no, and, no, was the answer he was given.

Ironically, Benn didn't work for some big monolith of a company; he worked for a hedge fund that he had co-founded. His partner was a more established New York financier. Benn, who lived in the San Francisco Bay Area, was the genius quant jock with a PhD in economics who co-managed the company's portfolio. Their partnership was a great blend of old school experience and new school smarts—that is, until it came to how they viewed their roles as fathers.

Benn's business partner had a wife who didn't work outside the home and took full responsibility for their family's needs while he focused exclusively on his career. Their traditional arrangement meant Benn's partner could be all-in, all-of-the-time professionally. He wasn't involved in the daily caregiving of the children, and his wife didn't have a career that required any kind of accommodations.

When it came to being a father, his partner told Benn the first year didn't matter. "And avoid any attempt to change a diaper. If they see you can do it, you'll never get off the hook," his partner said, only half-jokingly.

But Benn didn't want to be excluded from caregiving during his child's first year, including the diaper changing. He and Erin, a surgeon, wanted to share responsibility for their children. Not just because it was "the right thing to do" but because, as Benn told me, "being an engaged father is who I want to be. It's part of the legacy I want to leave my children. And, I know I'll enjoy it!"

Benn tried to find a solution, but his partner wasn't willing to make accommodations. He urged Benn to move to New York so there would be less travel and so they could work side-by-side. The business had been built with the understanding that he and his partner would be an East Coast/West Coast team, but the traditional world of finance was struggling with that arrangement.

"Can't your wife move?" his partner asked. Benn's answer was no. Erin's career was flourishing, and neither she nor Benn wanted to leave the Bay Area.

Not long after the flight, I received an email from Benn telling me he'd decided to quit. "It looks like the only way for me to really be there for Erin and the new baby is to leave the fund I started . . . pretty disappointing. But it's the right decision . . . On to new adventures :)."

OUR WORK-FIRST CULTURE IS HOLDING MEN BACK

For decades we have been hearing about how the workplace is a minefield for women. We are all fully aware by now of how glass ceilings, pay inequity, outright sexual harassment, and the more subtle unconscious bias have limited women's professional options. And, we women know how hard it is to manage that career and our family commitments. But we rarely hear about how the workplace is keeping men from achieving their goals as fathers.

How does it do that? You might ask. The same way it has hurt mothers. By insisting on face time and by reinforcing the notion that true success requires 24/7 commitment. You know the drill: Your unwavering devotion to your job shows you must display traits such as hard-charging ambition, single-minded focus, and tenacity. If you want to be part of the team, you have to forgo family, outside interests, even sleep. Women have been fighting against this for decades. But men? They've been quietly living under the weight of it all.

In 1997, *The Second Shift* author, Arlie Hochschild, wrote about the challenges women and men face in the workplace in her book *The Time Bind: When Work Becomes Home and Home Becomes Work.* She explored the rise of the work-first culture and defined the term "the ideal worker," who, as I explained in chapter 3, has a partner at home to focus on the children, the house, and all other non-office related activities. In a perfect world, the ideal worker also has a secretary to care for the non-essential workplace issues.

My guess is we'd all secretly love a wife and a secretary. But we know that's not our modern reality. In today's world few households can afford to have one person working full-time and one person devoted to the home. But the model that today's workplace is built on expects it. So when both parents are forced into a workplace that requires ideal workers, something has to give. For decades what has obviously given has been women's careers as we've tried to be both ideal workers and ideal mothers. And, what's given is the leaky pipeline that means there are few women at the top. It's a harsh penalty for working in an archaic model.

But men have also faced penalty. Joan C. Williams, who heads the Center for WorkLife Law and has written extensively on this issue, argues that maintaining an ideal-worker norm designed around traditional notions of male life patterns results in gender discrimination against men, too.[147] Joan wrote, "Expecting full-time, uninterrupted work from men has the effect of policing them into an outdated, stereotypical gender role, one that does not afford them the opportunity to be deeply engaged fathers."[148]

As I have shared, my own father lived his life in the ideal worker straitjacket. He had my mother at home who cared for the family and his devoted secretary who cared for workplace obligations. This allowed him to rise to great heights first as a lawyer and then in project finance. He was highly successful professionally. And while he will tell you he is proud of his professional accomplishments, he often shares how much he regrets missing our childhood as he toiled long into the night and traveled the world for work.

In her book *The Top Five Regrets of the Dying,* palliative care nurse Bronnie Ware wrote, "*ALL* of the men I nursed deeply regretted spending so much of their lives on the treadmill of a work existence."[149] It's not fair to limit the lives of men when we demand more for women.

THE NEW MALE MYSTIQUE

A myriad of studies has shown Millennial men are eager to be deeply engaged fathers[150] and, if time is any indication, they already are. Today's fathers spend an average of 4.1 hours per workday with their children under thirteen, significantly more than their same-age counterparts in 1977 who spent an average of 2.4 hours per workday with their children.[151] But fathers want more. A recent Pew Research report noted that 46 percent of fathers say they are not spending enough time with their children, compared with 23 percent of mothers.[152]

And when it comes to the mother of their children, men's attitudes have changed dramatically in just the past six years. In 2009, Pew reports that 54 percent of fathers with children under age seventeen said the ideal situation for young children was to have a mother who did not work at all outside the home;[153] today only 37 percent of fathers say that.

Even the future captains of industry are showing signs of a shift in perspective. Stewart Friedman, a professor of management at the Wharton School of Business, surveyed the class of 1992 and then followed up two decades later with a second survey of the class of 2012. He wrote about the results in his book *Baby Bust: New Choices for Men and Women in Work and Family.*

Stewart discovered a significant shift in the number of students who reported planning to have children. While 78 percent of the men of the class of 1992 wanted children, only 42 percent of the men in 2012 said they did (interestingly, the women matched their male peers in their responses regarding their desire for children: 79 percent in 1992 and 42 percent in 2012). But what was particularly interesting was that those modern men who did report wanting children were much more likely to believe two-career relationships work best "when neither partner has stereotypical or traditional ideas about men's or women's family roles."[154] These men also reported as being much more likely to value flexibility in work hours than those from the class of 1992.

Stewart Friedman wrote, "the young men in our study who expect to have children do not see the primary responsibility of fatherhood as bringing home the bacon. These young men expect and want to be involved dads."[155]

And they don't just want to be "helpful"; they are willing to do what it takes to ensure their children get the best care possible. In 2015, Boston College Center for Work & Family conducted a study of 1,100 Millennials.[156] The respondents were college-educated professionals who worked in the financial services or insurance industry. The goal was to uncover their attitudes toward their careers. The survey asked the married or partnered young adults if they would find it acceptable to stay home if their spouse or partner made enough money for the family to live on comfortably. Here's what was surprising: 51 percent of the men said yes, while only 44 percent of the women did.

However, that same Boston College study revealed that although men report a willingness to put family first, they also feel workplace pressure to be career focused. When asked about their own workplaces, 43 percent of the men said they believed to get ahead they were expected to work more than fifty hours per week while only 38 percent of the women agreed with this statement. When asked to agree or disagree with the statement "the ideal employee is the one who is available 24 hours a day," nearly a third of the men responded yes while only 22 percent of the women agreed with that statement.

Same workplaces, same professional cohort of men and women, and yet the men perceived the demands of work as being more intense. The researchers argued the male respondents internalized the pressure in ways that their female peers had not. Despite all of the rhetoric around "leaning in" for women, in all areas regarding ambition to move ahead, get promoted, and have influence, men reported higher levels of desire and drive than women. When asked about the statement "I would like to advance to a position where I can have a greater influence on policy decisions," nearly 85 percent of the men agreed, compared to only 71 percent of the women. As women have known for years, being both a hard-driving professional and a deeply engaged parent is challenging, and this may be what underlies the reported differences in male and female ambition. One wonders if modern fathers' desire for a deeper role in caregiving will change their desire to "get ahead." Only time will tell.

In 2011, the Families and Work Institute (FWI) issued a report on their ongoing National Study of the Changing Workforce entitled "The New Male Mystique."[157] In it, they revealed "The U.S. workplace is no longer a 'man's world' . . . Traditional, clear-cut gender roles are giving way to a 'new normal' that is both egalitarian and challenging . . . Our data suggests that men are experiencing significantly higher levels of work-family conflict than they did three decades ago." In other words, the report states, men are experiencing what women experienced when they first entered the workforce in record numbers: "the pressure to do it all in order to have it all."

Heath Black, a product manager at reddit, can certainly relate. He never imagined he'd find himself in a traditional marital structure. When I interviewed him, he said he and his wife, Sallie, have always been full equals professionally, trading off who followed whom as their careers progressed . . . until their son, Jeb, was born. Now Heath is the breadwinner father and his wife is home caring for their new son.

"We wanted to be sure at least one of us was there for Jeb and it just seemed to make sense for Sallie to be the one," Heath told me. "As a new father, I have felt this deep internalized pressure to make sure there is money in the bank and food on the table. Sallie keeps me grounded by reminding me that time with our family is most important, but that's not always easy." Heath paused and laughed when he shared, "It's ironic. Despite my deep passion and commitment to equality, here I am in this 1950s role."

As Stewart Friedman wrote in *Baby Bust*, "While 2012 men no longer identify their values with the breadwinner role, many men still identify with and worry about their ability to fulfill this role's financial obligations. These seemingly contradictory observations—that men no longer think of themselves as breadwinners but are still anxious about their ability to support their kids—indicates that we are in a period of transition as men's and women's roles converge." [158] Stewart later wrote, "Men aren't sure who they are or how to be." But what they do know is that they want to be a different kind of father than their own father was. The question is, will we let them?

"INAUTHENTIC" CAREGIVERS

In 1999, Kevin Knussman, a twenty-two-year veteran state trooper for Maryland, sued his employer for violating the Family and Medical Leave Act because he was denied parental leave after the birth of his daughter. His wife, Kimberly, had been ill, and Officer Knussman needed time off to care for her and their newborn. In court papers, it was revealed that a female personnel supervisor told Officer Knussman, "God decided only women can give birth," and "unless your wife is in a coma or dead," "because only women have the capacity to breastfeed a baby," he could not be considered the primary care provider, thus not eligible for leave.[159] The state of Maryland lost the case, but they were adamant in their position, so they appealed to the Fourth Circuit Court of Appeals. Again they lost. Men, the court decided, could be primary caregivers. And yet, in so many ways, they are still considered secondary.

While we still have a long way to go, much has changed in how we define womanhood. We women can be race car drivers, supreme court justices, neurosurgeons, astronauts, plumbers, construction engineers—the list goes on. Underlying all of this is a fundamental change in our attitudes of what it means to be a woman. Yes, we are still viewed as the primary caregivers, but we can also be successful professionals and primary breadwinners (which we already are in 40 percent of households).

That same expansiveness in terms of gender roles has not happened for men when it comes to caregiving. In her 2012 article entitled "The Gender Bind: Men as Inauthentic Caregivers," Kelli García, senior counsel at the National Women's Law Center and adjunct professor of law at Georgetown University Law School, provides a thorough analysis of attitudes and laws regarding men and caregiving. In it she wrote, "although many men no longer maintain the primary breadwinner role, they nevertheless retain a secondary role as caregivers; they are the helpers, not the ones responsible for caregiving."

Kelli detailed how our legal and governmental system places men in the secondary role when it comes to children. She reported,

> The United States Census Bureau considers caregiving by fathers while a child's mother is at work to be a 'child care arrangement.' The Census Bureau treats caregiving by mothers as the default by asking the question 'Who's Minding the Kids?' when mothers are not. Thus, the Census Bureau places a father's caregiving in the same category as a babysitter's, underscoring the way in which men's caregiving is treated as something done to help mothers rather than as a primary responsibility of fatherhood.[160]

Ask yourself how many times have you heard a man say he's "babysitting" his children or a woman say her husband "helps" her with the kids. This underlying belief that men aren't or can't be fully responsible and engaged caregivers is deeply embedded in our society and this conflict is playing itself out most clearly in the current debate around paternity leave.

PATERNITY LEAVE: THE FINAL FRONTIER

My brother, Chet, has always been passionate about renewable energies. Long before it was fashionable, he secured a college degree in environmental engineering. When he was in the Peace Corps, he was stationed in Rarotonga in the South Pacific, helping the island establish solar power facilities. He has since developed a career in the solar industry and is currently the vice president of business development at a residential solar installer in northern California. He also has always wanted to be an engaged father.

When his first child was born in 2003, Chet asked for two months of paid parental leave. They offered him two weeks' paid vacation time off. Then Chet's wife suffered severe postpartum depression. He needed more leave to care for his wife and new baby, but the company refused to give him any more time off, either paid or unpaid. Because they had fewer than fifty employees, they didn't fall under FMLA regulations. Chet could have lost his job at a time when his family needed his salary. Chet had no option, so he went back to work. Eventually, he left the company. He didn't want to work for a place that didn't support him and his family.

Chet's marriage to his first wife didn't last either. When his second partner became pregnant with twins, he didn't want to make the same mistakes. Chet reached out to his new employer to make sure he could take a paid leave of at least two months, preferably longer. The company had no policy, but they didn't say no to his request. They also didn't say yes. After the twins were born Chet took two weeks of paid vacation and then followed up to make sure he could take an extended paternity leave. They offered him six weeks of unpaid leave. Like his previous employer, they weren't large enough to fall into the FMLA guidelines and were under no obligation to give my brother any leave at all. They thought they were being generous.

Six unpaid weeks later when Chet was ready to return to work, his employer told him they had reorganized and didn't need him anymore. The company claimed they needed an employee who was "all in." Chet was angry and felt betrayed by a company that he'd helped build from $1 million in revenue to $4 million in just a few short years. My brother was forced to collect unemployment while looking for a new job to support his growing family—all because he needed some time to help his partner and new children settle into the world.

As I have already discussed, the Family and Medical Leave Act requires companies with more than fifty employees to provide twelve weeks of unpaid leave for new parents. It does not require companies to offer pay, but 14 percent of companies do. One of the hidden truths about the FMLA is that it actually had the greatest theoretical impact on men. Most of the companies that were required to comply already offered maternity leave. Of those that did have to make changes, the most common change, cited by 69 percent of the firms, was to allow fathers to take unpaid leave to care for a sick or newborn child.

Sounds all well and good, but here we are twenty-two years later and still most fathers are not taking or cannot take any extended time off. According to the United States Department of Labor, nine out of ten fathers do take off some time, but more than three-quarters of them take less than ten days.[161] The vast majority of college-educated fathers take less than one week off after the birth of a child. And yet, 75 percent report they would like to have more time off to be with their newborn child.[162]

Journalist Josh Levs certainly did. In 2013, he asked his employer, Time Warner, for parental leave when his third child was due to be born. The company gave ten weeks of paid leave to new mothers but only two weeks of paid leave for new fathers. Josh told me he just wanted equal treatment. Time Warner refused him, even after his daughter was born prematurely. Josh was forced to go back to work and was not there to care for his family. He was pissed. He decided to take action, something few men are willing to do, and filed a complaint of gender discrimination with the Equal Employment Opportunity Commission. When I interviewed him, he was adamant that "today's working fathers want to have time with our children. We shouldn't be punished for wanting that."

The case was eventually settled in 2015. Meanwhile, Time Warner announced it was changing its policy. It offered men not the full ten it gave mothers but at least six weeks of paid leave. Far better than nothing, but certainly not equal. Although Josh didn't benefit, he's thrilled he was able to enact change for his colleagues. He said, "I keep getting emails from my coworkers thanking me. One wrote me, 'I am saying a blessing to you every night I get to be with my kids.' My experience proves you really can take on city hall. You just have to take the risk."

Since then, Josh has gone on to become a passionate advocate for paternity leave. His must-read book, *All In: How Our Work-First Culture Fails Dads, Families, and Businesses—And How We Can Fix It Together*, details how our backward attitudes toward men and caregiving has hurt women, men, and America.

Josh argues that beyond keeping men from deepening their relationships with their children, refusing men paternity leave forces women to take more time at home and puts them at risk of leaving the workforce altogether. Research shows he's right. A 2015 study out of University of California at Santa Barbara looked at how workplace policies reinforce gender norms and found that while Millennial men and women have egalitarian attitudes about gender roles, when faced with a lack of family-friendly policies, most fall back on traditional roles at home and at work.[163]

The study's co-author, sociologist Sarah Thébaud, said, "The majority of young men and women say they would ideally like to equally share earning and caregiving with their spouse. But it's pretty clear that we don't have the kinds of policies and flexible work options that really facilitate egalitarian relationships."[164]

On a more positive note, a recent study of paternity leave in Canada revealed that when fathers take more paternity leave, mothers increase their level of full-time work, and another study in Sweden found increasing the amount of paternity leave has similar positive impacts on women's labor force participation.[165]

As Josh told me, "As long as we're pushing men to stay at work, we're pushing women to stay home."

Respondents of our *Women on the Rise* survey can certainly attest to this. As one wrote, "My husband has zero support to be involved with his family. They've flat-out told him, 'you are too involved with your family' (even though he works very long hours and is constantly 'on call')." Women finding opportunity, support, and balance in the workplace is in many ways tied to partners getting a similar flexibility and understanding." As more men are able to broaden their experience integrating work and family, they are more likely to be able support women who need and want this too.

> "As long as we're pushing men to stay at work, we're pushing women to stay home."

MEN, MASCULINITY, AND CAREGIVING

Let's be clear: Despite the way they're depicted in television shows, movies, and in advertising, men aren't stupid. They understand they face significant consequences when putting family first: Not only is their ability to provide called into question, but so is their very sense of what it means to be a man. Quite simply, we don't equate masculinity with caregiving, and so we punish men, like my brother, who break out of our expected notions of what it means to be masculine in our culture.

"Because workplaces are gender factories where men forge and enact their masculinity, a worker's manliness may be called into question when a man calls attention to his family care obligations," wrote Joan C. Williams in her book *Reshaping the Work–Family Debate: Why Men and Class Matter*.[166] She has conducted extensive research on the work–life debate, including the challenges men face when they do the "low status feminine work" of caregiving. Joan stated "Men who take leave or adopt flexible schedules are seen as bad workers. And that 'bad worker effect' is totally explained by the fact that they are seen as inappropriately 'feminine.'"[167]

A 2013 study out of the University of South Florida revealed that male students reported work–life balance as more important than their female peers, but when further asked if they planned to pursue work flexibility, men were less likely to indicate that they would. And, in fact, those men who reported believing they would be perceived as less masculine for seeking flexible work were the least likely to express their intention to do so. The authors of the study concluded that "men may believe that pursuing work–life balance may put their gender status at risk, and they may avoid work flexibility as a result" despite expressing their strong desire to have it.[168]

These young men understand what's at stake. Recent research shows that men who requested family leave were at greater risk of being demoted or laid off because they were perceived to have negative traits that are often used to stigmatize women, like weakness and uncertainty, not masculine ones like competitiveness and ambition.[169] And men who were described as having work–family conflict (causing them to miss work) received lower overall performance ratings and lower reward recommendations when compared to men who did not experience this conflict.[170] The few men who actually do take the twelve weeks of unpaid family leave mandated by the federal government often end up being demoted or let go.[171] It's no wonder so few men take paternity leave.

And it gets worse. As law professor Kelli García notes, "a man who takes paternity leave thus faces the problem of entering the 'mommy track' and engaging in gender atypical behavior. Further, by prioritizing family caregiving, he may be seen as abdicating the role of provider. Thus, because good fathers are those who take financial care of their children, he becomes, by definition, a bad father."[172] So if you put your family first and take your legally guaranteed right to parental leave, you could lose your job, not be seen as a "real" man, and then also end up regarded as a crappy father? Sounds like a no-win situation to me.

Which explains why men like Mark Zuckerberg really are heroes. Complain all you want about Facebook, one thing Mark has done right is use his position as a Silicon Valley icon to model what it means to be an engaged father in today's world. His two months of paternity leave after the birth of his first child has set a new standard. When leaders like him declare their priorities to their family in bold and public ways, our choices and options expand exponentially.

WOMEN HOLD MEN BACK, TOO

Have you ever read the book *William's Doll* by Charlotte Zolotow? She wrote it in 1972. In the story a little boy wants a doll, but his father is resistant, worrying that playing with dolls isn't manly enough. Why does little William want a doll? Because he wants to learn to be a good father. It is a sweet book that trumps gender norms and should be as outdated as refusing girls Legos. But it isn't—well, not exactly.

A few years ago, I was going to give a doll along with a copy of the book to the son of a friend of mine. I was more than a little surprised when the mother claimed she didn't think her husband would like her son to have a doll. When I asked the dad, he said of course, his son could have one. "I always wanted one when I was a boy," the dad told me, to his wife's astonishment.

How is it that men are finally feeling comfortable admitting their desire to be active fathers and we women are the ones slow to catch up? The workplace and our sense of what it means to be masculine are keeping men from being engaged fathers, but women are too.

There's a term for this: "maternal gatekeeping." In 2008, Sarah J. Schoppe-Sullivan, a professor of psychology at Ohio State, and her colleagues set out to prove what many of us experienced in our daily lives—that women were either consciously or unconsciously keeping men from being actively engaged fathers. She interviewed ninety-seven couples on their child-rearing beliefs and attitudes. She discovered there was a "poignant discord" between the kind of parents the couples claimed they wanted to be and the kind of parents they ultimately became. Most reported they wanted to share parenting, but that often didn't happen. Mothers generally assumed the larger role, and both the fathers and mothers were disappointed with that outcome. The study revealed that mothers became the de facto experts and often took over when fathers tried to take care of the children's needs.[173] Mothers, Sarah Schoppe-Sullivan explained, aren't consciously trying to shut fathers out. It's just something that happens.

Sheryl Sandberg wrote about this in *Lean In*: "I have seen so many women inadvertently discourage their husbands from doing their share by being too controlling or critical." She described the concept of maternal gatekeeping as "a fancy term for 'Ohmygod, that's not the way you do it! Just move aside and let me!'"[174]

Boy, can I relate. How often did I push Bill aside to make sure the job of parenting was done "right"? Too often to count, if I'm honest with myself. And yet, I'm reminded of those early days with our premature firstborn. Bill and I were at the Intensive Care Unit being trained by the nurse on how to care for William. We were trying to give him a bath and struggling to hold our tiny baby who mewed in terror—the loudest noise his little body could make. The nurse turned to my husband and asked if he'd ever played football. "Well, as a matter of fact I did," said Bill. He was a linebacker in high school, was recruited to play in college, and ended up playing on the varsity team.

"Then you know how to hold your son," the nurse told my husband, and, sure enough, he did. He pulled William in close as if he were a football and Bill were running toward the goal line. Our premature baby immediately calmed down as my husband gave him his first bath. From then on, Bill became the bathing expert. When our second and third were born, he took on the duty of bathing all of our children. Despite the rhetoric that women are biologically better caregivers (an argument that only serves to keep women in the home and men away from their children), we women aren't *naturally* good at parenting; like many things, we learn how to do it one day at a time.

As the lead parent in his family, Bill Romans couldn't agree more. "There is no training on how to be a parent. You just figure it out as you go along," he said, as we discussed his experience as primary caregiver.

Bill and his wife, Sue Barsamian, shared child care duties when their two daughters were babies. Sue worked for various technology companies in increasingly larger and more demanding roles, leaving her with limited flexibility. Bill's career as a strategic consultant meant he had more control of his time.

"Becoming the lead parent wasn't part of the plan. It was a natural evolution of what was happening in our careers and in our family life," Bill shared, "but I was surprised by the level of resistance to me in my role as primary caregiver."

Teachers, school nurses, and the other mothers wondered where Sue was, often assuming Bill was just "babysitting." He recounted a day that was hard to forget: "I remember I was on the sidelines of my daughter's soccer game. I was the only father amongst a group of moms. One of them asked where my wife was. I told them she was in India on business and the moms all said, 'Your wife certainly travels a lot. That's just so sad for the girls.' The implication of her comment was that my daughters weren't getting the best caregiving since their mom wasn't the primary parent. Frankly, it was insulting."

Bill's new hero is Andrew Moravcsik, husband of "Why Women Still Can't Have It All" and *Unfinished Business: Women Men Work Family* author Anne-Marie Slaughter. Andrew wrote his own article for *The Atlantic* entitled "Why I Put My Wife's Career First." When he was interviewed by CNN, Andrew said, "We have values in this country where we don't feel that a man who takes those child care responsibilities and becomes the lead parent has the same legitimate standing in society that a woman does and until we change those values not many people will take advantage even of the opportunities we make possible."[175]

Bill said, "In my experience, women prefer to believe that we men aren't equipped to do this job of being primary parent. And, men don't want to do the hard work of caregiving so they perpetuate the myth they aren't capable and that children really need their mother. But I firmly believe it isn't about gender; it's about who has the capacity and time and interest to take the leadership role in caring for the children."

Josh Levs likes to say, "Dads do it differently," and he's right. But he and Bill and Andrew are forgetting a key issue: Women have held the power in the home for years. Parenting has been the one thing where we women have been encouraged to excel. When we're told we're incompetent in the workplace, when we're castigated for not achieving our professional potential, at least we can be experts in parenting. It's hard to give that power up.

The truth is, we don't have a choice. Our work-first culture is based on the ideal worker model that demands us to be all-in, all-of-the-time, while our current economy means the vast majority of households need two incomes to survive. We women are too stretched by our many obligations to continue to hold dominion over the home. We need to get to 50/50 and the only way to do that is to let go of control and let fathers in. Trust me; it's a win for everyone.

Parenting has been the one thing where we women have been encouraged to excel. When we're told we're incompetent in the workplace, when we're castigated for not achieving our professional potential, at least we can be experts in parenting. It's hard to give that power up.

STAY-AT-HOME DADS: AN ELEVATED LIFE-FORM?

You can't have missed all of the articles lately about the increase of stay-at-home fathers. According to Pew Research, in 2013 7 percent of fathers with children under the age of eighteen did not work outside of the home, up from 4 percent in 1989.[176] These days, while nearly a quarter of stay-at-home dads report not being able to find a job, an equal number report they are home specifically to care for their kids. In 1989, only 5 percent claimed this as the rationale for why they were home. That means around 1 million modern dads have intentionally stepped back from their careers to push the strollers, change the diapers, and nurture the next generation.

These trailblazing men take pride in their roles as primary father. Raúl Castro certainly does. He said, "People think it is easy to take care of kids but it is one of the hardest jobs I have ever had. It certainly is the most important."

Originally from Durango, Mexico, Raúl met his wife, Julie Abrams, when they were both working at a restaurant in Chicago. Julie was waitressing to help pay for college. Raúl, who had recently immigrated, was trying to get his footing in his new country. Despite the cultural differences and the fact that Raúl barely spoke English and Julie barely spoke Spanish, they fell in love. It was obvious from the beginning that Julie's career would take precedence and that Raúl would be the one to offer support.

"She had more education and, as a result, more opportunities. Of course her career would come first," Raúl told me. I interviewed him over the phone with his daughter, Elizabeth, serving as interpreter. Although Raúl has been in the United States for more than twenty-five years, he prefers to speak in his native tongue. Elizabeth explained that he does this because it ensures his children are fully bilingual.

When the children were younger, Julie and Raúl both worked full-time. "We didn't have a choice," Raúl said. But when Julie was recruited to be CEO of a nonprofit, which came with a much bigger salary but also a family move, Raúl willingly gave up his job.

Like many women who have put family first and left the paid workforce, Raúl believes children need a parent as primary caregiver. He said, "If you want to do right by your kids, you need to have someone at home."

For Julie, having Raúl as stay-at-home father meant she has been able to focus on her career. Mirroring what so many successful men with spouses at home have said before her, Julie told me, "I am where I am today because he took care of the home front."

"In a way, it's almost like bragging for a woman to say she has a stay-at-home husband," said Diane Sollee, director of the Coalition for Marriage, Family and Couples Education. "Not only is she the breadwinner with a great job, but she's also got this highly evolved male person—a feminist, father, and husband who doesn't care what the gender roles are. It's really an elevated life-form."[177]

But is it really? There is no doubt the vast majority of senior women at the top of most professions have husbands who are the lead parents. These men often don't work or, like Bill Romans and Andrew Moravcsik, have careers that allow them to place family first. But does having a husband at home really mean we've come a long way?

In terms of gender roles, maybe. In terms of the workplace, no. What it really means is that the workplace hasn't changed to accommodate parenting. What it really means is that we haven't demanded our government provide systems and structures to support families. What it really means is that couples are forced to find individual solutions that may work for some but don't work for most.

And what of the men themselves? I interviewed nearly a dozen men who are putting family first in some way or another. Each of them expressed anger and resentment that, as caregivers, they were considered less masculine and less competent. Those who were still married and whose wives had careers that flourished had few regrets about the financial implications of their choice.

But what of the men whose marriages don't survive or whose wives have careers that don't flourish? Staying home for them brings the same financial and professional risks so many women who have opted out have faced these past few decades—in fact, probably more risks given the data on how men are penalized for prioritizing family over career. Imagine if a man was to tell an employer he'd been out of the workforce for a few years to care for his children. Talk about challenging the gender straitjacket.

These stay-at-home dads might be evolved feminists, but they are still locked in a system that doesn't allow them or their wives to integrate caregiving and careers. If it did, my guess is they wouldn't be staying home, at least not for very long. They'd do what so many trailblazing women have done before them and find work that allowed them both the flexibility of being an engaged parent and the rewards of a rich and meaningful career.

THE REAL NEW MAN

The good news is there are more and more men like Bill Romans and Andrew Moravcsik who are boldly placing family first and doing so without sacrificing their careers. Take Tim Cicero. I met him in London when I was helping run a conference on how to increase the number of women in creative leadership in advertising. Tim and I immediately bonded over our dreams for a more evolved workplace. He told me he had consciously constructed his career so he could be a fully engaged father, and that it wasn't easy. He gave up a rising career as a record producer with Universal

Music because the crazy hours and erratic schedule meant he was sacrificing time he could have spent with his children.

"It came down to realizing that my family was my priority. As a result, everything I do is compared against what it means for me in relationship to my kids. If I am going to give up one hour of time with them, I ask myself, what am I going to get back?"

He built off of his strong relationships in the music industry to launch his own executive coaching practice, something he said he had already been doing with colleagues on the side. His practice has morphed and, ironically, most of his clients now are senior women in advertising and media who are trying to figure out how to integrate their careers with their family obligations. He said he coaches them to do what he did.

"It takes courage to live your truth. For some, that means leaning in to the work and letting go of the guilt. For others that means giving up the big title, the fancy job, the outsized paycheck, and finding a life that has more flexibility. But make no mistakes, this isn't about gender," Tim said adamantly. "It's about courage. I believe true courage comes from being authentic to yourself. Women *and* men need to learn how to do that."

Charles Scott already has. Author Whitney Johnson wrote about him in her compelling book, *Disrupt Yourself: Putting the Power of Disruptive Innovation to Work*, recounting how Charles disrupted his own life and took a pause for parenthood. But because he's a man, he called it a "sabbatical." Whitney explained,

> Charles Scott had a plum job at Intel Capital's Investment Capital Fund, and had developed Intel's clean technology investment strategy. He also wanted to spend more time with his young children. He didn't quit his job right away. He took a two-month sabbatical to test-drive his steam: in the summer of 2009, he and his eight-year-old son cycled the length of mainland Japan, 2,500 miles in sixty days . . . Once he finished this endurance adventure, Scott had enough data to be certain he wanted to change career . . . So he saved and planned for two years before finally leaving Intel.[178]

Charles launched his new business, Family Adventure Guy, a for-profit-for-good effort that supports family endurance challenges and links them to charitable causes. Like so many women who found a way to integrate their kids with their careers, Scott worked, paused, and thrived.

MEN WANT A PLACE IN THE HOME

As of 2014, 90 percent of births were to women between the ages of eighteen and thirty-four. While we don't know the age of the fathers, we can assume the vast majority of them are also Millennials. And what do we know about Millennial men? Like Benn Eifert, they don't just want to be out there providing as men have been expected to do for, well, a millennium or two. The men of this generation also want to care for their children. The question is, will we women let them?

Michael Kimmel, distinguished professor of sociology at Stony Brook University and a leading expert on men and masculinity, often talks and writes about the "new real men." He wrote they are "animated by terrific relationships with their children" and expect their partners to be fully engaged in meaningful careers.[179] As we have seen, those expectations can be realized only if we allow men to take their rightful place in the home.

As Bill Romans said, "Caregiving isn't gendered; society's attitude toward caregiving is." Let's change that. But just changing attitudes isn't enough. We need to disrupt the workplace paradigm when it comes to caregiving and careers. It is good for men, good for women, good for children, and good for business.

> It's not fair to limit the lives of men when we demand more for women.

CHAPTER 7

The Workplace Is Changing, Slowly

"This isn't a women's problem; it's a business problem."
—Cathy Benko,
vice chairman/managing principal, Deloitte LLP

I first met Jenni Snyder when I moderated a panel on Moms in Tech for the 2015 Tech Inclusion Conference in San Francisco. The panel included women who had each struggled to figure out how to be a mom in the predominately male-dominated tech world.

The lack of women in the technology industry has been garnering headlines for years and came to a frothy head in 2014 when industry giants such as Google, Facebook, Microsoft, and others revealed their paltry employment statistics. Most of the biggest names in tech couldn't muster more than an 18 percent female headcount in tech-related jobs.[180]

"How could that be?" everyone asked.

"It's the pipeline," everyone answered.

There is no doubt there is an issue when it comes to the pipeline. The data shows that since the mid-1980s, the number of women graduating with degrees in science, technology, engineering, and math has dropped significantly.[181] Since there are so few "qualified" women to hire, well, of course, that must explain why there are so few women in the industry.

But women in tech are more than just technical professionals. There are marketers, product managers, customer support leaders, human resource executives, operations managers, and so on. These jobs typically don't have many women in them either, aside from the "pink collar" jobs of marketing and human resources. The data released by the Googles and Facebooks of the world revealed that there wasn't just a dearth of women in technical careers, but women in the tech industry overall. On average, the companies reported just 29.1 percent of their entire workforce were women.

"How could that be?" everyone asked.

"It's the sexist environment," everyone answered.

The argument goes that the industry is so sexist it won't hire women and when they do get hired the hostile workplace and "bro" culture sends them packing. In 2013, an app called TitStare that showed men staring at women's cleavage was released at a TechCrunch Disrupt conference (one of Silicon Valley's biggest annual events). At the same conference, one of the organizers simulated masturbating on stage. When TechCrunch organizers apologized for the incidents, another key technologist, Pax Dickinson, previously the CTO of Business Insider, tweeted out that he thought an apology was kowtowing and that it was just a little bit of "minor" misogyny.[182]

By 2014, women such as former GitHub software developer Julie Ann Horvath began sharing their stories of harassment and abuse via social media. Finally, the experiences of women in tech were shown to not be just isolated cases, but a pattern of more than "minor" misogynistic behavior.

And then there was the Ellen Pao lawsuit against venture capital firm, Kleiner, Perkins, Caufield and Byers, which became a lightning rod for the challenges many women in tech (and beyond) were experiencing. Ellen claimed she'd both been harassed and faced gender discrimination while she worked at Kleiner. They claimed she was a "bad fit" and didn't have the chops to be a successful venture capitalist. She eventually lost her case on all counts, creating more anger and resentment amongst women in tech.

The tipping point came during the Grace Hopper Celebration of Women in Computing conference in October 2014. The event, an annual gathering of women technologists, is hosted by the Anita Borg Institute. Over the past five years, the conference has gotten bigger and bigger. That fall's event was the largest they'd had with more than 8,000 women coming from all over the country.

One of the panels included four male CEOs who were dubbed "male allies" and who considered themselves avid supporters of women. Attendees were skeptical. A rogue group of women created fake bingo cards to keep track of each time one of the panelists said something sexist or clichéd. The boxes included things like, "'I've believed in women's rights my whole life'" and "Blames awkward geeks for abusive tech behavior." On a different panel, Satya Nadella, CEO of Microsoft, told women that instead of asking for fair pay, they should "trust" they will get the right raises as they advance in their career. "It's good karma" to let the system take its due course, he said; at that, one woman reportedly stood up and yelled, "Bingo!" The crowd cheered, mocking the panelists for their seeming unconscious bias.

Undoubtedly the tech industry has a problem. But it isn't only a pipeline problem or a toxic workplace problem. Women have been working in toxic workplaces for as long as we have been working outside of the home. The truth is, like just about every other industry, tech has a retention problem.

There are large cohorts of women who do manage to get into the pipeline and then weather the hostile work environments because they love the work. Sadly, a significant portion eventually leave. Various research has shown that somewhere between 50 percent and 60 percent of women in STEM careers will leave the workplace during the key mid-career period.[183] Why? Because they become mothers. One survey revealed that 65 percent left their jobs after becoming mothers.[184] As with women in other industries, it wasn't mothering per se, but the cumulative effect of dealing with a repressive culture that made motherhood the last straw. A former motion graphics designer said, "Motherhood was just the amplifier. It made all the problems that I'd been putting up with forever actually intolerable."

Which brings me back to the Mothers in Tech panel. Our goal was to give advice to women in tech who would soon be mothers. We knew their challenges would be manifold. Not only would they be dealing with their new roles as parents; they'd be dealing with a workplace that is hostile at worst or clueless at best when it comes to women in general and mothers in particular.

Jenni, who is the technical lead of the MySQL team at Yelp, was the only woman in the engineering department when she became pregnant with her daughter, Zelda. At the time, the average age of the engineers was between twenty-four and twenty-six years old. Her colleagues were young men not used to having women around and certainly not used to a colleague who becomes a mother. Jenni shared with the audience that she felt incredibly isolated and alone.

"It's not that they were purposely trying to discriminate against me; it's just that they had no idea how to deal with me," Jenni said.

So Jenni went on a campaign to change her company's culture. She launched the Yelp Mom's Resource Group, cajoled the company into providing a mothers' breastfeeding room and breast pumps, and collaborated with the human resources department to bring in consultants to reframe the company's thinking around motherhood.

Jenni is enthusiastic about how her company is evolving, but she knows how hard it is to be a trailblazer. "Until it becomes an everyday practice and we provide best practices for others, there will always be a first time," she told the audience. "You just have to deal with that reality."

So true. Jenni and other women in tech are following a long-held tradition of breaking new ground for women in the workplace. What is happening in tech right now has been happening in journalism, the financial services industry, and other industries over the last forty years. Sadly, despite all the hard work, we're still not much further along in any male-dominated industry. Change is happening, but these days we're seeing glaciers move faster.

> "Motherhood was just the amplifier. It made all the problems that I'd been putting up with forever actually intolerable."

DÉJÀ VU, ALL OVER AGAIN

In 1970, a group of women who worked at *Newsweek* sued the company for gender discrimination. Though they had attended elite women's colleges, had graduated with honors, and, like their male colleagues, were highly ambitious, they soon realized they were there only to support the "real" journalists: men. The women had been hired with the understanding that they would be allowed to write for the magazine, but soon discovered they were really there to "push carts of mail, clip stories from newspapers, fact-check, and occasionally mix a cocktail for an editor."[185] Lynn Povich, one of the women who participated in the *Newsweek* lawsuit, recounted in her book, *The Good Girls Revolt*, that they were told "women don't write here."

Unlike Ellen Pao, Lynn Povich and her team won their lawsuit. You'd think significant changes would be made in the ensuing years. And yes, women were added to the masthead and groundbreaking articles did get written by women. But is the culture all that different? Ask Jesse Ellison.

In 2009, Jesse was one of a new wave of female journalists at the magazine who found themselves experiencing some of the things Lynn and her colleagues dealt with all those years before. It wasn't until Jesse and her peers learned about the lawsuit that they realized nothing had really changed. As Jesse told Lynn Povich, "So much of the language and culture was still the same. It helped drive home the fact that it was still the same place, the same institutional knowledge, the same *Newsweek*."[186]

Jesse and her cohorts convinced the magazine to run a cover story entitled "Are We There Yet?"[187] In it they revealed that women made up 39 percent of the masthead, up from 25 percent in 1970, but that men still wrote the vast majority of the articles. In 2009, men wrote forty-three of the forty-nine cover stories, a pattern that was consistent over time despite the fact that a woman, Tina Brown, was the editor in chief.

Newsweek isn't the only place female journalists have faced discrimination. In the 1970s, *The New York Times* and other august newspapers and magazines were sued for how they treated women. Forty years later men still make up 69 percent of the bylines at *The New York Times*. In the field of journalism overall, men make up 60 percent of newspaper employees and 70 percent of newsroom editors, and men write 80 percent of newspaper op-eds. Men lead the way when it comes to "thought leader" magazines such as *The New Yorker*, too, typically garnering the vast majority of bylines. For example, in 2011, 242 bylines in *The New Yorker* were written by women; 613 were written by men. This pattern is standard for the magazine and others like it. As for "new media," the record is not much better. For example, The OpEd Project reports that during a 12 week period in 2011, only 33 percent of op-eds on the *Huffington Post* and *Salon* were written by women.[188]

Pipeline problem in journalism? Not according to the Journalism and Women Symposium, an advocacy group for female journalists. They report that, in the last decade, between 70 percent and 76 percent of all journalism and mass communications graduates have been women. Sigh . . .

Then, of course, there is the financial services industry. In the 1980s, it faced a similar set of lawsuits that the media industry had the decade before. Collectively, the lawsuits revealed a pervasive pattern of gender discrimination and sexual harassment against women that made working in the industry an utter hell.[189] I know this story well.

In 1984, three of my closest friends took jobs on Wall Street after we graduated from college. They were part of the new wave of women entering the financial services sector. They were paid exceptionally well but worked long hours and, though we lived in the same city, I rarely saw them. When I did, the stories they shared were enough to make you cry. Bosses who groped them, colleagues who mocked them, bonuses that paled in comparison to those of their male peers. They told me it was the price you had to pay for being a woman on Wall Street.

All three of my friends went on to business school—Wharton, Stanford, and Harvard. None are still in the financial services industry today. One is a stay-at-home mom, another a part-time art and math teacher, and the third changed careers completely and now works as a producer in Hollywood. When I asked them what they remember about their jobs at Goldman Sachs, Smith Barney, and Morgan Stanley, one said, "I was completely unprepared for how hostile and sexist it was. I still shudder at the memory."

Another said, "I'd like to believe it's different for the current generation of women, but I have my doubts."

You know it's not much different. In 2002, Laura Zubulake sued UBS Warburg for gender discrimination similar to the kind my friends experienced. She won her case and was awarded $29 million. In 2005, a group of female stockbrokers sued Smith Barney and won $33 million. In 2010, Charlotte Hanna, a former vice president, sued Goldman Sachs for motherhood discrimination, arguing they fired her after she asked to work part-time. The case was settled out of court. The list of similar cases goes on.

A 2014 global survey of 5,000 women in the financial services industry revealed the depressing truth: Not much has changed. A full 88 percent of respondents in the United States said gender discrimination is pervasive and nearly 90 percent say they believe they are paid less than men. And 59 percent of American respondents said they do not see it changing any time soon.[190]

After the 2008 Great Recession, women were laid off at a faster rate than men in the financial services industry and hired back more slowly.[191] Today, women in the top ranks are sparse. Women make up 54 percent of the financial services industry, but only 16 percent of senior executives and 0 percent of the CEOs. Only 13 percent of Goldman Sachs senior management team are women. JPMorgan has 17 percent and Bank of America boasts a full 36 percent, which is good compared to its competitors, but not great.[192] Here's the irony: Recent research[193] has shown that women are better investors. Female analysts' recommendations demonstrated a better rate of return when risk was taken into consideration. Female investors tend to be more risk averse and to deliver better long-term results.

According to Jay Newton-Small, author of *Broad Influence: How Women Are Changing the Way America Works*, "In the immediate aftermath of the global financial crisis, a panel of high-powered bankers gathered at the World Economic Forum in Davos, Switzerland, and debated whether, if Lehman Brothers had been Lehman Sisters, the investment giant would still have failed. In the end, they agreed, Lehman Sisters would've made much less money during boom times but would probably still be around today." Proving yet again why we need women in the workplace.

WOMEN MATTER (DUH)

As you saw in the previous chapter, having women in the workplace is good for the economy. It's also good for individual businesses. In case you haven't seen this data before, here's an overview:

- **Companies with a gender-diverse board perform significantly better than their competition.** A report by PwC states that "Studies suggest that companies with a gender-diverse board perform significantly better than their competition. This includes a 42 percent higher return in sales, 66 percent greater return on invested capital, and 53 percent higher return on equity."[194]

- **When senior management is more gender diverse, companies perform better on a number of key financial indicators.** A study by McKinsey showed that companies with more gender diverse senior management teams had a 10 percent higher return on equity, a 1.7 times higher stock price, and a 48 percent stronger operating performance (EBIT).[195]
- **When companies have more gender diverse workforces, they are more financially successful.** A McKinsey study of 366 public companies across a range of industries in Canada, Latin America, the United Kingdom, and the United States revealed 15 percent financial returns.[196]
- **Gender diversity leads to better innovation.** A study of more than 4,000 research and development teams found that gender diversity "generates dynamics that lend themselves to radical innovation, which causes a paradigm shift by the introduction of new features, resulting in the emergence of completely new markets."[197]

In other words, women are good for the bottom line.

Did you know that women account for seven tenths of global consumer spending and are responsible for over 80 percent of purchasing decisions in the United States?[198] Christine Lagarde, head of the International Monetary Fund, believes women are "the ultimate agents of aggregate demand." Why? Because companies that design and market their goods and services in ways that appeal to women are likely to sell more effectively, and companies that have women on their leadership teams and in their product development groups are more likely to understand the female consumer.

If we want healthy and vibrant companies and a healthy and vibrant economy, we need to get women to work. But we also have to get women to *stay at work*, and to do that we have to recognize that the vast majority will become mothers. It's time for companies to realize parenthood is a fact of doing business. Sadly, when it comes to supporting working parents, many companies are falling even further behind than they were less than a decade ago.

> **If we want healthy and vibrant companies and a healthy and vibrant economy, we need to get women to work.**

A 2014 National Study of Employers conducted by the Families and Work Institute revealed a disturbing post–Great Recession retrenching when it came to programs benefiting work–life integration and women.[199]

- Before 2008, 14 percent of employers offered full pay for parental leave. By 2014, that number had dropped to 9 percent.
- Before 2008, 20 percent of American companies formally offered flexible work arrangements. By 2014, that number dropped to 10 percent.
- Before 2008, 64 percent of companies reported they would support an employee if they needed a career break. By 2014, only half of the companies said they would welcome an employee back.
- Before 2008, 16 percent of employers offered targeted career counseling or management leadership programs for women. By 2014, that had dropped to 12 percent.
- Before 2008, 29 percent of employers expected their managers to rate employees based on face time. By 2014, that number had jumped to 38 percent.

In other words, on an aggregate basis, today's workplaces are getting less flexible, more political, and less supportive of women in general, and mothers in particular.

Millennial women currently account for over 60 percent of college graduates and 90 percent of new births, and it appears most companies don't seem to realize they are on the precipice of losing a significant portion of their best-educated talent pool.

Do they think smart, modern women are just going to accept a workplace that doesn't support work–life integration? Apparently they do.

Employers are more than willing to foster the narrative that you're lucky to have a job at all (so be grateful and stop making demands!). It's hard not to challenge that storyline. Read the headlines on any given day and you'd think Chicken Little was right—the sky is falling. We are all still trying to catch our breaths from the shock of the 2008 Great Recession. But here's a little secret most companies would rather you didn't know: The economy is growing and is expected to do so for years to come. The White House, the Federal Reserve, and the Congressional Budget Office all predict we will see unemployment rates in the area of only 4 to 5 percent through 2024.[200]

And that's for overall employment. Those with college degrees are likely to fare even better. According to the Bureau of Labor Statistics, in the next decade we can expect to see a 14 percent growth in jobs that require a college degree and an 18 percent growth in jobs that require a master's degree.[201] So if you are a college-educated Millennial, there is likely a job for you.

Surprising, I know, given the headlines such as "Millennials: Young, Educated, Jobless" that we've been seeing for years. The ongoing news stories of how hard it is to find a job for today's college graduates means many young women and men are scared about their prospects. But that narrative denies the reality that of course new graduates are expected to be jobless or underemployed in the early stages of their careers. It's part of the modern natural career evolution, one that is less linear than experienced by previous generations. In essence, it's how we find what we want and are able to do.

Consider what the New York Federal Reserve wrote in a 2014 report:

> Our analysis demonstrates that new college graduates typically take some time to transition into the labor market and find jobs that utilize their education. In fact, during both good and bad economic times, relatively high rates of unemployment and underemployment are not uncommon among college graduates just beginning their careers, and those rates can be expected to drop considerably by the time the graduates reach their late twenties.[202]

Consider also that over the next decade we will likely see millions of Baby Boomers retiring. The Social Security Administration reported that in 2015 almost 33 percent of our workforce, including 48 percent of our supervisors, became eligible to retire.[203] There are currently around

50 million people over the age of sixty-five. In the next decade, that number will increase to 60 million, around 20 percent of our population.[204] These aging men and women will likely pull back or fully retire, leaving room for the 80 million Millennials who want and need jobs. Finally, consider the fact that there is a growing realization women deliver bottom-line benefits *and* a growing movement to get women into leadership.

Frankly, it couldn't be a better time to be a college-educated woman looking for a job. Not only are you likely to find one, but you're in such high demand, you get to be choosy. Which means you can select a job working for a company that walks the talk when it comes to work–life integration.

The good news is that smart companies are finally seeing the light and realizing that attracting and retaining women is about creating cultures that support caregiving. Consider what Citibank has done. In 2006, it launched a new program called Maternity Transitions in its United Kingdom office. The program was multifaceted and included workshops for managers whose employees were heading out on maternity leave, workshops for the women themselves, and workshops for new fathers. This, in addition to expanding their maternity and paternity leave option, as well as offering flexible work solutions, has meant they have been able to retain 74 percent of new mothers, as measured within three years of giving birth—a vast improvement from the 40 percent who previously stayed without the support. The program was so successful, it was launched in the United States in 2009 and is seeing similar results.[205]

This fully integrated approach should be the gold standard, but it isn't. Sadly, most companies cry foul and argue it is just too expensive to deliver this level of support. But is it?

Frankly, it couldn't be a better time to be a college-educated woman looking for a job. Not only are you likely to find one, but you're in such high demand, you get to be choosy.

PARENTAL LEAVE: THE BENEFIT THAT MATTERS

As you've read, our parental leave policies in this country are nothing short of shameful. The research validating the importance of providing deeply engaged care that first year of life is by now undisputable, but rather than investing in the next generation, we have an unjust system that punishes children and their parents. Sure, those lucky enough to live in the right states or work for the right companies have paid leave, but the rest of us do not. Only 9 percent of companies offer full paid leave, although 56 percent of companies with at least fifty employees do offer some pay. Guess that's better than nothing.

COMPANIES THAT OFFER SOME PAY DURING PARENTAL LEAVE			
Type of Leave	**Total**	**Small (50–99 Employees)**	**Large (1,000+ Employees)**
Maternity	58%	56%	70%
Spouse/Partner Leave	14%	14%	14%

Source: Families and Work Institute, 2014 National Study of Employers. Sample size for percentages of employers

The reasons all companies don't offer full pay is that they claim paid parental leave is too hard a hit to the bottom line. But losing an employee because you don't offer this competitive benefit can be a significant financial hit as well. When an employee leaves, there are the costs to recruit, hire, and train their replacement, and the lost productivity while the new employee gets up to speed. According to the Center for American Progress, it costs at least 20 percent of an employee's salary to replace a white-collar worker.

Chris Duchesne, vice president of Global Workplace Solutions at Care.com, said companies "don't understand they'll often have to pay more if talented, skilled, and very valuable employees leave. These kinds of programs (paid parental leave) make employees all the more engaged, all the more loyal. For women, if they take leave available to them, they feel the company is more supportive and is invested in their future, and they will more than likely return to the same company."[206]

He's right. Research has shown again and again that women who take paid leave have strong attachments to work. Specifically, women who take paid leave are more likely to be working nine to twelve months after a child's birth than are those who take no leave at all.[207] So if companies want to keep women working and keep them working at their company, paid leave is one obvious solution.

Meanwhile, companies that do offer paid leave don't suffer financially. In my home state of California, where we've had a paid leave program since the mid-1990s, 89 percent of businesses report no increased costs as a result of the mandatory leave program. And, 9 percent report paid leave actually generated cost savings for their businesses by reducing employee turnover and/or reducing their own benefit costs.[208] Now, to be fair, California's leave program is paid via tax dollars, not from company coffers. But the state program covers only six weeks of leave at approximately 50 percent of one's pay. Many California companies cover the delta to ensure their employees are fully paid while out, and some even complement that state paid maternity leave with an extended one of their own. They wisely see it as a strategic cost of doing business.

The other thing to note is that there are benefits to society overall when women get paid leave. As we've seen, professional women are much more likely to return to work when they have paid leave. For those who are not working in professional jobs, there are still huge benefits to providing paid maternity leave. A study out of California revealed under-resourced moms have a 39 percent lower likelihood of receiving public assistance and a 40 percent lower likelihood of food stamp receipt in the year following the birth of a new baby when they have paid maternity leave.[209] Arguably, if we want to get rid of those "welfare queens," the best way to do that is to offer paid maternity leave.

The good news is our government is beginning to figure this out. Well, sort of. As of 2015, our military now offers women eighteen weeks of paid maternity leave,[210] up from six weeks previously. So across this country, we don't all get paid leave, but at least our military personnel do. When the government announced the change, Jane Waldfogel, a professor at Columbia University's School of Social Work, said, "This now sets a new standard which I think other companies, other employers and other employees will start paying attention to."[211]

They are. When Google expanded its paid maternity leave to four months, it saw a 50 percent reduction in women leaving the company after having a baby. Other tech companies are now extending paid leave to as much as a year.

This sounds great in theory, but there's a big potential problem with offering new mothers lengthy paid maternity leaves: It can increase motherhood bias. Managers may not want to hire women who might take the leave or may penalize women who do. So even if a company offers this seemingly great benefit, the net effect could be that we see fewer women hired and fewer women promoted.

How do we offer women longer leaves, but ensure we don't increase the risk of motherhood bias? Give men leave too. If men are just as likely to be out when a child is born, then penalizing women for taking leave becomes less of an issue.

And the benefits of paternity leave go on and on. As we saw in the last chapter, men who take it are more likely to be engaged fathers, and their wives are more likely to return to work and to stay working longer. A study by the Swedish Institute for Labor Market Policy Evaluation in 2010 found that a mother's future earnings rose 7 percent when their partners took paternity leave.[212] Additionally, a report from the Rutgers Center for Women and Work indicated that the families of men who took family leave have a significantly lower likelihood of receiving public assistance and food stamps in the year following the child's birth, when compared to those who return to work and take no family leave at all.[213]

Here's the challenge: We know that the vast majority of fathers don't take leave even when it's offered. So how do we get them to take it? It's simple: Give them a stronger incentive—money.

In the mid-1990s in Sweden, moms and dads could share leave, but fathers weren't taking the leave offered. Then the government instituted a use-it-or-lose-it policy targeted exclusively at dads. The country didn't make paternity leave mandatory, but couples lost a month of subsidized leave if the father took less than a month off. That meant he could no longer transfer all of his leave to his wife. The new policy also compensated fathers and mothers at 90 percent of their wages, making it harder for fathers to turn it down. It would be like throwing money away. Within five years, four out of every five new dads was taking paternity leave.[214] Similar use-it-or-lose-it programs were launched in Canada and Norway to equally robust results. On our shores, a 2015 study in California revealed that, if paid, a father was 46 percent more likely to take leave than if he was not offered pay.

Paid *paternity* leave may be THE key workplace benefit for retaining both male *and* female high-skilled workers.[215] In a 2014 study of highly educated professional fathers in the United States, nine of out ten reported paid paternity leave was "important" when considering a new job, and six out of ten considered it "very or extremely important." For Millennial workers, the data was even stronger, with over 90 percent indicating it was *extremely* important.

> Paid *paternity* leave may be THE key workplace benefit for retaining both male *and* female high-skilled workers.[216]

If we want to keep more moms working and if companies want to attract and retain Millenial talent, the single best benefit they can offer is paid parental leave.

CHILD CARE MATTERS, TOO

I quit my job at the advertising agency because the workplace was mother-phobic and I knew I couldn't be successful there. But that wasn't the only reason. When our caregiver quit, we were left scrambling for solutions. Child care centers that started at 7 AM and ended well after 8 PM didn't exist then (and rarely exist now). We interviewed a number of nanny candidates, but we weren't able to find anyone we felt confident could provide the kind of deeply engaged care we wanted for our two-year-old son and three-month-old daughter. Those who did fit the bill were way out of our budget. For me, the double whammy of a toxic workplace and inadequate child care meant I felt I had no choice but to downshift my career, at least for a period of time.

My story is not unique. Child care failures are often the tipping-point reason why women pull away from their careers. Nearly every woman I interviewed said either the cost of child care or the challenge of finding high-quality care was a key driver in her decision to pause her career. After paid parental leave, child care is the single most important retention tool for employees who are parents. Consider this:

- 93 percent of potential employees cite onsite day care as important when choosing an employer.
- Employee absenteeism due to child care breakdowns cost American businesses $3 billion annually.
- Almost two-thirds of employers found that providing child care services reduced turnover.
- Depending on the type of child care program offered, businesses reduced turnover by 37 percent to 60 percent.
- A University of North Carolina study found that companies with onsite child care get back between 50 and 200 percent of the cost of operation through reduced turnover and absenteeism, as well as increased productivity and engagement.[217]

And yet, only 7 percent of companies offer onsite child care support services (down from 9 percent before the Great Recession of 2008).[218] Fewer still offer backup support for unplanned child care needs.

Some companies are taking a forward-thinking approach and offering solutions to their employees. For example, Viacom offered its employees high-quality backup child care as a benefit and discovered its employees who were parents weren't the only winners.[219] The company ended up saving 528 days of unscheduled absences, resulting in substantial savings in productivity costs for the company.

Instead of onsite or even backup child care, some companies offer dependent care assistance programs. These programs give employees the chance to set aside tax-free dollars for child care to use as they see fit. Much like health savings accounts, these programs place the financial burden on the employee so the notion that they are an employer "benefit" is false. The employer is simply the conduit for the program. The financial burden is borne by the employee so the "benefit" isn't really a benefit at all. And, worse, the amount of money that can be taxed deferred is capped at 30 percent of the total expense of child care. So, some money can be saved through dependent care assistance programs, but not nearly enough.

In the tech world, where competition for talent is at an all-time high, smart companies are offering their employees meaningful child care solutions. Cisco Systems has two centers on its San Jose, California, campus and Google has four centers near its Mountain View headquarters. The "Googler Kids" enjoy low caregiver–child ratios, individualized attention and learning plans, and healthy, organic food. Unfortunately, there is already a three-year waiting list, so while it's a great perk, it doesn't work for everyone.

Facebook missed the mark on this one. When the company announced a $120 million new housing facility near its Menlo Park corporate offices, it made sure to include a pub, a laundry, a hair stylist, and a doggie day care. A place for employees' kids? Oops! Seems they forgot to include that in their extensive plans. They must have forgotten to get input from their CEO, new parent Mark Zuckerberg, or their COO, *Lean In* author Sheryl Sandberg. Surely, they would have wanted to make sure the parents amongst their employee base were supported with onsite day care. Wouldn't they?

TRENDS IN TECH IMPACTING HOW PARENTS WORK

As we've seen, the workplace hasn't changed much in the last thirty years since women started graduating on par with men from college, but in the last few years there has been a growing awareness of the need to offer family-friendly policies so we don't continue to lose female talent. Facebook's misstep aside, the field in which things are changing fastest today is the tech industry.

Here are a few key trends that will make a difference for parents in the workplace:

1) The Rise of the Gig Economy

There has been an ongoing debate about whether freelance jobs are on the rise, but debate no more. A recent study showed that, since 2000,

1099s (the tax form provided to freelance contractors by employers) have jumped a full 22 percent. Freelance jobs now account for over one-third of all new jobs in the country.[220]

This decade-long transition to a more flexible workforce has many concerned. Some have argued the rise of the "gig economy" is bad for business as company knowledge is lost by the spiraling in and out of new workers. Others have argued it is bad for workers who are not provided access to important benefits such as 401ks and parental leave. But the gig workforce is here to stay. A recent estimate is that by 2020, 40 percent of American workers will be freelancers.

The forces behind this sea change are many. For companies, relying on freelance staff can be highly appealing. First, it reduces the cost of overhead. Having fewer full-time employees enables companies to be more nimble in terms of reducing costs and reducing the pain of major layoffs when the company hits a downturn. Additionally, productivity per employee looks better when a company has fewer full-time employees, which is something Wall Street looks for when considering investing in a stock.

For individuals, the very definition of the workplace is changing given the rapid adoption of mobile technology, ubiquitous Internet access, and virtual technologies that support a distributed workforce. Add to that the waste of time, energy, and brainpower that commuting engenders and the general sense of malaise powered by the vague yet nagging notion that we're just not meant to work all day sitting in a cubicle, and it is understandable that some find freelance work appealing.

For those with caregiving responsibilities, freelancing can be the perfect solution to keep careers alive while downshifting to focus on family. Like many women who "pause" their careers, I became a gig worker after I left my job in advertising. I started my own marketing consulting practice and worked with small start-ups and large multinationals helping them develop business and marketing plans. I owned my time, became my own boss, and ended up making more money than I did when working full-time for one company. It was the perfect way for me to "stay in the game" and yet be able to put my family first.

Over 31 percent of *Women on the Rise* respondents are gig workers, working freelance on either a part-time or full-time basis. Some of the women I interviewed thought when they went freelance it would be a temporary solution, only to find out it was perfect for them and so became perennial gig workers.

There are downsides to freelancing, of course. While gig jobs offer flexibility, they are temporary, so gig workers need to be constantly selling their services. One gig worker told me she just wanted a job that she could rely on. "I'm tired of the constant hustle," she said.

Freelancing can be a risky career strategy for other reasons, too. For example, a lack of benefits means gig workers have no institutional support for emergencies, medical support, or retirement help (beyond the increasingly paltry "entitlements" provided by our government).

The good news is that as more men and women choose this path, it will become more of a standard way that we work, and systems will be put in place to mitigate those risks. Already, there is a new movement to unionize freelancers to ensure they get meaningful benefits such as health care and retirement plans. And, coworking spaces such as WeWork and Galvanize are likely to band together to offer their "members" joint access to health care and other benefits. They could replace the employer of today by providing not only office space but actual employer-related benefits. Only time will tell.

2) The Rise of Workplace Flexibility

As we have seen, lack of flexibility is often the key reason women leave after they have children. In the past, companies often offered flexibility to selected employees, but mostly by exception and often under the radar. I spoke to one senior executive of a branding and marketing agency who worked for more than eleven years in a part-time capacity. She agreed to keep her arrangement a secret from clients at the request of her agency's CEO. Why? Because he worried the clients would think they weren't getting the most committed talent. Of course, it simply wasn't true.

"Our clients had no idea I was working from home one day a week and that I was not available at all on Fridays. My team and I were able to structure our dynamic so that the clients never had to know. The work got done and we always delivered beyond the client's expectations," the woman told me.

I was completely surprised to learn of a friend from college who had arranged a similar work structure. I had admired her career in the luxury goods business from afar, marveling at how she "did it all," only to recently learn she did it by working three days a week and pretending to work five.

The senior team, of course, knew she wasn't working on two of those days, but they led the staff to believe she was working from another office and, occasionally, from home. She maintained the ruse by keeping up with email while on the playground with her kids.

"It wasn't a perfect situation, but it gave me the flexibility I needed," she told me. "I felt lucky they were willing to work with me."

She was. I spoke to numerous women who had these "special" arrangements. And while these customized arrangements might have been great for the individual woman, they do nothing for the greater good. First, this kind of exceptionalism can create discontent amongst other workers. The colleagues of these individuals aren't fools. They know something is up. Inevitably, the coworkers begin to wonder why person X has this special arrangement and they don't. In the end, the company may retain this one employee but often loses a number of others in the process either through disgruntled attrition or disengagement.

Additionally, if we hide these solutions, women (and men) won't realize there are options. They may leave the workplace rather than try to negotiate a situation that works for them *and* for the company. Again, good talent goes to waste.

Smart companies, like online media start-up Medium, are recognizing that being transparent about their work–life integration solutions can actually create more loyalty, not less. When Jean Hsu, a software engineer, was getting ready to take a leave for the birth of her second child, she approached her boss, Dan Pupius, the head of engineering at Medium, to discuss her return strategy. Jean knew she wanted time to ease back into the work world, but she wanted to be sure she would still be able to be of value to her boss and the team.

This was not new territory for Jean and the engineering team. As the first female engineer at Medium and, de facto, the first to get pregnant, she negotiated a three-day-week transition period after the birth of her first child. But Jean felt conflicted because she knew, as an individual contributor, this schedule had sometimes led to bottlenecks in the workflow. This time around, she and Dan decided it made more sense for Jean to move into an engineering management role where her work would be focused less on coding and more on guiding other engineers to accomplish their work.

After a twenty-week fully paid maternity leave, Jean returned to work but only two days a week. This flexible schedule was created with the entire engineering team's blessing and support. Jean hasn't had to hide her flexible schedule because at Medium they've baked work–life integration into their company's DNA.

In the decade to come, workplace flexibility is going to be the single biggest change in how we get things done. Why? Not because it's the "right thing to do" but because it's good for business. Companies need good talent and they are finally understanding that the way to recruit and retain good talent is by offering flexible work solutions—not just for women and parents, but across the board. In the end, it creates a culture of deep engagement and loyalty. As Jean Hsu told me, "Medium is the gold standard for how great companies treat their employees. Why would I want to be anywhere else?"

In the decade to come, workplace flexibility is going to be the single biggest change in how we get things done. Why? Not because it's the "right thing to do" but because it's good for business.

3) The Rise of Paid Parental Leave

The year 2015 couldn't have been a better year for parents in the tech world. In August, Netflix announced it was offering new parents up to twelve months of paid time off. Then Microsoft expanded its maternity leave to twenty weeks, and Adobe and PayPal announced a new sixteen-week paid leave for moms and dads. When eBay announced its twelve-week paid leave people joked it was just being stingy. It might seem to be a move toward enlightened corporate social responsibility—that is, until you realize the tech world is simply responding to the reality that its workforce is on the tipping point of parenthood.

According to the U.S. Labor Department, the average age of the American workforce is forty-two years old, but tech employees are much younger. The average age of employees at Facebook is twenty-eight; at LinkedIn it's twenty-nine; at Google and Apple it's thirty. At Microsoft, they're graying in at thirty-four.[221]

Now, consider the fact that the average age of a college-educated new mother in the United States is thirty.[222] If the average age of tech employees is around thirty, tech talent is on the precipice of new parenthood, and tech companies know this. They've been very public about their commitment to hiring and advancing women, but they need to figure out how to retain women once they have them. In particular, to keep aligned with their stated commitment to gender equality amongst their workforces, they are going to have to figure out how to avoid losing women once they become mothers. Offering extended parental leaves isn't generous; it's a strategic move intended to keep and attract talent.

Meanwhile, as the tech industry goes, so goes the nation. The expanded parental leaves in tech can only be a harbinger of things to come in other industries. In fact, the banking industry is already following suit. After the tech giants changed their policies, Credit Suisse and Goldman Sachs announced they too were extending their leaves, as did the United States military. To stay competitive, others are likely to follow.

4) The Rise of Returnships

Return-to-work internships that attract high-caliber talent who have been out of the paid workforce for a period of time are becoming more and more common. In 2016, PayPal launched its Recharge Program, a twenty-week paid internship. Their inaugural class included eight women and one man who stepped away from the paid workforce from two to twenty years. The participants are treated like full-time employees starting their first day with company-issued laptops, desks, and badges. At the end of the Recharge return-to-work internship, PayPal expects to offer each trainee a full-time job.

"It's such an obvious recruiting tool," said Thao Smith, director of the Recharge Program. "We get smart, eager, experienced employees and they get the training they need to get up to speed and be able to re-ignite their careers."

PayPal is part of a consortium of tech companies who are piloting mid-career internship programs as part of Path Forward, a nonprofit spin-off of Return Path, a New York–based software company. They had launched their own return-to-work program in 2015 to such great success they wanted other companies to get involved. Path Forward now has five technology companies piloting programs with ten to fifteen interns each. The companies don't guarantee employment, but they anticipate hiring around 80 percent of the cohort.

"We talk about wanting to solve the pipeline problem for women in tech," said Tami Forman, executive director of Path Forward. "What better way to solve it than to find talented employees who, with just a little bit of help, can hit the deck running."

In 2016, GTB broke new ground in the advertising industry by launching a formal ten-week paid "returnship" program for women who have cycled out of the workforce for more than two years. The goal, according to Traci Armstrong, senior vice president, global director of talent acquisition, at GTB, is "to eliminate the negative consequences of a resume gap by providing an on-ramp back into the ad world."[223]

These programs have been alive and well in the financial services industry for the past few years, used by forward-thinking companies as a means of attracting great talent. Consider the experience of Judith Galvin Casey. She started her career at Arthur Andersen and then went on to get an MBA from Duke University. She joined JPMorgan Chase as an associate after business school and worked her way up to vice president in the corporate finance department. She got recruited by a small capital bond insurer, where she spent six years managing $4 billion in assets as vice president of risk management. Then, like so many high-potential women, Judy paused to focus on her family.

Eleven years later, she knew it was time to go back to the paid workforce. But Judy had no idea how she was going to get "back on track." Lucky for her, investment banking firm Morgan Stanley had just launched its return-to-work paid internship specifically targeted to women who had paused their careers and who were ready to relaunch.

"I was lucky to have joined their inaugural class in 2014," Judy told me. "We spent twelve weeks in an intensive training program building our skills and getting reacquainted with the work world. It was a dream come true." Today, Judy is a vice president in wealth management at the firm and believes her "second" career is even more promising than her first.

"I don't have the distractions of young children and, as a result, feel much more engaged and able to perform at my peak," she said.

As more and more companies across industries look to hire highly qualified women to fill their leaky pipeline of female talent, we are likely to see return-to-work internships as ubiquitous as internships for college students. As Tami Forman told me, it is a great way for both company and potential employee to "try and buy" before a full commitment is required.

5) The Rise of Data as an Empowerment Tool

Finding the right company has gotten a whole lot easier thanks to technology. Before, if you wanted to really understand a company's culture, you had to call someone who knew someone who worked there. Today, most job hunters go straight to Glassdoor, an online database of over 8 million company profiles. The app crowdsources anonymous reviews that give CEO approval ratings, salary reports, standard interview questions, benefit details, office photos, and more. It distills the feedback using a five-star rating system.

Since it was launched in 2007, Glassdoor has become the de facto resource for potential employees to get a better sense of a company's character. Of course, those companies with low ratings hate it. Others claim it is a powerful recruiting tool.

Comparably is a new online database tool similar to Glassdoor. It is unique because it includes data regarding race and gender. For example, a recent analysis of Google revealed that while 89 percent of the company's male employees report it has a positive work environment, only 70 percent of Google's female employees do. This kind of data offers the job hunter clues as to what the culture is really like for those who aren't white and/or male.

Women now have their own tools to vet potential employers. Fairygodboss, another Glassdoor competitor, offers employer reviews for women by women. Georgene Huang, one of the co-founders, was inspired to start the company when she was job hunting while two months pregnant. She wanted a company that was friendly to women and wouldn't force her to "mommy-track" her career just because she was becoming a mommy. She couldn't find anything online to give her the real scoop about companies and how they dealt with moms. Georgene and her co-founder, Romy Newman, started Fairygodboss in the spring of 2015 and it immediately caught on with women. Within a few short months, the site had collected more than 19,000 reviews on more than 7,000 employers. Who's using Fairygodboss? American women between the ages of twenty-five and thirty-four who earn a median salary between $80,000 and $100,000 a year. In other words, the talent that every company now wants to attract.

The more data is available to potential employees about company culture, the more empowered we are to make smart decisions for ourselves and our families. In the past, employers held most of the power when it came to the hiring process. Job seekers were forced to rely on word of mouth or their personal networks to get insight into company culture, pay, and the like. Now, thanks to Glassdoor, Fairygodboss, and other rating services, we have more knowledge and, as a result, more power in the process. It couldn't be a better time to be a woman planning how she wants to integrate kids with her career because she can finally get insight into the reality of a given company's culture. With the click of a button, she can ascertain their level of female and family friendliness.

6) The Rise of the New Digital Class

This won't come as a surprise, but one of the fastest areas of job growth in this country is in tech. By 2020, employment in all computer occupations is expected to increase by 22 percent, according to the U.S. Bureau of Labor Statistics, and there will be an estimated 1 million new software engineering jobs that need to be filled.[224] As you also may have heard, the number of college graduates with computer science and engineering degrees is not increasing fast enough to meet the demand. Opportunity in these fields abounds.

Here's the great news: You don't need a college degree in computer science to become a programmer. All you need is a laptop and the ability to learn to write code. Why does this trend benefit those with caregiving responsibilities? Coding can be done from anywhere, including home while children are asleep or in school; and it is highly paid. Entry-level jobs for computer programmers run between $45,000 and $134,000 a year.

As a result, online programming courses like those offered by Treehouse and in-person bootcamps like those offered by Galvanize, a network of coworking and tech education spaces, give affordable access to training for those who might have not had it before. It's a fantastic backdoor into the heady world of tech. And it's growing exponentially. According to Course Report, which tracks and reviews bootcamps, there are now 250 programs across North America and last year there were 22,000 graduates—not nearly enough to fill the need.

"The number of open tech jobs has demanded some way to train developers that isn't the long, expensive route," said Liz Eggleston, co-founder of Course Report. "The demand is there, and it's been growing extremely quickly."

These coding schools typically range from eight to twenty-four weeks and cost around $10,000—not cheap, but certainly not as much as a four-year college degree. The in-person bootcamp experience means long days of instruction, extensive group work, and a major project at the end, such as an app or a game that enables the potential employee to show what they know.

However, many women, and mothers in particular, have found coding and coding camps out of reach. The technology is intimidating and these "backdoor" courses are typically filled with young guys who fit the "brogrammer" stereotype. Plus, if you are women with kids, the standard course can be untenable because the trainings often go on well into the night. Hard to manage that schedule if you have child care issues.

Enter targeted training programs like Hackbright Academy, intended to give women a leg up in the world of coding. Venture capitalist Sharon Wienbar joined Hackbright as CEO in 2014 because she is on a mission to change the ratio in tech.

"It's about breaking down barriers so nothing can prevent women getting into the tech pipeline and getting there fast," Sharon said.

The training is twelve weeks long with intensive 10 AM to 6 PM days, five days a week. The schedule is structured to ensure female students can get their children to school or child care before the class day starts. And, unlike other programs, Hackbright is committed to ending right on time. No hanging out with the bros for beers.

"The majority of our students are professionals in their late twenties and early thirties. A number of them have children. We are committed to ensuring our program allows them to meet their personal obligations while they are being trained," Sharon told me.

The demand for tech-savvy women means those who have these skills will be able to, as Sharon said, "write their own ticket."

7) The Rise of Male Allies

When Dave Goldberg, SurveyMonkey CEO and husband of Sheryl Sandberg, unexpectedly died in 2015, the women of Silicon Valley were deeply saddened. Not just because they had lost a well-regarded executive, a father, a husband, and a friend, but also because he had been a very public and proud male ally.

"Male allies"—men who support gender equality—have become all the rage in Silicon Valley. Brian Krzanich, CEO of Intel, won fans when he pledged $300 million to ensure diversity for the company's workforce by 2020.[225] When Blake Irving, CEO of GoDaddy, famous for their notoriously sexist Super Bowl ads, joined the company in 2012, he immediately put an end to the company's sexist advertising.[226] These are just two of the many senior leaders who are taking action to support women.

Consider the former vice president of corporate quality at Cisco Systems, Rich Goldberg. He recently left his company to devote his career to the issue of diversity and inclusion. In 2014, while at Cisco, Rich and a colleague launched the Cisco Men for Inclusion group. Enrolling key male stakeholders across the company in the steering committee, they hosted awareness trainings and workshops, asking participants to take a public pledge to make a difference.

"We wanted to create an allies network that was visible so others knew we were men who supported women," said Rich. Soon his passion for the issue convinced him to change careers, and now he is currently a Fellow at Stanford University's Distinguished Career Institute working in close partnership with the Clayman Institute for Gender Research.

Rich said, "It takes courage, the willingness to step out of the norm, and the humility to recognize your own role in the problem. Here's the thing. I'm a grandfather. If we men don't engage in this issue, nothing is going to change for the next generation."

These men and the hundreds of thousands like them who are standing up on behalf of women are also standing up for families. Not just for mothers, but for themselves. Take Max Schireson, ex-CEO of MongoDB. In a very public blog,[227] he announced he was stepping down from his post so he could spend more time with his children. It wasn't that well-worn euphemism for being fired. Rather, he was the first male tech leader to boldly say he was pausing his career for family. As men become more comfortable revealing their deep engagement as fathers, we'll likely see more and more men, too, working, pausing, and thriving.

8) The Rise of Gatekeepers

Not all of the new trends in the tech industry are positive. As we have moved to online recruiting systems, those with non-linear careers have struggled to "fit the bill" as defined by the algorithms created by mostly male engineers. Programs like Monster.com and Indeed.com are great if you have a conventional résumé, but not so great if you have danced in and out of jobs either because you paused for caregiving or because you became a freelancer.[228] And most companies today require you to fill out an online application, which again can result in an immediate rejection if you don't fit the narrow and outmoded concept of the traditional career path.

Beyond the technological gatekeepers, there are the recruiters and hiring managers themselves. Their own conscious or unconscious bias can keep nontraditional candidates from finding and landing a job.

Consider Lisa Tankersley. When she decided to pause her career, she never imagined she'd get divorced and end up struggling to find work. In 2000, she was pregnant with her second child and suffering from severe morning sickness, the kind that plagued Kate Middleton during her pregnancies. Lisa was working at a start-up in Silicon Valley. It was the beginning of the end of the Dot Com era.[229] Her commute was hell and the hours were punishing. When Lisa and her husband met with their accountant, he'd run the numbers and told Lisa, "You're barely making enough to cover your child care and expenses. You'd be better off staying home than working as hard as you are."

When her company announced layoffs, for Lisa it was the final straw. She quit working and stayed home with her children while her husband, an engineer, focused on his career. It was a good strategy—until it wasn't. Lisa and her husband divorced, and suddenly Lisa found herself in need of a full-time job. She couldn't find one.

She applied online via Facebook's contract portal for a position in the spam-filtering group. It was a data-entry job, something she had done at the very start of her career. As she was currently working part-time from home doing something similar for another company, meaning her skills were up to date and she had directly relevant experience, Lisa thought she was more than qualified.

So did an outside recruiter who was handling screening for Facebook. Lisa had a series of successful phone interviews and was invited to the company's headquarters to meet with the team. She had a few one-on-one interviews and a group interview as well. All of them seemed to go swimmingly.

"You know that feeling when people are smiling and nodding and you know you are in sync?" Lisa asked. "That's how my interviews went. That is, until the last one of the day and then it was like hitting a brick wall."

She met with a young man who was a leader on the team. His tone was negative. He swore a lot, complaining about the job and the "crap" they had to deal with in the spam arena. Rather than really get to know her, he spent the entire interview staring at her résumé, barely making eye contact, seeming to struggle to find something to ask her. He finally asked her how she went above and beyond "in the workplace," but Lisa didn't have a workplace to talk about.

He didn't ask about her twelve-year career break, but it was clear he was trying to make sense of it. And because he didn't ask the obvious question, he didn't find out she had worked for years (without pay) as a technical writer assisting her ex-husband on articles he "wrote" for engineering industry journals. He didn't find out she was an active and well-regarded blogger, without pay, on the highly successful Silicon Valley Moms blog, one of the first of its kind. He didn't find out she was a leader at her daughter's high school, serving as the vice president of fundraising, again without pay.

The recruiter called her that night and said Facebook had decided to pass. Lisa called to find out why, and the recruiter said she'd look into it but never called her back. Lisa didn't press the issue. She decided to move on and look elsewhere.

Sadly, because of one employee's biases (either conscious or unconscious) Facebook lost the chance to hire a strong candidate with an unconventional background. Lisa offered the company diversity that would have been directly in line with their stated goal of increasing the number of women on their payroll.

Facebook, at least, is very publicly trying to reverse this problem. They have launched a training series called Managing Unconscious Bias for their workforce.[230] The series includes four videos on the topics of first impressions, stereotypes, performance attribution bias, competency/likability trade-off, and . . . maternal bias.

By July 2015, more than half of their employees around the world had taken the course. But they didn't stop there. Rather than keep the training internal and use it as a competitive recruiting tool, Facebook has open sourced the training videos so anyone can view them and use them in their own workplace.

Lori Goler, Facebook's head of human resources, was quoted in an article on Recode as saying, "It isn't that we've figured it out or we have all the answers, but I would like to think that we're at a moment in time when any company that feels like it has something that's working will share it back with the ecosystem." She went on to say, "It's not a competition, it's part of making the entire industry better."[231]

The good news is the tech leaders at companies like Facebook, Google, LinkedIn, and others, which are largely staffed with data-driven, young men who see themselves as egalitarian and see Silicon Valley as a meritocracy, appear to be willing to acknowledge there is an issue with diversity and inclusion. When shown the statistics regarding gender (and race) discrimination at their companies, they didn't deny it; they acted by putting in place policies and programs to change the ratio.

Unfortunately, we won't know the true outcomes of their efforts for years. In the meantime, women like Lisa Tankersley who have taken extensive career breaks will likely continue to face overt discrimination and unconscious bias. And the first wave of Millennial moms like Jenni

Snyder at Yelp will likely have to go it alone given there so few women currently in engineering and other STEM-related jobs.

Still, the extensive attention on filling the pipeline with highly educated, highly skilled women means we will eventually see more and more female talent in these previously all-male bastions of work. The vast majority of these women will eventually have children. Importantly, they will have them with men who have a strong desire to be active, engaged fathers like Facebook's Mark Zuckerberg. As a result, the workplace will be forced to change. The problems facing parents won't be solved overnight, but I believe it will be better by the time my children have children of their own.

Part III

YOUR CAREER, YOUR WAY

CHAPTER 8

Conscious Careers, Conscious Choices

"Being able to know what matters to you and choosing that is what lets you live with authenticity and intention in your life."
—Jessica Herrin, founder and CEO of Stella & Dot

Late one night, after my brother and sister were finally asleep, I found my usually cheerful and seemingly happy mother crying in the kitchen. My father had been gone for two weeks of a three-week-long business trip, my younger siblings had been sick with the flu, and I had been "acting up" (puberty was getting the best of me). I thought she was just tired, but I learned it was much more than that.

"I thought I would be someone else, but here I am," my mother said. And then she cautioned me through her tears, "Don't make the same mistakes I did."

Like so many children, I had never thought of my mother as her own person. But that night I saw her in a different light. I realized she was lonely, far from her family, a housewife who was financially dependent on a man, living in country that was not her own. That night she went from being just my mother to a person with her own dreams, wishes, and regrets.

Years later, when she had her own career as a clothing consultant and became one of the leading salespeople for her company, she would tell me she regretted saying what she did that night, that it had all worked out in the end. And it did, but her words that night made a deep impression on me, as did society's message during the 1970s and 1980s, when I was growing up, that having a wildly successful career mattered more than anything, including having a family. I came to believe motherhood and marriage were patriarchal institutions in which women got the raw end of the deal. I wasn't going to let them get in the way of accomplishing my dreams and goals.

And then I met Bill. Talk about ruining my well-laid plans. I surprised my closest friends, my mother, and especially myself by marrying him the day before my twenty-fifth birthday. My mother asked me if I was sure, and I told her, "No, but somehow it feels right." It was.

In the years that followed, Bill and I never discussed kids in any real way. He assumed we would eventually have them, and I willfully ignored the subject. He went to business school and then I did. We got jobs, saved money, bought our first house. Life was going along swimmingly until Bill's mom and my mom started hinting they wanted to be grandparents.

Bill's mother, who rarely interfered, asked us one night, "You've been together for nearly seven years, what are you waiting for?" When I shared with my mother what my mother-in-law had said, she responded somewhat wistfully, "Well, all of my friends are already grandmothers. It does seem it's about time."

Time? I was in my early thirties; I had all of the time in the world. Or so I thought. I watched as one friend, and another, and then another, had problems with fertility. They spent months and even years getting shots, enduring in vitro fertilization, and suffering with miscarriage after miscarriage. Some were successful and had children; others were not.

"If you want children," one of those friends told me, "don't wait any longer."

And yet, I still I wasn't sure. If you have children, shouldn't you be sure? And then I unexpectedly got pregnant.

I'll never forget the bright blue line in the e.p.t. home pregnancy test. I hadn't told Bill I thought I might be pregnant before I took it, and as I stood in our bathroom staring down at my future, I wasn't sure what to tell him. I needed time to let this new reality sink in, to ponder what it meant for me, for us. I decided to keep the news to myself, at least for a while.

A few days later, I miscarried.

I was only seven weeks pregnant, so it seemed like a heavy period, not the loss of a potential human life. But suddenly I knew I wanted children, knew I wanted to be a mother, knew that if I didn't have that privilege, my life would not be complete.

It is funny to me now that I was in such denial about my desire to be a mother. The only way I can make sense of it is to recognize how deeply I had absorbed the negative narratives regarding career and motherhood. I believed I couldn't do both well, so I put my career ahead of everything, until I couldn't anymore. And, well, you know the rest of that story.

Looking back, the regrets I do have about how I handled my career are primarily focused on the fact that I didn't plan for motherhood. Or more specifically, I wasn't honest with myself about how important motherhood was to me. As a result, I didn't try to look at the ecosystem in which I was operating and didn't make a plan to navigate it in a way that could work for me and my family. I am not talking about derailing my career plans or downshifting my ambitions. I am talking about having a very clear understanding of the challenges women face in the world once they become mothers and developing strategies and tactics that would enable me to achieve my personal and professional goals. Because I didn't make conscious choices, I operated reactively, not proactively.

I write these words as a cautionary tale. To give you insight into how our unconscious choices lead to consequences that may not be what we intend. Yes, I worked, I paused, and now I feel as though I am thriving, but it happened largely by dint of luck. And, despite my sense that professionally I am on the right track, the financial consequences have not been insignificant. If one thing had gone another way (if my husband had lost his job or became ill and couldn't work or we had divorced or . . .), my life would have followed a completely different trajectory. Perhaps I would have thrived in that case as well; I'll never know. But I do know smart, modern women don't have to do what I did and gamble with their human capital or their family's financial well-being.

I am excited by the many ways the ambitious young women I meet are leaning in to their careers. They seem to truly believe nothing will get in the way of their professional dreams. I hope that is true, but I have my concerns. When I speak to these women, most aren't thinking about their options or evaluating their choices when it comes to integrating kids with their careers. They're winging it like I did.

Consider UC Berkeley Haas School of Business student Sarah Tait. She's well on her way to establishing her professional life. She has a fantastic job offer with an exciting start-up. She is also building the foundation of her personal life and will soon be married.

Sarah and her fiancé, Mark Kinnish, are committed to an equal partnership; they are busy planning their "feminist" wedding. They've decided on a destination event in Cabo San Lucas where they will walk down the aisle together because, as she says on their *Our Feminist Wedding* blog, "No one owns me, I'm not for being given away."

They've broken other traditions as well, such as advance viewing of the wedding dress (he's seen it) and the changing of her name (she'll keep it), but one tradition Mark found hard to break was the engagement ring.

He wanted to give her one as a sign of his "investment" in his love for her. She said she'd rather have a tattoo. Mark won Sarah over and now she proudly wears her solitaire diamond.

"We are committed to a marriage of equals, but I worried that if our marriage started out with a gift that is one-sided, it would set a precedent," Sarah said. "In the end, I realized you have to give and take to find a happy equilibrium."

So true. And yet, while Sarah has planned her career and is now busy thoughtfully planning a wedding that aligns with her and Mark's values, she's not planning how to be a mother. She told me, "I haven't really given mothering any thought. I guess I should, shouldn't I?"

Yes, Sarah (and Mark), you should.

I know motherhood is not the answer for all women. Many can't and many don't want to be mothers. However, despite the headlines about the declining fertility rate, the reality is the vast majority of us do, eventually, become mothers either biologically or through adoption. According to the U.S. Census Bureau, in 1976, 90 percent of American women were mothers. By 2014, that number had dropped to 85 percent.[232] However, looking ahead, researchers estimate that fertility will actually rise in the next ten to fifteen years in the United States.[233] Why? Well, because 80 million Millennials are entering their prime child-bearing years. And by many measures, they are more family focused than my generation. In fact, unlike Generation X, Millennials place marriage and parenthood far above financial and career success.[234] And yet, they don't seem to be doing much to prepare for how they are going to have both the careers of their dreams and the family they report they want.

I didn't plan for how to integrate kids with my career and, it would seem, neither did most of the other college-educated, high-potential women of my generation. It was, I believe, one of the biggest professional mistakes we made. In the course of my interviews, women told me they assumed "it wouldn't be a problem" and that "it would all work out." Then they told me they were blindsided when reality set in.

The second biggest mistake many of us made was to step off track and downshift our careers without a plan for how we were going to relaunch ourselves when the time was right. Again, we thought we would "just figure it out."

To our defense, we were bushwhacking new territory. Just as the women of my generation were trailblazing what it meant to try to break the glass ceiling, we were also trailblazing what it meant to step back for a period of time to care for our families. Yes, we were being innovators by disrupting the paradigm around linear careers, but putting our careers on the back burner without a plan was not very, well, professional.

If I could reel back my career to the period before I left my job in advertising, I would have taken the time to understand the personal, professional, political, and financial consequences of pausing my career. I would have recognized that because the workplace punishes those with caregiving responsibilities, if I wanted to place my family front and center (and I did), then I was going to have to embark on a non-linear career path. Then I would have put a plan into place that would allow me to achieve my professional goals even if my career didn't fit the traditional mold. I would have understood that pausing didn't have to mean I was abandoning my ambitions. I would have seen it was a temporary solution to an intractable workplace situation. By pausing, I was not failing; I was disrupting a flawed career model that didn't work for me. And, most important, I would have understood my pause for what it was: just one point of time out of a lengthy career.

Here's the good news: It has never been a better time to create a successful non-linear career. The workplace is changing, which means great things for women and men who want to integrate caregiving with their careers. But there is bad news, too: Things aren't changing quickly enough to make a real difference for the 80 million Millennials who are just now entering their prime child-bearing and child-rearing years. It will be up to each individual to figure out how to navigate the bumpy, curvy road ahead.

So what does a smart, modern woman do? She does what I didn't do; she takes the long view on her career and makes a plan. And, I believe, so should every man.

Women and men need to work together to find better solutions to our work–life integration issues. Planning together for the reality of children and the impact of caregiving is a powerful place to start.

Unlike previous generations, there is no question women will *have* to work outside the home, and there is no question men will *have* to be 50/50 partners when it comes to the house and children. Not just because we want equality, but because unless you are part of the "One Percent" and money is no object, you'll have no other choice.

Women and men need to work together to find better solutions to our work–life integration issues. Planning together for the reality of children and the impact of caregiving is a powerful place to start.

Part III of *Work PAUSE Thrive* offers insights, ideas, opportunities, and cautionary tales so you can thoroughly consider whether you should pause for parenthood and how to do so without killing your career. In the chapters ahead, I have written with career-driven women in mind—specifically, college-educated women who are married or plan to be married and who have or plan to have children. That said, as the mother of a gay son whom I hope will one day marry and have children, I don't mean to exclude other kinds of relationships, other kinds of parents, or men in general. The challenges of integrating kids with careers is ubiquitous. I believe what is written can apply to all couples, gay or straight, married or not, who are or will become parents.

As you read through the next section of the book, it will become clear that these strategies and tactics won't and can't work for everyone. At the very least, my research has shown that pausing requires you to have a partner who provides some measure of financial stability while you are putting your family first.

Additionally, for the women I spoke to and surveyed, a college degree was the foundation on which they were able to pause and then relaunch their careers. Pausing may not be a "choice" for women without college degrees because they are less likely to be able to afford a period of time in which they have reduced or nonexistent income. Single mothers also have few chances to pause because, in the vast majority of cases, they have no one to provide financial backup.

My dream is that we as a country will change our workplace and public policies so that all women and men can work to their fullest capacity over the length of their careers. This would include enabling them to temporarily pause to care for their families. But until that is the case, the population who will most benefit from the contents of this section of the book are women who have the personal and financial support in place that enables them to consider a pause.

As I have shared before, my agenda is to not encourage women to pause their careers, but to provide critical information for the many high-potential women who will inevitably ponder whether they should. Every woman must forge her own way, one that reflects the reality of her life and is aligned with her authentic dreams and goals. Doing so requires her to make conscious choices.

May the following pages help you on your journey.

CHAPTER 9

Working

The Foundation for Your Non-Linear Career

"We need a new home economics, one that helps women and men prepare for their dual roles as parents and professionals."
—*Women on the Rise* survey respondent

Melanie Wells grew up relatively poor in a small mountain community in North Carolina. Her singular goal was to "bust out of there" and build a career that would ensure she had the financial security she didn't have as a child. Melanie went to college at UNC Chapel Hill and fell in love with writing and journalism. After getting her degree, she built her career working for one high-profile media outlet after the next. Motherhood? Not on her radar.

"I have always been work obsessed," Melanie told me. "Kids weren't in my sights. As my colleagues put their careers aside to care for their children, I felt I was in a race and the horses were dropping out. I wondered if there was something wrong with me. I didn't want the same things they seemed to want."

Then things changed. When Melanie turned forty, she and her husband decided to adopt a baby girl. As the primary breadwinner, Melanie had no desire to slow down, but she did decide she wanted more control of her time. At first, her employer, Forbes, was "very accommodating," allowing

Melanie to work from home as she needed and even giving her a two-month sabbatical one summer when she and her husband moved. Then the industry began to shift as the transition from print to online changed the landscape for journalists. Melanie said she could see the "writing on the wall."

"I knew long term I would not have the career I wanted if I stayed in journalism so I pivoted and eventually launched my own content consulting company. Today, I'm making more money than I ever have and, most important, I have control of my time and destiny," said Melanie. "When you boil it down though, it was a professional decision based on a personal goal: I wanted to be more available to my daughter."

Melanie never "paused" per se, but by making smart decisions early in her career, she was able to create the job and life she wanted. How did she do that? She said, "I always had a plan and was thinking ten steps ahead of where I was at any given moment. It's impossible to anticipate what life will bring so I believe the single most important thing you can do for your career is think ahead and set yourself up for success."

In most of the books and blogs I've read about how to have a successful career, few talk about kids. We euphemistically talk about "work–life balance," but few say anything specifically about how ambitious women can be mothers in the deep and rich way so many of us want to be. It's like we're afraid to bring the idea up because we're afraid talking about it will somehow curtail women's ambition.

It won't.

We need to begin talking about this issue so the next generation of women (and men) have the knowledge and tools they need to build the life of their dreams, one that includes a great career AND a great family life. Not doing so is like asking women to follow the path men have been forced to be on for years: work all of the time and have no life outside of work. Who wants that?

Whether you think you might want to pause for parenthood or not, the best thing you can do is prepare yourself for a non-linear career. Not because you will have one, but because you might. The following are strategies gleaned from my interviews and from the responses to the *Women on the Rise* survey intended to give you options and allow you to take control of your career journey, whether you pause or not.

> We euphemistically talk about "work–life balance," but no one says anything specifically about how ambitious women can be mothers in the deep and rich way so many of us want to be. It's like we're afraid to bring the idea up because we're afraid talking about it will somehow curtail women's ambition.

STRATEGY #1: GET CLEAR ON WHAT YOU TRULY WANT

Our not-so-large living room was filled with women who had come for an all-day goal-setting workshop hosted by my friend Tara Sophia Mohr. Tara founded the "Playing Big Leadership Series" and is the author of the best-selling book *Playing Big: Find Your Voice, Your Mission, Your Message*. In the past five years, she has trained thousands of women around the world to achieve their "audacious" goals by helping them recognize what is holding them back and giving them tools to achieve their "big" dreams.

The ten women in the room were nervous, afraid to share what was in our hearts. Turns out, dreaming big is hard. The bigger the dream to you, the more vulnerable you feel. We went around the room timidly sharing our hopes and fears. Beth, who is an ordained minister, sensed she had a calling to be in service to women in some deep and meaningful capacity. Sally, who had spent years in local politics, wondered if she should recommit to her dream of political office at the state or national level. Tonya, who had just left her job and was considering her next move, imagined starting a company helping women become better investors. I wanted to write this book and share with others what I learned about integrating careers and family. Our dreams were big, but something was holding each of us back.

Tara asked us to fill out a card with those voices, or "inner critics" as she called them, that we heard when we tried to dream big. "These are the voices," she explained, "that keep you from achieving your goals."

Our voices said things like, "Everyone else has their act together. Why don't you?" or "You need to work harder if you really want to achieve that dream" or "Are you really willing to risk your financial security for something that is likely to fail?" or, as in my case, "Who is going to listen to your ideas?" In other words, who gives me the authority to speak on this complex and deeply emotional issue?

When we had each revealed our deepest fear, Tara said, "Now close your eyes. Today, we are going to find your inner mentor." That workshop helped me see something I hadn't before: We have been trained to look externally to find mentors to guide us, but we often forget or don't even know how to look internally to get clarity on what we want.

I am not here to discredit mentors. On the contrary, the wisdom of our elders is often dismissed in our youth-obsessed culture. I have been blessed with numerous mentors whose wisdom and guidance has had an incalculable impact on my life. The insights and experiences of mentors are valuable data points for helping you figure out your best path. And yet, their wisdom is rooted in their own life journeys.

You, too, have wisdom based on your experiences. Looking externally is useful to helping you get clarity on your options and your situation, and to give you insight on how you might navigate your life and career given the constraints you face, but *no one can tell you what is right for you.*

Living with clarity about your dreams, goals, constraints, and compromises allows you to walk your own true path. How you integrate your kids and your career will reflect your own unique set of circumstances. Reach out and find a mentor, and then reach in and find yourself. It's the best way to ensure you can live with authenticity and intention.

Living with clarity about your dreams, goals, constraints, and compromises allows you to walk your own true path.

I believe what holds most of us back is not *just* an inflexible workplace, a punishing public policy system, a millennia of patriarchy, a boss who won't promote us, a partner who won't do his fair share, a culture that says we must be a certain kind of mother to be considered a good mother. No doubt these are obstacles in our path. But they aren't insurmountable.

I believe what holds most of us back is fear.

Fear that if we truly ask for what we want—a full, rich life that includes work we love and the ability to develop and nurture relationships that are deep and meaningful—we might not get it. Here's the thing: We definitely won't get it if we can't even envision it.

Jennifer Mazella, who paused her career and then became a warrior championing the issues of the special needs community, shared her personal motto with me: "Don't lean in, stand up! When you do that it says you aren't leaning in to listen to someone else's authority, you are standing up and listening to your own inner truth."

I know it sounds clichéd, like some bad *Saturday Night Live* Stuart Smalley self-validation skit, but to successfully navigate the obstacles that are inherent when it comes to integrating kids and careers, you need to get clear on what *you* want and what you are willing to give up to achieve those personal and professional goals.

Do some deep work and ask yourself what attitudes and preconceived ideas you have when it comes to being a mother in general, and a mother in the workplace specifically. Ask yourself what attitudes and preconceived ideas you have when it comes to being a father. Ask yourself what a "life well lived" looks like. What are those deathbed regrets you want to be sure you don't have? What does it mean to be successful? What does it mean to be happy? What does it mean to be fulfilled? What trade-offs are you willing to make to truly thrive?

Now ask your partner the same questions. When you both have the answers, write them down. Then ask them of yourselves and each other again six months from now, one year from now, and all the years that follow. Get the Holstee Manifesto, frame it, and live with it each and every day. Eventually, you'll uncover what it is you really, really want.

Act accordingly.

STRATEGY #2: CHOOSE THE RIGHT CAREER

You've heard it before: When you are in the right career and in an environment that lets you thrive, what you do each day isn't work; it's passion. For the lucky women who live this reality, the guilt and doubt that can arise from privileging work over family often becomes less of an issue.

As a result, they are often not driven to pause. In fact, for them pausing can feel like a burden.

Consider the 28 percent of *Women on the Rise* respondents who did NOT pause their career. One of the key reasons they never slowed down professionally was because they loved their jobs. As one survey respondent said, "If you love what you do, why would you ever want to stop doing it?"

What is hidden in the stories of so many women who have paused their careers is that their first career wasn't the right one for them. Pausing for parenthood was the opportunity for them to step back and assess what they wanted professionally. As we saw in chapter 2, for many pausing was a much-needed opportunity to pivot their careers.

"My pause allowed me to reflect on who I am, what matters to me, and how I want to explore, cultivate, and express that through my work," one *Women on the Rise* respondent shared.

Another said, "I realized I had the confidence I didn't have earlier in my life to pursue work that I could be passionate about, not just work I fell into."

Their sentiments are not unique. But because career pauses are not seen as part of an overall plan or even part of a journey to find the right career, the power of the time away from the paid workforce is devalued. In reality, for women who pivot, leaving the workforce and their previous careers are often a critical part of their journeys to find the right professional path.

Consider women like Kriste Michelini, who left her job in software sales and became an interior designer; or Mary Page Platerink, who left a senior-level position at Coca-Cola and became an entrepreneur; or Patricia Nakache, who went from consulting to venture capital—the list goes on and on. Each of these women had achieved success in their previous work, but they weren't truly fulfilled. They left because, when they weighed the scales, time with their children felt significantly more meaningful than time at a job that didn't inspire them. Their pause was the break between two disparate paths.

No question there are long stretches of careers that can be a grind. Just like there are long stretches of caring for children that can be a grind. Neither will bring joy and inspire passion each and every day. And certainly, this is not to say one is more or less important than the other. This is only to say that when you are in the right career you are more likely to weather those tedious and frustrating days with resilience because the meaning you derive from your work over time is as important and as rich as the meaning you derive from your children. When that's the case, leaving your career simply doesn't make sense.

The right career is waiting. It's up to you to find it. Better to find it before you have children so you can be one of the lucky women who don't feel the strong desire to pause because the deep rewards of their work are too hard to give up.

STRATEGY #3: CHOOSE THE RIGHT COMPANY

Author, entrepreneur, and Twitter evangelist Laura Fitton didn't set out to find a company that could meet her work–life needs, but she says she is lucky to have found one in her current employer, HubSpot. She had built her career by helping companies harness the power of social media and digital marketing. In 2009, Laura co-wrote *Twitter for Dummies* and became an expert on all things Twitter. A year later, she made two key decisions: First, she decided to get divorced. Second, she decided to start a company that would be a marketplace for Twitter-based app developers. For Laura, it was her "lean in" moment.

Despite being a woman and a single mother of two young daughters, she managed to raise venture capital funding to help her build her business. Two "crazy" years later, Laura sold her company to HubSpot. It didn't mean she could retire for life, but it did mean she landed at a place that allowed her to thrive.

HubSpot[235] is a practitioner of results-only work environment (ROWE). ROWE is a human resources strategy that puts the emphasis on getting the work done, not on working long hours just to prove you are the most committed employee. ROWE is a relatively new way of structuring how we work at work. The focus is on empowering employees and treating them like, you know, adults. ROWE workplaces don't have structured work hours; they let employees work when and where they can be most productive.

Because the leadership team at HubSpot valued results and not "face time," Laura was given the flexibility she needed as a single mother and a professional. Laura could have left HubSpot after they purchased her company, but she loved the culture. She's been there ever since.

"I feel so lucky to have such fantastic work–life balance," Laura told me. "I don't just *get* to be at this company, I *want* to be here."

Laura's enthusiasm reflects the tone and tenor of women (and men) who manage to land in the right place for their personal and professional needs. And it doesn't have to be luck. Smart planning and foresight can help ensure you land in the right place too.

Because there is a growing demand for well-educated, high-potential employees and for women in particular, you have options. If you're ready to have kids or already have them and want to find a workplace culture that supports your needs, you are much more likely to find it today than were women in previous generations.

One of the major reasons respondents to the *Women on the Rise* survey left their jobs after they had children was because they couldn't get the flexibility they needed. Many of those who stayed were those who had companies and/or bosses that empowered them to integrate their careers with their lives. These women were already in situations that allowed them to thrive.

The good news is more companies than ever are committed to creating cultures that support caregiving needs and flexible working solutions. Look carefully at your company or workplace's culture and make sure it supports its employees as they head into the intense years of parenthood. Online company rating systems such as Comparably, Fairygodboss, and Maybrooks allow women to evaluate a company's female- and family-friendly policies.

Do the research and decide if you are in the right place or not. If not, find a new job and settle in. You may discover you don't need to take a career pause because you have what you need to integrate work and life.

That's the dream. Now, more than ever, you can live it.

STRATEGY #4: CHOOSE THE RIGHT PARTNER

Yeah, I know. No pressure. But choosing the right partner can make all of the difference when it comes to your career. We failed to ask respondents

CHOOSING THE RIGHT COMPANY FOR YOU

Want to make sure you can integrate kids and careers?

Ask these questions of your future employer (after you have received the offer, but before you commit to the job!).

- Do they have a diverse senior management?
- Do they have a diverse board?
- Do they have mothers in leadership?
- Do those mothers have spouses who work outside of the home?
- Do the male leaders have spouses who work outside of the home?
- Do they have a generous paid parental leave policy?
- Do women take their full maternity leave?
- Do men take paternity leave? For how long?
- Does the company offer sabbaticals? Do people take them?
- Does the company operate with a ROWE culture?
- Does their culture support flexible work hours?
- Do they offer part-time opportunities?
- Does needing flexibility curtail future advancement?
- Do mothers there feel supported?
- How many women leave after they have children?
- Do they have a "returnship" program for people who have paused their careers?
- Do they welcome back employees who have left in good standing?
- How is your future boss integrating work and life?

of our *Women on the Rise* survey about their partners, but boy did they tell us in the comments section.

"My husband's job was too demanding and I had to quit," one wrote.

"When it came down to it, my husband's career came first," another shared.

"He was traveling all of the time and someone had to take care of the kids," yet another told us.

And it wasn't just the weight of *his* career that mattered; many of the women shared the reason their own careers stalled was because they married men who expected them to be responsible for all of the traditional duties of a housewife despite the fact that they too were working full-time. This "double bind" of being full-time at home and full-time at work means, as Arlie Hochschild wrote in her book *The Second Shift: Working Parents and the Revolution at Home*, that women suffer professionally and personally. In her book, she found that often women "privileged" their husband's careers and well-being over their own needs. Many did this to keep their marriages from failing. Sadly, Arlie observed that many of these marriages failed anyway.

As one woman I interviewed told me, "I supported my husband while he went to graduate school. I supported him when he started his company. I supported him when he was too busy to take care of the house or the kids. I gave up my work to support him, but in the end, he had a great career and all I got was a divorce."

On the flip side, the women who had chosen well had partners who shared the household and caregiving duties 50/50. I'm not just talking laundry; I mean who's responsible for scheduling the dentist appointments, who's following up on the kids' vaccinations, who's taking the dog to the vet. And it wasn't just the day-to-day duties, these women had husbands who recognized that a career break was just that, a temporary professional pause in the overall course of a lifetime. These men assumed their wives would eventually return to the paid workforce and supported them when they did.

One woman said, "My husband was the single biggest reason my career is back on track. He has always believed in me."

Another shared, "I don't know how women do it if they don't have husbands who pick up the slack. We're a team and that's made all of the difference."

Sounds like a fairy tale, but it doesn't have to be. Your career depends on having a partner who supports it. Find him and then take Sheryl Sandberg's good advice: "If you want an equal partnership, you should start now."[236]

When we were first married, I was surprised to discover Bill assumed I would be buying, writing, and sending birthday cards to his family members. Huh? He was in graduate school and I was working full-time to support us. I barely had enough time to stay connected with my own family.

So I suggested the following: "Since you expect me to send the cards to your family, how about you send the cards to mine?"

"What?" he said, incredulously. "That doesn't make any sense!"

Really?

I explained to Bill that if I took this added responsibility on not only was he adding extra burden on me, he was also missing the chance to truly connect with his own relatives. A card from him would mean so much more than a card from me *for him* (or for us).

He saw the light. In the twenty-nine years we've been married, Bill has always been the one to send the cards, the flowers, and the gifts to his extended family. The funny thing is, all these years and his mom still thinks I'm the one doing it. Bill laughs when his mother calls to thank me. He jokes that I tricked him. Of course, that was not the goal, but I do appreciate his good humor about it (and am happy to get the bonus daughter-in-law points!).

Once you have the right partner, talk about how you both envision integrating kids and careers. Once you have kids, check in and make sure you are both comfortable with your roles. Keep the communication lines between you open or you might get blindsided by unintentionally falling into traditional gender roles. He might become primary breadwinner without wanting to, and you might end up bearing the burden of all of the home duties. Splitting responsibilities that way is not a good or bad choice, but it is an important one to be conscious about.

STRATEGY #5: BUILD YOUR FOUNDATION

It might seem obvious, but to build a non-linear career, you need to have a career to start from. In essence, you need to have established yourself professionally so you *can* pause.

Ask Kella Hatcher's father; he'll tell you. He had a career in human resources. He told his daughter that if she wanted to be able to navigate having a family and having a career, she should build a professional foundation on which to grow.

"My dad taught me to establish myself first because he knew my experiences, skills, and contacts would be the lifeblood I needed to accomplish my long-term goals," Kella explained to me during our interview.

She took his advice, and today her life path could be a model for working, pausing, and thriving. Kella's career, like that of so many of the other women I interviewed, zigged and zagged. She worked full-time, paused for kids, worked full-time again, worked part-time, paused again, worked part-time again, and now is working full-time at her "dream job."

Kella had always been a passionate advocate for disadvantaged youth and went to law school with the idea that she would focus on the juvenile justice system. After law school she became an assistant district attorney in Orange County, North Carolina. She loved her work, but struggled when she was forced to prosecute juvenile cases. The trauma of seeing children commit "horrible" crimes or be the victim of other equally horrible crimes became too much and so after her second child was born, Kella paused her career.

"I wanted to step back and figure out how I could be part of the solution," Kella shared with me during our interview. While she relished her time at home with her two young children, it didn't take long for her to realize she wanted to be back in the paid workforce. Kella got the word out to her network. It was her sterling reputation as a skilled lawyer that inspired a former colleague to invite her to apply for a job as the legal counsel for North Carolina's Guardian ad Litem program, a statewide government child advocacy program representing abused, neglected, and dependent children in the court system.

"I worked there full-time for a number of years, then I was able to negotiate a part-time work schedule. Eventually, I transitioned to a job-share. My boss was absolutely willing to work with me to find the optimal work–life solution. It made all of the difference," Kella said. But Kella's family demands eventually proved too imposing, so she decided to leave her job.

"I had a great situation, but my children were having issues in school and I felt I needed to be more present for them," Kella said.

She didn't stay out of the paid workforce for too long. One of her colleagues at the Guardian ad Litem program was working on a project for the University of North Carolina School of Government. The school wanted someone to create a manual for judges and attorneys who worked with juvenile cases. Kella's experience was perfect for the job, and the job was perfect for her. She could work part-time on her schedule and still be available to her family. For the next six years, Kella worked for UNC completing the report and others like it.

When her children got older and she was ready to return to full-time work, Kella again reached out to her network. One of her past coworkers was an advisor to the North Carolina Department of Health and recommended she apply for an opening they had. Today, Kella is the executive director of the North Carolina Child Fatality Task Force.

"In many ways, this job brings together so many of my previous roles. I wouldn't be here if I hadn't had those earlier experiences and the contacts I made that allowed me to keep moving my career forward. Like always, my father was right."

He was right. To pause, you need to build a foundation. None of the career planning seminars I attended as a young woman nor any that I've heard of today ever mentioned this as a career strategy. Perhaps it's because, as my generation of women entered the workforce, we didn't have enough data to know about how to integrate a pause into one's career. Or, perhaps it's because we hesitate to seemingly encourage women to pause their careers for their families at a time when we need to keep the pipeline filled to the top with highly qualified women.

Refusing to address the reality that women can and do pause means the millions of women who leave the workforce each year to become primary caregivers to their children or who pull back to work part-time are getting insufficient career planning advice. Not discussing the importance of building one's professional foundation does a disservice to all women, whether they think they want to pause or not.

Much has been written about how Millennials are taking longer to settle into their chosen careers. Some of this has to do with the fact that they have come into the workforce as it is trying to recover from the Great Recession and jobs have not been as readily available. When they actually do get jobs, Millennials have proven they are more committed to trying on different careers before settling into one defined path. In fact, a 2015 report by Ernst & Young noted that over two-thirds of Millennials expect to leave their current job in the next three to four years.[237]

This job hopping can offer a multitude of benefits, including building a wide set of skills and contacts. But job hopping does not necessarily help you establish your career. By not settling into a career path before you launch into parenthood, you may well be risking your ability to pause, even if it is one from which you pivot after you pause.

Why?

Because your reputation, your skills and abilities, and your credibility as someone who can deliver the needed results in a given workplace is the foundation that supports your career as you move ahead, no matter if you are working or pausing. It takes a number of years and some measure of stability to build this foundation. So job hop at first, but settle in for a few years *before* you have children. It may just be the ticket to the professional freedom you want and need.

Finally, as you build your foundation, remember to also build your ability to integrate work and life *before* you have children. If you are always all-in and then suddenly have a baby, you won't have the necessary skills to set boundaries, manage your time, and prioritize the myriad of demands on your schedule. Debbie Lovich, partner and managing director at Boston Consulting Group, tells women, "If you wait until you have kids, you won't know any other way to work but to work all of the time. That's not a recipe for success."

Learn to work smart, not hard. This ability will help you whatever your life priorities may be.

> Refusing to address the reality that women can and do pause means the millions of women who leave the workforce each year to become primary caregivers to their children or who pull back to work part-time are getting insufficient career planning advice.

STRATEGY #6: BUILD YOUR LATTICE

For decades now, career advisors have been telling women the key to a successful career is to "build your network." We're told we need to get out there and join a professional group, go to conferences, learn to golf! Their advice is well intentioned and not necessarily wrong, but it can be misguided. First, networking in this context can backfire for women.

Mingling the personal and the professional through social interactions can be ripe with mixed signals between women and men. Numerous young women have told me they would rather avoid the bar scene than send the wrong message to a coworker by grabbing a drink after work.

On the flip side, studies have revealed that women who network extensively can be seen as unlikable and overly ambitious. In a famous study, business students at Columbia University were asked to rate the likability of a well-connected entrepreneur. The students were divided into two groups and then given two identical profiles, the only difference being the person's name: Howard versus Heidi. The students rated Howard as the more appealing colleague. Meanwhile, Heidi was viewed as more power hungry and self-promoting than Howard.[238] What did she do so wrong? She was a woman who used her network to advance her career.

Finally, networking takes time. If you have children or other caregiving responsibilities, spending hours with colleagues trying to expand your network can be prohibitive. As one woman said to me, "I've kids, parents, and a household to take care of. When I am supposed to fit in a game of golf?"

Women often spend their time heads down at work just trying to get the job done, which can actually hurt us professionally. In their 2014 *Fortune* article, former Yahoo! CEO Carol Bartz and Upward founder Lisa Lambert urged women to stop doing more work and start doing more connecting. They wrote, "leadership today is increasingly defined not just by how many hours you spend at your computer, but your ability to connect to others, how you incorporate outside perspectives, and how you navigate groups. Networking takes time, but it matters."[239]

Study after study[240] has shown that men and women network differently. Men tend to have vast networks that include mostly men. Women usually have smaller networks with deeper relationships. As a result, when women are hunting for a new job, they may have fewer contacts that lead them to their dream job.

What's the solution? For women it may well be a different kind of networking. Rather than focusing on what others can do for them, women who focus on what they can do for others often are the most likely to be successful. Lori Goler, head of human resources at Facebook, has shared that when Sheryl Sandberg took on the role of COO at the company, she called Sheryl to ask how she could help. Lori didn't call for career advice; she called to offer her services. It was this difference in approach that appealed to Sheryl, who in turn hired Lori to run human resources.

Another tactic is to not think about it as networking per se, but rather as building a lattice of interconnectedness. Lattices offer support through their interlacing points. They are strong because of those points of connection. We each have something to offer, and others have things to offer us. If we can come to our professional relationships with the idea that we have something they might need, then we lose the sense that we are being self-serving and realize that we are supporting them as they are supporting us.

One woman I interviewed shared, "When I needed a job, my network helped me find one and now I am helping them find jobs and opportunities. I learned to not view networking as self-serving, but as an act of giving back to those with whom I'm connected."

Building a lattice of interconnectedness doesn't only happen in person. It also happens online. We are told social media allows us to build our brand, but I believe its best use is allowing us to build our professional lattice. Those who understand this typically view themselves as offering a service to their community, be it access to great articles, insight to important research, or hilarious commentary on the issues of the day. They engage (in a productive manner) to move the conversation forward and in doing so reveal who they are to their community. Yes, they build their brand online, but their real goal is to build a web of connections that is mutually beneficial.

So step away from your desk, overcome your fear that you will be perceived as overly ambitious, and reach out to others in person and online. They need your help just as you might one day need them to help you.

STRATEGY #7: UNDERSTAND YOUR WORKPLACE ECOSYSTEM

Elena Malykhina is a journalist who early on recognized the power of the Internet for her industry. She graduated from college with a degree in journalism and a minor in media studies. Her first job covered the mobile and wireless space for *InformationWeek*. She went on to become the online editor for Prometheus Global Media, which owns *Brandweek*, *Adweek*, and other key properties.

Elena worked long hours and many weekends in the beginning phase of her career. And then she got pregnant. "I was afraid to tell my boss because I was worried I wouldn't be given as many assignments," she told me.

Her instincts were right. When she was twenty weeks pregnant, the company announced layoffs. You can guess what happened to Elena.

"There were two of us managing the website," she said. "A guy who was young and newly married and me who was pregnant and would be heading out on maternity leave. The company decided to keep him on staff and lay me off."

Elena considered suing the company for discrimination, but decided it wasn't worth the time, money, and effort. Instead she launched a successful career as an independent journalist. Now that her second child is ready for preschool, Elena is considering a number of different job opportunities. But this time, she is being more careful.

"I learned my lesson," she said. "As a mother you can't succeed in a workplace that doesn't value all that you have to offer. I should have looked around me and realized there were very few mothers at that time at the top of the company and as a new mother I wasn't going to succeed in that environment."

Understanding the realities of your company's culture is one way to be sure you are prepared; another is understanding the realities of what it means to be a woman and a mother in our country. Re-read Part II of this book, and then get angry. Elena chose to go her own way, but if every woman does the same, no real change will happen. We must collectively understand the ecosystem in which we are operating and together change it so bright, talented women like Elena don't get pushed to the side simply because they are bringing forth the next generation.

Meanwhile, it is critically important to recognize the workplace environment in which you are operating. You may think nothing can hold you back, but you just might be surprised. One young woman recently reached out to ask for advice. She is a woman of color who works as a creative at a high-profile advertising agency—in other words, someone any smart company truly committed to inclusion and innovation would be loath to lose. She has been working at her agency for a number of years and is about to get married. She wants children, but she is dismayed by what she is seeing in her company. She wrote,

> Maternity leave used to be six weeks with 100 percent pay. Most of the women I've been talking to around the agency that have had babies usually take their maternity leave plus short term disability (that was optional for a small cost per paycheck for the employee) which used to be six weeks at 60 percent pay. Now they got rid of maternity leave and the agency is paying short term disability for all the employees. The only change I noticed is that short term disability says it could go up to thirteen weeks depending on the severity of the disability (so I am guessing if you have a c-section or a complication) but it remained at 60 percent pay.
>
> They are hiding behind the excuse of "equality" because not everyone could use this benefit (maternity leave) and now everyone can (short term disability). If it was about equality why not just open it to paternity leave as well?

Good question. The reality is that changes like these are not about equalizing opportunity for all employees; they're about punishing new parents. If this agency truly cared about its talent, it would offer a fully paid meaningful (four months or more) maternity leave AND a paternity leave. It would also extend short-term disability to all employees so those with other nonparenting-related needs can get the support they need. But this agency cared more about managing the short-term bottom line than retaining the talent it already has on its team.

The young woman went on to write, "How can I stay in to a job that will not support me being a mother if I get pregnant in a year? The same company that I have put so many hours of effort into? While the world is moving forward with maternity leave policies, we seem to be going backward."

The advice I gave her? Leave. A smart, highly employable woman like her is in high demand.

Companies who view their employees as expendable, rather than as a competitive advantage, are not places mothers thrive. Put your human capital to work in a place that views your talents and abilities as the key to their success. When you do, you will have a much higher likelihood of integrating your personal and professional goals.

STRATEGY #8: IF YOU WANT CHILDREN, DON'T WAIT (UNTIL IT'S TOO LATE)

Rose Gutierrez never planned on having children. She'd spent years working at Robert Half International, a leading executive recruiting firm, growing their finance and accounting division and eventually managing a staff of twenty-three. In 2010, she launched her own recruiting company and then in 2013, she married the man of her dreams. Rose believed she'd finally arrived. So you can imagine how this self-described "shoe-a-holic" who is most at home in her beloved Louboutins felt when she became unexpectedly pregnant three months after getting married.

"I was forty years old, fully established in my professional life and looked forward to traveling the world with my new husband. Children? So not on the agenda!" Rose laughingly shared with me when we spoke.

Three years in and Rose's life has completely changed. She's downshifted her career and now is a contract recruiter for a company that allows her to work from home two days a week. She even traded in those Louboutins for sneakers on the days she's home with her young son.

"I am so grateful for this happy accident," Rose told me. "All of my friends are committed professionals, none have children, and all are now suffering deep regrets. It's too late for them and now they tell me they realized they made a mistake."

One of her friends did manage to freeze a batch of her eggs, but now, at forty-five, she's found it impossible to get pregnant and is considering hiring a surrogate—a costly endeavor, to say the least.

Rose enjoys meeting all of the ambitious, committed young professional women in her role as an executive recruiter and loves placing them in jobs that will allow them to shine. But she's worried about their futures. "I hear them tell me they'll think about kids later. But, if my friends are any indication, wait too long and there won't be a later."

Because the age at which most men and women are at the peak of their careers also happens to be the same age most women have children, one "solution" that has recently gained traction is the idea of harvesting your eggs so you can postpone motherhood. In fact, Facebook and Apple now offer their female employees the chance to freeze their eggs so they can continue to stay on track professionally.

I was surprised to learn that a number of young women I spoke to loved the idea, seeing it as an important tool for managing their careers. When I challenged them to consider why they had to gamble with their fertility to fit into a paradigm that doesn't honor the reality of their bodies or lives, few told me they had even questioned the issue. But understanding the reality of fertility is critical for a woman planning her career.

According to Nick Raine-Fenning, a clinical associate professor in Reproductive Medicine and Surgery at University of Nottingham, fertility remains relatively stable until the age of thirty with about 400 pregnancies for every 1,000 women (40 percent) not using contraception for one calendar year. It then begins to decrease until around the age of forty-five, when only 10 percent of women will be able to conceive. Meanwhile, as pregnancy gets harder, miscarrying gets easier. About 10 percent of women will miscarry at age twenty, compared with 90 percent at forty-five.[241] I know we each like to believe we are the exception, but we most likely won't be.

Another thing to consider is the health of the mom and the baby. Hypertension and diabetes increase for older women who are pregnant, as does the risk of death. Stillbirths and babies born with cognitive and physical issues also increase along with the mother's age. In short, you can postpone pregnancy, but not for too long.

I know having children isn't on everyone's agenda. It certainly wasn't on mine and it wasn't on Rose Gutierrez's. Now she advises younger women to think carefully about whether they want to have children and to be conscious about the consequences of postponing that decision.

As Rose said, "Your body has a timeline; your career does not."

STRATEGY #9: GET OVER THE MYTH OF WORK-LIFE BALANCE

As chief operating officer and co-founder of mLab, a cloud-based hosting platform, Angela Kung Shulman is living the entrepreneur's dream. As the parent of two young girls, she is living a mother's nightmare. She had always wanted to be a housewife and mother, but skill, luck, and timing meant she is also busy with her other baby, her start-up company.

"There is no other way to say it. Right now my work–life balance sucks," Angela told me over coffee at Starbucks in Noe Valley, a San Francisco neighborhood filled with young kids and harried parents.

It's true. It does. Angela rarely sees her daughters, who are five and two years old. She is too busy putting out fires and managing the rocket ship growth of mLab. Her main focus at work is product management, technical operations, and customer support. Her main focus at home is trying to see her daughters before they go to bed. Angela's days are not her own and they certainly aren't her family's.

Angela was an applied math major in college and got a job as a business analyst at a start-up called Scient. It didn't take long for her to see that the company wasn't doing well financially and that if she wanted job stability, she needed to be working on the technical side of the business. She taught herself programming and became a software developer. When Scient, like so many high-flying start-ups, closed its doors, Angela quickly got a job at Oracle as a software engineer. She hated the big company life, so after two and a half years she jumped ship and went to another start-up, Merced Systems. That's where she met her husband, Will.

At Merced, Angela switched from software engineering to product management. Turns out she had a knack for leading teams to get the best product to market. While she loved the job, she decided she needed more business training and went to Dartmouth College's Tuck School of Business to "flesh out" her résumé.

"Then I decided to try something completely new and went into investment banking, but that wasn't the career for me, so I quit," Angela explained. "I was pregnant and what I really wanted was to stay home with my daughter. I launched a small web development company, but Will had the idea for mLab. We'd worked together before and knew we were a good team, so it made sense for me to help him."

Help him she did. In 2010 they built their first product, had their first daughter, and landed their first customer. In 2011, they raised $3 million in venture funding and then a year later raised an additional $5 million. By 2015, the company had grown to twenty employees, and their family had grown to four.

If you're exhausted listening to her story, imagine how Angela feels. "I just want to spend my days at a slower pace, actively involved in my daughters' lives. Instead, I am always working. I just hope it's worth it," she said.

As the COO of her own company, Angela should well be able to set her own agenda. But she can't. Or rather, she *feels* she can't. When I asked her why, she told me, "We are striving for the entrepreneurial dream of the big IPO. That means we have to be all hands on deck. But we haven't built our company to scale with our growth and are desperate to hire the right team. Until we do that, I can't just abandon ship."

Here's the truth: At any given time, true work–life balance is impossible. In the current system of how we work, how we structure child care, how we mythologize the role and duty of mother, no woman can "do it all." The demands of one will always overshadow the demands of the other.

Angela may be an unintended entrepreneur, but her work–life challenges are not unusual. Combine small children, a job, and a working culture that requires 24/7 engagement and it's a recipe for work–life chaos. How do you get work–life balance then?

You don't.

Here's the truth: At any given time, true work–life balance is impossible. In the current system of how we work, how we structure child care, how we mythologize the role and duty of mother, no woman can "do it all." The demands of one will always overshadow the demands of the other.

Interestingly, the pressures of "doing it all" appears to impact women more intensely than men. Recent research on how women and men view the future as it relates to their goals reveals that men have narrower life goals and give themselves a longer time to achieve them.[242] In other words, women feel the challenges of work–life imbalance more strongly because we want more out of life and we want more out of it today.

Changes to the workplace and our cultural attitudes toward prioritizing work aren't going to happen anytime soon. So it comes down to you. You have to decide what you can live with. But, if you can make peace with your choices and recognize that while today the scales are tipped to one side, on another day they'll tip to the other, and over time you will accomplish a certain equilibrium.

Like so many of us, Angela struggles with the day-to-day imbalance. As a result, an ongoing sense of dissatisfaction and failure sets in. High-achieving women like Angela often quit their jobs because if something has to give, it's not going to be their children.

But the workplace needs Angela (and women like her) and Angela (and women like her) need the workplace. So what's a smart, modern woman to do? She can see that today's problems are not a lifetime of problems. They are temporary. She can recognize that her daughters (and sons) will more than likely thrive, even if their mother is not there every day. And by understanding that it is not her children who are suffering, but rather she who is suffering the loss of them, she will be able to make choices and decisions that take the long view on her career and life.

Does it make sense for Angela to leave the workplace right now when her company is in high-growth mode? The answer is no. She is likely to never have this professional chance again. She'll have others, but not *this* one. That said, Angela is missing precious moments with her children. How can she solve this?

The immediate solution is to create boundaries when it comes to work. She can insist on taking one afternoon a week off. The company will not fold if she is not there for five hours each week. Or, she can decide to commit to working 24/7 for a set period of time (two years, for example) and then make it clear she will no longer be in the role of COO. Two years is more than enough time to help the company find a replacement.

It's time for Angela, and millions of women like her, to realize daily work–life balance is a myth, but that over a lifetime work–life integration is possible. The short-term intensity of her career is not likely to hurt the long-term success of her family. What will hurt it is the anger, resentment, self-doubt, and frustration that results from believing she should be doing it differently.

The most important thing, the thing that soothes the fear and anxiety and stress inherent in temporary work–life imbalance, is making a conscious choice about how you spend each day. Whether that means deciding to be all-in, all-of-the-time or deciding to pause for a period of time, owning your decisions is the best way to live a life free from regrets.

CHAPTER 10

Pausing

The Innovator's Solution

"People told me that if I paused it would be 'career suicide' and I would never be able to re-enter in a way that would be satisfying. I am so delighted to say that they were SO wrong. People were eager to welcome me back in. [This] is a story I wish more young women could hear instead of the fear-inducing narratives that were presented to me . . ."
—*Women on the Rise* survey respondent

We know the narrative: Opt-out moms kill their careers. But if you've read this far, you already know this simply isn't, or rather doesn't have to be, true. Women re-ignite their careers all of the time. We dismiss them as isolated examples because they challenge our preconceived notions about those who pause: that they lack ambition and are destined for failure. That is simply wrong.

As many of the 186 women I interviewed and the 1,476 women who responded to the *Women on the Rise* survey have shown, you can take the path less traveled and find not only career success but also life satisfaction. When we asked the *Women on the Rise* respondents how their career pause impacted their lives, 79 percent said it enabled them to gain better work–life balance, 80 percent said they felt more confident as a result of their career break, and, as I've shared before, 78 percent had *no regrets at all.* Encouragingly, 95 percent felt they were good role models for their children. In other words, by disrupting the traditional career paradigm and innovating to find their own unique paths, these women proved you can work, pause, and thrive.

> As many of the 186 women I interviewed and the 1,476 women who responded to the *Women on the Rise* survey have shown, you can take the path less traveled and find not only career success, but also life satisfaction.

We asked them what advice they would give a younger woman who wanted to pause for parenthood without killing her career. Here are some of the things they told us:

"Think carefully."

"Do what feels right to you and your family."

"Follow your heart."

"Stay current."

"It's *your* life, live it the way *you* want."

"Believe in yourself."

"Beware of the risks."

"You CAN do it!"

Yes, you can. But how? The following are the key recommendations for how to pause for parenthood without killing your career from the women who have done it.

STRATEGY #1: DON'T SKIMP ON YOUR MATERNITY LEAVE

In 2015, when Yahoo! CEO Marissa Mayer announced she was only going to take two weeks of maternity leave after the birth of her twins, she sent shivers down the spines of many women in the tech industry and beyond. It became all the more confusing when at the same time tech giant Netflix announced it was offering its employees a full year of paid parental leave. Weeks later, Microsoft announced twelve weeks of fully paid leave for both men and women. And then, not to be outdone, Adobe announced sixteen weeks for men and women and an additional ten weeks for women who had given birth.

The list of companies to follow suit goes on and it would seem to be a bounty of riches, but here's the rub: It remains unclear whether employees will actually take the full leave offered them. Men, as noted in chapter 6, are highly unlikely to take their full leave, if they take leave at all.

And women? Marissa isn't the only one cutting offered/available leave short due to workplace pressures. The current message about maternity leave tells women that if they want to get to the top they have to work up to the day they give birth, take as short a leave as possible, and race back to the office. Often, women worry that they'll seem no longer as committed to their careers if they take their full leave. As a result, many ambitious women have followed Marissa's strategy and taken as little leave as possible.

Remember Symantec vice president Carolyn Herzog, from chapter 3? She is the primary breadwinner in her family and has a stay-at-home husband who cares for their two daughters.

I met Carolyn when I moderated a panel on women and their careers at LinkedIn's Mountain View, California, campus. She shared with the audience that she was inspired by her grandmother, a successful career woman and Holocaust survivor who worked every day of her life.

"My grandmother taught me if you want to get ahead, you have to work and work hard," Carolyn said.

So Carolyn took the minimum time possible during each of her two maternity leaves. In fact, when she gave birth to her second child in 2006, she was back in the office after six weeks and is proud to say she was promoted the day she returned.

Carolyn's actions are what used to pass for corporate loyalty and ambition. Even today, for some women, short maternity leaves are a badge of honor signaling to the boss that work is more important than anything, including the birth of one's child.

But what if a woman wants more time with her newborn and still wants to climb the corporate ladder? Does she follow Marissa or Carolyn and take a truncated leave to make sure her employers and other key stakeholders know she is committed? Or, does she take an "extended"[243] leave and risk sending the message that family does comes first, at least sometimes?

In my interviews I learned that rather than follow an outdated model that gives them little chance to bond with their new babies, many smart, modern women are arranging for and taking longer maternity leaves. Yes, they are ambitious and committed to their careers, but they also want to spend those first precious months with their children. If they find the company isn't as supportive of them and their careers when they return, these women feel empowered to move on to companies that offer more inclusive cultures.

Consider Vidya Peters. Perhaps it was because she is from India and her husband is from the Netherlands, but there was never a doubt in her mind that she would take a six-month leave after her first child was born in the spring of 2011. Vidya loved her job in marketing at Intuit, a financial services software company, but she wanted as much time as she could afford to be with her newborn. When her friends worried she might be sending her employer the wrong message, she told them that was ridiculous.

"I was very pragmatic about it," Vidya told me. "Because I work in the state of California, I knew my job was protected. They couldn't fire me, so why wouldn't I take as long a leave as I could? That time gave me a great chance to step back and consider what I wanted as a mother and as a professional."

What Vidya realized she wanted was a new, more challenging opportunity. While she was on leave, she learned that a job as a group marketing manager was opening in a different division at Intuit. It was a more senior role, but she thought it couldn't hurt to interview for the job; at the very least, she would be able to show her company she was still committed to her career.

"I realized all they could say was no, so I decided to throw my hat in the ring," Vidya said.

It worked. She came back from maternity leave to a promotion and more pay. Even though Vidya took a longer-than-standard leave, she was still able to signal to her company that she was passionate about her career by actively engaging in her own professional advancement.

A few years later, Vidya became pregnant with her second child. Again, she took a six-month leave. And again, she was promoted when she came back. When Vidya returned to work, she moved over to be director of marketing for a key product line, a job with increased influence, responsibility, and exposure.

Vidya stayed in that job until she was recruited by another company for an even more senior role. Today, she is the vice president of corporate marketing at MuleSoft. Her new bosses don't care how long she took off for maternity leave. It's likely they don't even know. What they care about is how she is performing now.

Like Vidya, I too took a longer-than-standard leave after my first child was born. It was a risk. The longest leave anyone had taken at my company was three months, and even that was frowned upon. Six weeks was standard, shorter was even better.

But I had preemie baby who needed round-the-clock care. The idea that I would return to work after only six weeks was completely beyond consideration. During those first few months of his life, my baby needed me, and because of that, I was willing to risk everything.

While I had originally told my employer I would return three months after my son was born, I asked for an additional month (unpaid). To my relief the company agreed. That "extended" leave was essential for me as a mother *and* as a professional. My son grew quickly and by the end of my four-month maternity leave, he was on track with babies his age who had been born full-term. I was confident he would not only survive, but thrive.

I believed I would, too, professionally. While I was on leave, I kept the communication lines open with my manager regarding my dreams and wishes. She understood what I wanted and worked with me to make sure I could accomplish my goals. Like Carolyn and Vidya, when I returned to work, I was promoted to the next level and placed on one of the company's flagship brands. Sadly, my bosses were two men who held deep biases against mothers who worked outside the home. Because I knew the value of my human capital, I knew working for them was not a good use of my time and effort. So I left and found a new job making more money and working for a more supportive boss.

"I would encourage every woman to take as much maternity leave as they can afford and as they are allowed by law. If your company doesn't like it, then take your leave and find a new company where the culture is a better fit for you and your family," Vidya told me.

I couldn't agree more. Your maternity leave is a necessary time for you to heal from pregnancy and birth, a critical time for you to bond with your new baby, and an important time for you to adjust to your new role as a mother. For many it may be the only pause you will get, so take as long as you can. You won't regret it.

STRATEGY #2: CREATE THE POST-MATERNITY LEAVE ONRAMP THAT WORKS FOR YOU

One of the most challenging times for mothers in the workplace are the days, the weeks, and even the months that follow their maternity leave. The vast majority of leaves are way too short and, as a result, women are often forced to place their babies in the care of others, often before both mother and baby are ready. Between lack of sleep, the challenges of trying to pump breast milk at work, and their newfound feelings of attachment, a mother's commitment to work can be tenuous at this time.

The best way to solve this is to create the onramp that works for you. For some women this means getting right back in. For others, this means extending their maternity leaves. For still others, this means working a reduced schedule for a few months until they feel fully ready.

A number of the women I interviewed had negotiated a flexible onramp schedule. They worked three days a week at first, then four, then eventually five. Their reduced work schedule often didn't last more than three months, so within the year they were back to being all-in.

Smart companies already offer transitional onramping to their new mothers. Traci Armstrong, senior vice president, global director of talent acquisition, at GTB, an advertising agency headquartered in Detroit, said, "The cost of replacing a valuable employee is far greater than the few months it can take to transition a new mother back in. It is such an obvious win for all. It's good for the mom and good for the business."

But most companies aren't this forward thinking—yet. As a result, most women are afraid to ask for what they want and need now that their life has changed. It takes confidence to ask for what you want.

In their book, *The Confidence Code: The Science and Art of Self-Assurance—What Women Should Know*, authors Katty Kay and Claire Shipman wrote, "We might like to believe that keeping our noses to the grindstone, focusing on every detail, and doing everything perfectly are the materials that build a career . . . It's confidence that sways people."[244]

During my interviews, I learned that confidence in their abilities and an understanding of their value to their employers were essential to the women who had successfully navigated the work–life conundrum. In fact, for those who wanted a flexible schedule, having confidence made all of the difference.

Why? Because they knew if their current company wasn't a good fit, there would be another one that was. As a result, they went into their negotiations with the goal of finding a mutually beneficial solution, one that worked both for them and their employers. Their confidence in their value infused the discussion and enabled them to secure the onramping situation that met their needs. But confidence is elusive and hard to have if you are worried you might lose your job or, as in my case, the company has not offered flexible solutions before.

When my first maternity leave was nearing its end, I asked to meet with the head of my division. I told him I wanted to figure out a way to work a reduced schedule so I could have Fridays off with my son. I offered to reduce my salary by one-fifth or to work longer hours on the four workdays. I promised this would not be a long-term arrangement; rather, I would keep this schedule until my son's first birthday when we could evaluate its pros and cons.

It was a bold move, as the company had never had someone in management who worked an untraditional schedule. But that leader was willing to take a risk. Together, we decided a forty-hour, four-day workweek was best for the company and for me. I spent the next year enjoying Fridays with my son and continuing to offer value to my company.

How did I get the courage to make the ask? Quite simply, my baby gave it to me. Watching him fight for his life made me realize I had to fight for ours. I didn't go into that meeting making demands. I went in fully understanding it was a negotiation. And to find a solution that would work, both I and my employer had to be committed to creating a solution that worked for both of us.

In preparation for asking for what I wanted, I took a page out of Professor Amy Cuddy's playbook on power poses (this, of course, was decades before Amy presented her famous TED Talk on the topic of body language). I wrote what I was going to say and practiced in front of the mirror. I wanted to show I was confident in myself and to make sure my delivery didn't reveal my inner doubt about the validity of my request.

Each woman's script will be different, but here's what one who successfully negotiated a part-time schedule said to her employer:

> I am a committed employee who has repeatedly delivered results. I would like to continue bringing my talents to bear at this company. In order for me to do so, I temporarily need a flexible schedule. Let's discuss how we can make this a win for everyone.

Figure out what you want and need. Practice your script and then make the ask. I've said it before: You can't get what you want unless you ask.

STRATEGY #3: STAY IN THE GAME (IF YOU CAN)

When we asked what piece of advice they would give a woman who was contemplating pausing her career, the vast majority of *Women on the Rise* respondents recommended she "stay in the game." Work part-time, consult, do something that keeps your professional life alive and well.

Remember those "Cruisers" who had pulled back by working part-time but did not completely leave their careers? They reported the highest levels of overall satisfaction in the *Women on the Rise* survey. Over 90 percent felt they were a good role model for their children, 83 percent had no regrets at all about their decision to work part-time, 85 percent said doing so enabled them to have better work–life balance, and, interestingly, 60 percent reported that pulling back allowed them to gain important skills and experiences that helped them be better employees when they recommitted to their careers full-time. Finally, the vast majority maintained a reduced schedule for only a few short years. Nearly 80 percent had returned to full-time work by the time their children were in elementary school.

Lisa Johnson's career path is perfect example of how one can "stay in the game" by being a Cruiser. Today, she is an executive vice president and division manager at Wells Fargo in Chicago, a mother of three (including a set of twins), and a proud board member of the United Way. But, like many of the women I interviewed, her career path hasn't been a direct shot to the top. She worked part-time when her children were young and then recommitted to full-time work when she was ready and able.

Lisa graduated from Baylor University in 1983 with a degree in finance and took a job in commercial banking with a company out of Denver that was later acquired by Norwest. She became a commercial lending officer for Wells Fargo and was a top sales person in the company. In 1994, when she became pregnant with her first child, she approached her manager and asked for a part-time schedule. The company had no part-time offerings, but her boss agreed to let her work three days a week as a trial. If it didn't work, they agreed they would renegotiate after a year.

"I was determined to prove it could be done," Lisa said during our interview. "I became highly efficient on those three days and managed to generate more sales that year than I had ever in my career. The next year, I did even better. It was a win for everyone."

Lisa was recruited by a boutique investment banking firm and agreed to take the job if, and only if, she could continue on her reduced workweek schedule. They agreed and so she left Wells Fargo to try her hand in a new type of finance. But two years later, Lisa's husband was offered a plum job in Chicago, so she went back to work, still part-time, for Wells Fargo working out of their Chicago office. When Lisa became pregnant with her twins, she told her new manager she was going to quit working and focus on her family. He begged Lisa to stay.

"My boss was an incredible mentor. He said, 'Tell me what you want' and I told him I wanted to work from home while the kids were young. So we created a staff role that focused on training and recruiting," she said.

Again, Lisa outdid herself, far exceeding her manager's expectations. Soon, she was managing a team of fifteen who were distributed across the country, all while she continued to work part-time from home. Lisa led this team until her twins entered kindergarten. Then, when her boss offered her a larger job with profit-and-loss responsibility, Lisa decided she was ready for the new challenge. She took that job, but only after negotiating to have a modified schedule that allowed her to have Fridays off as needed.

Today, Lisa's oldest daughter is in college and her twins are finishing high school. It may have taken her longer than others to get to a leadership position, but Lisa has no regrets about her scenic route to the top. Lisa is very public about her choices because she wants to be a model for how flexibility can work for companies and employees.

"In many ways, my career path is a business case for flexible solutions. I gave 110 percent to the company and the company rewarded me by supporting my need for flexibility while still helping me grow and advance," Lisa said. "I want others to know this is possible."

A longitudinal study by the Pew Research Center shows that between 1997 and 2012 the vast majority of mothers consistently reported they would prefer to work part-time while their children are young.[245] However, the sad truth is that even today with the advent of technology that allows for a distributed workforce, meaningful part-time jobs that require the skills of a professional are hard to come by. The women who have managed to secure those coveted slots have done so only after having proven themselves to their employers—and by having the courage to ask.

As Lisa told me, "Because I had proven myself to be a hard-working, committed employee, when I went in to ask for a flexible schedule, I was able to confidently say, 'I'm worth it.'"

Women who "stayed in the game" by working part-time found re-igniting their careers relatively easy. For those, like Lisa Johnson, who had negotiated a reduced schedule, it simply required signaling to their boss and/or to the human resources department they were ready for more responsibility. For those who decided they needed to move on to a new company, their part-time schedules could easily be buried in their résumés if needed.

Because the typical résumé or LinkedIn profile does not distinguish between full-time and part-time work, potential employers have no idea if a candidate has been working a reduced schedule. The women I interviewed who had taken the Cruiser path were evenly split on whether to be fully honest or selectively mute about the topic. Some expressed concern that women who have temporarily downshifted could struggle to overcome the flexibility stigma.

However, as one woman who had successfully relaunched after working part-time for years said to me, "Would you ever really want to work for the person who cares that your previous job was part-time? How can you be true to yourself and your future employer if you start the relationship out with a lie? I recommend being fully authentic and then finding the boss and company who can support you to be your very best."

Only you can decide what feels right for you. But be strategic in what you decide to communicate about your career progression. Sometimes less is more. Then again, what parent wants to work for a boss who doesn't value family?

Pulling back on your career and "cruising" for a while is often the first choice for many women who are struggling to integrate kids and careers. Sadly, most workplaces don't offer flexible work solutions, and so many women either struggle as they work full-time or they leave the workforce entirely. As one woman I interviewed said, "It's a nice gig if you can get it."

Unfortunately, most women can't, and so what happens when the challenges of integrating kids with careers become insurmountable? Often, they just quit.

STRATEGY #4: DON'T JUST QUIT

Ask a hundred women why they left their careers and the vast majority will tell you their "So I quit" story. Here are a few I heard in writing this book:

> I was on a United flight from New York City to San Francisco a few days before 9/11. I realized I could have been on that flight and decided being with my family was more important than a big career. So I quit.
>
> I had to miss an event at my son's school to go to a meeting. Nobody in my office would help me out. So I quit.
>
> Our nanny left and we couldn't find a good replacement. So I quit.
>
> I was traveling extensively and kept missing major milestones in my son's life. His first word, his first step, his first trip to the zoo. So I quit.
>
> My colleague lost his sixteen-year-old son in a car accident. That left an impression on me. I didn't want to miss out on my baby's life. So I quit.
>
> My boss didn't respect my work and then I discovered I was being paid significantly less than the men around me. So I quit.

When we got the results back from the *Women on the Rise* survey, I was astonished by the large number of women who reported they "just quit" their jobs and then "one thing led to another" and they found themselves becoming stay-at-home mothers, as if it happened almost by accident. All of these women had college degrees and many of them had at least one graduate degree—they had put much time, money, and effort into building their careers—and yet, they seemed to have lost their agency when it came to battling for the right to be both engaged mothers and professionals. It was as though they were running from, rather than toward, something.

I don't judge them. How could I? I'm one of them. Don't make the same mistake we did. If you feel you have no other option, then create a plan that will allow you to incorporate an extended pause into your career. When ready, set about to implement that plan. Communicate your career plan with your boss, your mentors, and your professional network so they too can support your dreams. Be proactive and strategic about your pause, just as you would be about any other phase of your career. Whatever you do, don't just quit.

STRATEGY #5: LIVE WITHIN YOUR NEW MEANS

There are many reasons a person may choose to prioritize work: to gain prestige, to feel useful, to make an impact. But one of the biggest reasons many of us put our all into our careers is so we can fund our lifestyles. And what is often at the heart of that? Keeping up with the Joneses. It's one of America's favorite pastimes.

In his groundbreaking book, *The Price of Inequality*, Nobel Prize–winning economist Joseph Stiglitz wrote about trickle-down behaviorism, "People below the top 1 percent increasingly aspire to imitate those above them . . . And for those in the third percentile, the second percentile provides aspiration, and so on down the line . . . Individuals say they are working so hard for the family, but as they work so hard there is less and less time for the family, and family life deteriorates." In the end, Joseph wrote, "It may be we are working more to maintain our consumption relative to others"[246] rather than for our families.

Public relations guru Kristin Kiltz knows this only too well. She had a thriving career and a big salary working for a well-regarded agency when she decided to pull back her career to spend more time with her children.

It didn't take long for Kristin to realize she missed the lifestyle her paycheck offered, so she went back to full-time work.

"I liked the flexibility," Kristin told me, "but the lifestyle cuts meant we couldn't do as much as we wanted. So I went back to full-time work at the agency. I was working crazy hours, but the money was good. We could afford anything we wanted. We traveled, we ate out, we even did a big remodel on our home."

Things might have continued on as they were, but Kristin began to get severe headaches. She went to doctor after doctor, but none seemed to be able to diagnose her. Because she felt so ill, Kristin took numerous days off from work. She missed meetings and had to push back deadlines. Kristin was scared about her health; her boss was less than supportive about her lack of focus.

One day, after a particularly harrowing set of doctors' appointments, Kristin's boss came into her office and complained, "I've seen more tears from you in the last two weeks than all of the years you've worked here. I'm sick of seeing all of these tears." That lack of support might have been the final straw, but Kristin still didn't leave her job; she had the big remodel to pay for.

Eventually, the doctors discovered Kristin had a brain tumor. She had surgery and was relieved to discover the tumor was benign. Kristin felt she had been given a new chance at life and decided things had to change.

"I knew I could never go back to the way things were. I was working for the money and the status, but I learned that terrifying lesson: Life is too short," she told me.

Kristin wanted to quit and launch her own agency, one that would allow her more control of her time and provide a less toxic work environment. But when she and her husband crunched the numbers, they realized they would have to make serious changes if she was going to leave her job. They decided changing their lifestyle was worth it. She launched her own agency and they made choices: No more dinners out, no fancy vacations, and, eventually, they even sold their newly remodeled home.

"It was a beautiful house. Truly a dream home," Kristin said. "But we couldn't afford it anymore. So we ended up downsizing and moving to a smaller home in a better school district."

These days, even though money isn't as tight, Kristin and her husband are happy with their new lifestyle.

"In the end, we realized we didn't need all of the things we thought we needed. The fancy trips, the cars, the chasing the Joneses. We're done with that. We downsized to do better," Kristin said.

Unless you are part of the One Percent, making the decision to temporarily leave the paid workforce or downshift to part-time work requires you to ask yourself what you are willing to give up—now and in the future—to accomplish this goal. For some, the trade-offs are not worth it. For others, it's about gaining the life they truly want.

Human resources professional Mary Heeney understands this. She and her husband are passionate sailors and envisioned a radical life change: home schooling their children while the family sailed from the United States to New Zealand.

Mary had been working part-time as an independent human resources consultant. The work was steady but not high paying. Her husband made good money, but they had not put enough away to have both of them stop working for an extended period. So Mary took a full-time job and they saved. No dinners out, no fancy clothes. They whittled their lifestyle down to essentials.

"It's all about priorities," Mary told me. "We saved and then sold our house to buy the boat. We sailed for three years accomplishing our goal of traveling from the United States to New Zealand and many places in between. I like to joke that we took a sailing trip rather than doing a remodel on our house."

Not everyone will feel comfortable embarking on an extreme lifestyle change so they can take a pause and only you can decide what feels right to you and your partner. But you may want to take stock, serious stock, of what you have and what you want. You know how the Rolling Stones song goes: "You can't always get what you want, but if you try sometimes, you just might find, you get what you need." Only you can decide what you "need."

However, let me reiterate: You MUST focus on the financial implications of pausing your career. Do you have enough in savings to be out of the paid workforce for one, two, three, or more years? Are you planning long-term for that loss in income? If not, then you are either filled with magical thinking or you are a trust-fund baby.

Sure, your husband's career may flourish, making money a non-issue. He may never lose his job. The economy might not suddenly blow up and decimate all of the savings you put aside for college and/or retirement.

You may never get divorced or become ill or be forced to care for your elderly parents. But these things can and do happen. Before, during, and after your pause, you must get and keep your financial house in order so you can thrive (read chapter 12 for more on how to make sure a career pause won't kill your bank account).

STRATEGY #6: KEEP IT SHORT

In 2015, the Federal Reserve Board of St. Louis released a study[247] that looked at unemployed women by age group. It revealed that women in their fifties were disproportionately affected by the Great Recession of 2008. This cohort was taking longer to find jobs and were much more likely to fall into the "long-term unemployed" category used to describe those who have been out of the paid workforce for more than six months. Specifically, the research showed, before the 2008 recession, less than a quarter of the unemployed women over the age of fifty were members of the long-term unemployed. But by 2012, nearly half of older jobless women were in that category.

Why? According to study co-author, Alexander Monge-Naranjo, taking an extended career break was at the top of the list. *The New York Times* wrote about the study, saying, "When it comes to women over 50, one theory that makes sense to Mr. Monge-Naranjo is that those who dropped out of the labor force to take care of children when they were younger can't easily get back in. 'They did not see that the labor market was going to be so tough and it's taking quite some time to go back to normal,' he said."[248]

My research both one-on-one and via the *Women on the Rise* survey corroborates this observation. Women who had paused their careers for extended periods of time and who, as a result, were older when they tried to re-enter the workforce faced the double whammy of caregiver bias *and* age bias. When we asked respondents what their primary concern was about re-entering, the vast majority said, "Age discrimination."

While 78 percent of our survey respondents who had paused their careers had no regrets, the longer they were out, the more they regretted their decision to pause. Nearly 50 percent of those who had been out for eleven years or more *did* regret their decision to leave. One key reason was the challenge they faced when trying to re-enter. In fact, 68 percent of those women who were out of the paid workforce for more than eleven years indicated the reentry was *very* difficult. On the inverse, 63 percent of women who had paused for two years or less considered the reentry *very* easy.

Those who had a shorter pause (fewer than five years) were also more likely to say they did not make any compromises when they re-entered, whereas those that were out of the paid workforce for more than five years were more likely to say they compromised by taking lower compensation and a lower status position so they could get back in.

Without a doubt, there are women who truly do want to be full-time mothers and housewives. No judgment here. In a world that values paid work above all else, it takes courage to be true to your values. It also takes courage to trust your financial security to someone else.

Unless you truly do want to be out of the paid workforce for the remainder of your life or are willing to risk the myriad of challenges the long-term unemployed face, keep the time you pause your career short. Some would argue six months is too long. Our research indicates pausing no more than two years is optimal and five years is doable, but six or more and you'll likely need to rethink your options. It's definitely not impossible to re-enter, as I have shown repeated examples of women who paused seven, ten, even fifteen years and still managed to relaunch to great success. But you're rolling the dice at that point, and gambling is not a great way to manage a career.

Unless you truly do want to be out of the paid workforce for the remainder of your life or are willing to risk the myriad of challenges the long-term unemployed face, keep the time you pause your career short.

STRATEGY #7: VOLUNTEER STRATEGICALLY

As discussed in chapter 4, our schools, communities, and nonprofits rely on the unpaid help of stay-at-home parents. These jobs range from things as simple as baking cookies for the annual school picnic to running major fundraising campaigns. While you are pausing your career, you get to choose with whom and where you share your talents. Smart, modern women understand that unpaid volunteer work can be a powerful tool in their career development.

Consider Atsuko Jenks. She was born and raised in Japan before coming to the United States to study business, where she met her American husband. After graduating, Atsuko worked for Williams-Sonoma assisting them in their efforts to reach the Japanese market. After her second daughter was born, she decided to pause. Atsuko knew she would eventually want to re-enter and knew she needed to keep up her skills and network so she joined the education foundation of her daughters' school district to help run its multimillion-dollar fundraising campaign.

"I knew I wanted access to high-profile executives, but I was out of the paid workforce. I realized one of the best ways for me to do that was to talk with them about our schools," Atsuko said. "I was invited as a guest into the homes of some of the biggest names here in Silicon Valley. That network has been essential for me in my current business."

Today, Atsuko is a strategic advisor to Japanese companies that want to do business in the United States and to American companies interested in doing business in Japan. She sits on the board of the U.S.–Japan Council and is working to help the Japanese government increase more women in its workforce. Given her current success, you'd never know she was out of the paid workforce for nearly a decade. Atsuko understood the importance of setting herself up for future success while she was pausing her career.

For many women I spoke to it was the connections they made while they were volunteering that helped them relaunch. Take Alison Cormack, for example. She left a satisfying career at Hewlett Packard after the birth of her second child. She knew it was risky, but she felt her family needed her. Like many stay-at-home moms, Alison was an active community volunteer. But rather than focus on in-classroom efforts, Alison used her time and talents to strategically advance her skills, network, and marketability. She joined the Palo Alto Library Foundation board and chaired its Better Libraries campaign formed to pass a $76 million bond to rebuild and modernize the town's libraries.

It was a Palo Alto Library Foundation board colleague who helped Alison land a job at Google. "He worked there and knew I was job hunting.

I told him I had found a job posting at the company online. He helped me navigate the recruiting process and recommended me to my current boss. It was, without a doubt, my new network and that leadership role as a volunteer that helped me onramp."

Alison not only used her volunteer experience to help relaunch her second (paid) career, she also used the expanded group of contacts she made while she volunteered. This strategic use of her time and human capital enabled Alison to work, pause, and thrive.

STRATEGY #8: MAINTAIN (AND EXPAND) YOUR NETWORK

One of my favorite lessons from Sheryl Sandberg is the idea that you shouldn't leave your career until you have actually left. In other words, "lean in" until you don't need to anymore. But I think Sheryl misses a critical point: If our careers aren't just about the job at hand, but about the way what we are doing fits into the arc of our lives, then we are always leaning in, whether we are in the paid workforce or not.

Women who understand that their pauses are part of their careers recognize that it is a temporary strategy, so they continue to "lean in" by maintaining, and even expanding, their contacts and connections. What does this look like? First, it means regularly checking in with past colleagues, previous bosses, and others in your professional network. One woman I interviewed made sure she had lunch with a professional contact at least once a month. Others continued to attend professional events and programs specifically targeted to help advance women's careers.

We asked the *Women on the Rise* respondents if they had attended networking events while they were pausing their careers. I was surprised to learn only 29 percent had. A number of women told me they feared having to explain that they didn't have a job and were "just" stay-at-home moms. I understand that. It takes courage to get out there and promote yourself whether you have a job or not.

In the fall of 2014, I hosted the TEDx Sand Hill Road Women's conference in Menlo Park, California. Sand Hill Road is the avenue in the heart of Silicon Valley where the vast majority of venture capital firms have offices. If you aspire to be an entrepreneur, this is your Mecca. On that fall day, more than 100 women gathered at an event space along that famed avenue to hear fantastic speakers and be inspired. The room was filled with incredibly impressive women who held senior positions at some of the tech industry's most storied companies. I know I was intimidated by the group, and I heard from others they were too.

I shared this at the start of the event: "There is a reason you are here today. You are meant to meet someone, hear something, or gain an insight that is intended to move your life and career forward. Today, it is all about connection, not perfection."

At the break, three women approached me. They were each relaunching their careers and had come to the conference together because they thought they might find a job or a contact. They were uncomfortable and worried they didn't fit in with these "rock stars." When we broke into small group exercises, I made sure they separated and invited them to ask their small group for support in their endeavors. A few weeks later, I learned that one of the women had a job offer from someone she had met at the event and another was busy conducting informational interviews and was confident something would arise for her as well. The third realized she wanted to pursue a different career after hearing one of the speakers talk about her work with indigenous populations. This one networking event changed those three women's lives.

One of the TEDx attendees told me later, "It took all of my courage to attend the conference. I worried what I would say about my lack of career these past five years. I didn't think I would have anything to offer. I realized I was wrong."

Staying connected in person matters, but these days staying connected online matters just as much. Keeping a live profile on LinkedIn is essential, as is engaging on Twitter, Facebook, Instagram, and other social networks in ways that go beyond just posting yet another adorable baby picture. Posting about successes with your volunteer work can show the world you continue to have professional wins even if those wins are unpaid. Commenting on articles or even posting blogs can be a way to stay engaged. Your online presence can even be the key to a new job.

One *Women on the Rise* respondent shared she had set up a blog and became active in online women's groups. By building a voice and presence on issues that mattered, she was able to show potential employers she could "get the word out" and secured a job in marketing communications when she relaunched.

Women who have paused their careers often internalize the narrative that they are no longer valuable to the workplace and so completely step away from engaging in a professional manner with their networks, either online or in person. But to successfully set yourself up to get hired, you need to get out there. Attend networking events with pride and confidence. Post your key unpaid milestones on LinkedIn and elsewhere online. And, own your pause. You are doing something that matters even if you are not being paid for it. Remind your network that your pause will be brief and is part of your overall career plan. Keeping your network alive will make your re-entry much easier.

> Women who understand that their pauses are part of their careers recognize that it is a temporary strategy, so they continue to "lean in" by maintaining, and even expanding, their contacts and connections.

STRATEGY #9: KEEP YOUR SKILLS CURRENT

Meredith Miller Vostrejs is not afraid of much. After college, she spent two years with the Peace Corps in a tiny village in the Caribbean focusing on issues related to maternal health and women's economic development. Then she worked as a child abuse prevention advocate seeing cases of such horror it could break a person's heart. Eventually she landed her dream job in Africa as the Swaziland Country Manager for the Clinton Foundation.

Along the way Meredith married and had two children. The stress of work, living the life of an expat, and parenting without the support of extended family was "intense," Meredith told me when I interviewed her. When her husband had the opportunity to return to the Bay Area from Africa, allowing them to be closer to family and for Meredith to take time off and "just be a mom," she jumped at the chance.

After four "glorious" years, she was ready to return to paid work. Her biggest fear wasn't finding a job; it was overcoming the vast changes in technology that had occurred while she paused.

"I'm afraid I'm a technical dinosaur," Meredith said.

Her fears are not without merit. Given the rate of technological change in the past decade, taking a career break without maintaining one's skills can be one of the biggest impediments to career re-entry. But programs like Silicon Valley's ReBoot Accelerator, co-founded by Diane Flynn whom I wrote about in chapter 1, are helping women overcome their deficiencies with technology.

"So much has happened and continues to happen in terms of how work gets done," said Diane. "If you are not on top of it, you can quickly become overwhelmed. That said, it doesn't take long to gain technological competence. It just takes confidence to know you can."

Petrice Espinosa has that confidence now, but she didn't always. She took thirteen years off from full-time paid work. Then, in 2009, the unthinkable happened: Her husband became seriously ill and could no longer support the family. They lived on savings while he recovered, but by 2011 they needed benefits. Petrice went on Craigslist and found a role as a customer service manager for a start-up clothing line.

"I wasn't looking for the perfect job," Petrice told me. "I just wanted to get back in the game." That experience laid the foundation for her next job as office manager at ZOOM Marketing. Now Petrice is the co-founder of an outdoor apparel line. She said, "I am so much more with it now than I was when I first went back. My technical skills weren't up to speed and I had to learn everything from scratch. It would have all been so much easier if I had stayed current."

Put simply, if you value your career, stay abreast of the latest technology. By this I mean not just the latest social media craze, but also productivity and connectivity tools such as Slack, Evernote, UberConference, Dropbox, and the like. Doing so will make your re-entry much smoother and help you overcome potential biases employers may have about your ability to be immediately productive.

STRATEGY #10: RELISH YOUR PAUSE (BUT DON'T FRITTER AWAY YOUR HUMAN CAPITAL)

One of my favorite Sunday morning pleasures is to read the blog *Brain Pickings* by Maria Popova. She scans the breadth of literature, culture, art, and ideas, and opines on the issues at hand. She is always witty, insightful, and honest. Unlike many modern writers, she is never snarky or unkind.

A few years ago, she ran a piece on British philosopher and writer Alan Watts,[249] who is largely attributed with bringing Eastern philosophy to the West. His 1951 book, *The Wisdom of Insecurity: A Message for an Age of Anxiety*, is considered a classic. Of the book, Maria wrote, "What keeps us from happiness, Watts argues, is our inability to fully inhabit the present." She, and he, could easily have been writing about the challenges many of us face when we try to juggle work with family: how to be in the here and now of childhood when we are tasked with the demands of daily life.

If you have decided to pause your career, you have said with your actions that you believe slowing down and getting on "kid time," as one women I interviewed called it, is worth investing your human capital.

And yet when we asked the respondents of our *Women on the Rise* survey how they felt *during* their pause, the words "guilt," "self-doubt," "fear," and "anxiety" were repeated again and again. These highly educated, highly skilled, highly capable women were riddled with negative emotions that undermined their ability to enjoy their decision to focus on their families. In other words, they couldn't inhabit the now and so weren't truly happy.

As one said, "I spent most of my time worried I wouldn't be able to get back to my career so I was never fully present with my children."

I remember one sunny afternoon when my then-four-year-old son was lying in the middle of our small backyard lawn. We lived not too far from the airport, and he liked to watch the planes circle above as they prepared to land. He begged me to come and lie down with him, but I was pacing back and forth, worrying about the consulting client I had just lost, and trying to decide if I should go back to full-time work. We needed the money.

"Mom, come here," William whispered. I ignored him.

"Mom, you gotta see this." His voice was slightly louder, but I still ignored him.

"MOM!"

"What?" I snapped at him.

"Hummingbirds. Tons of them. All over the flowers," William said, his voice quivering. "They're gone now. You missed it."

He was right. I did miss it, and so much more—not because I was working and not present, but because I was worrying and not present. Don't do as I did. Stop worrying. You'll get back your career, but you'll never get back that moment when your son shows you a swarm of hummingbirds dancing from flower to flower.

During my pause, the time spent with my children was life changing. I am a better person for the hours we chased butterflies, imagined faces in the clouds, and built castles from wooden blocks. But I also frittered away my time on activities that kept me busy but didn't add value to my life or my career. Why? Because I was worried that if I wasn't busy, I wasn't doing something of importance. I know I am not alone.

Washington Post journalist Brigid Schulte spent years overwhelmed by the demands of work and caring for her family. Even though she negotiated a reduced workweek, she still found herself buried by the constant busyness of her life. Her best-selling book, *Overwhelmed: How to Work, Love, and Play When No One Has the Time*, was the result of her personal and professional journey to understand how it is we never seem to have enough time.

In the chapter entitled "Too Busy to Live," she wrote,

> Somewhere toward the end of the twentieth century . . . busyness became not just a way of life, but *glamorous*. Now, they say, it is a sign of social status . . . What changed is the cultural imperative not just to *have* it all, but to *fit* it all in on the fast track, packing in a multitude of work, activities, and obligations until life feels, as one researcher put it, like an exhausting "everydayathon."[250]

She went on to write, "Busyness is now the social norm that people feel they must conform to . . . or risk being outcasts."

Think about how we catch up with our friends. "How have you been?" you might ask. "So busy!" she's likely to answer. This intense need to prove our worth through the churn of activity is, I believe, one of the reasons we suffer work–life imbalance. Choosing to pause and to get off the fast track requires you to buck the trend, follow your own path, become an outcast in a busy, busy world. It takes courage.

That said, being smart about your time away from the paid workforce is vitally important. Frittering away your human capital on activities that don't help advance your skills and talents or help you expand your network is not the best use of your human capital. You don't have to be PTA president (as I was) or queen of classroom volunteering (as I was) to prove your time with your family is well spent.

It just is.

I know these might be fighting words for some, but engaging in less-than-useful activities to validate our roles as stay-at-home mothers harms our careers and undermines our value. I remember one day when I spent hours creating gift bags for the children in my daughter's class who were all heading out on a field trip. These children already lacked for nothing, and yet I felt compelled to use my hard-earned talents and abilities to ensure they had a special treat on their adventure. Why? I see now it was because I felt a powerful need to prove that I was a "good" mother and that my time and effort was being put to "good" use. I realize now, for me and my personal and professional goals, it wasn't.

Think about it. How many working mom/stay-at-home mom conflict narratives have focused on silly things like baking (rather than buying) cookies for the class party? Too many to count. We need to recognize that baking cookies is great, but so is supporting the women who are adding their talents to the school in other important ways.

My friend Katie Snodgrass is a senior vice president of wealth management at UBS Financial Services. She is also a committed mom who uses her volunteer time wisely. She is always the first to agree to pull together the classroom email contact list, the online schedule of classroom activities, the field trip volunteer schedule, and so on. On most days, she can't be in the classroom, but she can be actively involved.

Katie's best friend, Sarah Cleasby, is a full-time, stay-at-home mom. She is an active classroom volunteer who is there to help teach the kids math, co-run the school bake sale, and lead important PTA volunteer efforts. Katie and Sarah have different professional goals, but both are passionate about being engaged in their kids' schools. They support each other in their choices and how they can each best contribute given their personal and professional realities.

The author Annie Dillard once wrote, "How we spend our days is, of course, how we spend our lives. What we do with this hour, and that one, is what we are doing."[251] Being present, freeing one's self from worry, having courage and faith to know that what you are doing truly matters, are essential to a successful pause. But so is being smart about your time. If you have the "luxury" to take a career break, don't waste that time on needless activities. Make sure how you spend your time is chosen with intention and thought.

As one *Women on the Rise* survey respondent said, "I was out of the paid workforce for seven years. I could have completed a PhD program during that time. Instead, I focused exclusively on my children. While I loved being with them, I did nothing to help move my career forward. What a missed opportunity."

> If you have decided to pause your career, you have said with your actions that you believe slowing down and getting on "kid time," as one women I interviewed called it, is worth investing your human capital.

STRATEGY #11: FIND YOUR PURPOSE

The walls of the conference room at the corporate offices of NerdWallet in San Francisco were filled with poster-sized paper. The brightly colored drawings on each one looked like complex mazes filled with images of cars and houses and stick figure humans. At the front of the room a seven-year-old girl named Athena shared details about her team's new strategy for saving money. She and the twenty or so other elementary school–aged children were here to learn how to problem solve using design thinking. While the kids were being trained to unleash new ways of thinking, their mothers were being introduced to the basics of coding. The day was hosted by MotherCoders, the brainchild of post-pause Warrior Tina Lee.

Tina spent the first half of her career working to support Fortune 500 companies, government entities, philanthropic foundations, and non-profits in their efforts to integrate technology in their business systems. She also worked as a recruiter, helping companies find great technical talent to solve their business problems. Tina was often frustrated by the lack of women in technology, but she did not actively work to change it. And then she had children.

While she was making good money as a recruiter, according to Tina, the work was less than inspiring. She felt strongly she was supposed to do something else, so she decided to pause her career after her first child was born to figure out what that was. Tina enrolled in a one-year master's program that allowed her to integrate her love of technology with education. After that, she worked with governmental agencies to assist them in their efforts to innovate and empower citizens through technology. She was working in the California State Controller's office on policy issues regarding technology and innovation at the governmental level when her second child was born. Again, Tina decided to take a pause. Her reason was the same as before: She didn't feel she was doing the work that she was meant to do.

Tina realized that rather than analyze technology and innovation, she wanted to be part of the booming technology economy. She enrolled in a coding bootcamp and was dismayed to find she was the only woman in the group and the only parent. While the young, eager men gathered at lunch to talk about what they'd learned, Tina hid in the unheated women's bathroom and pumped breast milk for her baby. For Tina it was an epiphany.

"I realized we're never going to change the ratio of women in the tech industry if we don't figure out a way to make it more mother friendly," she told me when I met her at the MotherCoders event at NerdWallet. "Coding seemed like a great way to tackle the issue. First, the demand for coders is huge. Building the skills and knowledge of coding offers solutions for mothers who want to change careers. Plus, coding is also a perfect way for mothers who want flexibility to do part-time work until they are ready to onramp to full-time work. But the coding eco-system is oriented to young men who generally don't have children. I wanted to create a program for mothers like me."

In the fall of 2013, Tina launched a nonprofit dedicated to creating a more inclusive tech economy by expanding the talent pool to include mothers. She donated her time and managed to raise enough money to design the MotherCoders training program. The nine-week Saturday-only course with onsite child care introduces moms to the coding ecosystem so they can decide which coding language and career they would like to pursue. After being trained at MotherCoders, they can then move on to a full software-training program like Hackbright Academy.

In 2015, MotherCoders participated in the Points of Light Foundation Civic Accelerator and was the winner of a $100,000 grant from Google Impact Challenge. After hosting two training programs, Tina has refined the curriculum and is now offering an additional course specifically designed for returning female military veterans who are looking to relaunch into the civilian economy.

"Thanks to my children, I am finally doing what I was meant to do," Tina told me recently. "Being a mother and having a chance to realize the challenges other mothers face has finally enabled me to find my path."

Google the term "Find Your Purpose" and 612,000,000 results pop up. Wade through a few of them and they'll give you plenty of lists and how-tos all intended to offer you a quick fix on the path to a meaningful life. But quick fixes are not the solution. It isn't easy finding your purpose.

The real power of the pause is the opportunity to have time and leisure to ponder the course of your life, to meditate on what brings you joy, to reflect on your values and what it means to have a life well lived. I am sure busy stay-at-home moms are laughing into their much-needed coffee or wine glass as they read this, but if you elect to take a professional pause, I encourage you to use the time not just to focus on your family, but to also focus on yourself.

We so often lose ourselves in our roles as mothers and wives and daughters and employees and community volunteers and . . . In fact, losing ourselves is one thing most women have in common. We become so outwardly focused, we forget our inner truth. And as a result, we often end up living inauthentic lives working in careers that are unsatisfying. It's no wonder then that so many women leave the paid workforce to be with their children. For some, motherhood may be the first time they have found true meaning in their lives.

But while our children give our life meaning, they are not our sole (or soul) purpose. To find our life's work, we need to look beyond what we can bring to our families and consider how we can utilize our talents, trainings, and abilities to make a difference in the world. Getting clarity on our inner truth, our values, and that which most deeply matters to us ensures we will find meaningful work.

My pause allowed me to realize I loved writing, making change through the sharing of ideas, and, at the heart of it all, empowering women to bring their full talents to bear at work and at home. Early in my career, if you had asked me would I become a journalist or an author, I would have scoffed at the notion. And yet here I am.

My friend Monica Laurence told me she sees it this way: "We each have a legacy. The question is, do you want to wait until the end of your life to leave it or do you want to live it each and every day?"

As I have said before, I am not here to advocate that you *should* take a pause. But if you do take time away from the paid workforce, I encourage you to make the most of the time you are giving yourself. Yes, be immersed in your family, but also be immersed in your own evolution. Taking the time to pause, however that looks for you, can empower you to get clear on your legacy. Don't wait until it is too late to live it.

> The real power of the pause is the opportunity to have time and leisure to ponder the course of your life, to meditate on what brings you joy, to reflect on your values and what it means to have a life well lived.

CHAPTER 11

Thriving

The Career You Deserve, the Life You Want

"It's never too late to reinvent yourself."
—Maryanne Perrin,
forty-eight-year-old PhD candidate

The main auditorium at Columbia University was buzzing with excitement. The audience included MBAs, JDs, PhDs, and others with equally impressive credentials and concomitant work experience. They represented a cross segment of some of the highest-caliber talent available. You would have thought the 600 women (and handful of men) in attendance were at the height of their careers. Instead, the packed room was filled with people who were desperately trying to unlock the secrets of how to relaunch their professional lives after stepping back to focus on their families.

Attendees had come in from all over the country to participate in the 2015 iRelaunch conference, yet another sold-out event hosted by the leading company dedicated to helping career pausers power forward. Since its inception in 2008, iRelaunch claims to have served more than 16,000 women and men in their journey to re-enter the paid workforce. And, importantly, by championing the untapped talent of the returner market, the company has helped employers understand the value proposition this segment of the population brings to the workplace.

iRelaunch was co-founded by Carol Fishman Cohen, a Harvard MBA who herself managed to enter the paid workforce after an extended career pause. She is a trailblazer who, like me, launched into the workforce in the 1980s ready to grab the brass ring we'd been told was ours for the taking. She worked on Wall Street, went to business school, and then worked her way up the ladder at Drexel Burnham Lambert, an investment banking firm. But Carol's career was derailed just after her first child was born. Midway through maternity leave she was blindsided when her prestigious Wall Street company unexpectedly went out of business. That confluence of events left her with no job and a newborn child. Rather than try to find a job immediately, she decided to do what so many of us have done: She freelanced.

For the next five years, Carol worked part-time on limited engagements with financial services companies. Eventually the birth of three more children and the challenges of trying to integrate work and family forced her to leave the paid workforce completely. For six years, Carol committed herself to her children and to being a leader in her community. She became a Parent-Teacher Association president, active classroom volunteer, and, of course, being chauffeur to her four children kept her busy. And then it was time to re-enter. After extensive networking and numerous job interviews, Carol managed to find work at Bain Capital. Her career re-entry experience has been well documented in a Harvard Business School case called "The-40-Year-Old Intern."

Carol could easily have continued to commit to her career in the financial services industry, but her journey inspired her to take action. In partnership with a business school classmate and friend, Carol launched iRelaunch so other well-educated, highly skilled women (and men) could find their path back to the paid workforce after a career pause. Today, Carol Fishman Cohen is the poster woman for the re-entry movement.

iRelaunch is just one of a number of companies and organizations that have sprung up in recent years to meet the growing demand by women and men eager for help as they work to navigate the choppy waters of career re-entry. In Silicon Valley, I am an advisor to ReBoot Accelerator, a spin-off from tech incubator GSVlabs. ReBoot hosts training sessions providing women with the technical skills, the connections, and the confidence they need to get up to speed after a career break. In Boston, reacHIRE takes it one step further by not only offering training but also providing internships. And a recent start-up out of New York, called Après, is billing itself as *the* online platform for women who want to re-ignite their professional lives after a personal pause.

The question for participants in these programs is almost always the same: How do I get my career back on track? Here are the top ten strategies recommended from the trailblazers who worked, paused, and thrived before you.

STRATEGY #1: KNOW YOUR VALUE

At that 2015 iRelaunch conference, I moderated a panel with four women who had participated in company-specific return-to-work internships. At the end, I turned to the audience for questions. Many wanted to know if these "returnships" were part of corporate social responsibility programs—programs designed to help the community, not a given company's bottom line.

What?

Companies aren't being socially responsible when they hire relaunching women; they are being fiscally responsible. Why? Because they need smart, talented, engaged employees to help their businesses grow and thrive. And, given the latest research that has proven companies with diverse workforces and companies with women in leadership do better than those without, they need us. But our lack of confidence about our employability after a career break has us convinced otherwise. We have come to believe that when companies hire relaunching women, they are doing us a favor rather than realizing we have something of deep value to offer them.

Companies aren't being socially responsible when they hire relaunching women; they are being fiscally responsible. Why? Because they need smart, talented, engaged employees to help their businesses grow and thrive.

Penny Locey is vice president at Keystone Associates, a firm that specializes in helping laid-off executives find jobs. She says, "No matter the reason for your career break, the most important thing a job hunter can do is to know their value and to remember it's not about you, it's about what the business needs."

And what the business needs is committed, *engaged* employees.

Engagement, or rather *dis*engagement, is a hot topic these days. In 2013, Gallop released its Workplace Survey on Employee Engagement. According to their research, 70 percent of the U.S. workforce reports feeling disengaged, resulting in $550 billion in lost productivity in this country alone. Employees who are excited to be working and ready to commit themselves have, as Ruth Ross, author of *Coming Alive: The Journey to Reengage Your Life and Career*, wrote, "a true competitive advantage."[252]

Ruth spent her career in human resources, most recently as an executive vice president at Wells Fargo. She saw employees come and go, but the ones she had no doubt would be successful were the women who had paused their careers.

"Women who are re-entering have a leg up on people currently in the workforce because they have had the chance to sit back and find their truth. This leads to authentic engagement with work," Ruth told me.

Bob Plaschke, CEO of Sonim Technologies, sees this in the relaunchers he has hired. "In the past three years, I've hired three women who took career breaks. Without a doubt, they are some of the hardest working, easiest to manage, and most committed employees I have."

It's time to reframe the narrative that says college-educated, professional women who pause their careers have nothing to offer the workforce. If you have paused your career, the best thing you can do as you are job hunting is have confidence in what you bring to the table. Once you have that, you are ready to find the right job with the right company—it's out there waiting for you.

STRATEGY #2: BE OUT AND PROUD ABOUT YOUR PAUSE

Joanna Pomykala isn't one to shy away from her truth. She's a triathlete who trains early in the morning before her children rise and spends her days studying human behavior as the senior director of Insights for LinkedIn's sales division. She leads a team of eighty people and has helped the company launch its Women's Initiative (WIN), intended to get more women into senior management positions. Joanna is on the fast track to being one of them.

Sure, her career is on fire now, but not so long ago, Joanna was home caring for her two children. She had been at Microsoft and then, after the birth of her second child, used her maternity leave to evaluate her next career move. She wanted to try the start-up route and decided to take first one job and then another at a series of early-stage companies. While she loved the fast-paced experience, she decided the risks were not worth the reward at that point in her career. Plus, her husband was at a start-up and was traveling extensively. The family needed some stability.

So, for almost two years, Joanna paused her career. She stayed in the game by taking on small consulting projects while she assessed her next move. She relished her time with her kids, but she knew she didn't want to stay home indefinitely. She wasn't "opting out," just taking a career pause.

Because her husband was spending more time in San Francisco than Seattle, they decided to move down to the Bay Area. Once they settled in, Joanna embarked on an intensive job search. When she interviewed for various positions, Joanna didn't hesitate to tell them she had paused her career to focus on her two young kids. She believes her pause not only gave her family a much-needed break, she says it also helped advance her career.

"Employers didn't think twice about my time out because they saw it was more than 'opting out.' They understood I was willing to take risks and try new things," Joanna told me. "I had something to talk about that helped my employer see I was making thoughtful choices about my life and my career."

This empowered attitude is what women with successful non-linear careers have when it comes to their pauses. They aren't apologetic. They explain their career break for what it is, a career strategy that enables them to take risks, try new things, build new skills, and come back stronger than ever.

> This empowered attitude is what women with successful non-linear careers have when it comes to their pauses. They aren't apologetic. They explain their career break for what it is, a career strategy that enables them to take risks, try new things, build new skills, and come back stronger than ever.

A new study by Joni Hersch, professor of law and economics at Vanderbilt, revealed that when female candidates gave personal information about why they paused their careers, they raised their chance of being hired by up to 40 percent compared to a comparable female candidate who provided no personal information.[253]

Study co-author Jennifer Bennet Shinall said, "We have a significant number of highly educated, highly qualified women who take a few years off to raise children, and want to come back into the labor market. And the fact of the matter is they seem to be getting bad advice from recruiters and career websites urging them to pretend their private lives don't exist."[254]

As I have shared before, there is a reason we hide our personal lives: caregiver bias. We have been trained to smooth over gaps in our résumé because, we've been told, employers don't want to hire women with children in general, and particularly women who have paused. It's no wonder we are uncomfortable being forthcoming about our career breaks. But, as the latest research shows, hiding your truth hurts you.

It also hurts the rest of us. As we saw in chapter 3, the research of Professor Pamela Stone and other experts has revealed when women take time away from the paid workforce and don't give voice to why they are leaving, they reinforce the notion that they are the ones that have failed, not the system itself.

If you decide to become a non-linear career trailblazer and pause briefly to care for your family, do it proudly. Tell your family, your friends, your business colleagues, and your employer what you are doing and why.

You can say (as one woman I interviewed told me she *wished* she had said), "I want to be able to give 100 percent to all that I do, but the way work is currently structured, I don't feel I am truly able to do that. So,

I've decided I'm going to take a *brief* career break. I'm doing this because I want to be the primary caregiver to my children when they are young. Then, I plan to recommit 100 percent to my career. I'd love your support."

It is hard to argue with those who are authentic with their dreams and goals. By enlisting the support of others and being clear on what you want, you may find you have allies you didn't know existed. Sure, there's no doubt there will be many people who believe you are making a mistake by pausing your career, but having clarity *and* a plan can empower you to be true to your own path despite them.

Just think, if every woman who paused spoke her truth about why she was pausing, we would help change the narrative that says *women* need to change, and put the focus on how the system needs to change to accommodate caregiving. As Anne-Marie Slaughter so brilliantly detailed in her book *Unfinished Business: Women Men Work Family*, we live in a cultural, political, and professional environment that doesn't value caregiving. It is time we named it, owned it, and changed it.

STRATEGY #3: USE YOUR NETWORK

In the previous chapter, you read of the importance of keeping your network alive. If you have done this well, they'll be there to help you when you relaunch. Just ask lawyer Karen Dienst.

She had an enviable career, first clerking for a judge in the Third Circuit Court of Appeals, then working her way up to partner at the prestigious law firm of Morrison & Foerster. She went on to become vice president and general counsel for ADAC Laboratories. And she managed to have four children during it all. After nearly five years in her role as general counsel, Karen decided to pause her career.

"I had accomplished everything I set out to do professionally and I decided I wanted to put my energies into my family," Karen told me.

She spent eight years at home, and then it was time to re-ignite her career. Karen went on a "listening tour" to find out which jobs might be well suited given her skills, abilities, and interests. She loved the law, but she had no passion for working in a large firm. It was a past colleague who introduced Karen to her current business partner, Kathy Woeber Gardner.

"My colleague knew us both and believed we'd work well together," Karen said. He was right. Karen and Kathy launched Montgomery Pacific Law Group, a boutique law firm focusing on the needs of emerging and later-stage companies.

Karen might not want to be compared to Alicia Florrick of the television show *The Good Wife*, but the comparisons are apt. For both, it was a colleague who knew them before they paused—in Alicia's case, an old law school classmate—that helped them relaunch.

Penny Locey says this is very common. "They remember you as you once were, not as you are. For them, you have been frozen in time and so the professional skills and abilities you had are still alive in their memory of you. As a result, they can be your best resource for a new job."

Your network isn't limited to past colleagues; what about those who know you today? A significant portion of women who pause their careers donate their extensive skills and talents to volunteer work. The women and men they meet as a result are often exactly the new network they need to re-ignite their careers.

As one woman told me, "At my children's preschool, a group of ten women had been meeting regularly to help raise funds for a new playground and to create an endowment so we could offer scholarships to under-resourced children. Somehow the conversation came up about our pre-mother life. Of that group of ten, I learned that four had MBAs, two were previously lawyers, one had her PhD, and another was a successful entrepreneur. They became my network when I was ready to relaunch."

It was Kim Drew's new network that helped her find her dream job. After building her professional foundation, she left a senior position in business development for Charles Schwab to care for her three young children. For two years Kim threw herself into her role as stay-at-home mom. She volunteered in school, took her kids to the park, and proudly made organic, nutritious dinners. She found a job working part-time as a strategy consultant but eventually she was ready to be all-in again.

During her pause, Kim had served on the board of the Friends of the San Francisco Library. One of her colleagues from the board told Kim about a job at JVS, a vital nonprofit committed to helping under-resourced and under-prepared people find jobs in the Bay Area. For Kim, it was a natural fit. She wanted to make sure others could find great jobs just as she had. Today, Kim is the vice president of business development of JVS.

"I wouldn't be where I am today if the network I developed as a volunteer hadn't supported my efforts to re-ignite my career," Kim said. "You never know who will be there to help you make that next big leap."

STRATEGY #4: CONSIDER THE CONSTRAINTS

In 2007, Carol Fishman Cohen, co-founder and CEO of iRelaunch, co-wrote a how-to book entitled *Back on the Career Track: A Guide for Stay-at-Home Moms Who Want to Return to Work.* In it, she argues that a career relaunch is a different kind of job search.

> Your early job searches may have been driven by needs for prestige, advancement potential, or résumé building, as well as money. But this time around, although you still may be motivated by financial concerns, you have the chance to do what you really *want* to do rather than what you think you *should* do or what someone else is telling you to do.[255]

In other words, you get to choose your next career path. You can boomerang back to your previous job and/or industry, or you can pivot to something new. Like some Pivoters (see chapter 2), you can become an entrepreneur or fight to make a difference and become a warrior for a meaningful cause. That's the good news.

The not-so-good news: As Carol wrote, "As a relaunching mother, however, you may face a lot of constraints" on your ability to find your ideal job.

Carol called these constraints the "Three C's of a career relaunch." These include how much control of your time you have, doing work (content) that is personally meaningful, and getting compensated in a way that rewards you accordingly.

She argued that relaunchers are often forced to find a two-thirds solution. You may find work that gives you control and content but doesn't pay you as much as you might like. Or, you may find work that pays well and is intellectually stimulating, but forces you to give up control of your time. In essence, Carol Fishman Cohen says relaunchers have to manage their expectations.

She's right, but I believe her lessons apply to the vast majority of professional women and men, not just those who are relaunching their careers. Think about it: How often does your career have that perfect blend of meaningful pay, manageable hours, and exciting and rewarding work? Rarely, as far as I can tell.

Does that mean that those who have paused and are now re-igniting their careers don't face additional challenges? They absolutely do. But don't fall into the thinking that it is only because you paused that you are facing these limitations. The reality of work for most of us is that, whether you pause or not, you must decide what you are willing to trade.

When we asked the *Women on the Rise* respondents what compromises they had to make when they re-entered the workforce, lower pay and lower position were the two most frequently cited challenges. But, surprisingly, for 48 percent of our respondents *this was part of their plan.*

This intention goes against the common assumption about women who are trying to re-enter. In her book *Off-Ramps and On-Ramps: Keeping Talented Women on the Road to Success*, economist Sylvia Ann Hewlett reported that women who paused their careers often re-entered to lower-paying jobs, which, along with other similar reports, suggests that women can't get back on track. But it seems no one asked if these women *intentionally* took a slower onramp.

Why did nearly half of the women who paused their careers intentionally take a less-demanding job with lower pay when they went back to the paid workforce? A significant majority (66 percent) indicated they wanted "control of their time" and took a less-demanding/lower-paying job because it would allow for greater flexibility.

As one respondent shared, "Yes, I entered with lower pay and lower responsibilities, but I also had the choice to take jobs with higher pay and responsibilities. Flexibility was more important to me."

Encouragingly, since re-igniting their careers, 58 percent of *Women on the Rise* respondents reported their compensation has increased, and 37 percent indicated they have been promoted. And, 69 percent shared they felt back on track professionally within a year. So much for a pause killing their careers.

STRATEGY #5: ADAPT AND EVOLVE

You may have noticed that in many of the stories I've shared about women who have worked, paused, and thrived, there is a sub-theme about being able to continually improve and refine their careers. And because they were constantly adjusting, their non-linear careers were more emblematic of a jungle gym or a lattice, as Deloitte's Managing Partner and previous Head of Talent Cathy Benko has called them, than the traditional ladder. These women zigged and zagged professionally, and along the way they built skills, acquired knowledge, and forged relationships. At the heart of it all was a willingness to try and fail, and then adapt and evolve.

Maryanne Perrin knows this only too well. After she got her MBA at the University of North Carolina at Chapel Hill, Maryanne worked in business and finance operations for KPMG Peat Marwick, a big six accounting firm. She was recruited from there to work in-house at a fast-growing software company running the IT department. When she was pregnant with her first child, the company built a nursery for her and two other new moms so they could bring their babies to work at the onsite day care. But when she unexpectedly got pregnant with her second child just nine months after her first, Maryanne decided to pull back and negotiated a reduced workweek. At this point it looked like her career would end up like that of other "Cruisers" where she would pull back temporarily and then reengage when the children were older. But then she became pregnant with her third, and Maryanne knew it was time to take a "career sabbatical."

For more than four years she served as an active community volunteer, but the whole time, she told me, she was "itching" to get back in. So were many other women who were just like her, she realized. Maryanne decided to pivot and become an entrepreneur. With a close friend, Maryanne started a company called Balancing Professionals. They connected employers with high-caliber part-time consultants, talented professionals like herself who needed flexible work arrangements.

When the company floundered after the Great Recession of 2008, Maryanne stepped back. She took six months to explore what she really loved and realized she'd always been fascinated by how food drives our health, so she shifted again to pursue her dream.

"My real passion has always been around the power and importance of nutrition," Maryanne told me as we talked over the phone about her career, her choices, and her newfound mission in life. "So I decided it was time to focus on it." She enrolled in a master's program with a focus on nutrition and was hooked. She loved the vibrancy of the academic world, the energy of her younger classmates, and the intellectual challenge of science. She said, "I never realized I was a scientist at heart!"

Maryanne went on to secure her PhD at North Carolina State University. While there, she found a mentor who saw beyond the fact that she was a forty-five-year-old mother of three with no real experience in the field. Professor Jack Odle offered Maryanne a fifteen-month fellowship, which, she said, changed everything for her. Today, Dr. Perrin is proud to say she has a two-year $150,000 grant to support her research on nutrition for medically vulnerable infants.

"Never in my wildest dreams did I think I would be doing this," she told me. "I'm the model that says it is never too late to reinvent yourself."

Katie Kelley, director of people development at the Fuerst Group and author of *Career Courage: Discover Your Passion, Step Out of Your Comfort Zone, and Create the Success You Want*, believes the only way to truly thrive is a willingness to adapt and evolve

She told me, "I studied to be an MSW and worked in a psych ward in New York. It wasn't the right job for me so I took a job in pharmaceutical sales, which blended my experience in treating patients with my passion for giving doctors the tools they need to treat those patients. I was on the fast track at my company, but I felt I had gotten what I needed from that job and experience. Plus, I wanted to get back working directly with people, so I quit."

Katie started her own leadership consulting practice helping women find their professional dreams. She became a media personality offering career tips on a morning show in Portland, Oregon, which led to her book and to her current job.

"I've never been happier," she told me. "But it wasn't a straight line to here. I had to be willing to take risks and be innovative."

Adapting and evolving can mean trying different careers and different jobs; it can also mean changing how you work. Tiffany Cummins knows this only too well. Today she works full-time as the co-owner of Cross Marketing, a successful public relations agency. While her career has always been in PR, Tiffany adapted and evolved her work schedule to meet her personal and professional goals. She's worked as an in-house full-time executive, as a full-time contractor, as a part-time consultant, as a stay-at-home mom, and now she's back to full-time again.

"No one told me this was an option. I had to figure it out myself," Tiffany said.

Katie Kelley told me she counsels others to "remember it is so hard to be the one that marches to the beat of their own drummer, but you'll never know what you might be capable of unless you have the courage to try. Giving yourself permission to follow your own path is essential to having a truly rewarding career."

In other words, adapt and evolve.

STRATEGY #6: DON'T GIVE UP

I interviewed one woman whom I'll call Sara. In many ways she should be the Silicon Valley dream hire. Sara was born in Iran and came to the United States for college. She has a degree in electrical engineering with a minor in computer science. She spent the bulk of her career working as a program manager for Sun Microsystems and then she decided to pause her career. For six years, Sara stayed home. Much to her surprise, when she was ready to break back into the paid workplace, she struggled.

"All these tech companies claim they want to hire women in STEM, but apparently they only want young women with no children," she told me.

Sara was deeply demoralized. She explained she'd had job interviews with Amazon and Google, both to no avail. When I asked her to provide details, it turned out that Sara fell into a trap I have heard from a number of relaunchers who struggle to get back in. It's not that she couldn't find a job. She'd done a number of consulting gigs and had been offered full-time jobs, but felt the positions weren't right for her. She wanted to hold out for the perfect job and since she couldn't find it, she gave up.

Holding out for your ideal job is a valid strategy, although it's one that requires you to have the financial resources and the fortitude to wait for something that meets your criteria. But rather than own that strategy, many women who don't immediately get hired convince themselves that the system is stacked against them. Arguably, it is. But for some that can become an excuse to avoid continuing to look for work.

No doubt Sara faced age bias and motherhood bias and the bias faced by the long-term unemployed. But she also faced something else: her own internal beliefs about the employability of "opt-out" moms. Sara believed the narrative that it is too hard to get back in.

"Everyone told me it would be hard. Everyone told me my skills were outdated and that because of my career break, I was unemployable. They were right," she said.

I challenged Sara to think back on her post-pause job-hunting process. She'd done many things right. She found consulting work that helped bring her skills up to speed. She'd used a few of her contacts to help make introductions to companies. But when the perfect job didn't immediately materialize, Sara stopped trying.

"I realize now I wasn't persistent enough. I could have widened my net to look at other companies and talked to more of my contacts. I could have taken something just to get back in the door. I could have taken my skills and applied them to another industry or career path. I could have, but I didn't," Sara said.

Sara and so many other women who have taken extended career pauses undoubtedly face obstacles to relaunching their careers. But it is important to recognize what role the system is playing and what role you are playing in limiting your options. Are your expectations unrealistic? Are you open to taking a job that might not be perfect to get your "foot in the door"? Are you considering what else you might do that could fit your skills, abilities, and interests? Have you given up because the perfect job hasn't landed in your lap rather than work your way into that perfect job?

I'm not trying to blame the job hunter. I am simply trying to highlight that relaunching your career takes an equal measure of grit and persistence. Don't give up.

And yet, it is important to not diminish the challenges a relauncher who has taken an extended pause can face. A number of *Women on the Rise* respondents said they believed age bias was as challenging an issue for them as motherhood bias. One said, "I'm only forty-five and look younger than my age, but the recruiters and hiring managers are very young. It is hard to break their preconceived ideas."

Catherine Richards knows this only too well. She is currently the global lead for cyber security messaging at Dell Computers. After an eight-year career pause, she onramped via a series of part-time consulting projects and then a seven-month full-time stint at Alcatel-Lucent where she was hired by a woman who needed a fixed short-term marketing project completed. Notably, it was that same "sister" at Alcatel-Lucent who recommended Catherine for the Dell job.

Catherine said, "She went to bat for me and I will always be grateful."

Catherine invited me to lunch when she heard from friends I was writing this book. She was intrigued and wanted to discuss my thesis: that pausing for parenthood won't kill your career, particularly if you are strategic about your choices. Like many of the *Women on the Rise* respondents, she believes it isn't just motherhood, but ageism that can hurt women who want to re-enter.

When we met, I thought Catherine was much younger than her years. She has a high, girlish voice that adds to the overall impression of youth. With her bright smile, smooth skin, and trim build, Catherine could easily pass for someone in her early thirties, but she is actually fifty-two years old, something she has kept a professional secret until now.

"I don't intentionally lie about my age, but I think of it as career stewardship," Catherine told me. "Most of my colleagues are much younger than I am, so to blend in I rarely talk about my children and I certainly don't mention that they are college aged."

When I asked why she wanted me to interview her for the book and "out" herself as a woman of certain age, Catherine said, "It's time we women start being more authentic about our lives. I took a career break and now I'm a team leader at a fantastic technology company. I want to model for other women that it can be done, that you're never too old to have a successful career. But I also want them to understand they need to be smart about how they do it."

And how do they do it? They don't give up!

STRATEGY #7: MAKE PEACE WITH YOUR SLOW CAREER

Articles about slow careers, downshifting, and alternative ways of living started showing up en masse after the 2008 financial meltdown. And for good reason—many women and men who had given up so much of their personal lives so they could be all-in at work were suddenly finding themselves with the proverbial pink slip and a walk to the door.

I'd seen it before. On Monday, October 19, 1987, the stock market crashed. The Dow Jones Industrial Average lost 23 percent in a single day—the largest one-day percentage drop in history. Over the next few days, $1 trillion in total wealth was lost.

At the time, I was working as a product manager at Fidelity Investments while Bill was at business school. With hundreds of thousands of dollars in school loans, my salary and benefits were the only things between us and that financial cliff.

At Fidelity, it was an all-hands-on-deck day. Managers like myself who had never "manned" the customer service phone bank were called in to calm the nerves of terrified retirees, housewives, and primary bread-winning husbands.

I'll never forget one woman's anxious call. She begged me to tell her if they should sell everything so they would be assured to save something. "My husband is the only one earning a salary now because I'm home with the kids. If we lose this money, I'll have to go back to work. That is if I can even get a job!"

A few months later, Fidelity announced major layoffs. We managers were told to sit in our offices while our bosses would individually inform us of our "employment status." I could hear grown men shouting in disbelief down the hall and I saw one colleague crying as he was escorted out the door. I didn't lose my job that day, but I came to understand how precarious job security can truly be. I vowed to make sure I would always have a job with a good paycheck. As you know, I didn't keep that promise to myself, largely because I didn't foresee what it was like to be a professional and a mother.

The lessons of the financial collapse of 2008 rang differently to the respondents of the *Women on the Rise* survey. Rather than convince them one should never leave the workforce, the Great Recession convinced many of them that their choice to pause was exactly the right decision.

As one woman wrote, "If you can lose everything you have worked so hard for in the blink of an eye, you better make sure the sacrifice was worth it."

Another said, "I knew I had made the right choice when I watched my friends who worked long hours and never saw their children lose so much of their savings. They stayed working non-stop to earn all of that money and then it was gone. Because I had paused my career, we didn't have as much savings to lose, but I had time, which was much more valuable to me."

Time and how you feel about what you do with it is at the heart of working, pausing, and thriving. In a 24/7 work world where it's about getting to the top as fast as you can, choosing to take control of your time by meandering along on your own path can be incredibly difficult. Making peace with a slow career means you have to accept that those who stay all-in, all-of-the-time, are going to reach the top before you. For many women, that can be a huge challenge.

It takes courage to push back and confidence to make peace with the consequences. Venture capitalist Patricia Nakache remembers how hard it was to stay true to her personal goals when she decided pull back and work part-time. She told me, "I felt like the tortoise in the race to be successful. My women friends were moving along and, in my mind, I was doing the same work as my male colleagues even if I was working a reduced schedule. But they were the ones getting promoted. You have to swallow your pride as you watch others succeed around you to keep your goals on track."

As Patricia, and so many others, have proven, a slow career doesn't need to be slow forever. When you are ready, you can re-ignite your professional goals, most likely catching up far more quickly than you might have expected. Despite taking a career breaks between two and ten years, it took fewer than twelve months for the vast majority of the *Women on the Rise* respondents to feel they were "back on track." In all likelihood, it won't take long for you either.

> Time and how you feel about what you do with it is at the heart of working, pausing, and thriving.

STRATEGY #8: MANAGE THE DYNAMICS OF MONEY, POWER, AND MARRIAGE

Here's the deal: If you leave the paid workforce for an extended period of time or pull back thereby significantly reducing your income, two things will happen. First, you will become financially dependent on someone else. And second, that person will bear the daily burden of being the primary provider for you and your children.

While we'd like to imagine our partners' careers will be steady and secure, sometimes life gets in the way. Companies downsize, start-ups fail, the economy tanks, your savings dry up. The stress of these financial challenges can be overwhelming and, as in so many cases, can lead to divorce. These things are hard to plan for, but smart couples understand the risks and have a financial plan for the worst-case scenario.

But there is more at risk than your financial freedom and security if you take a career break. There is also the question of your power and independence. You need to look at yourself and your partner and ask some important questions. What does it mean to you to become financially dependent? Are you willing to lose the power that comes with bringing in money to the household? How will you feel when you suddenly find yourself in a marriage that resembles something out of that 1950s television hit, *Leave It to Beaver*?

Yeah, I know you don't think that will happen to you, that you and your beloved will fight against the cultural norms and create new models that go beyond capitalism and patriarchy. But the truth is, for my generation at least, that's as rare as a snowflake in Phoenix.

Ann Crittenden, author of *The Price of Motherhood: Why the Most Important Job in the World Is Still the Least Valued*, gave a thorough analysis of this conundrum in a chapter called "The Dark Little Secret of Family Life." She wrote,

> In every household a certain amount of explicit and implicit bargaining goes on: over how to spend the family's resources, who does the housework, who takes off work for a sick child. The outcome of each of these family decisions is strongly influenced by what social scientists call the "threat point"—the point at which a spouse's threats become credible . . . When fathers make much more money than mothers, and when alimony and child support are skimpy at best, the wife is likely to put up with a lot more than the husband.[256]

In brief, the loss of power due to the shift in one's economic status means the parent who has become the primary caregiver has a lower "threat" point. I remember the day this lesson was brought home to me. It started out with me rushing to get our children to preschool, then spending the morning in back-to-back meetings with my consulting clients. Afterward, I raced to pick up groceries, dropped off the dry cleaning, bought a birthday gift for my mother, and then zoomed back to pick up the kids from school. The children and I arrived home not long before my husband.

Bill walked in the door, went to the bedroom to change out of his business suit (yes, this was back when men still occasionally wore suits in Silicon Valley), came to the kitchen, sat down at the table, and said, "Man, what a day I've had. I'm exhausted." Then he turned to me and asked, "So, what's for dinner?"

I could have clobbered him. Instead, I burst into tears.

My husband is not an inherently sexist man. When we were dating, one of the most appealing things about him was his belief and commitment to equality. He loved, and still loves, empowered women. But in that moment, I realized my bargaining power (my "threat point") when it came to the housework, the kids, the myriad of demands of home and family, had been significantly reduced. Somehow after I had changed my life from work-first to family-first and my paycheck shrank in proportion to his, I became the thing my mother had warned me against: a housewife.

I am not alone. Many of the women I interviewed were blindsided by how their seemingly equal marriages became lopsided seesaws once they paused their careers. When we asked *Women on the Rise* survey respondents what compromises they had to make to pause, many of them shared they took on all of the burdens of the household when they left their jobs.

"My husband's career was so demanding I was forced to take on all of the household responsibilities. So much for equality," one wrote.

Sue Tachna, a member of my Not-So-New Mothers Group, thought she and her husband Steve had it figured out after their first son was born. Both committed feminists, they agreed to split the housework and child care down the middle.

Steve was working as a high-tech consultant and Sue was working in communications for a pharmaceutical company. Her job required extensive face time, but Steve was able to create his own hours. He staggered his schedule so that three mornings a week he stayed home with the baby and then worked from mid-day late into the evening. Sue was in charge of night-time duty on those days. Their son Daniel was in day care the other two days a week.

"It seemed like a perfect solution, but we were always exhausted and our work demands kept getting in the way," Sue told me. So they both "leaned in" and put Daniel in full-time day care. Sue didn't enjoy her job so she found a new one, hoping that would solve her dissatisfaction. She still wasn't inspired by the work, but they needed the money. When she became pregnant with their second son, Avi, Sue had had enough. They agreed to rework their finances so Sue could work part-time.

"Steve loved his job and I didn't. It seemed to make perfect sense for me to be the one to step down for a while," Sue said. Steve's career started to take off and the family's financial situation improved, so Sue stopped working outside the home altogether. She, too, became what she least wanted to be: a housewife.

Sue can laugh about it now. She's since found the work she loves and feels she was always destined to do: She's an elementary school science teacher. But those years when she and her husband fell into a more traditional marital structure, Sue pondered if you could truly be a feminist if you gave up your economic independence. Today Sue is more resolved about their life choices. She says, "We are living the traditional thing, but we're not traditional thinkers."

In situations like Sue and Steve's, the first power shift in a marriage often happens when one person's career takes priority and that person becomes the primary breadwinner. The second shift happens when the person who paused reengages her career and suddenly she is not focused on the needs of the family anymore. The women I interviewed told me again and again it was challenging for the family to adjust to their new roles now that they were back in the workforce.

When you pause your career and then again when you relaunch it, the dynamics will change in your marriage and in your family. Be conscious of how your actions and choices align with the reigning ideas about gender roles and be conscious of the inevitable guilt that comes when a mother puts her goals and dreams first.

STRATEGY #9: MANAGE YOUR GUILT

I met Grace Zales, like Sue, at my New Mothers Group at Stanford Hospital in 1996. Her daughter, Ellie, was born just days after the birth of my daughter. Grace, who was slightly older than I, had spent years trying to get pregnant. She knew she wanted to be as available as possible to her new daughter and was able to negotiate a part-time schedule with her company, Cornerstone Research.

Grace always came to our Not-So-New Mothers gatherings with exciting talk of her job as a litigation consultant. The company was growing exponentially, and Grace loved her work. She also loved her new BlackBerry that allowed her to be available to her clients when she was not in the office. But Grace and her husband wanted another child. They struggled with infertility; it took eight more years for Grace to give birth to their second daughter. It was then that she finally decided to leave the workforce altogether.

"The large gap between my first and second child allowed me time to consider how I wanted to mother differently," Grace said. She was out of the paid workforce for more than ten years and then, when her oldest entered high school, Grace was ready to relaunch. She reached out to her old boss and is now working as a litigation consultant again. The transition wasn't easy.

"I struggled with the guilt," Grace told me, "convincing myself my children needed me and I was failing them. It took a while, but now they're flourishing. I realized part of going back to work is also about letting go and allowing your children to make their own path. It's the guilt though that can tear you apart."

Guilt. I don't know why it isn't in the definition of "mother" in the dictionary. It should be. Women leave their careers because they feel guilty for not putting their children first and then when they relaunch, they feel guilty they are no longer focusing on their families. You can't win. Do yourself a favor and have confidence your children will be fine. You took a risk and sacrificed your career to be with them; now that you are back at work, they can step in and help you thrive.

As Grace said to me once, "Maybe, in the end, all of that hovering and helicoptering wasn't good for either of us."

Jodi Detjen is professor of management at Suffolk University and co-author of *The Orange Line: A Woman's Guide to Integrating Career, Family & Life.* She believes one of the biggest things holding women back is that we are constrained by our "Feminine Filter."

The "Feminine Filter" as described in her book is "a commonly adopted belief system for what makes an ideal woman in our culture." Be nice, look good, do it all. You know these tropes. The number one way we limit ourselves within the "Feminine Filter," Detjen wrote, is through guilt. "Guilt is a very effective at keeping behavior in line because it constantly saps energy . . . As long as women still believe deep down in the ideal woman, guilt will work to keep the assumptions real."[257]

The "ideal woman," like the "ideal mother," is a barrier to our personal growth and life satisfaction. We'd be a better off, and the world would be a better place, if we could all figure out how to let those little voices in our heads go. So hard to do, but I believe it is the only way to get the life you want.

STRATEGY #10: SPIRAL WITH YOUR SPOUSE

Some couples truly do seem to have figured it out. Take Molly Anderson and her husband, Richard Berger. Molly worked at Deloitte as a strategy consultant before and after her children were born. She did what many career-driven women do: She worked long hours to support her clients' needs, traveled extensively, and rarely got home in time to kiss her babies good night. As a young mother, she didn't mind because Richard's career as an engineer meant he worked more stable hours. He could be home early to cook the family dinner, bathe their two children, and read them their nightly bedtime stories.

Eventually, Molly's priorities changed. She knew she wanted and needed time with her children, so she decided to pause.

Molly said, "When I left Deloitte, I didn't have an intentional well-thought-through plan. I wasn't thinking about my long-term career. I just knew I had had enough."

So, like me, she scaled back her career and became a "single shingle" consultant working part-time from home. For eight years, she managed the playdates, the grocery shopping, the doctors' appointments while Richard committed himself to his career. It was, as she says, "marvelous" and "frustrating." She had worked hard to establish herself professionally, and there didn't seem to be a path for integrating her role as mother with her role as professional.

While Molly was away from Deloitte, the company had spent time realizing they had a "brain drain" problem. Bright, talented women were leaving in droves once they had children. Deloitte had invested time and money in these women. Rather than view it as a "woman's problem," Deloitte viewed it as a talent retention problem.

In 2004, they created a new program called the "Initiative for the Retention and Advancement of Women." They placed their rising star, Cathy Benko, as the head of the initiative. Cathy and Molly had worked together before so when Cathy took on the job, she reached out to Molly and asked her to come back and help launch the program.

Molly and Richard knew this would mean she would have to be "all-in, all-of-the-time," so Richard decided to scale back his career and become the lead parent. Now he was the carpool king, the homework helper, the playdate manager, and Molly was the power-suit-wearing, always-gone-on-business primary breadwinner. Richard continued in his role as lead parent until their children were in high school. Then Richard relaunched his own career and is now working as an engineering lead at a health care start-up.

Molly and Richard were able to spiral their roles as lead parent and lead breadwinner because they both had workplaces that allowed them to thrive. Neither were penalized for their career pauses and, as a result, both have had the benefit of experiencing the joys and challenges of being primarily responsible for the children and primarily responsible for financially supporting their family.

"My husband and I spiraled our careers in a way that allowed us to truly have the best of all worlds. It wasn't easy and we made many sacrifices and compromises along the way. But we feel we have managed to find our own version of having it all," Molly told me.

The good news is that we are seeing more and more couples approach their partnerships in this way. One *Women on the Rise* survey respondent shared the following:

> My husband and I agreed when we married that we both wanted to work and raise our children. We are both in a creative field that offers more flexibility than most in stepping in and out of "career" mode, and in working part time from home. When one of us takes on a major project, the other one steps more into the parental role. So in this case, I paused my work while my husband was researching and writing his book. Then, the day after his book tour ended, we moved to another state so I could

> start my book research . . . We have learned the hard way that each switch creates new challenges and uncertainties. But it has allowed us to build "pauses" into our lives together.

For other couples, spiraling hasn't meant leaving the paid workforce, but rather taking turns with who serves as lead parent. Jodi Detjen works full-time as an author, a leadership consultant, and a professor of management for Suffolk University. But when her children were young, she downshifted her career to around twenty hours a week and became the number one parent. These days, it is her husband, Mark, who has taken the role of lead parent.

"My husband worked hard when our kids were younger and now that his career is more firmly established, it's his turn to have the chance to pick them up from school, be in charge of their various activities, and serve as the go-to parent. We've shifted parenting responsibilities back and forth over the years. It's been a win for the entire family," Jodi told me.

Spiraling requires a constant commitment to equality and a willingness to break traditional gender roles. For men like Richard, it means getting comfortable being the only guy in the "moms" group. For women like Molly, it means giving up control of the household. Conscious couples understand these challenges and proceed in ways that allow each partner to work, pause, and thrive.

CHAPTER 12

Money Matters, Plan Accordingly

"As long as you can handle the consequences, the time focused on your family is the best investment you will ever make."
—*Women on the Rise* survey respondent

One of the biggest gifts my parents gave me was the ability to graduate from college with no debt. But I didn't fully understand the power of that gift until I married my husband. Bill was the first in his family to graduate from college. His grandparents on both sides came from Italy. In fact, the name of one of his grandfathers can be found on a placard on Ellis Island. His father, a mechanic, and his mother, a secretary, gave everything they could to help their son succeed.

Bill entered college with scholarship money, financial aid, and a job working in the school cafeteria. During summers he worked as a house painter, an air-conditioning installer, and a busboy. The first job he had that was more reflective of his future professional life was when he worked as an intern at Analog Devices, a semiconductor company based outside of Boston. He didn't make much more than he did when he was a house painter, but at least it was a step in the direction of his eventual career in the tech industry.

As a child, Bill rarely traveled. When I met him, he didn't have a passport and had only once been on a plane. He fondly remembers the one big family vacation they went on when he was eleven. He, his two sisters, and his parents drove from Massachusetts to Disney World crammed together in their Chevy Impala, bickering over who got to sit next to the window. He loved that trip.

After college, Bill decided to get an advanced engineering degree and then went on to business school. Those seven years of education cost him (us) just over $300,000 in pre-tax money. We married the day before my twenty-fifth birthday and finally paid off those loans just before my thirty-fifth.

So you can understand what I mean when I say I truly know the power of the gift my parents gave me when they paid for my college education. My dream has always been to give that same gift to our three children. We've tallied it up and the pre-tax cost to send the three of them to a private college like the one Bill and I attended (including tuition, living expenses, travel back and forth, and the attendant hidden charges that surprise even the best financial planners) will run around $1,500,000(!).

I didn't think about that when I called my boss at the advertising agency to say I wouldn't be coming back. The first few years I worked as a freelance consultant I made as much as I did working full-time at the agency, but when I transitioned first to become a social entrepreneur and second to become a writer and journalist, my income plummeted. For over ten years, it didn't match what I made at my big agency job.

Paid sick leave? 401k? Disability insurance? I haven't had those since 1998. My ability to do what I do professionally rests fully on my husband's shoulders.

That is a lot of burden for one person to bear.

We live in Silicon Valley, home of the gazillionaires you read about with their Teslas and private jets. But for every rich guy whose good idea, hard work, perfect timing, and dollops of good luck landed him with more money than he could possibly throw away in a lifetime, there are thousands of men and women who are doing well, providing for their families, and still counting their pennies.

Bill and I were incredibly lucky to be part of the Dot Com era. He was at a start-up that was bought by Cisco Systems. That money allowed us to buy a home and build a life for our family. But the Great Recession hit us, as it did the rest of country, hard. Much of our savings suffered. The money we had set aside for our kids' college tuitions all but dried up. After careful thought, we have decided to downsize and sell the family home to pay for our children's education.

When I left my big job with the upwardly mobile salary and hefty benefits, I never imagined that one day I would be making this kind of trade-off. Yes, our children could get loans and financial aid, but Bill and I would rather give them the gift of financial freedom. Launching our children into their glittering futures with no debt versus continuing to live in a house that is too big with too much stuff in it? As far as we are concerned, it's an easy trade.

Please don't misread this as whining or complaining. I know I am incredibly lucky to even have a house to sell, and my children will be even luckier to not start their adult lives burdened with the weight of student debt. My broader point is that I didn't anticipate the financial consequences of my career choices. In fact, I didn't even think about them.

Bill and I could never have predicted the second largest stock market crash in history, nor how it would affect our financial well-being, but we are lucky we have options. Many women who leave their careers and don't properly plan for financial contingencies are not so lucky.

When we asked respondents of our *Women on the Rise* survey what advice they would give a younger colleague or their own child about pausing, a key sub-theme was "be prepared" because "life happens."

Connie Weisman can relate. She and I met when I moderated a panel on women who've paused and then re-entered the workforce. Like Bill, Connie came from a working-class Italian Catholic family. Her father was a police officer, her mother a homemaker. Connie dreamed of being a nurse. After she secured her degree, she worked at Cornell Medical Center. Soon Connie met her future husband, who was studying to be a doctor. They married and she followed him to New Haven where he embarked on a fellowship at Yale.

It turned out nursing wasn't a good professional fit, so Connie decided to try her hand at business. She secured a job working in the health care division at Marsh & McLennan, an insurance company. Connie flourished. When she and her husband moved out to California, her company happily transferred her. Not much later, Connie was recruited as vice president of business development for Arisco, a small insurance brokerage firm. Again she proved herself a star. Connie's career was flourishing.

When her first child was born, she negotiated a part-time schedule while maintaining her senior position. Like many of the other women I interviewed, Connie's "special" arrangement wasn't something the company broadcast and you'd never know from her LinkedIn profile she was working fewer than thirty hours a week. But the schedule worked for her and for her employer.

Even though she was working part-time, her career still flourished. In fact, while Connie was pregnant with her second child, she was aggressively recruited by a competitor to run the North America sales office. Connie turned it down. At that stage, she needed time and flexibility more than the additional money and a bigger job. Plus, she was loyal to her company. They had done right by her when she needed support.

It wasn't until her husband caught the entrepreneurial bug and launched a start-up that Connie decided to make a change. Rather than move back to full-time work as her company was asking her to do, she decided to leave the workforce altogether.

"My husband was traveling non-stop. I was pregnant with our third child. It was like I was a single mom trying to work and raise my kids. It was just too much," said Connie.

She stayed out of the paid workforce for seven years. Connie admits she may have never gone back. She was an active volunteer, managed her kids' soccer teams, and helped with school fundraising events. And then her husband's company failed. Not much later the marriage did, too. After all of that time, Connie now had to figure out how to support herself and her children.

"I hit bottom," said Connie, "a place I never imagined I'd be. It was humbling, but it gave me perspective. You can't sit at your kitchen table and boo-hoo your life. You have to get on with it."

She took a job in retail at Pottery Barn just to get back into the work world. She'd gone from vice president to cashier, and the new job was so far below her previous career as to be, as Connie told me, "laughable." But, it gave her confidence. She could manage the kids' schedules, get to work, be productive, and make money again even if her salary was the same as her caregiver's.

"That initial job was exactly what I needed to get me back in the groove. I wouldn't recommend it for everyone, but it worked for me," Connie said.

A part-time job at Pottery Barn wasn't the end goal for Connie; it was a stepping stone. When she was ready to be all-in, she reached out to her network and asked for help.

"The husband of a friend of mine was starting a company. He knew me from my days as the manager of my daughter's soccer team. He said he was confident I would be a great employee because I was organized, collaborative, and always got things done. We negotiated an hourly job as a recruiter for his new company, an incubator for technology start-ups. I knew nothing about recruiting or about high tech. But that CEO took a risk on me. I'll be forever grateful," Connie said.

Within months, Connie proved herself indispensable and was quickly promoted. Now, she is the director of Strategic Partnerships & Community Development for Plug and Play Tech Center, a job she said is perfect for her skills and interests.

"While I don't regret the years I spent at home with my children, if there is one thing I have learned in my life, it's that money matters, so plan accordingly."

Connie's story is rich in so many ways, but at its heart, it's a cautionary tale of the importance of planning for the worst. In reality, pausing without a financial plan is, well, so 1990s. When it comes to money management, the women I interviewed and surveyed offered the following as things they wish they had done or considered before they downshifted their careers.

DO A PROFORMA

Guy Kawasaki, the original Apple evangelist and modern-day start-up guru, calls children "the ultimate startup. And when they leave for college, it's their IPO. And when they get married, it's an M & A deal. And like most startups, these milestones usually take longer and cost more than you predicted."[258]

I raised my children in the heart of Silicon Valley, so start-up analogies are hard to avoid, but Guy is right. Crass as it may sound, it's not so outlandish to think of your family as a business and your children as the products. Like any business, you have income and expenses, assets and liabilities, profits and losses. I'm not talking about the intangibles of love and worry and care. I'm talking real money here. To determine if you (or your partner) can afford to leave the paid workforce, I recommend doing an eighteen-year pro forma to assess the financial implications. This will help you both decide if one of you can truly can afford to pause and, if so, for how long.

1) Run the Numbers: Consider the Real Cost of Raising a Child

Look, we all know children are expensive and the costs of raising them doesn't stop when they are eighteen, but you need to start somewhere. The U.S. Department of Agriculture has been tracking the cost of raising a child since 1960.[259] The data, which includes food, housing, child care, and education, is used by state governments to determine child support guidelines and foster care payments. As of 2013, the U.S. Department of Agriculture estimates it will cost $304,480[260] (adjusted for projected inflation) to raise a child from birth to eighteen. That's around $17,000 a year.

Seventeen thousand dollars a year? Perhaps in some parts of the country, but in California where I raised my kids, child care alone runs around $12,000.[261] And, what about the thousands of dollars you'll spend on their "enrichment" programs such as art class, summer camp, soccer club fees, piano lessons, tutoring, braces . . . the list goes on and on. Then they hit high school, and there is a myriad of big and little ways you'll blow your well-intentioned budget: "All my friends have a phone." "No one I know pays for gas when they drive the car, their parents do." "Everyone's got a private college counselor, why can't I get one?" My guess is that for many families who want to give their children the "best" foundation for success, the annual costs will be much, much higher. I know ours were.

And what about college itself? Well, the USDA doesn't take that into account. As I shared, for our three children, college alone will cost us around $1,500,000 before taxes. If you plan to send your children to college, an eighteen-year pro forma is not enough, but it is a good place to start. You can use the USDA's Cost of Raising a Child Calculator to help you get a sense of the estimated expenses. You'll be shocked at how quickly they add up.[262]

In your financial planning as you and your partner consider the implications of living on one salary for a period of time, ask yourself if you have the resources to cover your expenses. Can you really afford to live on one salary? If yes, for how long? And, what are the long-term financial implications if you do pause your career?

For the vast majority of women we surveyed, a two-year break was doable. Beyond five years and they were forced to make major life changes such as downsizing or significantly reducing their lifestyle, or they were part of the One Percent.

Yes, they are adorable and worth every penny, but don't deny the reality of how much it will cost to raise your children. Do a pro forma that takes into account the full breadth of these expenses and then plan accordingly.

> In your financial planning as you and your partner consider the implications of living on one salary for a period of time, ask yourself if you have the resources to cover your expenses. Can you really live on one salary? If yes, for how long? And, what are the long-term financial implications if you do pause your career?

2) Run the Numbers Again: Child Care Is a Joint Expense

In 2000, when Lisa Tankersley and her husband sat down with their accountant to review their family finances, he told them the high cost of day care was putting an undue burden on their bottom line.

Lisa was a project manager at a telecommunications start-up. The financial rewards were not in the salary at hand but in the hoped-for bonus that would come when the company was either acquired or went on the public stock exchange. Meanwhile, her husband was an engineer at a semiconductor company. His job was stable, the benefits were good, and, at that time, he made more than she did.

When I interviewed Lisa, she said, "The accountant told me, 'It's probably not worth it for you to work,' and I believed him." Her voice cracked with anger, indignation, and self-reproach as she spoke.

In hindsight, Lisa said she was shocked the accountant didn't discuss the long-term financial implications of leaving the workforce. He didn't suggest alternative ways the family could cut expenses during the burdensome preschool years. He didn't recommend she find a more lucrative job at another company. He looked at their tax returns and told them her salary was not worth the cost.

The truth is the accountant, her husband, and Lisa herself viewed her career as secondary even though she was working as many hours as her husband and the theoretical upside was potentially much greater given she was working in the high-risk, high-reward start-up world. As a result, the cost of child care was compared against *her* salary, not half against his and half against hers.

Couples make children together. The cost of caring for those children should be spread across both incomes, not against the income of one member of that relationship. But in the vast majority of cases, that is not how couples do the accounting. The cost of child care is measured against the mother's salary, rather than against the salaries of *both* parents, when determining what changes, if any, need to be made in terms of work–life integration

We know two things. First, women are much more likely to be making less than their male spouses. Oh yes, we've heard that 40 percent of wives are primary breadwinners. But that's ALL wives, not college-educated wives married to college-educated husbands. In the professional world, where a college degree is usually required, fathers are still likely to be the primary breadwinners.

Second, we know that despite decades of collective effort and great books like *Getting to 50/50: How Working Parents Can Have It All* that offer tools and strategies for, well, getting to 50/50 when it comes to housework and child care, women still bear the burden of being the *perceived* primary parent. When couples look at their finances, they are often likely to look at the salary of the wife as the one that offsets child care expenses. Many, like Lisa, her husband, and their accountant, assume the mother is the one who would otherwise be caring for the children.

Even if you can't get beyond the notion that your salary is the one that should cover the cost of child care, don't forget to consider your future child care needs. Unless you are planning to never return to work again, the notion that leaving because child care costs are too high obscures the reality that those costs don't go away. And, when you do return to work, you'll still need child care because standard school hours, holidays, and summer vacation means children will be unsupervised for extended periods of time.

Plus, if you have more than one child and you wait until they are in school, then depending on how many children you have, you could be out for more than a decade. A choice, but one that, as we have seen, makes it all the more challenging to relaunch into the paid workforce. Reducing your child care expenses by quitting your job is one solution, but consider the financial consequences before you decide to do so.

Finally, remember that old adage that how you spend your money reflects what you value? If we want men to take more responsibility in doing the care, shouldn't we expect them to take more responsibility in paying for the care? Until we do, they will continue to view their role as helper, not equal partner. Make sure your partner puts his money where it matters and he applies his salary 50/50 to the cost of care of the children you two are raising.

Your career is as important to the family's well-being as your partner's, even if he is making more money at this moment. Spread the expense of child care across both salaries when you do your pro forma and then decide if it is truly "not worth it" for you to work.

> Couples make children together. The cost of caring for those children should be spread across both incomes, not against the income of one member of that relationship.

3) Run the Numbers: Consider the Long-Term Cost of Leaving

When I left the paid workforce, I never took into consideration what the real cost of leaving would mean for my personal bottom line. Frankly, even if I had considered it, it would have been hard to truly calculate. Not anymore.

Michael Madowitz, an economist for the think tank Center for American Progress, and his wife were trying to determine the financial implications of a career pause. He was astounded to discover there were no systems to conduct this analysis, so he created a net price calculator that includes the cost of lost wages, lost wage growth, and lost retirement and benefits when one leaves the workforce to care for children.[263]

The result: The average American woman taking a five-year break from her career starting at age twenty-six will lose out on $467,000. The average American man of the same age will lose $596,000. He loses more because he earns more and his lifetime earning potential is higher, which explains why so many couples decide it makes more sense for the woman to pause her career.

I plugged in my data. I was making just over $100,000 when I left my job in advertising at the age of thirty-five. If I had stayed out five years, I would have lost $590,000 in actual income and $1,600,000 in potential income (!). That's a lot of money that I and my family could have used.

Of course, as Sachi DeCou noted when I posted the net price calculator of a pause on my LinkedIn page, "The decision to stay home and take care of children isn't purely a financial one," but not understanding the financial implications of your choices is, well, not very smart. I should know; I didn't understand them.

Don't make my mistake. Check out the net price calculator at http://interactives.americanprogress.org/childcarecosts/ and decide if the income loss from pausing for parenthood is a trade-off you are willing to make.

4) Run the Numbers Again: Child Care Is a Career Tool

As I have previously shared, for the 186 women I personally interviewed and the 1,476 who responded to the *Women on the Rise* survey, the number one piece of advice they offered was "stay in the game." They didn't necessarily mean don't pause; they meant keep your industry knowledge up to date, volunteer in ways that build your skills and are advantageous to your re-entry, and, perhaps most important, stay connected to your professional network. But doing all of this takes time away from caring for your children.

Many of the women I spoke to who had volunteer leadership positions that enabled them to stay engaged professionally found that they were working nearly as hard as if they had full-time jobs. Alison Cormack who raised millions of dollars for her town's library foundation worked nights and weekends in her role as chairwoman of the foundation. She had child care because she could not have done her unpaid job without it.

Sharon Meers believes one of the smartest things a woman who pauses her career can do is to keep her child care arrangement or to secure one before she pauses if she doesn't already have one in place. As I shared in chapter 2, Sharon left her big job at Goldman Sachs, decided to use her time away from her full-time job to write a book, and then pivoted to the tech industry. Throughout it all, she never gave up child care.

"It's about human capital," Sharon told me over coffee one day. "I valued my contribution and therefore it made sense for the five years I was not working full-time to keep the same support systems in place. I shared the cost of household help and child care with my husband. I didn't consider it a luxury. I considered it a requirement for my future career."

Before you just dismiss this as a solution for the One Percent, think about it: It's true most of us can't afford to keep our child care situation while we lose an income. But if you consider your pause as a temporary blip in the lifetime arc of your career AND if you and your partner recognize that child care is a shared expense, not just something to be docked against your salary alone, then it might just make sense to keep some type of care, even if only part-time, available to you.

I know of women who've traded care with other mothers, switching days on a regular basis so they could each devote part of their time to volunteering and/or skill development. I've heard of others who've pooled their money and hired a caregiver a few days a week to give them freedom. I have heard of still others who have used drop-in day care at their local YMCA or gym. The reason smart women who pause use child care isn't so they can perfect their yoga pose; it's so they can use the time to commit to activities that keep them relevant and employable while they're out of the paid workforce.

Consider maintaining some sort of child care while you pause so you can be sure to continue to keep your career alive and well.

Consider maintaining some sort of child care while you pause so you can be sure to continue to keep your career alive and well.

5) Run the Numbers Again: Your Value Is More than Your Replacement Cost

My friend, Deb, and I have a joke. "How much is a mother worth?" one of us will ask.

"Priceless," the other responds and we guffaw at the deep truth and the deep deception of that punch line.

In actuality, valuing a mother's worth is no laughing matter.

Back in the mid-2000s when the world was scandalized by all of those well-educated women who were "opting out," a series of articles started touting the "real value" of motherhood. Feminist economists tried to evaluate the replacement cost of the stay-at-home mother. Now, without fail, each May you'll see some insulting article touting the Mother's Day Index.[264]

As of 2015, the Mother's Day Index based on a compilation of tasks from the U.S. Bureau of Labor, lists the annual salary of stay-at-home mothers as $65,283. That assumes the position is salaried. If the wage was hourly and included overtime pay, SAHMs would be making more than double that. Great pay, if you can get it.

However, those Mother's Day Index calculations are based on replacement cost. In other words, they trade in one person for the entire tribe it would take to replace her in today's dollars. You know, the cost of hiring a nanny, a housekeeper, a chauffeur, a financial analyst, a tutor, a chef, a party planner, and so on. But this subsumes the real issue. It's not the value to the family that truly matters when a woman pauses her career; it's her value to herself. In other words, what's most important is the cost to her opportunity when leaving the paid work world.

If you spent the first twenty-five years of your life and hundreds of thousands of dollars getting a college education, then spent the next decade or more applying your skills and knowledge in the paid workforce, by the time you pause your career, the issue isn't your value today, but the future earnings you forgo.

A 2004 longitudinal study of male and female workers by Stephen J. Rose of Rose Economic Consulting and Heidi Hartmann of the Institute for Women's Policy Research revealed that "when actual earnings are accumulated over many years . . . the losses to women and their families due to the wage gap are large and can be devastating." Their research revealed that over the fifteen years of the study the average man earned $722,693, while the average woman earned only $273,592, a gap of 62 percent. Even acknowledging the reality that women tend to work in lower-paying professions (nursing, teaching) and that even in the same jobs we know women face a pay gap, the authors concluded the biggest hit came because of the "continued unequal division of family labor, with women having to make most of the adjustments of time in the labor market to perform family work."[265] In other words, they found that the biggest contributor to the lifetime wage gap between men and women is due to the fact that women move in and out of the paid workforce.

Lisa Tankersley knows this only too well. When they decided it was not "worth it" for her to work, they didn't take into account the long-term benefits of having Lisa stay in the workforce. As she was relatively new to her career, it is likely she would have been promoted and made more money. Given the high need for well-trained talent in the frothy start-up world, Lisa's experience may well have been transferable to other start-ups. Along the way, she would also have been contributing to her retirement via her 401k and Social Security.

Fast forward to 2016: Lisa, who didn't collect a paycheck for years, is struggling to find a full-time job. She's patching together part-time work until she can land something better. Because she is divorced, she has no one to provide backup financial support while she tries to relaunch her career. Meanwhile, she has little saved for retirement and, because unpaid child care is not measured and counted as labor by our government, she has earned nothing toward her Social Security benefits since she left her telecommunications job.

"I try to stay optimistic, but the reality is I'm living with the consequences of that bad advice," Lisa told me. If she could do it again, she says she would have paused for a year or two and then re-entered when her children were slightly older and the job market was booming again.

It is these stories of woe that permeate the national media. And there is a reason for it. Things will go wrong. You will face unexpected obstacles. You will, most likely, need a job at some point in the future. Pausing may seem like a brilliant solution at the moment, but consider your risk tolerance and plan accordingly. While my research has shown an alternative narrative for women who take extended pauses—that they can and do relaunch successfully—the reality is that being one of the long-term unemployed can make relaunching difficult. Only you can decide if the professional and financial risk is worth the personal reward.

Your worth is more than what you are making today. When you run the numbers, consider your lost future earnings and then decide if you can truly afford to pause *and* for how long.

Your worth is more than what you are making today. When you run the numbers, consider your lost future earnings and then decide if you can truly afford to pause *and* for how long.

VALUE YOUR LIFE

As you saw in chapter 4, we don't count women's unpaid work in our GDP. This means there are no governmental safeguards for your retirement or to support you and your family in the event of illness or death. Since no one else will value your human capital as an unpaid caregiver, you must, which means you need to give special consideration to the long-term financial implications of stepping away from the paid workforce. Much as we may want Prince Charming to magically solve our problems, only you can take care of you. The following will help protect you if you do choose to pause your career.

1) Plan for Your Retirement

OK, so you've run the numbers and have decided you can pause. What's your strategy for taking care of the wise old woman you will become? Or, more specifically, the wise old widow (or divorcée) you are unfortunately likely to become? The average life expectancy for American men is seventy-six years. For American women, it is eighty-one years.[266] According to a 2014 Gallup poll, the average age Americans expect to retire is sixty-six, but the average age they actually do retire is closer to sixty-two.[267] Based on the average, you're likely to live about twenty years after the last paycheck comes in.

What does it mean if that paycheck has come in only intermittently in the forty or so years before you retire? What does it mean if that paycheck is part-time or from freelance gigs that don't allow the worker to have access to a company savings plan? For women, it means that we aren't saving enough.

A 2014 Vanguard study revealed that men have average and median retirement account balances that are 50 percent higher than that of women's.[268] According to a 2014 article in *The Atlantic*, data from Fidelity Investments' 13.6 million participants tell a similar story: "While men have an average 401(k) account balance of $98,700, women lag at $67,400."[269] This is largely because men earn more money more consistently over time, but this also happens because most women don't set money aside for their retirement while they are pausing.

If you do choose to pause, value your future self and continue to plan for your retirement. When I paused, I promptly set up a Roth IRA. I transferred all of the retirement savings I had accrued through my various full-time jobs into the account. Since then, I have consistently put the highest allowable amount each year into my IRA. On those years when I did not earn any income, I still transferred money to my account. Yes, that money came from my husband's salary, but we valued my unpaid contribution to the family and paid into my retirement accordingly. I hope we both live a long time and die together, preferably in our sleep on the same night. But, I know the statistics are against me on that one, and while I joke with my children that I plan to move in with them once their dad is gone, I'd rather do it because I *choose* to, not because I *have* to.

2) Get Life Insurance

I was dismayed to learn from a close friend that while her husband has a hefty life insurance policy that will ensure she is very, very well cared for if he were to pass away, she didn't have a policy at all.

"What if you died first?" I asked her. "How will your husband support the family while he is grieving? What if he doesn't want to return to work for a period of time so he can care for your children?"

I know of what I speak. My neighbor and friend lost his wife to a lengthy battle against breast cancer. He was heartbroken and his kids were inconsolable. He chose to pause his career while he and his sons grieved. It was the right choice for him. He has since remarried to a remarkable woman, and now his sons are all off to college. But while it all looks rosy now, he will tell you it was painful and hard at the time and that those years that he paused were essential to his family's well-being. He needed financial security during those years and was lucky enough to have planned accordingly.

The Life Insurance Marketing and Research Association reports that, as of 2015, only 52 percent of American women have life insurance and when they do their policies are likely to be 31 percent lower in terms of dollar coverage than men's.[270] Nilufer Ahmed, senior research director for the research association, said in an article in the *Omaha World-Herald* that wives are more likely than husbands to be underinsured or to not have life insurance at all.

"There's still the whole idea that if I don't earn an income, maybe I shouldn't be buying insurance, or there's less of an impetus to buy," Nilufer said.[271]

My neighbor would likely tell you that is a horrible mistake. Remember that old Mother's Day Index? Your replacement value in the case of your untimely death truly does have a significant financial impact on your family.

3) Don't Forget Disability Insurance

Look, it may be that you will never pause your career. But if you do plan to have kids, you'll want, at the very least, to have maternity leave after they're born. Unless you are one of the 13 percent of Americans who work for a company that provides paid leave or you're lucky enough to live in one of the three states that offers it, you're basically out of luck.

The only option you have then is to get short-term disability insurance (STDI). These insurance programs typically cover a six-month period and replace some of the wages lost by people who cannot work because of a disabling injury or illness that is not work-related.

Don't get me started on why maternity leave is considered a disabling event that requires insurance. How could it be that 50 percent of the population is considered disabled and therefore needs insurance when they give birth to the next generation? And yet, that's how our paltry maternity leave system has been set up. As a result, the vast majority of women must purchase disability insurance if they want to be financially covered for maternity leave. Men? They can't get disability insurance for paternity leave because they're not "disabled" by the birth of their new child. However, men can purchase disability insurance to cover their wives during maternity leave.

Most companies with more than 100 employees offer STDI as a benefit, but only 39 percent of employees who are eligible and who work at these companies take advantage of it. This means that either the remaining 61 percent weren't women in their prime child-bearing years, weren't husbands of women in their child-bearing years, or didn't realize the benefit's importance for getting paid while out on maternity leave.

There is some concerning evidence that the next generation of potential parents aren't valuing the STDI benefit. The 2014 Hartford Millennial survey[272] revealed that over half of respondents thought STDI was "nice to have" but not a deal breaker when it came to choosing where to work. It may be those respondents were men, since they really aren't the primary beneficiary of short-term disability insurance. However, since men can get coverage for their wives under their policy it is more, much more than a "nice to have."

Many employees forgo this benefit because they would prefer to optimize their take-home pay. Big mistake. If your company offers it and children are in your future, sign up for it. It may cost you a modest amount each month, but it can save you thousands in the end. If your company doesn't offer it or you're a gig employee, consider buying into a group plan offered by AAA or your alumni association.

Smart financial planning means you value yourself. Invest in your future and don't ignore the importance of getting the right insurance for yourself and your family. Why? Because you're worth it.

SHARE THE FINANCIAL BURDEN

We've all heard the statistic that 50 percent of marriages end in divorce. Did you know the statistics are completely different if you graduated from college? The truth is eight out of ten college-educated women can expect their marriages to last at least twenty years.[273] Those that don't? It's most often money that kills the vibe.

In her study, "Examining the Relationship Between Financial Issues and Divorce,"[274] Sonya Britt, a Kansas State University researcher, reviewed data from 4,500 households. The research revealed that arguments about money lasted longer and were more intense than other types of disagreements between spouses.

Sonya said, "Arguments about money [are] by far the top predictor of divorce. It's not children, sex, in-laws, or anything else. It's money—for both men and women."[275]

So, if you want to stay married, you and your partner need to get on the same page when it comes to money. One way to do that is to share the burden of breadwinning. The reality is pausing does not share the financial burden. Yes, you may become the one that is responsible for the family obligations, but your partner will be the one who has to continue with the paid work grind. He has to make sure money is coming in to clothe, feed, and house you and your children.

Today, many of the Millennial men I spoke to told me they are finding themselves in breadwinner roles they didn't expect or necessarily want. Why? Because their partners are leaving the paid workforce to be the primary caregivers for their kids. Which is fine if those roles, and the consequences of taking on those roles, are what you and your partner want. Not so fine if you each aren't willing to be fully responsible for the paths you have chosen. You need to be clear, very clear, that you *both* agree this is the right thing to do. If not, you may find yourself in a traditionally gendered marriage that doesn't work for either of you.

Also, make sure you both are willing to risk your long-term financial well-being should the unexpected occur, for the short-term gain of having one of you at home with your children. If he loses his job or in some way cannot deliver financially, are you both willing to accept the financial consequences? If not, you may find yourself in a situation you never imagined you would be: divorced.

Taking a pause is not without risks and only you can decide if the risk is worth the reward. But if you do decide to pause your career, as Connie Weisman cautioned, "money matters, plan accordingly."

CONCLUSION

United We Stand

"It takes more than a village. It takes an army."
—*Women on the Rise* survey respondent

So here we are. Much like that rollicking plane I rode all those years ago when I was pregnant and my future was unknowable, I have landed safely. As I write the conclusion of this book, my children are well on their way to being independent adults. After years of the push-me, pull-me of work–life imbalance, I can again be fully engaged in my career without the constant distractions of having children at home. Looking back, only now do I see that the answer to that issue of "balance" isn't trying to have it, but knowing that the imbalance we feel at any given moment is temporary. Careers are long; pauses are short. I couldn't be more excited about what is ahead.

And yet, as I have shared, I do have regrets. One stands out above them all: I've spent the last few decades hunkered down, focused on my own issues, worrying unceasingly about how I alone could navigate the challenges of work and life. Meanwhile, in the more than twenty years since I became a mother, as I obsessed in my personal silo, we as a nation have not moved the needle on how we support families. And like our government, I did nothing to help.

The long list of strategies and ideas I uncovered as I wrote this book are solutions that may help relieve work–life integration for women who are college-educated and privileged with resources that can enable them to find personal solutions. But there are many more millions of American women who do not have the resources or support they need to overcome their burdens. The daily challenges of trying to support their families in a system that dismisses the realities of caregiving are heartbreaking. So while this book was written for women like me, in writing it, I have come to see we desperately need solutions that work for *all* Americans.

I've said it before and I'll say it again: It is shameful that our country does not offer its citizens paid parental leave, paid sick leave, and universal child care. We are better than this. I take ownership for my role in letting our country abandon its citizens. You can, too.

Ask yourself: Do we want women (who are generally tasked with being the primary caretakers) to be prevented from bringing their talents, experiences, and skills to the workforce as fully as they are able? Do we want men to be locked into the role of primary breadwinner and miss the chance to be fully engaged fathers?

And this isn't just about our fulfillment as individuals. Do we want our economy to suffer because one-half of the population is handicapped by a culture that doesn't allow them to be fully engaged? Do we want our country to fall behind other industrialized nations because of outdated models of employment and old-fashioned ideologies of what it means to be a parent? Put simply, if we want to remain competitive as a nation, how we work has to change.

We can argue about working mothers and stay-at-home mothers and One Percent mothers and welfare mothers, but all of that arguing doesn't get us the solutions we collectively need. Rather than privilege our differences, we need to come together to find solutions that can work for all of us.

Anthropologist Margaret Mead is famously quoted as saying, "It takes a village to raise a child." Today, we need more than a village; we need an army. It's time to start fighting for the rights of the next generation, because if we don't, women's careers won't be the only thing that suffer. Our country will, too.

The following are recommendations for how we can begin to support the women, the men, and the families of America. It starts with you.

Rather than privilege our differences, we need to come together to find solutions that can work for all of us.

WHAT CAN I DO?

Recognize: *Caregiving is about more than just me and my family.*
Reframe: *I have a responsibility to advocate for under-resourced families and to help other women so we all can thrive.*

Be an Advocate for Paid Parental Leave

We know we have a growing class divide in our country. Paid leave may well be a powerful antidote.

The United States is one of two developed countries that does not offer government-sponsored paid maternity leave. Sure, the Family and Medical Leave Act gives nearly 40 percent of workers access to (unpaid) leave, but the vast majority don't take the leave offered to them because they can't afford the loss of income.[276] As a result, nearly 65 percent of workers who qualify do not take the full leave they are eligible for under FMLA[277] and over one-quarter of new mothers take no more than two weeks off after the birth of a child.

What does that mean over the long term? It means these already under-resourced women are exhausted and can't function properly in their jobs. It means they often eventually lose those jobs or have to quit because they literally cannot afford to keep working. One of the fastest-growing groups of stay-at-home moms are those below the poverty line. In fact, today over 30 percent of mothers who are unemployed are those at the bottom rungs of the economic ladder. These women have made it clear they want to work, but they need support to enable them to do so. Paid parental leave is the place to start to ensure they have the foundation they need to stay engaged in the workforce.

Of those women who do have paid leave, for most it's the luck of location. If you live in California, New Jersey, New York, or Rhode Island, you can get some measure of compensation after the birth (or adoption) of your child, but it is only half of your salary and only for about six weeks. In 2002, California became the first state to guarantee paid family leave, followed by New Jersey in 2008, Rhode Island in 2013, and New York in 2016. While the California, New Jersey, and Rhode Island programs are all in effect already, New York's will take effect on January 1, 2018.[278] Washington state has also passed a paid family leave law, but the implementation has been delayed.

In other countries, paid leave is funded through taxes, which means the entire country is supporting mothers as they give birth to the next generation. In each of three states that currently offer it, the paid family leave program is part of the state's existing temporary disability insurance system. Employees finance the paid family leave program through payroll deductions. So the leave is paid for by the individual worker herself—with the help of her employer if she is lucky enough to work for one of the few companies that do offer paid leave. But leave is not financed by the population as whole.

In most cases, the companies that do offer paid leave are bigger, more established firms. Deloitte, PWC, Coca-Cola, and many of the other Fortune 500 companies have offered paid leave for years, typically in the six-week to three-month range. Recently, the tech industry has been garnering headlines for offering paid parental leaves of up to a year. A nice gig if you can get it, but remember the numbers: Only 13 percent of private-sector workers have access to paid leave in the United States.[279] So, well-educated, well-paid mothers and fathers who work for big companies have it good. The rest are in dire straits.

This has to change. We need a national policy. Sadly, the powers that be in Congress have little will to make progress on this issue (or on many other issues, for that matter). Because of congressional gridlock, local municipalities are beginning to take up the call to arms regarding paid parental leave. In Washington, D.C., in 2015, city council member Elissa Silverman introduced the Universal Paid Leave Act. It provides sixteen weeks of paid leave funded largely by a 1 percent payroll tax on private-sector employers in the city. The law continues to languish and has yet to pass.

In June 2016, San Francisco voters passed a proposed paid leave plan to require employers with more than twenty employees to cover the difference between what the state pays and the individual's full salary. Beginning in January 2017, companies who operate in San Francisco will be required to offer their employees the additional 45 percent that is currently not covered under the state's disability law, which currently covers 55 percent for six weeks. Full pay for six weeks is not enough, but it is far better than what the vast majority of workers have.

These are just two examples of local governments trying to solve the problem our national or state governments refuse to address. It's a step in the right direction, but it's obviously not nearly enough. We need an army of one-issue activists.

The good news is we've already got one in the making. In 2006, Joan Blades and Kristin Rowe-Finkbeiner published the *Motherhood Manifesto*, in which they wrote, "Despite all the media chatter about the so-called Opt-Out Revolution—and all the hand-wringing about whether working moms are good for kids—women, and mothers, are in the workplace to stay. Yet public policy and workplace structures have yet to catch up."[280]

Joan and Kristin didn't stop there. They recognized the need for collective action, so they gathered a team together and founded MomsRising, a non-partisan group determined to change public policy for families in this country. Since inception, MomsRising has garnered more than 1 million members who collectively advocate to improve how caregivers are treated in this country. Now MomsRising has partnered with PL+US (Paid Leave for the U.S.), a grassroots organization with one goal in mind: to secure universal paid leave in this country.

Join MomsRising and PL+US to help make a difference for all families. While you are at it, lobby your city, state, and federal politicians to ensure they understand the importance of this issue. Paid parental leave for both women and men is the single biggest way we can enable women to stay in the workforce. When fathers take paternity leave, their partners are less likely to quit their jobs and the dads are more likely to be engaged with their kids over the long haul. Good for children, good for women, good for men, good for the workplace. Seems so obvious, doesn't it?

Help Under-Resourced Mothers

Ensuring mothers have time to bond with their new babies is one way of empowering them to stay engaged in the workforce; so is providing those in need with daily essentials. If you're a new parent, you're probably as shocked as I was by the high cost of diapers these days. Did you know that providing one child with regular changes through potty-training (which typically occurs around the age of three) can cost as much as $3,000—a burdensome expense for many and a devastating expense for the 46 million people living in poverty today.

Inexplicably, public assistance programs like food stamps and Special Supplemental Nutrition Program for Women, Infants, and Children (WIC) benefits can't be used for diapers. Shockingly, they are dubbed "non-essential" items and get grouped with pet food, cigarettes, and alcohol. Meanwhile, most child care facilities require parents to supply diapers for their children and reusable cloth diapers aren't usually allowed. So what's an under-resourced mother to do? It's a classic Catch 22: Here you are trying to support your family, but you can't afford the very diapers that will allow you to drop your baby off at day care so you can actually go to work and support your family.

Lisa Truong had always been passionate about social causes and had built her career working in nonprofit management, but it was after the birth of her second child when she decided to take a pause that she became aware of this issue. She told me, "I believe every mother who wants (or needs) to work should have the support and resources to do so. When I discovered that something as basic as diapers was keeping women from providing for their families, well I knew I had to get involved."

And get involved she did. Lisa (in partnership with another stay-at-home mother) started a nonprofit called Help a Mother Out. Their mission is simple: provide free diapers to any mother in need. Since its inception in 2010, her nonprofit has partnered with companies like Huggies and the National Diaper Bank Network to deliver 3 million diapers to more than 10,000 women.

Lisa argues, "It's not just about diapers, it's about breaking the cycle of poverty. By helping these mothers with a practical solution, we are not only giving them the opportunity for economic empowerment, we are giving them dignity."

When I asked Lisa if she felt it was ironic that a "stay-at-home mother" is helping other mothers to work, she said, "Yes, but isn't that the point? We mothers have to support each other to do what we feel is right for us and our families. If something as basic as diapers is holding you back, let's work together to get rid of that barrier."

Lisa's efforts are showing real results. In 2015, California Assemblywoman Lorena Gonzalez introduced AB 1516, the first bill in the entire country that would help families who receive welfare benefits pay for diapers. It gives families who qualify for CalWORKS, the state's welfare program, $50 a month for the necessity. An estimated 120,000 children would get the assistance. The bill was passed in August 2016. Other states are considering similar solutions.

We can't all become warriors for change on the same scale as Lisa, but we can all consider what an under-resourced mother needs and find a way to help her. Donations to programs like Help a Mother Out is a start. Lobbying your city and state politicians to get diapers included as a welfare benefit is another way to get involved. If we truly want to help an under-resourced woman be engaged in the workforce, something as simple as providing her children with diapers can make all the difference.

Be Authentic About Your Path

Groups like Help a Mother Out show there are many ways we can be of service to under-resourced mothers, but one big way we can help *all* women is to be authentic about our own journeys and choices. Those who are just now embarking on motherhood need to know how the women before them did it. The myth of the woman who "does it all" serves no one. The truth of women who didn't do it all (at least not all at once) but who still fashioned rewarding careers while fully owning their passion for and commitment to family along the way are the stories all of us need to hear.

That's exactly what motivated Kathryn Rotondo to launch her podcast, *The Motherboard*. When she returned to her job as a software developer after giving birth to her son, Max, she struggled with the re-entry. She had had emergency gall bladder surgery seven weeks after her son was born and spent most of her unpaid maternity leave trying to recover. When she went back to work three months after Max was born, she was forced to pump her breast milk in a unisex bathroom without a lock. There was only one other woman at her small company and no women on the technical side. And, since she was one of the first amongst her friends to have a child, Kathryn had no one to turn to for guidance and advice. It all became too much, and she soon developed postpartum depression.

Then she was asked to speak at a tech conference. Kathryn was one of two women on the dais. She knew the other woman, also a developer, was a new mom, so Kathryn asked her how she was handling it all. This other woman explained she had negotiated a part-time schedule to ease her transition back in.

"It was like the clouds parted and the angels started singing," Kathryn told me. "I had no idea that was even an option. I promptly went back to my manager and asked for a reduced scheduled. He readily agreed and suddenly my life changed. I would have never known what was available to me if I hadn't bumped into that other new mom."

It was that feeling of isolation and craving for shared wisdom that inspired Kathryn to start *The Motherboard* podcast in 2013. She has since interviewed scores of women about their journeys and won a "Systers Pass-It-On" award from the Anita Borg Institute for her efforts. She has thousands of listeners who tune in to the podcast to find comfort and guidance.

"We need to be authentic about how hard this is and we need to share our stories so others can know they are not alone," Kathryn said.

She's right. If I had known that women who, from the outside, looked like they "had it all" were also struggling to figure out how to integrate work and family, I wouldn't have harbored so much self-doubt or felt so much anxiety, and I would have had more confidence about my career journey. When we hear the non-linear career stories of everyday women like Kathryn Rotundo, of trailblazers like venture capitalist Patricia Nakache, of celebrated entrepreneurs like Tory Burch, and of august change-makers like Supreme Court Justice Sandra Day O'Connor, we come to see that we too can work, pause, and thrive. Their journeys reveal how they honored their commitment to their family and their careers and give us confidence that we too might realize a life that allows us to have "it all," whatever our personal "all" might be.

Radio journalist Amy Westervelt wrote a hilarious essay in the *Huffington Post* called "Having It All Kinda Sucks." She detailed how she was barely keeping it together after the birth of her second child. Dishes in the sink, laundry stacked in the corner, dinner nowhere to be had. Amy was damn proud of herself for being able to hide her new motherhood from clients while working remotely from home, but her "aha" moment came when she realized that, in an effort to "have it all," she'd negated her son's life. In the essay Amy wrote,

> Let's redefine "having it all," or better yet let each woman define for herself what the best version of her life might look like. Because when you think about it, reflecting back on the first month of my son's life and reveling in what a good job I'd done at covering up the fact that he exists is pretty fucking sad.[281]

Yes, it is. It's tragic when we have to deny our motherhood to appear professional. How can we be fully authentic if we deny this essential part of who we are all in an effort to meet some outmoded concept of success? It is way past time we women stopped denying our families and hiding the true narrative of our career journeys to look like we "have it all." Let's show our life paths for what they are: non-linear, nontraditional, and fully our own.

We need to let the world know: This is what *my* success looks like.

Pay It Backward (and Forward)

Another way to make a difference for moms and families is to mentor, advocate for, and hire women who have paused their careers. As I learned from my many interviews and from the respondents to the *Women on the Rise* survey, the reasons a woman leaves the paid workforce are manifold. Let's not waste their time or ours by needlessly judging them. Let's help them get back into the paid workforce so their talents can be used to help our businesses, economy, and country grow.

Remember Diane Flynn, the chief marketing officer of GSVlabs? She was so passionate about supporting other women to relaunch their careers that she co-founded ReBoot Accelerator. It's a program that works to ensure women who have paused have the technical savvy to interact with those who have not left the paid workforce. Their motto: Current, Confident, Connected.

As I have shared, ReBoot Accelerator is just one of a number of programs committed to ensuring women who have paused their careers can relaunch. Carol Fishman Cohen, CEO and co-founder of iRelaunch, was the trailblazer in this area. Her company offers conferences and online training to women who are ready to reengage. Carol also championed the notion of return-to-work internships and, because of her advocacy, many companies, including IBM, Goldman Sachs, Morgan Stanley, and others, are bringing talent back into the paid workforce.

Women like Diane and Carol are part of a growing sisterhood who are working, pausing, thriving, AND making sure others can too. But so are many women who never paused. Marlene Williamson is just such a woman. She proudly says she never wanted or needed to pull back from her career. The reason why? She had supportive bosses and a supportive spouse, and she loved her job as a chief marketing officer for a number of high-technology companies. As she told me, "My north star always started with my husband and my children. In every job I worked in, I made that clear and was lucky enough to have employers who supported me."

Now Marlene wants to pay it forward and has taken on the role of chief executive officer of Watermark, a leading women's networking organization based in the San Francisco Bay Area. "My vision has been the same since I began my career. I want women to have the opportunity to be the kind of leaders they want to be. We're committed to helping advance women at whatever stage they are in to get to the next level." Marlene may have never "opted out," but she is excited to help women "opt in."

There are scores of ways you can offer support to women who are rebooting their careers, from introductions, résumé advice, and interview practice, to just plain old "you go, girl" cheerleading. It's time we debunk the myth that women are each other's worst enemies. The more we can help each other, the more we all benefit.

Recognize (and Name) Caregiver Bias

Meghann Foye stepped on a landmine when she published her 2016 book, *Meternity*. It's a fictionalized account of a woman who fakes being pregnant so she can get maternity leave. The protagonist, who has never had children, believes that maternity leave is like getting a much-needed extended vacation.

In promoting the book, Meghann wrote in *The New York Post*, "I couldn't help but feel envious when parents on staff left the office at 6 p.m. to tend to their children, while it was assumed co-workers without kids would stay behind to pick up the slack."[282]

You can imagine the firestorm she created. Mothers were up in arms. As one successful entrepreneur and mother of three said to me, "Vacation? Is she kidding? Between the colic, the waking every two hours to breast-feed, I was more exhausted than I had ever been during the seventy-hour workweeks I put in to launch my company!"

Another said, "Maternity leave is for getting your body and family back on track and bonding with your newest little one. Someone who does not have a kid does not need that. But what EVERYONE needs is a chance to take a break. Let's not confuse these things."

The explosion Meghann created isn't about maternity leave or sabbaticals; it's about the resentment employees feel at being forced to "pick up the slack" when those with caregiving responsibilities have to put their home life first. Rather than get angry at the system that requires those without children (or ill family members) to fill in for those with pressing personal priorities, we blame and fight amongst each other.

Journalist Kathryn Jezer-Morton nailed the issue in her column for online magazine *Jezebel*. She wrote, "Until we stop griping at each other for failing to understand each other's struggles, all of which are very real, nothing will change. It's hard, because the common enemy of burned-out single women and burned-out working moms is invisible, spread diffusely over our entire culture, impossible to isolate or pillory."[283]

Humans care for others. It is the essence of who we are. Whatever our relationship status, we will in the course of our lifetimes have caregiving responsibilities, whether for children, elderly parents, ill siblings, troubled friends, even beloved animals.

It's time we stopped getting mad at each other and started getting mad at the workplace culture that pits us against each other. You may not have noticed it until you had children and were forced to leave early to pick up a sick baby from day care or missed an important meeting because your nanny quit and your spouse was traveling for business, but caregiving bias permeates our workplaces. But now that you see that bias, it's your responsibility to call it out.

When colleagues complain that the new mom who just got back from her "vacation" is leaving early again, explain to them about caregiver bias. Tell them you hope someone is there to help them one day when they need to leave early to support a loved one. And, if you see a colleague who is always filling in for others (or filling in for you), take the time to express your appreciation.

One close friend who has no children told me, "I don't mind picking up the slack. I just wish they would thank me once in a while. It would mean so much if they would just recognize the extra help I'm putting in on their behalf."

A little appreciation goes a long way.

Help Men Help Us

As you read in chapter 6, men want a place in the home. Once they become fathers, they face bias regarding their competency as caregivers just as women who become mothers face bias regarding their competency as workers. We women need to let go of control when it comes to being the parenting expert and let men become our true partners at home. It's a win for them, for our children, and for us.

It's time to recognize that when their wives are forced to downshift or pause their careers, men become saddled with the role of primary breadwinner. For most, this is not what they signed up for when they married their equal. My husband married me in part because he believed I would be his financial partner and would consistently earn a salary on par with his. Neither of us were prepared for the challenges of integrating kids and careers. My decision to pause impacted not just me, but him as well.

Helping your male coworkers understand the impact of the current 24/7 workplace culture *on them* can help facilitate change for us all. Do an unconscious bias training workshop around caregiving bias and how the consequences of that bias means they may be locked into a traditional role they may not want. For many who thought work–life balance was a "women's issue," they may be surprised at how they are held back too.

Finally, take blame out of the equation. As women advocate for change, men often hear it as though we are blaming them. They often feel as if they are at fault.

I moderated a panel on diversity and inclusion at the annual conference of a leading Silicon Valley tech company. After the event, the CEO approached me and said, "I was hesitant to have this panel. So often it comes across as a blame game. As though we men are the reason there isn't more diversity. Today you made me and the other men in the room feel like we're part of the solution."

That CEO has now launched an unconscious bias training program for his senior executives. He wants them to see they can change and that in doing so they can be part of the solution. He plans to roll it out to the rest of the company over the next year. He's just one of many enlightened men who are eager to help us change the way we all work.

WHAT CAN COMPANIES DO?

Recognize: *This isn't a women's problem; it's a business problem.*
Reframe: *Businesses thrive when they have inclusive cultures that attract, retain, and promote women.*

Revamp the Culture

When Blake Irving joined GoDaddy as their CEO in 2012, he knew something had to change. The company was notorious for their raunchy Super Bowl ads filled with scantily clad women and the geeks who love them. Blake decided enough was enough. He decided to "hack the culture."

First, he focused on the internal environment. After reviewing the abysmal staffing ratios (they mirror the rest of the industry, with women making up only 18 percent of their engineering talent), he hired Elissa Murphy from Yahoo! as the new CTO and added Betsy Rafael, former chief accounting officer at Apple and finance vice president at Cisco Systems, to the board of directors. He also looked at the customer demographics and realized the company was missing out on a critical customer base: women entrepreneurs.

"It turns out 58 percent of tiny companies with one to five employees are run by women in the United States. This is our target customer. Why would we want to piss them off?" Blake told me. So he turned his attention to GoDaddy's advertising.

Instead of having supermodels tonguing chubby nerds, the GoDaddy Super Bowl 2014 ads made a major shift by showing women starting and running companies. In their current campaign, three of the four feature ads highlight women entrepreneurs. Blake said the customer response has been "Good. Very good."

"I grew up in a household in which men and women were equal," said Blake. "My wife, mother, and sisters are feminists. I consider myself one, too. But it wasn't only a personal commitment to equality that led me to make these changes. It was simply good business."

You've heard it before, but why not say it again: Focusing on recruiting and retaining women and increasing the number of women in leadership is not part of corporate social responsibility; it's an essential part of the bottom line.[284] As I shared in chapter 7, when companies have more women on their boards, they have a 42 percent higher return in sales, 66 percent greater return on invested capital, and 53 percent higher return on equity.[285] When 30 percent of senior management is made up of women, companies have 6 percent higher net profit margins than companies that don't. When companies have more diverse workforces, they are 35 percent more financially successful.[286] When companies employ women, they provide paychecks to the demographic that overwhelmingly makes the purchasing decisions in this country (80 percent of purchasing decisions are made by women). These women are the very consumers they want and need for their products. Employing women becomes a virtuous circle and a profitable one.

It's time to recognize: It's not about women; it's about business.

But here's the thing: Companies have spent millions of dollars and many years trying to attract and retain women. They've instituted women's initiatives, established mentoring programs, created support networks. It's not working. When you look across almost every industry, there are plenty of women at the entry level, but once they hit middle management, they start winnowing out. By the time they should be at the top, the vast majority of women are gone.

Yes, it's about sexism. Yes, it's about wage inequality. Yes, it's about toxic workplaces. Yes, it's about conscious and unconscious bias. Solve all of these *and we will still have a leaky pipeline problem.*

Why? Because unless we face the foundational issue that constrains women in the workplace, we will see the same thing happen again and again. We need to recognize that if we want to attract, retain, and promote more women so we have a full and robust pipeline to leadership, we need to address the lack of support we offer those who bear the primary responsibility of caring for children and other loved ones: women. Until we solve this issue, women will continue to leave. Their exodus speaks to the truth that workplaces just don't work for families.

> Yes, it's about sexism. Yes, it's about wage inequality. Yes, it's about toxic workplaces. Yes, it's about conscious and unconscious bias. Solve all of these *and we will still have a leaky pipeline problem.*

So what's a smart company to do? You can follow Courtney Buechert's lead and change everything. In 2012, Courtney realized he had a problem. As CEO of Eleven, a full-service marketing agency whose clients include Apple, Facebook, NetApp, and others, he saw that his company had 150 employees and was growing, but women were not part of that growth.

"I always thought of myself as someone who supported gender equality, but then I looked at our agency and saw that we had no female creative directors, no female partners, and no women in senior management. Despite all our good intentions and stated commitment to equality, we weren't walking the talk," Courtney told me. "We realized we can ask women to change and we can individually help them make that change. But until we fundamentally change the way we do business, nothing is going to change."

So Courtney and the other (male) senior leaders got down to business and decided the only way to truly disrupt the issue was to completely alter how their company was structured right down to the articles of incorporation. They changed their human resource policy to allow for more flexible work solutions, increased their parental leave policies, and revamped how they reviewed and evaluated talent.

In just two years, Eleven added one female partner, promoted a woman to creative director, and expanded the pipeline to management for women in all areas of the company. On the creative side where agencies make their bread and butter, 46 percent of their staff is now women.

And here is the best news of all: Although the intention was to "do the right thing," Courtney shared he is also seeing a significant increase in talent retention. "We made changes we thought would be good for women, but we're finding these strategic solutions also meet the complex lifestyle needs of Millennials. In the end, our good intentions have turned out to be very good for our business."

Companies are finally figuring out that mothers have been the "canaries in the coal mine" when it comes to workplace culture. The changes companies make to meet our needs are exactly what businesses need to thrive in the twenty-first century. Those who have the courage and the ability to make significant changes are likely going to see the greatest results both in terms of a more diverse workforce and bottom-line results.

But most companies can't be as nimble as Eleven and disrupt everything to innovate. So what can those companies do? First and foremost, stop thinking of this as a female problem and recognize it for what it is: a workplace culture problem.

This requires extensive soul searching and a willingness to look at long-held intractable unconscious biases. The great news is that some companies have already started to do so and are sharing their efforts by "open sourcing" their learning and training. Check out Facebook's Managing Bias series[287] and Google's Unconscious Bias @ Work program.[288] If you want to look at your own unconscious biases, a good place to start is Harvard University's Project Implicit,[289] which tests your social attitudes. It's eye-opening, I assure you.

As Debora Spar, president of Barnard College, wrote, "Fixing the women's problem is not about fixing the women, or yanking them onto committees, or placating them with yet another networking retreat. It's about fixing the organization—recognizing a diversity of skills and attributes, measuring them in a concrete way, and rewarding people accordingly."[290]

I don't believe the way to solve the issue of attracting, retaining, and promoting women into leadership is to ask women to work harder or to expect us to continue to change ourselves to fit into a system that doesn't honor our commitments to family and community. I believe the way to solve the problem is to change the system itself. Recognizing the workplace constraints that keep true inclusion from becoming a reality is essential. So is establishing policies and systems that reflect these goals.

> Companies are finally figuring out that mothers have been the "canaries in the coal mine" when it comes to workplace culture.

Thaw the "Frozen Middle"

CEOs like Blake Irving and Courtney Buechert are examples of senior leaders who are committed to advancing women. And no doubt the women at the bottom are eager to advance. Often it is middle management that keeps change from actually happening.

Ask Lori Nishiura Mackenzie, who is yet another work, pause, thrive role model. She had a lengthy career in marketing as a brand manager for Procter & Gamble, a vice president of marketing for a natural products start-up, and a division head of a global marketing agency. Then she decided to pause to care for her two young children. Six years later, Lori relaunched her career. She worked at PayPal and eBay, but she knew she wanted to do more. Frustrated by the intractable challenges faced by women in the workplace, Lori decided to pivot her career from marketing to becoming a Warrior for change.

"I recognized that the only way I would be truly satisfied in my career was if I could help others overcome the resistance to workplace inclusion," Lori said. Today, she is the executive director at the Clayman Institute for Gender Research at Stanford University. At Clayman, they work extensively with companies to unpack what Lori calls "the frozen middle."

"For many companies, the sticky place for change management is not the top or the bottom of organizations, but in the 'frozen middle,' where managers are responsible for hiring and promoting," Lori told me.

In late 2013, the Clayman Institute launched a corporate partnership program to work with companies who are truly committed to making deep, sustainable inroads to foster true diversity and inclusion. Google, Cisco, and eBay are just a few of their current partners.

"We focus on three key areas," said Lori. "First, we work to unlock unconscious bias.[291] That's the collection of beliefs that we carry about ourselves and others coupled with the tendency to gravitate to those who are similar to us. Second, we facilitate company-specific solutions to block that unintentional bias. Third, we partner with selected middle managers who help serve as change agents within the organization. This multi-pronged approach becomes infused into the DNA of the organization and that allows them to capitalize on a key benefit of diversity and inclusion: unparalleled innovation."

Unconscious bias training is one way to help revamp the culture, but there is nothing better than data. The following three recommendations can help your company get clarity on what can be done to attract, retain, and promote women.

Use Data to Drive Change

1) Do a Staffing Audit; Make It Public

Tech companies have broken new ground by declaring their deep deficiency when it comes to diversity and inclusion. By releasing their employment data, they have made it clear they can and want to make a difference in their staffing ratios.

In 2014, Google, Apple, Facebook, Twitter, and other leading tech companies made headlines when they revealed their employee demographic data.[292] That data confirmed what we here in Silicon Valley intuitively knew: Women and minorities were deeply under-represented in the single most influential industry in modern times. At just about every company who reported their results, women made up no more than 30 percent of the employee rolls. Drill down to technical jobs and the numbers were even more discouraging. Men typically held 80 percent of those jobs. And in management? Google had no women in senior management. Neither did Apple. Microsoft had two. Amazon boasted it had eighteen women amongst its 120 top managers.[293] But then, not much later, an investigative report by *The New York Times*[294] indicated that the Amazon workplace culture was so toxic, people could often be found crying in their cubicles. It wasn't unusual to hear about employees having nervous breakdowns. And God forbid you get sick. The company apparently didn't think a serious illness was a good enough excuse to miss work. So Amazon may be able to boast it has more women at the top than other tech companies, but its culture clearly needs to be improved for all employees.

Smaller, more nimble tech companies are now taking the lead on changing the ratio on gender equality in the workplace. Take Buffer, for example. They're a software company that has an application for managing your social networks. If you're active on Twitter, Instagram, Facebook, and more, you use Buffer. The leadership team is so passionate about "moving the needle" on diversity, they've created a live feed that tracks their employee statistics.[295] At any given time, you can see the demographic make-up of its current employees and the make-up of the candidates who apply for open jobs. They know transparency is the only way prove to under-represented populations that they mean business.

And other industries are finally following suit. Accenture was the first big consulting firm to release its data in January 2016. The company revealed that of its 48,000 employees only one-third are women. Why'd they share their dirty laundry? Because they, too, understand the power of transparency. Julie Sweet, CEO of Accenture, North America, said, "Transparency creates trust . . . allows us to track our progress and hold ourselves accountable."

We are beginning to realize our good intentions are not good enough to empower women in the workforce. We need public accountability. In the end, this concrete data might just enable us to actually "move the needle" in attracting and retaining women and other under-represented groups.

2) Do a Wage Audit; Make It Public

One of the leading issues women face is unfair pay. And, as we've seen, women with children face an even bigger pay penalty. Most companies don't realize there is an imbalance because they haven't compared employee pay based on gender. And, if they have done a wage audit at all, they are highly unlikely to have compared pay based on parental status. Myths are rampant about the pay gap for women, but data is data. The

U.S. Department of Labor offers a few myth-busting statistics about the pay gap. For example,

> **MYTH:** There is no such thing as the gender pay gap—legitimate differences between men and women cause the gap in pay, not discrimination.
>
> **REALITY:** Decades of research shows a gender gap in pay even after factors like the kind of work performed and qualifications (education and experience) are taken into account. These studies consistently conclude that discrimination is the best explanation of the remaining difference in pay. Economists generally attribute about 40% of the pay gap to discrimination—making about 60% explained by differences between workers or their jobs.
>
> **MYTH:** Women are responsible for the pay gap because they seek out flexible jobs or choose to work fewer hours. Putting family above work is why women earn less.
>
> **REALITY:** Putting aside whether it's right to ask women (or men) to sacrifice financially in order to work and have a family, those kinds of choices aren't enough to explain away the gender pay gap. The gender gap in pay exists for women working full time. Taking time off for children also doesn't explain gaps at the start of a career. And although researchers have addressed various ways that work hours or schedule might or might not explain some portion of the wage gap, there may be a "motherhood penalty." This is based on nothing more than the expectation that mothers will work less. Researchers have found that merely the status of being a mother can lead to perceptions of lowered competence and commitment and lower salary offers.[296]

In other words, the single biggest factor determining gender pay inequity is not being female; it's being a mother. So, if companies really want to figure out how to keep women engaged, they should look at how they are paying them and then look even more closely at how they are paying mothers. At the very least, they should consider following the lead of companies like tech giant Salesforce.com, start-up SumAll, and advertising powerhouse The Martin Agency. Each conducted extensive wage audits and then used that data to rebalance salaries. SumAll went so far as to make the data internally public so transparency about pay would keep employees from wondering if they were being treated fairly.

> In other words, the single biggest factor determining gender pay inequity is not being female; it's being a mother.

SumAll's Chief Executive Officer Dane Atkinson said, "Gender pay gaps and discriminatory salary practices are awful. I used to do these things at my other companies. I would hire someone for one amount and someone else for another amount. At the time, I thought I was creating shareholder value—but it ended up hurting me down the road."[297]

How? Through lowered engagement and employee churn.

"People discover that they're not being treated fairly," said Dane. "Their only method for resolution is to self-compensate by underperforming or leaving altogether." Now employees can see what their peers are making and are empowered to negotiate their pay accordingly. This knowledge helps avoid uncomfortable conversations during salary discussions and supports women who tend to ask for lower salaries and for fewer raises.

It takes guts for a company to do the hard work of a wage audit. It takes even more guts to face the reality that your company just may have discrimination baked into its DNA. But you can't argue with the facts, and the fact is, mothers are underpaid.

3) Do a Motherhood Retention Audit

Like men, women leave jobs all of the time. They get better jobs. They move. They stop working to travel the world, to care for ailing family members, and to care for themselves. But the truth is that women are most likely to completely leave the workforce to care for children.

For example, in the tech industry, according to the National Center for Women & Information Technology, 56 percent of women in STEM leave their jobs mid-career.[298] This is double the turnover rate of men. Of the women who leave, 24 percent take a non-technical job in a different company, 10 percent go to a start-up, and the remaining 42 percent either freelance or stop working altogether. Why? We don't have actual data, but it's safe to assume these women are leaving to care for children. And the same mass exodus happens in advertising, financial services, law, and business. It's one of the key reasons we don't have enough women at the top. With fewer women to choose from, it's harder to find women to promote into senior leadership.

Historically, most companies haven't actually tracked where women go, much less why they leave. Exit interviews don't typically ask detailed questions about work–life integration. This lack of information means we can imbue a woman's exit with our own biases. If she says she is leaving to focus on her children, we assume she "opted out" rather than recognize circumstances likely forced her out. Because we see this as her "choice," we don't realize she might not have left if she had the right support, such as flexible work options or an environment that recognized that leaving at 5 PM didn't mean you weren't committed to your career.

If a meaningful exit interview had been done when I left my advertising agency, I would have explained I was leaving because I knew I couldn't be successful as a mom in that environment. I would have explained how the punishing hours meant I couldn't be home to put my child to bed. I would have explained how uncomfortable it was trying to pump in the bathroom. I would have explained that I had one too many male executives ask me why I wasn't at home with my child rather than working late into the night, implying as they did that I wasn't a good mother.

This data might have enabled my company to put into place a retention plan so the next time a new mom was considering leaving the agency, they would have the tools and information to figure out a way to keep her. But our biases about "opting out" means we don't challenge our thinking about why moms leave. Data changes that.

There are a number of talent software systems like PeopleInsight and Talent Chaser that allow employers to track when a woman takes maternity leave, the length of that leave, and when she leaves the company. However, most of these software systems don't drill down to understand *why* she leaves. It requires a forward-thinking human resources leader to ask that question and connect the dots. Conducting a motherhood retention audit is the only way to truly unpack the motivations behind why a mother leaves a job and figure out what could have been done to keep her.

Motherhood retention audits aren't just exit interviews. They are detailed questionnaires with inputs that uncover the true motivations behind leaving. They offer the talent manager the chance to track these trends to identify if, in fact, the company has a motherhood retention issue. This data can offer critical insight into why we have a "leaky" pipeline.

Ask any woman who has paused her career, as I did with the *Women on the Rise* survey, and she can tell you the exact moment she knew she would leave her job—that "tipping point" moment when she looked at the balance of her life (caring for beloveds on one side and a rewarding career on the other) and decided the scales were completely askew and something had to give. If we truly want to keep women engaged in the workforce, then let's understand their tipping point moments. If motherhood retention audits were standard, it wouldn't take long for companies to figure out why and when women hit that tipping point moment at their company. Intervening before that moment comes can keep a talented employee from abandoning ship. Do this enough times and there will be plenty of women to fill that pipeline to the top.

Provide a Meaningful Paid Maternity Leave and Onramping Support

A colleague recently asked me what the "right amount" of maternity leave should be. It's a hard question to answer. Right for whom? For companies—because they don't take into account the fact that productivity, engagement, and retention are all affected by short maternity leaves—the standard six weeks is too long. I have heard many women say twenty-four weeks should be the minimum. Meanwhile, studies out of Europe show that forty weeks is optimal for the health of the baby.

Two studies (one[299] published in 2005, the second[300] five years earlier) examined the longitudinal results of paid leave in sixteen European countries, starting in 1969. The result? A 20 percent drop in infant deaths directly attributable to a ten-week extension in paid leave. The biggest drop was in deaths of babies between two and twelve months, but deaths between one and five years also went down as paid leave went up. According to Christopher Ruhm, the author of the first European study, paid leave of about forty weeks saved the most lives.[301] If the optimal length of parental leave for the health of the baby is forty weeks, how is it we are willing to tolerate six weeks as the standard?

In many ways it is not surprising that the standard pregnancy is forty weeks long and that forty weeks is the optimal time to help a baby adjust to this new world. But in the business climate of the United States, forty weeks is an eternity. So, what's a company to do?

I'd like to suggest twenty weeks as the standard paid maternity leave and then offer women an additional twenty weeks of onramping support. For some this could mean working part-time; for others, this could mean working one day a week at home. Each woman and her company could figure out the strategy that worked best for them.

By institutionalizing a forty-week postpartum "pause" that was collectively understood as standard, babies, women, and their companies would all benefit. Children would have optimal health outcomes, women would have optimal career outcomes, and companies would have employees who were more loyal, more engaged, and more productive.

And it's a great retention tool. Remember Medium's software engineer Jean Hsu, mentioned in chapter 7? Because her company worked with her to ensure she would thrive as a new mother and a professional, she was able to stay committed to both her career and her company. As Jean said, "Why would I want to be anywhere else?"

If the optimal length of parental leave for the health of the baby is forty weeks, how is it we are willing to tolerate six weeks as the standard?

Offer Paternity Leave and Encourage Dads to Take It

We know maternity leave is good for moms, babies, and business, too, but new research shows that paid paternity leave is not only good for dads but also for moms, babies, and businesses.

Fathers who take two or more weeks off after the birth of a child stay more involved in the child's care[302] (changing diapers, feeding, bathing) nine months later than fathers who don't take leave. Men who take paternity leave end up being more competent and committed fathers as their children grow older. And when dads take leave, mom's income rises and the burdens of household chores are more evenly distributed.[303]

Around the world, more than seventy countries offer dads paid leave,[304] but in the United States, few men have access to it. As noted in chapter 6, fathers who work in companies with fifty or more employees have the right to take unpaid parental leave thanks to the FMLA, but few actually do take it. Those few who did have paid leave available to them took only two weeks on average, whether they had more paid leave available to them or not.

Josh Levs, author of *All In: How Our Work-First Culture Fails Dads, Families, and Businesses*, said, "Companies who offer paid parental leave are paying you to take a pause. Not taking paid leave is like throwing money away."

Some have advocated a "Daddy Quota" to get dads to take paternity leave. They suggest offering money to men if and only if they take a leave after the birth (or adoption) of their new child. As I shared, since Sweden and Norway began offering this use-it-or-lose-it policy in the mid-1990s, men's use of paternity leave has skyrocketed.

Throwing money at the problem is one way to entice men to take leave; another is to simply make sure senior leaders model support of it. As noted in chapter 6, Mark Zuckerberg did wonders for paternity leave when he took two months off after the birth of his daughter. As more men are willing to boldly place family first by taking paternity leave, we are likely to see more women staying in the paid workforce because they will have partners who are more willing to share caregiving duties and, arguably, male coworkers who support their needs as mothers in the workplace.

Getting men to take their paid leave is one issue, but companies need to offer it in the first place. Those companies looking to attract top talent should take this into consideration: In a survey of 1,000 employed fathers, 90 percent said if they were thinking of having another child and considering a new job, it would be important for a new employer to provide paid leave, with 60 percent saying it's extremely or very important.[305] Another study revealed 93 percent of Millennial men said *paternity leave* was crucial in deciding whether they took a job.[306] If companies want to stay competitive in today's market, offering paternity leave isn't a nice thing to do, it's a must-do.

Provide Child Care Solutions

So the baby comes and daddy and mommy have taken their respective leaves. What do parents need now? Child care. In the *Women on the Rise* survey, not having access to quality child care or confidence in their child's caregiver was a major reason women left the workforce. It was certainly true for me. But as we have seen, few companies provide onsite child care, leaving parents forced to cobble together suboptimal solutions. That strategy may have worked for my generation, but that's not going to fly with the next one.

Here is the issue: Millennials are becoming parents at the rate of 11,000 new babies every day, and they have been very clear that they place family above their careers. If we want to keep women in the workforce, one way to do it is to provide them with high-quality child care.

We know few companies offer onsite child care. In fact, of the top ten companies to work for on the rating website Fairygodboss, which tracks which companies are the most female friendly, only two are listed as offering child care: Google and Cisco Systems. Some companies are offering direct cash gifts to parents to help cover child care costs. Facebook gives new parents $4,000 to help defray expenses, but in California where they are headquartered, the annual average cost of child care runs over $12,000, so that one-time gift is not enough by a long shot.

Rather than writing a check, many companies turn to dependent care spending accounts for employees.[307] These allow employees to put aside tax-free dollars to be used exclusively for child care services. The companies don't give anything, so it really isn't a "benefit" at all and the employee can only put aside up to $5,000 of tax-free money. Given that child care costs on average around $11,000 per year in this country, this "benefit" offers little real relief.

We know the government will not get traction on this issue anytime soon, so it is up to companies to take the lead. Providing onsite child care is one of the most powerful solutions. There are many reasons why onsite child care makes sense, not the least of which is the benefit to the bottom line. According to a recent study in the *Journal of Managerial*

Psychology, employee performance was higher and absenteeism was lower for those employees using onsite child care versus those employees using an off-site center.[308] Interestingly, their performance was even higher than those employees who had no children.

It's time for twenty-first century companies to add onsite child care to their list of employee benefits. Not just because it is the right thing to do, but because it is the fiscally smart thing to do.

Focus on Results, Not "Face Time"

"Face time" (not the app, but the get-in-early, stay-late kind) may well be the number one killer of mothers' careers. We, who need flexibility to perform our caregiving duties, are unduly penalized by a culture that requires us to be in the office all of the time. The ideal worker construct means those with caregiving responsibilities cannot succeed. Changing the workplace to focus on results opens the door to empower employees to be productive on their terms.

As noted in chapter 9, companies are beginning to realize that embodying a results-only work environment (ROWE) offers extensive benefits. Employees are reporting higher levels of satisfaction, deeper engagement, better work–life balance, and more loyalty.[309] In fact, an eight-month study of 775 companies that had employed the ROWE managerial system reduced employee turnover by 45 percent.

Shifting focus toward results benefits all employees, not just mothers, but without question those with caregiving responsibilities benefit most deeply. The good news is technology is helping us when it comes to the issue of "face time." Collaboration tools such as Slack, Evernote, Asana, and virtual meeting systems such as Google Hangouts and WebEx, enable teams to stay on track without having to be in the office to meet face to face. This opens up the opportunity for a distributed workforce and remote teamwork. It's how I work with most of my consulting clients and how the vast majority of other "gig economy" workers stay connected. Companies that use these tools probably aren't thinking about the shift to a results orientation, but it is happening anyway.

It takes courage and commitment to restructure how we work, but companies that figure it out set themselves up to win the battle for talent.

Revamp the Recruiting System

I hear it all the time: "I can't grow my business because I can't find talent." It's why the recruitment industry is a $400-billion global business and growing 7 percent year over year.[310] Companies want and need talent. But here's the problem: Most jobs these days, especially those at mid-sized and larger companies, require an applicant to use an online application system. But because of the way they are designed, these systems are inherently built to reject people, not actually find them.

Think about it. To answer many job postings, you have to fill out a form. Usually that form goes through a software application that looks for keywords, rejecting or ignoring those that don't include said keywords. Those applications that actually make it through the software are then reviewed by a junior recruiter who also looks for key terms. Those early vetting systems (be they human or computerized) look for reasons to get rid of a candidate. It's their job. Recruiters and their processes are paid to weed people out.

As a result, those with nonstandard résumés don't get past the front gate, and mothers are the most likely to have a non-standard résumé because many of them have non-linear careers. And the résumés of women who have paused their careers to attend to their caregiving responsibilities are even more non-standard, so the application system rejects them even though they might be exactly the candidate who can fill the leaky pipeline.

Remember Alison Cormack? She had an impeccable résumé for the first twelve years of her career, and then she spent ten years at home with her children. She was strategic with her human capital by using her time to spearhead a hugely successful fundraising campaign, raising millions of dollars to expand the libraries in her town. But her ten-year résumé gap meant that when she first applied online to her job at Google, the system rejected her. Undeterred, Alison went around the system by enlisting the help of a library board colleague who was a Google employee to get her application the attention it needed. Once past the online filtering system, she was able to quickly get hired.

If companies want to attract candidates with non-linear careers, they need to find ways to help these potential employees break through the recruiting barriers. Some companies are setting up a separate job application process focused on those who have paused. PayPal has launched a "return to work" internship program in which the applicants are required to have been out of the paid workforce for at least two years. As a leader in the tech industry, the company is sending the message they value experience that happens beyond the cubicle.

The truth is software isn't the only problem; so are people. Remember Lisa Tankersley? Despite her decade-long pause, she did manage to get through the recruiting software at Facebook. Then she hit a wall when she was interviewed by the hiring manager. He was a young, single man who couldn't understand why she would leave the workforce. Despite the fact that she worked part-time doing exactly the work required for the full-time job for which she was interviewing, Lisa couldn't overcome his bias against women who paused for caregiving.

Another way to disrupt the barriers to hiring is to take a deep-dive look at how bias in the recruiting process may be keeping nontraditional candidates from applying in the first place. Buffer's Chief Technology Officer Sunil Sadasivan recognized they had a problem in recruiting. A careful analysis revealed that when their job descriptions had the word "hacker" in them fewer than 2 percent of the applicants were female.[311] That inspired the company to create more gender-neutral language in their job descriptions, as well as insist their interviewers participate in unconscious bias training. Since these changes, they've managed to add two female engineers to their team. Might not seem like much, but for a small company with only fifty employees, even a change that small can have huge consequences.

Offer "Returnships" to Re-Entering Talent

One powerful way companies can attract high-caliber talent who have paused their careers is to take a cue from PayPal, GTB, and other forward-thinking companies and offer return-to-work internships.

These internships could be formalized, like the ones Goldman Sachs, Morgan Stanley, and others have created. These are typically three- to six-month training programs that are focused on the specific needs of relaunching women who have paused their careers for more than two years. Other programs might be less formal, more akin to consulting projects that allow companies to test out a potential employee's skill and fit.

According to Penny Locey, vice president of career placement firm Keystone Associates, more and more companies are employing this method of hiring talent. She told me, "These days, companies are more inclined to offer potential employees short-term projects on a 'try and buy' basis. As a result, the time has never been better for those who have paused to re-enter with great success."

A company that is unsure if someone who has paused her career has kept her skills up to date can set up a consulting project and treat it like a return-to-work internship. If the fit's not right, then the company isn't locked in to hiring her full-time. Meanwhile, the woman working to reboot her career gains important skills and the confidence to know she can get back in. It's a win/win.

Bob Plaschke, CEO of Sonim Technologies, has taken this strategy to heart. "I heard the mother of one of my son's friends was interested in returning to work. She'd been an active volunteer in our community and I knew she was more than qualified. So I reached out and offered her an internship," he said. "I'll never forget the first day she showed up. She had a huge box with her. Turned out she didn't have a laptop so she brought her desktop computer. She told me she wanted to be productive and knew the only way to do that was to have all of the tools necessary. I wish all of my twenty-five-year-old new hires had that level of commitment!"

Since then, he has hired two more "return-to-workers" and continues to be thrilled with the results. He told me, "I get the smartest, most committed, and easiest to manage employees when I hire returners. I don't know why everyone hasn't caught on to this incredible and eager pool of talent."

Neither do I.

Create Alternative Paths to Leadership

In 2010, when Deloitte's head of talent, Cathy Benko, and Molly Anderson, head of Deloitte's Women's Initiative, co-wrote their book *The Corporate Lattice: Achieving High Performance in the Changing World of Work*, their goal was to convince companies to recognize that those with non-linear career paths were equally strong candidates for top leadership. Put simply, if you want to solve for the dearth of women who are on the ladder to senior management, you need to look beyond the traditional paradigm. Women, they argued, don't climb the ladder; they swing on the lattice.

When it comes to celebrating female leadership, companies typically trot out their token woman in senior management and say, "We love women. Look, she did it!" And how did she do it? In most cases, she did it by keeping her head down, performing like the "ideal worker," and behaving and acting like the men around her. If she has kids, then it's not unusual for her partner to have put his career on hold and to stay home and focus on the family. We do need to celebrate those women (and to the men who supported them); they broke on through. But their direct line to the top meant they played by the traditional (typically male) rules. That works for some of us, but not for most.

We want to see women who didn't rise in lockstep to the top. Show us the woman who paused her career for a few years and then relaunched to great success. Promote *her* to senior leadership, make *her* the poster woman for what success looks like, and then we'll begin to believe our non-linear career paths and our family-focused choices are truly valued.

The good news is that it's beginning to happen. Global strategic consulting company PricewaterhouseCoopers LLP (PwC) has 195,000 employees across 178 countries. It's launched the Full Circle Program, which allows both women and men to take up to five years off for dependent care needs and still be assured they can return to the company. While these men and women pause their careers, they are given a sponsor at the firm, are invited to attend events, and can participate in other "alumni" events as they see fit. The company expects to see a number of the Full Circle Program participants in senior leadership in the near future.

The effort is part of an overall retention strategy launched by Mike Fenlon, PwC's global and U.S. talent leader. In 2004, PwC conducted an extensive retention study[312] of its employee base. They knew they were losing women once they hit a certain level in their firm. PwC thought money was the problem; they discovered it was time. Put simply, employees who left wanted better work–life balance. So the company reframed how they developed and nurtured their talent. "We realized it's not about the here and now," Mike Fenlon told me. "It's about the long term. We want to build a life-long relationship with our talent. So, if an employee needs to leave temporarily, they can have the confidence we'll welcome them back."

As more enlightened companies see the value of supporting "lattice" or non-linear careers, we are likely to see more women pulling back from their professional commitments and working a reduced schedule for a period of time, which may mean we'll see a temporary reduction in their productivity. But over the arc of their careers, wouldn't it be better to keep them engaged in the workforce rather than have them leave completely? And, as I heard from Karen Catlin, Patricia Nakache, Lisa Johnson, and the many other women who were given the option to become "Cruisers," their loyalty to their companies was unparalleled.

The women I interviewed for this book and many of the respondents to the *Women on the Rise* survey are just a small number of the millions of shining lights whose non-linear careers prove you can work, pause, and still rise to the top of your field. The more a company can honor and celebrate these nontraditional paths to senior management, the more they send the message that a pause is not a career killer.

Bake Work–Life Integration into Your Company's DNA

Ryan Carson is chief executive officer of Treehouse, an online training company that focuses on building individuals' coding and software development skills, and he's passionate about work–life integration. He launched Treehouse in 2010 with the goal of ensuring employees can "have a life" while doing great work. The entire staff of 110 employees (and growing) only work Monday through Thursday. Ryan is in the office at 8:30 AM and leaves no later than 6:15 PM. He doesn't believe in "face time."

He's not alone. We are seeing more and more companies bake work–life integration their DNA and, in doing so, redefine what productivity and success looks like. Consider Menlo Innovations,[313] a software development firm based in Ann Arbor, Michigan. The company was founded by Rich Sheridan, a self-described "refugee" from Corporate America who believed things could and must be different for the American worker.

He and a team co-founded Menlo Innovations to be different in every way. Rich said, "We spend too much of our work lives trying to deny our humanity. We have to deny the fact that we are parents, deny that we have aging parents . . . For me, this is personal."

Menlo Innovations is built on the belief that joy is a business imperative. "If you have time for your life, you are joyful. And when you come to work in the morning, you're more creative, more imaginative, more excited to be here," Rich said. "There is, in fact, a tangible business value to joy. You get better relationships. Better quality. Better productivity."

The proof is in its success. Menlo Innovations has not only won numerous awards for being a great place to work, it is one of the fastest growing software companies. But Rich Sheridan doesn't look at success in a conventional way; he measures it in employee and customer satisfaction. For him, profits are just one measure, not the only measure, of a great company.

Making the workplace work for American families isn't easy. It requires us to view culture as a competitive advantage. It means we need to think of productivity in a new way. We need to look beyond the notion that employees are replaceable commodities to viewing employees as the greatest asset. Modern companies are coming to realize that it is no longer about how much can get done as fast as it can get done, but how we can do it in a way that doesn't burn out the talent.

John Gerzema, co-author of *The Athena Doctrine: How Women (and the Men Who Think Like Them) Will Rule the Future*, believes twenty-first century leadership isn't about competition, wining at all cost, secrecy, or privileging productivity over people. After surveying 64,000 business and community leaders from around the world, he wrote that leaders of the future embody a commitment to collaboration, empathy, authenticity, and purpose-driven shared goals.

At the heart of this leadership is a deep and abiding commitment to empowering each person to live their best life. As PwC's Mike Fenlon told me, "In today's competitive market, it's really quite simple. There is nothing more important than your team. And that means having an environment that is flexible and teams that are diverse. Creating workplaces and support structures that allow our employees to integrate their personal and professional priorities ensures we can attract and retain the best talent. That's just smart business."

Let's hope other companies figure this out soon. Not just for our sakes, but for theirs.

WHAT CAN POLICY MAKERS DO?

Recognize: *It isn't a women's problem; it's an economic problem.*
Reframe: *Our country is stronger when we keep all people working. We need programs in place to support them so they can.*

If you're reading this book, it's likely you're looking for immediate answers to how you can integrate your career with parenthood. You can dream of living in Norway and getting the support you need and deserve, but short of moving there, you're going to have to figure it out on your own. Why? Because the gridlock that is our current political system, both at the state and federal levels, means little movement on public policy issues that support parents in the workforce is likely to happen in the near future.

This gridlock is emblematic of the fraying of the social contract that is at the heart of how our country works. We can't even agree on how to support the most basic of human endeavors: parenting. If our lawmakers actually cared about the next generation, they would get beyond partisan politics to create programs to support those with caregiving responsibilities—in other words, all of us. Programs like paid parental leave and high-quality child care aren't "entitlements"; they are essential to ensuring the next generation thrives.

I don't see a change anytime soon, but that doesn't mean we can't dream. I've created the *Work PAUSE Thrive* Manifesto, a list of what our country can do to be truly devoted to our children, their children, and all of the children to come.

Imagine living in a country that so valued its citizens that it used its resources to actually help provide for their well-being. We don't, yet.

Rather than do what I and so many other women and men of my generation have done, which is to hunker down and do our best to meet the needs of ourselves and our families, I encourage you to join me in fighting for change. At the very least, it's time we demanded paid parental leave, paid sick leave, and universal, high-quality child care. Maybe if we do, our children and their families will have the support they need to work, pause, and thrive.

WORK PAUSE THRIVE MANIFESTO

We believe a great country provides the following to its citizens:

1. Paid parental leave for all new parents
2. Paid sick leave for all workers
3. Universal child care
4. Universal health care for all citizens
5. Job security for those with caregiving responsibilities
6. Social Security benefits for unpaid caregivers
7. Paid vacation days for all workers
8. Limits on overtime for salaried and non-salaried workers
9. Affordable college tuition and the ability to refinance student loan debt
10. Marriage rewards (not penalties) on taxes

When I started writing this book, a friend pulled me aside and cautioned me against it. "We don't want to encourage women to leave the workforce," she insisted. "What happens when all that brainpower goes home?"

I understood her concern. She was expressing what so many have expressed for years. We need women in the workforce. Women need to be in the workforce. Why would you argue for a different path?

Think for a moment about the values that underlie that point of view. At the heart of the notion that women (or men, for that matter) should work uninterrupted for their entire careers is the deep belief that what is done outside the home is of more value than what is done within the home.

And yet, what happens when a woman goes home? She cares for her family.

When did we become a society that believes caring for family is of no value? When did we become a society that doesn't celebrate those who nurture and support the next generation? When did we become a society that doesn't honor those who care for the previous generation as they make their way toward the ends of their lives? Why is caregiving so devalued?

I am not arguing women should pause. I am arguing that because we have a country that does not have universal policies that value caregiving, women (and men) must be supported to care for their families in the way that meets their personal and professional goals.

We must come to recognize that mothers work, but, because we lack support through our public policies and our workplaces, they don't and can't work all of the time. As a result, many put their careers on pause. It's time we recognize pausing isn't "opting out" or abandoning one's ambitions; it is simply a temporary break in the arc of one's career to meet the pressing needs of one's family.

In researching this book, I discovered a multitude of trailblazing women who have proven it is possible to integrate kids and a career. They are innovators whose resilience and fortitude and clarity of goals empowered them to disrupt convention. Their non-linear career paths are models of how it can be done, not in the way we've been told to do it, but in ways that worked for them and could work for you.

Which brings me back to my Journalism and Women Symposium colleague Lauren Whaley's question, "How did you do it?"

My answer? I worked, I paused, and, like my friends in the Not-So-New Mothers Group, the hundreds of women I interviewed, the nearly 1,500 who responded to the *Women on the Rise* survey, and the millions whose stories we don't know, I thrived.

I wish that for all of us. I wish that for you.

Appendix

WOMEN ON THE RISE SURVEY

WOMEN ON THE RISE SURVEY

In the fall of 2015, my research partner, Erin St. Onge-Carpenter, and I launched the *Women on the Rise* survey. Our goal was to determine how college-educated women with children were navigating the challenges of work and life. With the guidance of Pamela Stone, Hunter College Professor of Sociology; Erin Reilly, doctoral candidate at University of Texas at Austin; and Carol Fishman Cohen, founder and CEO of iRelaunch, we[314] conducted the most comprehensive modern survey of the career paths of highly qualified women.[315]

The goal of our study?

- To ascertain how highly qualified women are integrating kids with careers.
- To assess whether pausing for parenthood does actually kill a career.
- To understand the motivation of women who pause and how they feel about their choices.
- To unearth potential strategies and tactics for creating a successful non-linear career path.

THE "CREAM OF THE CROP"

The 1,476 women who responded to our survey were college-educated women who had spent an inordinate amount of time and money to ensure they could have the careers they wanted by investing in their human capital. In fact, over 60 percent had graduate degrees. They were professionals who had careers in business, medicine, academia, technology, law, and other traditionally male-dominated fields.

They were also married mothers (88 percent) in the center of their child-bearing and child-rearing years. The majority were between the ages of thirty-five and fifty-four, and 84 percent had children under the age of eighteen living at home.

While they may have been mothers, they were also committed to their careers. When we asked the respondents how career driven

THE *WOMEN ON THE RISE* RESPONDENTS

They are married, Gen X moms

- 76% are between the ages of thirty-five and fifty-four
- 88% are married
- 84% have children under the age of eighteen living at home

They are highly educated

- 99% have college degrees
- 61% have graduate degrees

They are mostly white and well-off

- 81% are white
- 78% live in homes with combined incomes of over $100,000

They are (or were) professionals

- 23% work or worked in Business
- 12% work or worked in Health Care/Medicine
- 12% work or worked in Academia/Education
- 11% work or worked in Technology
- 8% work or worked in Law
- 7% work or worked in Financial Services
- 7% work or worked in Nonprofit/Government
- 6% work or worked in Media/Journalism
- The remaining respondents listed "other" as their career/ industry

they would describe themselves, 60 percent told us they were "very" ambitious and 36 percent reported they were "somewhat" ambitious. They are (or, at least, were) the very women we would have expected to be at the top of their professions given their academic training and self-reported drive.

AND YET . . . THEY PAUSED

While the respondents to our *Women on the Rise* (WOTR) survey had the education, ambition, and life foundation that should have ensured they would "lean in," only 28 percent of these high-potential women had *never* paused their careers.

In fact, at some point 72 percent had either left the paid workforce completely for a period of time (52 percent) or had temporarily downshifted by working reduced hours (20 percent). Of the 52 percent who had completely left the paid workforce, 79 percent had relaunched their careers. Of the 11 percent of respondents who are still pausing, 83 percent plan to return to work. In other words, these women have not abandoned their careers. Rather, they are disrupting the traditional path by incorporating a temporary break in their careers in order to meet their personal goals.

Of the *Women on the Rise* respondents, 72 percent paused their careers by either working part-time or leaving the workforce altogether.

WOMEN ON THE RISE **SURVEY**

Since You First Began Working, Has There Ever Been a Time When You Took a Voluntary Pause from the Paid Workforce?

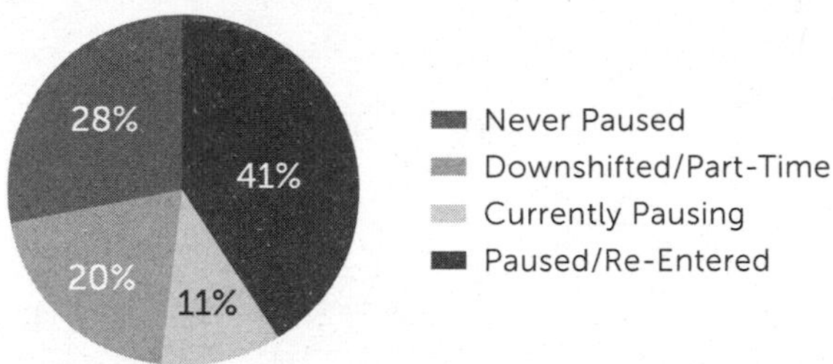

Despite being highly ambitious and having invested extensive time and money into their careers, the majority of *Women on the Rise* respondents did pause their careers.

EXPECTATIONS VERSUS REALITY

Was this part of their plan? Previous research out of Harvard Business School and other elite institutions found that while most of their alumnae did not expect or plan to pause their careers for kids, many ultimately did. At HBS, 42 percent of alumnae who have two or more children reported they left the paid workforce for a period of time, but most had not expected they would do so.[316] We wanted to know if our respondents had similar experiences. They did.

We asked them their thoughts about career and family when they first entered the workforce. Overall, only 11 percent of respondents expected to fully pause their careers when they had children, but as noted above, 20 percent of respondents eventually downshifted by working part-time or on a reduced schedule and 52 percent left the paid workforce fully for a period of time. In other words, for a significant segment of respondents, their expectations did not meet their reality.

Only 11 percent of *Women on the Rise* respondents planned to leave the paid workforce, but 52 percent actually did.

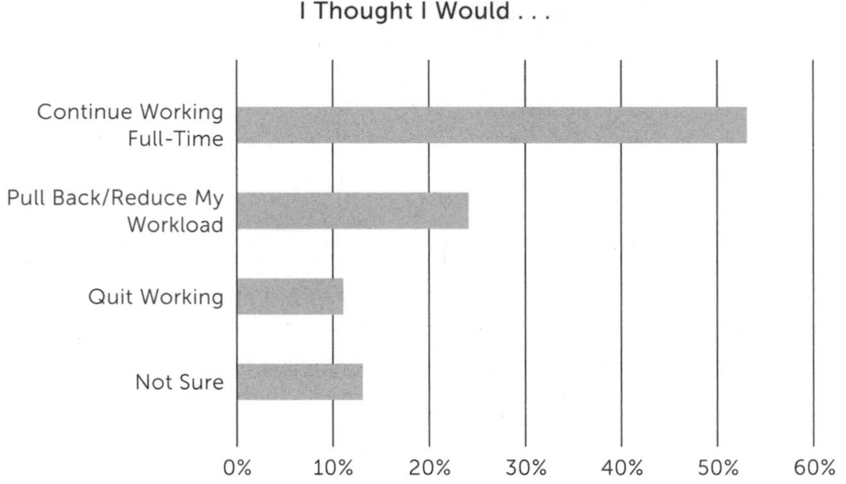

"I never imagined I would leave my job. I had big plans for my career . . . and then I had kids."

—*Women on the Rise* survey respondent

Once they had kids, the actual career paths of the *Women on the Rise* respondents did not align with their original goals and expectations.

WOMEN WHO STAYED THE COURSE

The answers from the 28 percent of respondents who followed a more traditional career path by never pausing gave us fascinating insights into why some women stay in the paid workforce.

First, they found deep satisfaction and personal validation in having a career. Over 90 percent told us this was a key driver for why they never left the paid workforce. Additionally, 82 percent reported they loved their jobs. Finally, and arguably most important, 59 percent said having a flexible workplace situation that allowed them to integrate their kids and careers was a key driver for them. In other words, beyond their personal motivations, they had work situations that supported them as mothers.

Of those who stayed in the paid workforce, 59 percent said workplace flexibility was a key reason they did NOT pause their careers.

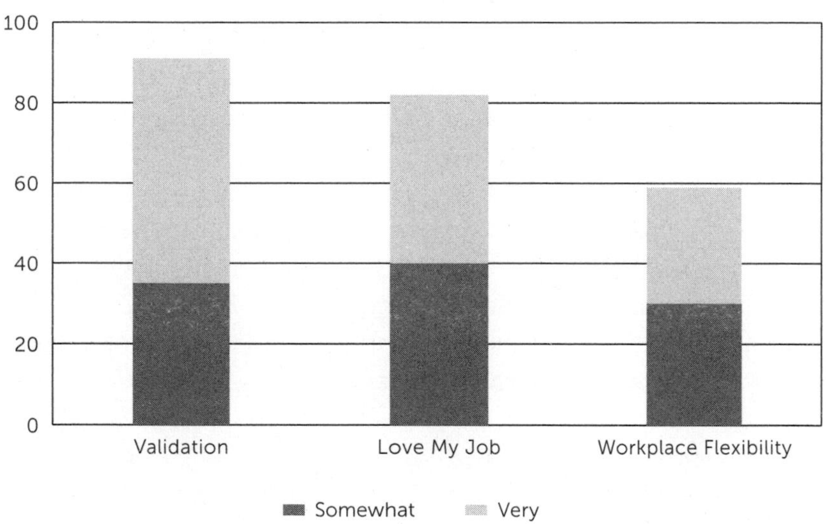

Respondents were given the opportunity to choose multiple responses

> *"Flexibility has been key. I don't feel like I've missed much with my children in terms of school programs, parties, sports activities, etc. Without the flexibility to get to do all of these things, I may have been bitter about working."*
>
> —*Women on the Rise* survey respondent

Most of the *Women on the Rise* respondents who never paused their careers didn't want or need to pause because they loved their jobs and had the flexibility to integrate work and life.

However, despite the fact that the vast majority of women who never paused reported they loved their jobs and found personal validation in having a career, nearly 40 percent of those who did not pause said they would have paused if they could have. Of those who never left the paid workforce, whether they wished they had paused or not, 73 percent said "I did not feel I had a choice" to pause. This could be because 45 percent of respondents who never paused were the primary breadwinners of their families. These women were married (81 percent) and had children at home (79 percent). While we did not ask them if their spouse was also working, many of these women reported in the comments section that their husbands had paused so they could continue their climb to the top.

As we see more women becoming the lead earners, we may see fewer mothers pausing. This may be because they will feel they don't have the option. Or, it might be because they have spouses who can serve as primary parent, freeing them up to focus on their careers. These husbands face challenges similar to those faced by women who have paused their careers.

> *"My career journey has been fully enabled by my husband. He has been home with our children for the past twelve years. Now he is trying to re-enter."*
>
> —*Women on the Rise* survey respondent

WOMEN WHO PAUSED AND WHY

We want to believe women who have devoted themselves to their professional development by securing college and graduate degrees will follow the same path as men who have marched directly up the ladder. Some do, as we saw with the 28 percent of respondents who never paused. But most of our respondents disrupted that paradigm and trailblazed a decidedly non-linear career path. We wondered why. Did they lack ambition? Were they forced out? We wanted to know what motivated them to leave.

Not surprisingly, the women who reported they never paused were also more likely to report they considered themselves "very" ambitious: 66 percent indicated they viewed themselves that way. But interestingly, when we asked the 72 percent of women who had paused (either by leaving the paid workforce completely or by downshifting and working part-time) how they viewed themselves, 63 percent of them indicated they too were "very" ambitious.

Of the *Women on the Rise* respondents who paused and relaunched their careers, 63 percent viewed themselves as "very" ambitious.

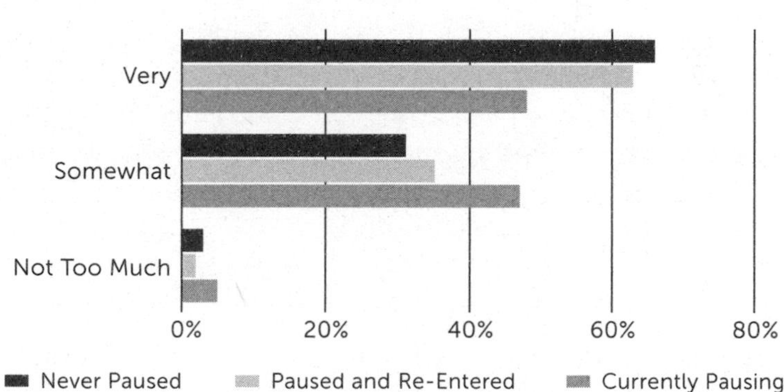

If it wasn't lack of ambition that drove them out, what did? Researchers have argued toxic workplaces have been at the heart of why women leave the paid workforce. No doubt pay inequity, sexist bosses, the constant fight to get credit for ideas, the sense that male colleagues who are less qualified are moving up the ladder faster, the never-ending feeling of not being good enough, the overt and covert sexual harassment, the frustration that comes with putting your heart and soul into your career and realizing you still won't rise to the top, has fueled the decision to leave for many.

In fact, 65 percent said workplace "intensity" and dissatisfaction were key reasons for why they left. They also reported they left because of a lack of workplace flexibility (56 percent) and pressures put on them by the demands of their partner's career (53 percent).

But, our research also revealed something deeper, something that many who are committed to seeing women in leadership seem loath to acknowledge: The number one reason these very ambitious, well-educated, highly qualified women paused their careers was because they wanted to be the primary caregiver of their children for a period of time, particularly when their children were young. Over 85 percent reported this as the biggest motivator for their decision to step off the well-trodden path and embark on a non-linear career journey.

Respondents who downshifted or left the workforce completely and then relaunched told us they cared for more than "just" their careers—that having a rich and rewarding family life was as important to them as being professionally successful. Given the workplace didn't support their needs as mothers, they decided to take a risk and temporarily prioritize family.

The majority told us they viewed their pause as the logical solution to an unyielding work culture. In other words, when forced to choose, these trailblazers were unwilling to sacrifice their family for their careers.

> While the vast majority of respondents considered themselves "very" ambitious, over 80 percent of women paused their careers did so because they wanted to be the primary caregiver to their young children.

WOMEN ON THE RISE SURVEY

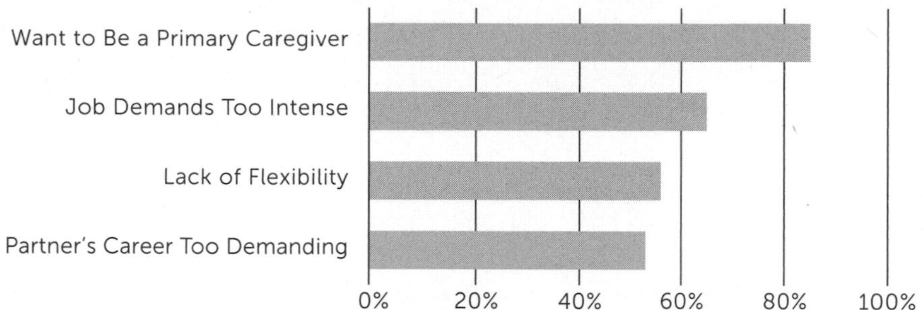

Respondents were given the opportunity to choose from multiple responses

> *"I believe that advancement in the workplace is extremely important, but should never be more important than family."*
> —*Women on the Rise* survey respondent

The myth of the "opt-out" mom who leaves the workforce because she lacks career motivation was not validated by our research. In many cases, they were the "canaries in the coal mine" whose actions revealed a deeper truth: The workplace does not support families in general and mothers in particular.

HOW HARD WAS IT TO RELAUNCH?

The assumption about pausing is that it is difficult to get back in. For those who paused longer than six years, this seems to be true. In fact, the vast majority of those who paused eleven years or longer reported it was difficult to relaunch. For those who had paused between two and five years, their career break did make re-entry more challenging, but not impossible. Re-entry was "easy" for those who took a brief two-year pause.

HOW CHALLENGING WAS YOUR RE-ENTRY?				
	<2 years	**2–5 years**	**6–10 years**	**11+ years**
Easy	**63%**	44%	31%	19%
Neither easy nor difficult	14%	22%	29%	13%
Difficult	23%	34%	40%	**68%**

Finding a job took relatively little time for those who had paused fewer than five years. The vast majority of them were able to be in the paid workforce within six months. Those who had taken more than five years out of the paid workforce were able to get back in, but it took longer—for over one-fifth it took as long as two years.

Overall, 66 percent of *Women on the Rise* respondents were able to find a new job in fewer than six months no matter how long they had paused.

HOW LONG DID IT TAKE TO GET YOUR FIRST POST-PAUSE POSITION?				
	<2 years	2–5 years	6–10 years	11+ years
Fewer than 6 months	**91%**	69%	56%	44%
6 months–1 year	8%	19%	31%	17%
13 months–2 years	0%	6%	10%	17%
More than 2 years	1%	6%	3%	**22%**

Overall, 69 percent reported they were in full swing in fewer than twelve months, and the shorter the pause, the faster respondents were able to feel back on track. However, it is important to note that a not insignificant percentage still struggled once they had relaunched. Is this because the workplace has not changed and so the issues they faced before they paused are still front and center, or is this because their pause negatively impacted their career? Our data did not give us insights into this important issue.

Overall, 69 percent of *Women on the Rise* respondents felt "back on track" within a year.

HOW LONG DID IT TAKE TO FEEL "BACK ON TRACK"?				
	<2 years	**2–5 years**	**6–10 years**	**11+ years**
Fewer than 6 months	62%	48%	50%	43%
6 months–1 year	18%	22%	10%	18%
More than a year	20%	30%	40%	39%

Here's the good news: Since re-igniting their careers, 67 percent of all relaunchers reported their compensation has increased and 35 percent indicated they have been promoted. And, 9 percent reported they had started a successful company. With so many indicating they have increased both their salary and responsibility, it is no wonder the majority feel "back on track" professionally in such a short period of time.

Relaunching was relatively easy for most women who paused for less than five years. And, no matter how long they had paused their careers, the vast majority of respondents felt "back on track" within a year of re-entering the paid workforce.

DID PAUSING KILL THEIR CAREERS?

Apparently not. The single biggest surprise from our *Women on the Rise* survey was the number of women who had paused, relaunched, and currently report being in senior-level roles at their companies. We know not every woman or man is going to rise to the top of his or her profession; only 35 percent of those who never paused listed their title as "director" level or higher. But here's the surprising news: When we looked at the data, we were encouraged to learn that one-third of women who had paused *also* had titles of "director" or above. In others words, rising up to a senior position was almost equally attainable whether a woman had paused or not.

We wondered if this was because those who paused had started their own companies and were able to give themselves the titles of their choice. The data did not bear this out. While 27 percent of those with high-level titles who paused and relaunched were entrepreneurs, an equal number worked for large companies. The rest worked for small or mid-sized companies.

Interestingly, we found that those women who never paused were much more likely to work for big companies than were relaunchers. Is this because big companies are less likely to hire relaunchers? Is it because relaunchers are more entrepreneurial? Is it because women who never paused have a lower risk tolerance and prefer the comfort and structure of a big institution? Our research did not unpack this issue.

While 35 percent of the women who had never paused their careers reported being senior managers, a full 30 percent of women who had paused also reported being senior managers.

WOMEN ON THE RISE SURVEY

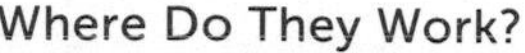

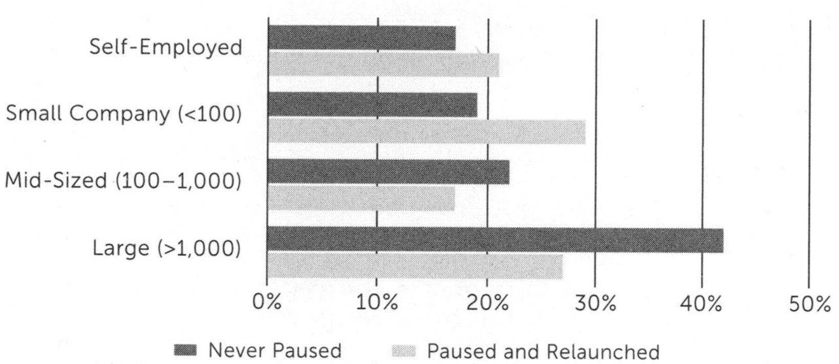

"People told me that if I paused it would be 'career suicide' and I would never be able to re-enter in a way that would be satisfying. I am so delighted to say that they were SO wrong."

—*Women on the Rise* survey respondent

Whether they paused or not, a comparable percentage of respondents rose to senior levels in their professions, debunking the myth that pausing or pulling back is career suicide for ambitious women.

PAUSING DOES HAVE CONSEQUENCES

Previous research[317] has noted that women who pause their careers often re-enter to lower-paying jobs. Our research validated these findings. While a quarter reported they did not have to make any compromises when they re-entered the paid workforce, 48 percent indicated they were forced to take lower pay and 41 percent took a lower position.

But, surprisingly, for nearly half our respondents this was part of their plan. Nearly 50 percent of women who paused their careers reported *intentionally* taking a less-demanding job with lower pay when they went back to the paid workforce. Why? A significant majority (64 percent) indicated they wanted "control of [their] time" and took a less demanding/lower-paying job because it would allow for greater flexibility.

Of the *Women on the Rise* respondents who paused their careers, 49 percent *intentionally* chose to relaunch to lower paying jobs with less responsibility because they wanted flexibility.

Respondents were given the opportunity to choose multiple responses

> *"Yes, I entered with lower pay and lower responsibilities, but I also had the choice to take higher pay and responsibilities. Flexibility was more important to me."*
>
> —*Women on the Rise* survey respondent

We did not ask respondents to specifically tell us about the financial implications of their career pause; however, many did in the comments section. While they claimed they had no regrets, many commented on the negative financial ramifications of their pause.

> *"I have done a number of things and all have worked out well financially. However, I am still not at the level of financial success (stock portfolio, executive bonuses, likely high-level salary at big company) that I would have attained had I not paused my career."*
>
> —*Women on the Rise* survey respondent

The *Women on the Rise* respondents may have innovated their own self-defined career path, but as many told us, the financial consequences are not insignificant.

Another issue many of these ambitious women commented on was the psychological challenges they faced as they watched their peers continue to rise up the ladder. This seemed to become particularly frustrating when those who had paused tried to regain professional footing. Having to re-enter at lower levels and taking longer to rise up the professional ladder nagged at some women.

When asked to expound on some of the biggest compromises they had to make as a result of their pause, one woman wrote, "Putting up with bullshit from less-experienced men who had not paused their careers" was a serious source of frustration. Why hadn't those men paused? She wrote, noting the irony, "they were supported and enabled at home by someone who had [paused]."

Loss of confidence for those who had paused their careers and not yet re-entered the paid workforce was another powerful sub-theme in the survey. Many wrote in the comments that they suffered from self-doubt. They didn't think they were going to be able to relaunch or wondered how they were going to do it. When asked what concerns they had about re-entering, the women who paused but had yet to relaunch reported they worried they had lost contact with their professional networks and had skills that were no longer relevant. They were also concerned about their résumé gap. As one woman wrote, "I'm worried that employers will think I've taken a 'holiday' rather than been doing the important work of caring for my children."

WOMEN ON THE RISE SURVEY

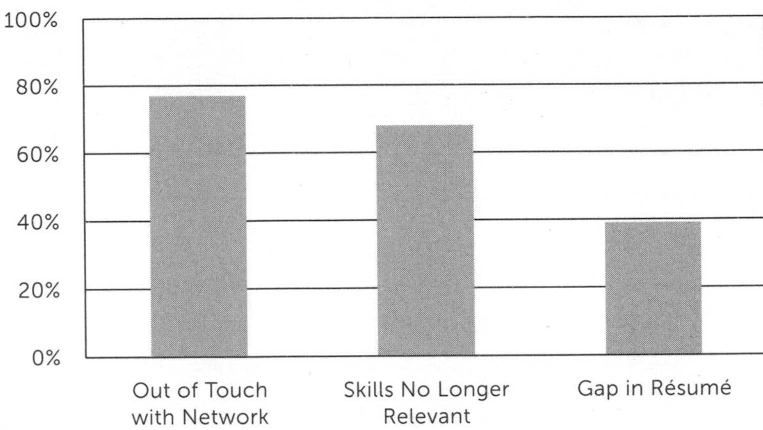

Respondents were given the opportunity to choose multiple responses

> *"I know what I have done matters, but does an employer?"*
>
> —*Women on the Rise* survey respondent

Another issue many women who had relaunched mentioned was the impact their second careers was having on their families. Guilt over how their children were faring now that their mother was not as readily available to them and frustration that they were still expected to be full-time mom and housewife even though they were now full-time employees were major issues for the women who were back in the paid workforce.

One powerful mitigating factor for these issues was the role their husbands played in their relaunch efforts. A number of women noted their husbands became more active in household and child care duties when they went back to the paid workforce.

> *"The key reason I was able to successfully get my career back on track is because my husband picked up the slack. I don't know how women do it otherwise."*
>
> —*Women on the Rise* survey respondent

> Pausing one's career requires a willingness to take risks, the confidence to create your own path, and a family who supports you along the way.

REGRETS?

We know the assumptions about how hard it is to "onramp" and the dire warnings that you'll have regrets if you "opt out," but that simply wasn't the reality for our respondents. Of those women who had left the paid workforce and then later re-entered, the vast majority reported they had no regrets. In fact, 78 percent reported they had no regrets AT ALL. And of those women who didn't leave the paid workforce entirely but pulled back to work part-time, 82 percent had no regrets.

Not surprisingly, the longer the respondent was out of the paid workforce, the more they regretted their decision to pause. For those out more than ten years, nearly 50 percent indicated they did regret their decision to leave the paid workforce.

> Of the *Women on the Rise* respondents who paused their career, 78 percent had NO regrets at all.

DO YOU HAVE ANY REGRETS ABOUT PAUSING?

	<2 years	2–5 years	6–10 years	11+ years
Yes	**3%**	14%	20%	**46%**
No	97%	86%	80%	54%

While the vast majority of those who paused their careers didn't regret a thing, of the 22 percent who did have regrets, 57 percent viewed pausing as a mistake. They reported it took longer for them to find work and when they did their pay was lower than they expected.

Of this 22 percent who indicated they regretted pausing their careers, 62 percent were between the ages of forty-five and fifty-four. These women were more likely to have older children and to have been out of the paid workforce longer. As a result, many reported they believed they faced not only motherhood bias but also ageism in their efforts to return to the paid workforce.

Those Who Believe Pausing Was a Mistake Also Faced the Following . . .

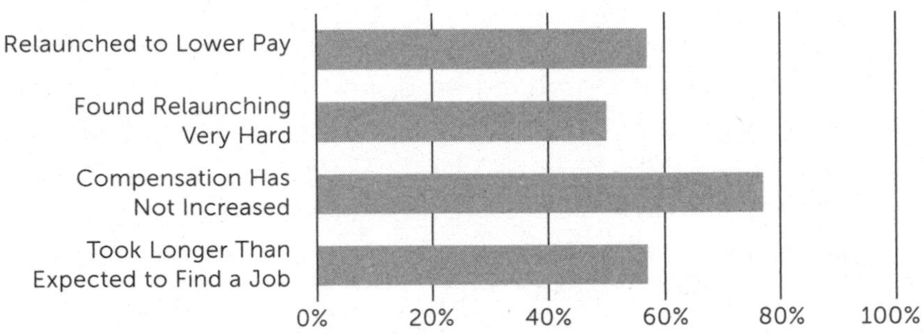

Respondents were given the opportunity to choose multiple responses

> *"Ageism was the biggest thing I faced when I relaunched my career. The recruiters and hiring managers are all very young. It's hard to break their preconceived ideas of what makes the best candidate especially if you have taken a career break for family."*
>
> —*Women on the Rise* survey respondent

Most respondents had no regrets about the path they took. However, the longer they paused, the harder it was to relaunch because of the twin challenges of motherhood bias and ageism.

REWARDS!

When we asked respondents who had paused about the benefits of their career path, they were enthusiastic, with 94 percent reporting they view themselves as good role models for their children even though they "opted out" for a period of time. Eighty-five percent said they felt more confident as a result of their pause, perhaps because 63 percent believe their paused enabled them to gain valuable skills that made them a "better, more engaged worker." For most, pausing was the optimal work–life integration solution, with 78 percent agreeing that doing so enabled them to gain the balance they wanted and needed.

> **The vast majority of *Women on the Rise* respondents (94 percent) who paused their career reported they viewed themselves as good role models for their children and 78 percent reported that pausing them helped them gain better work–life balance.**

Women on the Rewards of Pausing and Re-Igniting Their Careers

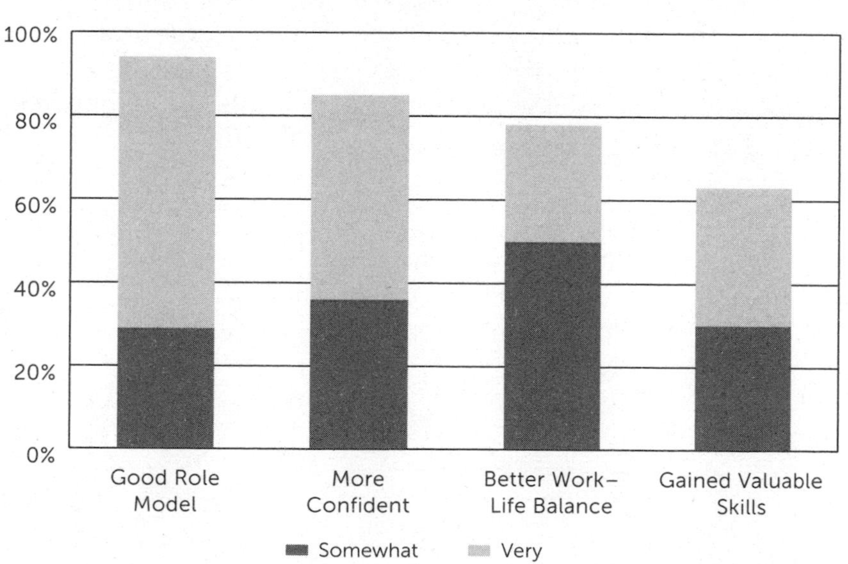

"I discovered I could have it all, just not all at once."
—*Women on the Rise* survey respondent

The trailblazers who paused their careers and then relaunched had high life satisfaction and considered themselves powerful role models for the next generation.

SUMMARY

Our *Women on the Rise* survey offers a different narrative about how very ambitious, highly qualified women navigate the challenges of work and family. Despite the assumption that pausing is a career killer, for most it was not. And for some, it was a needed break on their path to the top. The women who paused their careers proved to have a higher tolerance for risk and a deep commitment to their roles as mothers and caregivers, which empowered them to disrupt the traditional paradigm and find innovative ways to integrate kids with their careers. Their choices led to a higher sense of self-confidence, a belief that they were good role models for their children, and greater work–life balance. As a result, the vast majority had no regrets.

For further information and a deeper dive into the results of the survey, visit www.workpausethrive.com.

ACKNOWLEDGMENTS

When I became pregnant with my first child, I dreamed of giving him a gentle home birth with candles, soft music, and only my husband and a doula nearby for encouragement and support. William's birth story was so far from my fantasy it is, even today, almost laughable. It took an extended tribe of doctors, nurses, family, friends, neighbors, and coworkers to help bring him into this world. How I became a mother wasn't according to plan, but nothing ever really is, is it?

So, too, with this book. No candles, no music, no single doula brought *Work PAUSE Thrive* to life. It took a tribe of women and men who dedicated their time and support to give it birth. Words can never express my gratitude to each of you, but special thanks goes to the following:

To my intern, "Rebooter" Denise Donnelly, for tirelessly scouring the internet for resources and ideas.

To my research assistant, Aparajita Pande, for always saying yes and always delivering beyond my wildest dreams.

To my research gurus, Professor Pamela Stone, Carol Fishman Cohen, Erin O'Reilly, and Erin St. Onge-Carpenter, for keeping it real and right.

To Holly Payne, Katrina Alcorn, Amanda Enayati, Sarah Granger, and all of the other Authoresses, for providing support in ways too numerous to count.

To Josh Levs, for being one hell of a manbassador.

To my sisters at the Journalism and Women Symposium, for welcoming me as one of your own.

To Sarah Pollock and Kat Rowlands, for guiding, coaching, and encouraging me.

To Diana Henriques, for assuring me, "Yes, you could write a book. Why not?"

ACKNOWLEDGMENTS

To the Amazing Chix—you know who you are.

To Margarita Herrera, who has been there for me from the beginning.

To The 3% Movement CEO and founder, Kat Gordon, who champions change for women and men each and every day, for championing me.

To the incredible women in my Not-So-New-Mothers Group, for being there at the beginning, the middle, and the now. You are my guiding lights.

To Brooke Warner, for being the best book proposal doula an aspiring author could ask for.

To my agent, Brandi Bowles, who lives the reality of this book each and every day, for being an invaluable advocate.

To my publisher, Glenn Yeffeth, and the entire team at BenBella Books, for believing from the beginning and for having been better partners than I could have dreamed possible.

To my editor, new mother Leah Wilson, for making this book far better than I ever imagined it could be. I am so grateful for your vision, your advocacy, and our partnership. May a full night's sleep be yours again soon.

To the 1,476 respondents to the *Women on the Rise* survey and to the nearly two hundred women and men I interviewed—I am awed by your willingness to reveal your truths. Your passionate commitment to making sure the next generation has insight into the opportunities and challenges ahead continues to inspire. You are the trailblazers that show there are a myriad of ways to work, pause, and thrive.

Finally, to men. If you've gotten this far, you know this book isn't about complaining or finger-pointing, it's about solutions, and you are part of the solution. Here's to working together to co-create a future that allows each of us to lead our best lives.

In gratitude,
Lisen Stromberg

ENDNOTES

1 Professor Pamela Stone was the first to apply the term "canaries in the coal mine" to high-caliber women who left the paid workforce to care for children in her 2007 book, *Opting Out? Why Women Really Quit Careers and Head Home.*

2 While there are 80 million Millennials, not all will be parents. For a great read on the subject, check out this *Wall Street Journal* article: Zumbrun, Josh. "Coming Soon: Millennials Married with Children." *WSJ.* August 12, 2015. Accessed July 14, 2016. http://www.wsj.com/articles/coming-soon-millennials-married-with-children-1439371801

3 Sandberg, Sheryl. *Lean In: Women, Work, and the Will to Lead.* 14. New York: Random House, 2013.

4 Burch, Tory. "Commencement Speech." Speech, Class of 2014 Commencement, Babson College, Babson Park, Massachusetts, May 2014. http://www.babson.edu/news-events/events/commencement/2014-recap/pages/burch-tory.aspx

5 "Table 4. Families with Own Children: Employment Status of Parents by Age of Youngest Child and Family Type, 2014-2015 Annual Averages." U.S. Department of Labor Bureau of Labor Statistics. 2016. http://www.bls.gov/news.release/famee.t04.htm

6 "Happy Mother's Day from BLS: Working Mothers in 2012." U.S. Department of Labor Bureau of Labor Statistics. 2013. http://www.bls.gov/opub/ted/2013/ted_20130510.htm

7 Cohn, D'vera, Gretchen Livingston, and Wendy Wang. "After Decades of Decline, a Rise in Stay-at-Home Mothers." Pew Research Center. April 8, 2014. http://www.pewsocialtrends.org/2014/04/08/after-decades-of-decline-a-rise-in-stay-at-home-mothers/

8 "Fast Facts: Educational Attainment." U.S. Department of Education, National Center for Education Statistics. 2015. https://nces.ed.gov/fastfacts/display.asp?id=27

9 Cohen, Carol F. "The '40-Year-Old Intern' Corporate Reentry Internships." iRelaunch. Last modified January 25, 2016. http://www.iedcevents.org/Downloads/Conferences/Leadership_16/cohen.pdf

10 Hersch, Joni. "Opting Out Among Women with Elite Education." *Review of Economics of the Household* 11, no. 4 (2013): 469–506. doi:10.1007/s11150-013-9199-4

11 Ibid.

12 Ibid.

13 "Life and Leadership After HBS." Harvard Business School. Last modified May 2015. http://www.hbs.edu/women50/docs/L_and_L_Survey_2Findings_12final.pdf

14 Cohn, D'vera, Gretchen Livingston, and Wendy Wang. "After Decades of Decline, a Rise in Stay-at-Home Mothers." Pew Research Center. April 8, 2014. http://www.pewsocialtrends.org/2014/04/08/after-decades-of-decline-a-rise-in-stay-at-home-mothers/

ENDNOTES

15 Friedman, Stewart D. *Baby Bust: New Choices for Men and Women in Work and Family.* Philadelphia: Wharton Digital Press, 2013.

16 Newport, Frank, and Joy Wilke. "Desire for Children Still Norm in U.S." Gallup. September 25, 2013. http://www.gallup.com/poll/164618/desire-children-norm.aspx

17 Bowers, Katherine. "A Mother's Work: Special Report." *Working Mother.* March 19, 2014. Accessed July 15, 2016. http://www.workingmother.com/special-report/mothers-work-special-report

18 *Millennial Careers: 2020 Vision.* ManpowerGroup, 2016. http://www.manpowergroup.com/wps/wcm/connect/660ebf65-144c-489e-975c-9f838294c237/MillennialsPaper1_2020Vision_lo.pdf?MOD=AJPERES

19 "Work-Life Challenges Across Generations: Global Study." Ernst & Young. Last modified 2015. http://www.ey.com/US/en/About-us/Our-people-and-culture/EY-work-life-challenges-across-generations-global-study

20 Steinmetz, Katy. "Help! My Parents Are Millennials." *Time.* October 26, 2015. http://time.com/help-my-parents-are-millennials-cover-story/

21 "Life and Leadership After HBS." Harvard Business School. Last modified May 2015. http://www.hbs.edu/women50/docs/L_and_L_Survey_2Findings_12final.pdf

22 "On Pay Gap, Millennial Women Near Parity—For Now." Pew Research Center. December 11, 2013. http://www.pewsocialtrends.org/2013/12/11/on-pay-gap-millennial-women-near-parity-for-now/

23 Belkin, Lisa. "The Opt-Out Revolution." *The New York Times.* October 26, 2003. http://www.nytimes.com/2003/10/26/magazine/26WOMEN.html?pagewanted=all

24 Warner, Judith. *Perfect Madness: Motherhood in the Age of Anxiety.* New York: Riverhead Books, 2006.

25 Warner, Judith. "The Opt-Out Generation Wants Back In." *The New York Times.* August 7, 2013. http://www.nytimes.com/2013/08/11/magazine/the-opt-out-generation-wants-back-in.html?pagewanted=all&_r=1

26 The women I interviewed were all college-educated middle-class and upper-middle-class mothers. Most were married. They lived across the country from Silicon Valley to Texas to Florida and New England. What they had in common was a mutual commitment to their careers AND to their families.

27 Stone, Pamela. *Opting Out? Why Women Really Quit Careers and Head Home.* Berkeley and Los Angeles: University of California Press, 2007.

28 Hewlett, Sylvia A., and Carolyn Buck Luce. "Off-Ramps and On-Ramps: Keeping Talented Women on the Road to Success." *Harvard Business Review.* March 2005. https://hbr.org/2005/03/off-ramps-and-on-ramps-keeping-talented-women-on-the-road-to-success

29 Special thanks go out to Erin Reilly, doctoral candidate at University of Texas at Austin, who provided additional insights and to Aparajita Pande, my intrepid intern. Her dogged commitment to the project was essential to its success.

30 Catlin, Karen. "Thinking About a Part-time Role in Tech?" *Global Tech Women.* January 7, 2013. http://www.globaltechwomen.com/blog/thinking-about-a-part-time-role-in-tech

31 I had the pleasure of profiling Kriste for the San Jose *Mercury News* in an article entitled "Back on the Fast Track: How 3 Execs Opted Out for Motherhood, Then Opted Back In."

Stromberg, Lisen. "Back on the Fast Track: How 3 Execs Opted Out for Motherhood, Then Opted Back In." *The Mercury News.* September 11, 2014. http://www.mercurynews.com/bay-area-living/ci_26508289/back-fast-track-how-3-execs-opted-out

ENDNOTES

32 The term "single shingle" comes from the French term *une enseigne*. It was used as a sign for a shop owned by one person. For women, the term has been converted to "cupcake" business and is often said in a derogatory manner to indicate a small, unambitious avocation.

33 Cantwell, Maria. "21st Century Barriers to Women's Entrepreneurship." U.S. Senate Committee on Small Business and Entrepreneurship. July 23, 2014. http://www.sbc.senate.gov/public/?a=Files.Serve&File_id=3f954386-f16b-48d2-86ad-698a75e33cc4

34 Fetsch, Emily, Chris Jackson, and Jason Wiens. "Women Entrepreneurs Are Key to Accelerating Growth." *Entrepreneurship Policy Digest*. Ewing Marion Kauffman Foundation. July 20, 2015. http://www.kauffman.org/what-we-do/resources/entrepreneurship-policy-digest/women-entrepreneurs-are-key-to-accelerating-growth

35 *Women-Owned Businesses (WOBs): NWBC Analysis of 2012 Survey of Business Owners*. National Women's Business Council, n.d. https://www.nwbc.gov/sites/default/files/FS_Women-Owned_Businesses.pdf

36 "New OPEN Report Shows Phenomenal Growth for Women-Owned Businesses." American Express OPEN. April 2013. https://www.americanexpress.com/us/small-business/openforum/articles/latest-trends-in-women-owned-businesses/

37 Robb, Alicia, and Dane Stangler. "Sources of Economic Hope: Women's Entrepreneurship." Ewing Marion Kauffman Foundation. November 19, 2014. http://www.kauffman.org/what-we-do/research/2014/11/sources-of-economic-hope-womens-entrepreneurship

38 Brush, Candida G., Patricia G. Greene, Lakshmi Balachandra, and Amy E. Davis. "Women Entrepreneurs 2014: Bridging the Gender Gap in Venture Capital." Arthur M. Blank Center for Entrepreneurship, Babson College. September 2014. http://www.babson.edu/Academics/centers/blank-center/global-research/diana/Documents/diana-project-executive-summary-2014.pdf

39 Cross, Lindsay. "I Hate 'Mompreneurs' But I Support Women in Business." The Grindstone. October 3, 2011. http://www.thegrindstone.com/2011/10/03/career-management/i-hate-mompreneurs-but-i-support-women-in-business-327/

40 Casserly, Meghan. "'Mompreneur:' Own It, Ignore It or Prove It Wrong." *Forbes*. October 4, 2011. http://www.forbes.com/sites/meghancasserly/2011/10/04/mompreneur-own-it-ignore-it-or-prove-it-wrong/

41 Casserly, Meghan. "Female Founders: Overcoming The Cupcake Challenge And 'Mompreneur' Stigma." *Forbes*. March 22, 2011. http://www.forbes.com/sites/meghancasserly/2011/03/22/female-founders-cupcake-challenge-gilt-groupe-learnvest-zipcar/

42 "Meet the Woman Who's Shaking Up Silicon Valley with Stella & Dot." TODAY.com. December 10, 2015. http://www.today.com/video/meet-the-woman-whos-shaking-up-silicon-valley-with-stella-dot-583496771506

43 Casserly, Meghan. "Female Founders: Overcoming the Cupcake Challenge and 'Mompreneur' Stigma." *Forbes*. March 22, 2011. http://www.forbes.com/sites/meghancasserly/2011/03/22/female-founders-cupcake-challenge-gilt-groupe-learnvest-zipcar/

44 Robb, Alicia, and Dane Stangler. "Sources of Economic Hope: Women's Entrepreneurship." Ewing Marion Kauffman Foundation. November 19, 2014. http://www.kauffman.org/what-we-do/research/2014/11/sources-of-economic-hope-womens-entrepreneurship

45 Stone, Lisa. Women.com. Accessed August 2, 2016. http://www.women.com

46 Wallbridge, Wendy. *Spiraling Upward: The 5 Co-Creative Powers for Women on the Rise*. Brookline, MA: Bibliomotion, 2015.

47 Slaughter, Anne-Marie. *Unfinished Business: Women Men Work Family*. 6. New York: Random House, 2015.

ENDNOTES

48 Stone, Pamela. "The Rhetoric and Reality of 'Opting Out.'" *Contexts* 6, no. 4 (2007): 14–19. doi:10.1525/ctx.2007.6.4.14

49 "Act II." Bloomberg.com. March 29, 2004. http://www.bloomberg.com/bw/stories/2004-03-28/act-ii

50 For more data on the ideal worker, check out this report by Catalyst: Carter, Nancy M., and Christine Silva. "The Myth of the Ideal Worker: Does Doing All the Right Things Really Get Women Ahead?" Catalyst. 2011. http://www.catalyst.org/system/files/The_Myth_of_the_Ideal_Worker_Does_Doing_All_the_Right_Things_Really_Get_Women_Ahead.pdf

51 Blair-Loy, Mary. *Competing Devotions: Career and Family Among Women Executives.* Cambridge, MA: Harvard University Press, 2003.

52 Trae Vassallo, in partnership with market research guru Michele Madansky, conducted a survey of senior women in Silicon Valley called the "Elephant in the Valley." For a complete review of their research, visit http://www.elephantinthevalley.com/

53 For a deep dive into the survey results, visit http://www.elephantinthevalley.com/

54 For a thorough overview of the issue, visit http://www.catalyst.org/knowledge/sex-discrimination-and-sexual-harassment-0

55 Kitroeff, Natalie, and Jonathan Rodkin. "The Real Payoff from an MBA Is Different for Men and Women." Bloomberg.com. October 20, 2015. http://www.bloomberg.com/news/articles/2015-10-20/the-real-cost-of-an-mba-is-different-for-men-and-women

56 Correll, Shelley J., Stephen Benard, and In Paik. "Getting a Job: Is There a Motherhood Penalty?" *American Journal of Sociology* 112, no. 5 (2007): 1297–1339. doi:10.1086/511799

57 Williams, Joan C. "The Maternal Wall." *Harvard Business Review.* October 2004. https://hbr.org/2004/10/the-maternal-wall

58 Halpert, Jane A., Midge L. Wilson, and Julia L. Hickman. "Pregnancy as a Source of Bias in Performance Appraisals." *Journal of Organizational Behavior* 14, no. 7 (1993): 649–663. doi:10.1002/job.4030140704

59 Euben, Donna. "Working Mothers and Gender Discrimination." *The Chronicle of Higher Education.* May 27,2005. http://www.aaup.org/issues/women-higher-education/working-mothers-gender-discrimination

60 Ibid.

61 Williams, Joan C., Mary Blair-Loy, and Jennifer L. Berdahl. "Cultural Schemas, Social Class, and the Flexibility Stigma." *Journal of Social Issues* 69, no. 2 (2013): 209–234. doi:10.1111/josi.12012

62 Williams, Joan C., Mary Blair-Loy, and Jennifer L. Berdahl. "The Flexibility Stigma: Work Devotion vs. Family Devotion." Center for WorkLife Law. Winter 2013. http://worklifelaw.org/pubs/TheFlexibilityStigma.pdf

63 Matos, Kenneth, and Ellen Galinsky. "2014 National Study of Employers." Families and Work Institute. Last modified 2014. http://www.familiesandwork.org/2014-national-study-of-employers/

64 Bernard, Tara S. "The Unspoken Stigma of Workplace Flexibility." *The New York Times.* June 14, 2013. http://www.nytimes.com/2013/06/15/your-money/the-unspoken-stigma-of-workplace-flexibility.html?_r=0

65 Kuttner, Robert. "She Minds the Child, He Minds the Dog." *The New York Times.* June 25, 1989. http://www.nytimes.com/1989/06/25/books/she-minds-the-child-he-minds-the-dog.html?pagewanted=all

66 Meers, Sharon, and Joanna Strober. *Getting to 50/50: How Working Couples Can Have It All.* 76. New York: Random House, 2009.

ENDNOTES

67 Parker, Kim, and Wendy Wang. "Modern Parenthood." Pew Research Center. March 14, 2013. http://www.pewsocialtrends.org/2013/03/14/modern-parenthood-roles-of-moms-and-dads-converge-as-they-balance-work-and-family/

68 Miller, Claire Cain. "Mounting Evidence of Advantages for Children of Working Mothers." *The New York Times*. May 15, 2015. http://www.nytimes.com/2015/05/17/upshot/mounting-evidence-of-some-advantages-for-children-of-working-mothers.html

69 Lucas-Thompson, Rachel G., Wendy A. Goldberg, and JoAnn Prause. "Maternal Work Early in the Lives of Children and Its Distal Associations with Achievement and Behavior Problems: A Meta-Analysis." *Psychological Bulletin* 136, no. 6 (2010): 915–942. doi:10.1037/a0020875

70 Warner, Judith. *Perfect Madness: Motherhood in the Age of Anxiety*. 91-92. New York: Riverhead Books, 2005.

71 Ibid., 54–55.

72 Friedan, Betty. *The Feminine Mystique*. New York: W. W. Norton, 1963.

73 Gino, Francesca, Caroline A. Wilmuth, and Alison W. Brooks. "Compared to Men, Women View Professional Advancement as Equally Attainable, but Less Desirable." *Proceedings of the National Academy of Sciences* 112, no. 40 (2015): 12354–12359. doi:10.1073/pnas.1502567112

74 Levy, Jessica. "I Wanted to Stay Home with My Son. So Why Would I Lie About It?" *The New York Times*. November 1, 2015. http://parenting.blogs.nytimes.com/2015/11/01/i-wanted-to-stay-home-with-my-son-so-why-would-i-lie-about-it/?smid=fb-nytimes&smtyp=cur&_r=0

75 Cox, Daniel, and Robert P. Jones. "How Race and Religion Shape Millennial Attitudes on Sexuality and Reproductive Health." Public Religion Research Institute. Last modified March 27, 2015. http://www.prri.org/research/survey-how-race-and-religion-shape-millennial-attitudes-on-sexuality-and-reproductive-health/

76 Friedan, Betty. *The Second Stage*. 71. New York: Summit Books, 1981.

77 "The Condition of Education 2012." National Center for Education Statistics. Last modified 2012. https://nces.ed.gov/fastfacts/display.asp?id=72

78 This information was compiled using statistics from the U.S. Department of Labor's list of "Non-Traditional Occupations," U.S. Census Bureau, Catalyst, Congressional Research Service, and NALP diversity statistics.

79 For a complete list of those professions that women dominate, check out the U.S. Department of Labor's list of traditional occupations: http://www.dol.gov/wb/stats/TraditionalOccupations.pdf

80 McKinsey & Company, in partnership with LeanIn.org, conducted an extensive analysis of women's careersacross nine industries in 118 North American companies. For more information, visit http://www.mckinsey.com/business-functions/organization/our-insights/breaking-down-the-gender-challenge

81 Warner, Judith. "The Opt-Out Generation Wants Back In." *The New York Times*. August 7, 2013. http://www.nytimes.com/2013/08/11/magazine/the-opt-out-generation-wants-back-in.html?pagewanted=all&_r=1

82 "What Women Want: Results from Our 3% Community Survey." The 3% Movement. Last modified 2016. http://www.3percentconf.com/downloads/what-women-want-results-our-3-community-survey

83 Slaughter, Anne-Marie. *Unfinished Business: Women Men Work Family*. 58. New York: Random House, 2015.

84 Applebaum, Eileen, Heather Boushey, and John Schmitt. "The Economic Importance of Women's Rising Hours of Work." Center for American Progress. April 15, 2014. https://www.americanprogress.org/issues/labor/report/2014/04/15/87638/the-economic-importance-of-womens-rising-hours-of-work/

ENDNOTES

85 Guilford, Gwynn. "The Economic Case for Paternity Leave." *Quartz*. September 24, 2014. http://qz.com/266841/economic-case-for-paternity-leave/

86 "LFS by Sex and Age—Indicators." OECD Statistics. Accessed July 16, 2016. https://stats.oecd.org/Index.aspx?DataSetCode=LFS_SEXAGE_I_R#

87 Ibid.

88 Cook, Lindsey. "These Charts Show the Insane Cost of Child Care." *U.S. News & World Report*. October 8, 2015.

89 Holland, Kelley. "The High Economic and Social Costs of Student Loan Debt." CNBC. June 15, 2015. http://www.cnbc.com/2015/06/15/the-high-economic-and-social-costs-of-student-loan-debt.html

90 Kantor, Jodi. "Working Anything but 9 to 5." *The New York Times*. August 13, 2014. http://www.nytimes.com/interactive/2014/08/13/us/starbucks-workers-scheduling-hours.html?_r=0

91 Graff, E. J. "The Opt-Out Myth." *Columbia Journalism Review*. March/April 2007. http://www.cjr.org/essay/the_optout_myth.php

92 "Transcript: Michelle Obama's Convention Speech." NPR.org. Last modified September 4, 2012. http://www.npr.org/2012/09/04/160578836/transcript-michelle-obamas-convention-speech

93 Cottle, Michelle. "Leaning Out." *POLITICO Magazine*. November 21, 2013. http://www.politico.com/magazine/story/2013/11/leaning-out-michelle-obama-100244

94 Kingston, Anne. "'Mom-in-Chief' Provokes Debate on Feminism and Gender Roles." *Macleans*. September 13, 2012. http://www.macleans.ca/news/world/mommy-wars/

95 Cohn, D'vera, Gretchen Livingston, and Wendy Wang. "After Decades of Decline, a Rise in Stay-at-Home Mothers." Pew Research Center. April 8, 2014. http://www.pewsocialtrends.org/2014/04/08/after-decades-of-decline-a-rise-in-stay-at-home-mothers/

96 And it should be noted, these new immigrants are much more likely to be college-educated than Americans. In 2013, a full 41 percent of recent immigrants had graduated from college versus only 30 percent of native-born Americans. For further information, read: Fry, Richard. "Today's Newly Arrived Immigrants Are the Best-Educated Ever." Pew Research Center. October 5, 2015. http://www.pewresearch.org/fact-tank/2015/10/05/todays-newly-arrived-immigrants-are-the-best-educated-ever/

97 Obama, Michelle. "What Women Owe One Another." *More* magazine. July/August 2015.

98 Donnelly, Kristin, Jean M. Twenge, Malissa A. Clark, Samia K. Shaikh, Angela Beiler-May, and Nathan T. Carter. "Attitudes Toward Women's Work and Family Roles in the United States, 1976–2013." *Psychology of Women Quarterly*. June 26, 2015.

99 Parker, Kim, and Wendy Wang. "Modern Parenthood." Pew Research Center. March 14, 2013. http://www.pewsocialtrends.org/2013/03/14/modern-parenthood-roles-of-moms-and-dads-converge-as-they-balance-work-and-family/

100 "Parenting in America." Pew Research Center's Social & Demographic Trends Project. Last modified December 17, 2015. http://www.pewsocialtrends.org/2015/12/17/parenting-in-america/?utm_source=Pew+Research+Center&utm_campaign=aeceff44ba-12_16_2015&utm_medium=email&utm_term=0_3e953b9b70-aeceff44ba-399756373

101 Kurtzleben, Danielle. "New Data Show Women, More Educated Doing Most Volunteering." *U.S. News & World Report*. February 27, 2013. http://www.usnews.com/news/articles/2013/02/27/charts-new-data-show-women-more-educated-doing-most-volunteering

102 Crittenden, Ann. *The Price of Motherhood: Why the Most Important Job in the World Is Still the Least Valued.* 65. New York: Metropolitan Books, 2001. Ann Crittenden provides a thorough overview of how traditional women's work has been devalued.

ENDNOTES

103 Budig, Michelle J., and Paula England. "The Wage Penalty for Motherhood." *American Sociological Review* 66, no. 2 (2001): 204–225. doi:10.2307/2657415

104 Crittenden, Ann. *The Price of Motherhood: Why the Most Important Job in the World Is Still the Least Valued.* 77. New York: Metropolitan Books, 2001.

105 Ibid., 73.

106 "Volunteering in the United States News Release." U.S. Department of Labor Bureau of Labor Statistics. 2016. http://www.bls.gov/news.release/volun.htm

107 "Volunteering and Civic Engagement Among Women." Corporation for National & Community Service. Accessed July 18, 2016. https://www.volunteeringinamerica.gov/special/Women

108 O'Donnell, Liz. "The Crisis Facing America's Working Daughters." *The Atlantic.* February 9, 2016. http://www.theatlantic.com/business/archive/2016/02/working-daughters-eldercare/459249/

109 Tumlinson, Anne. Accessed August 2, 2016. http://daughterhood.org

110 Abrahms, Sally. "Help! Who Will Care for Baby Boomers When They Need it?" AARP. August 26, 2013. http://blog.aarp.org/2013/08/26/sally-abrahms-help-who-will-care-for-baby-boomers-when-they-need-it/

111 Fry, Richard. "Millennials Overtake Baby Boomers as American's Largest Generation." Pew Research Center. April, 25, 2016. http://www.pewresearch.org/fact-tank/2016/04/25/millennials-overtake-baby-boomers/

112 Bergersen, Kristin. "Report from Norway by Our Transnational Partner." European Database: Women in Decision-Making. Accessed August 2, 2016. http://www.db-decision.de/CoRe/Norway.htm

113 O'Donnell, Paul. "20% of Employers Violate FMLA, Study Concludes." *Cleveland.com.* May 27, 2008. http://blog.cleveland.com/business/2008/05/20_of_employers_violate_fmla_s.html

114 "Parental Benefit." Norwegian Labour and Welfare Administration.. https://www.nav.no/en/Home/Benefits+and+services/Relatert+informasjon/parental-benefit

115 Shepherd-Banigan, Megan, and Janice F. Bell. "Paid Leave Benefits Among a National Sample of Working Mothers with Infants in the United States." *Maternal and Child Health Journal* 18, no. 1 (2013): 286–295. doi:10.1007/s10995-013-1264-3

116 Lerner, Sharon. "The Real War on Families: Why the U.S. Needs Paid Leave Now." *In These Times.* August 18, 2015. http://inthesetimes.com/article/18151/the-real-war-on-families

117 "Maternity/Paternity Leave." MomsRising. Accessed August 2, 2016. http://www.momsrising.org/issues_and_resources/maternity

118 "Parental Benefit." Norwegian Labour and Welfare Administration. https://www.nav.no/en/Home/Benefits+and+services/Relatert+informasjon/parental-benefit#chapter-3

119 Rindfuss, Ronald R., David K. Guilkey, S. P. Morgan, and Øystein Kravdal. "Child-Care Availability and Fertility in Norway." *Population and Development Review* 36, no. 4 (2010): 725–748. doi:10.1111/j.1728-4457.2010.00355.x

120 Story, Mary, Karen M. Kaphingst, and Simone French. "The Role of Child Care Settings in Obesity Prevention." *The Future of Children* 16, no. 1 (Spring 2006): 143–168. doi:10.1353/foc.2006.0010

121 Grose, Jessica. "What It's Like for a Working Mom in Oslo, Norway." *Slate* magazine. August 21, 2014. http://www.slate.com/blogs/xx_factor/2014/08/21/child_care_in_norway_an_oslo_mom_on_how_working_parents_manage.html

122 "Cash-for-Care Benefit." Norwegian Labour and Welfare Administration. Last modified August 8, 2016. https://www.nav.no/en/Home/Relatert+informasjon/cash-for-care-benefits-for-the-parents-of-toddlers--805369180#chapter-2

123 "Leaving Children to Chance: 2012 Update." Child Care Aware. Last modified 2012. http://usa.childcareaware.org/advocacy-public-policy/resources/reports-and-research/leaving-children-to-chance-2012-update/

124 Laughlin, Lynda. "Who's Minding the Kids? Child Care Arrangements: Spring 2011." U.S. Department of Commerce, Census Bureau. April 2013. http://www.census.gov/prod/2013pubs/p70-135.pdf

125 "Child Care in America: 2014 State Fact Sheets." Child Care Aware. Last modified 2014. http://www.ks.childcareaware.org/wp-content/uploads/2014/09/2014-Child-Care-in-America_State-Fact-Sheets.pdf

126 Rose, Jenn. "Child Care Costs Are So High, Many Of Us Can't Actually Afford Them, Says New Report." *Bustle*. October 20, 2015. http://www.bustle.com/articles/115229-child-care-costs-are-so-high-many-of-us-cant-actually-afford-them-says-new-report

127 Matos, Kenneth, and Ellen Galinsky. "2014 National Study of Employers." Families and Work Institute. Last modified 2014. http://www.familiesandwork.org/2014-national-study-of-employers/

128 Schulte, Brigid. *Overwhelmed: How to Work, Love, and Play When No One Has the Time*. 99. New York: Picador, 2014.

129 Ibid., 100.

130 Ibid., 101.

131 "Fact Sheet: Helping All Working Families with Young Children Afford Child Care." The White House—Office of the Press Secretary. January 21, 2015. https://www.whitehouse.gov/the-press-office/2015/01/21/fact-sheet-helping-all-working-families-young-children-afford-child-care

132 "POP1 Child Population: Number of Children (in Millions) Ages 0–17 in the United States by Age, 1950–2015 and Projected 2016–2050." Forum on Child and Family Statistics. 2016. http://www.childstats.gov/americaschildren/tables/pop1.asp

133 Powell, Bonnie. "Framing the Issues." *UC Berkeley News*. October 27, 2003. http://www.berkeley.edu/news/media/releases/2003/10/27_lakoff.shtml

134 Cohn, D'vera, Gretchen Livingston, and Wendy Wang. "After Decades of Decline, a Rise in Stay-at-Home Mothers." Pew Research Center. April 8, 2014. http://www.pewsocialtrends.org/2014/04/08/after-decades-of-decline-a-rise-in-stay-at-home-mothers/

135 Wesley, Daniel. "How Countries Spend Their Money." Visual Economics. CreditLoan.com. Accessed August 2, 2016. http://visualeconomics.creditloan.com/how-countries-spend-their-money/

136 "Norway's Petroleum History." Norwegian Petroleum. Accessed August 2, 2016. http://www.norskpetroleum.no/en/framework/norways-petroleum-history/

137 Kim, Susanna. "Why Norwegians Are Millionaires and Americans Are Paupers." ABCNews. January 11, 2014. http://abcnews.go.com/Business/norwegians-millionaires-norways-sovereign-wealth-fund/story?id=21488085

138 McGregor, Jena. "The Average Work Week is Now 47 Hours." *The Washington Post*. September 2, 2014. https://www.washingtonpost.com/news/on-leadership/wp/2014/09/02/the-average-work-week-is-now-47-hours/

139 Ray, Rebecca, Milla Sanes, and John Schmitt. "No-Vacation Nation Revisited." Center for Economic and Policy Research. May 23, 2013. http://www.issuelab.org/permalink/resource/15349

ENDNOTES

140 Adkins, Amy. "Majority of U.S. Employees Not Engaged Despite Gains in 2014." Gallup. January 28, 2015. http://www.gallup.com/poll/181289/majority-employees-not-engaged-despite-gains-2014.aspx

141 Dishman, Lydia. "Millennials Have a Different Definition of Diversity and Inclusion." *Fast Company*. May 18, 2015. http://www.fastcompany.com/3046358/the-new-rules-of-work/millennials-have-a-different-definition-of-diversity-and-inclusion

142 Stiglitz, Joseph E. *The Price of Inequality: How Today's Divided Society Endangers Our Future*. 132. New York: W. W. Norton & Co, 2012.

143 Cohn, D'Vera, and Andrea Caumont. "7 Key Findings About Stay-at-Home Moms." Pew Research Center. April 8, 2014. http://www.pewresearch.org/fact-tank/2014/04/08/7-key-findings-about-stay-at-home-moms/

144 Johnsen, Sigbjørn. "Women in Work: The Norwegian Experience." *OECD Observer*. November 2012. http://www.oecdobserver.org/news/fullstory.php/aid/3898/Women_in_work:_The_Norwegian_experience.html

145 Hsieh, Esther. "What Universal Child Care Does for Norway." *The Globe and Mail*. May 16, 2013. http://www.theglobeandmail.com/report-on-business/economy/canada-competes/what-universal-child-care-does-for-norway/article11959366/

146 "World Happiness Report." United Nations Sustainable Development Solutions Network. 2016. https://en.wikipedia.org/wiki/World_Happiness_Report

147 García, Kelli K. "The Gender Bind: Men as Inauthentic Caregivers." *Duke Journal of Gender Law & Policy* 21, no. 1 (September 2012). http://scholarship.law.duke.edu/cgi/viewcontent.cgi?article=1234&context=djglp

148 Ibid.

149 Ware, Bronnie. *The Top Five Regrets of the Dying: A Life Transformed by the Dearly Departing*. Carlsbad, CA: Hay House, 2012.

150 Galinsky, Ellen, Kerstin Aumann, and James T. Bond. *2008 National Study of the Changing Workforce*. Families and Work Institute. Last modified August 2011. http://familiesandwork.org/downloads/TimesAreChanging.pdf

151 Claire Cain Miller has written extensively about work–life issues. Her article on how Millennial men find work and family hard to balance reviews some of the statistics and challenges facing fathers today: http://www.nytimes.com/2015/07/31/upshot/millennial-men-find-work-and-family-hard-to-balance.html?_r=0

152 Parker, Kim, and Wendy Wang. "Modern Parenthood." Pew Research Center. March 14, 2013. http://www.pewsocialtrends.org/2013/03/14/modern-parenthood-roles-of-moms-and-dads-converge-as-they-balance-work-and-family/

153 Ibid.

154 Friedman, Stewart D. *Baby Bust: New Choices for Men and Women in Work and Family*. 31. Philadelphia: Wharton Digital Press, 2013.

155 Ibid., 33.

156 Harrington, Brad, Fred Van Deusen, Jennifer Sabatini Fraone, Jeremiah Morelock. "How Millennials Navigate Their Careers: Young Adult Views on Work, Life and Success." Boston College Center for Work & Family. Last modified 2015. http://www.bc.edu/content/dam/files/centers/cwf/pdf/BCCWF%20Millennial%20Careers%20FINAL%20for%20web.pdf

157 FWI has been studying changing attitudes toward work since 1992. See http://www.familiesandwork.org for more insights into their ongoing study.

ENDNOTES

158 Friedman, Stewart D. *Baby Bust: New Choices for Men and Women in Work and Family*. 37. Philadelphia: Wharton Digital Press, 2013.

159 "ACLU Wins $375,000 Jury Award in Case of Dad Denied Leave to Care for First-Born Child." American Civil Liberties Union. February 3, 1999. https://www.aclu.org/news/aclu-wins-375000-jury-award-case-dad-denied-leave-care-first-born-child

160 García, Kelli K. "The Gender Bind: Men as Inauthentic Caregivers." *Duke Journal of Gender Law & Policy* 21, no. 1 (September 2012). http://scholarship.law.duke.edu/cgi/viewcontent.cgi?article=1234&context=djglp

161 "Paternity Leave: Why Parental Leave for Fathers Is So Important for Working Families." U.S. Department of Labor. n.d. https://www.dol.gov/asp/policy-development/PaternityBrief.pdf

162 Harrington, Brad, Fred Van Deusen, and Beth Humberd. *The New Dad: Caring, Committed and Conflicted*. Boston College Center for Work & Family. 2011. http://www.bc.edu/content/dam/files/centers/cwf/pdf/FH-Study-Web-2.pdf

163 Pedulla, David S., and Sarah Thébaud. "Can We Finish the Revolution? Gender, Work–Family Ideals, and Institutional Constraint." *American Sociological Review* 80, no. 1 (2015): 116–139. doi:10.1177/0003122414564008

164 Miller, Claire Cain. "Millennial Men Aren't the Dads They Thought They'd Be." *The New York Times*. July 30, 2015. http://www.nytimes.com/2015/07/31/upshot/millennial-men-find-work-and-family-hard-to-balance.html?_r=0

165 "Paternity Leave: Why Parental Leave for Fathers Is So Important for Working Families." U.S. Department of Labor. n.d. https://www.dol.gov/asp/policy-development/PaternityBrief.pdf

166 Williams, Joan C. *Reshaping the Work–Family Debate: Why Men and Class Matter*. 88. Cambridge, MA: Harvard University Press, 2010.

167 Ibid., 62.

168 Vandello, Joseph A., Vanessa E. Hettinger, Jennifer K. Bosson, and Jasmine Siddiqi. "When Equal Isn't Really Equal: The Masculine Dilemma of Seeking Work Flexibility." *Journal of Social Issues* 69, no. 2 (2013): 303–321. doi:10.1111/josi.12016

169 Ibid.

170 Butler, Adam B., and Amie Skattebo. "What Is Acceptable for Women May Not Be for Men: The Effect of Family Conflicts with Work on Job-Performance Ratings." *Journal of Occupational and Organizational Psychology* 77, no. 4 (2004): 553–564. doi:10.1348/0963179042596478

171 Rudman, Laurie A., and Kris Mescher. "Penalizing Men Who Request a Family Leave: Is Flexibility Stigma a Femininity Stigma?" *Journal of Social Issues* 69, no. 2 (2013): 322–340. doi:10.1111/josi.12017

172 García, Kelli K. "The Gender Bind: Men as Inauthentic Caregivers." *Duke Journal of Gender Law & Policy* 21, no. 1 (September 2012). http://scholarship.law.duke.edu/cgi/viewcontent.cgi?article=1234&context=djglp

173 Schoppe-Sullivan, Sarah J., Geoffrey L. Brown, Elizabeth A. Cannon, Sarah C. Mangelsdorf, and Margaret S. Sokolowski. "Maternal Gatekeeping, Coparenting Quality, and Fathering Behavior in Families with Infants." *Journal of Family Psychology* 22, no. 3 (2008): 389-398. doi:10.1037/0893-3200.22.3.389

174 Sandberg, Sheryl. *Lean In: Women, Work, and the Will to Lead*. 108. New York: Random House, 2013.

175 Zakaria, Fareed. "Moravcsik on Male Lead Parents." *The Global Public Square*. CNN. October 17, 2015. http://www.cnn.com/videos/tv/2015/10/17/exp-gps-moravcsik-sot-men-at-home.cnn

ENDNOTES

176 Parker, Kim, and Gretchen Livingston. "6 Facts About American Fathers." Pew Research Center. 2015. http://www.pewresearch.org/fact-tank/2015/06/18/5-facts-about-todays-fathers/

177 Stout, Hilary. "Real-Life Stay-at-Home Husbands." *Marie Claire.* August 9, 2010. http://www.marieclaire.com/sex-love/advice/a5100/stay-at-home-husband-status-symbol/

178 Johnson, Whitney. *Disrupt Yourself: Putting the Power of Disruptive Innovation to Work.* 87–88. Brookline, MA: Bibliomotion, 2015.

179 Kimmel, Michael. "How Can We Help Women? By Helping Men." *The Huffington Post.* January 17, 2014. http://www.huffingtonpost.com/michael-kimmel/how-can-we-help-women-by-helping-men_b_4611523.html

Michael Kimmel has written extensively on men and masculinity. His book *Angry White Men: American Masculinity at the End of an Era* (Nation Books, 2015) offers a fascinating analysis of the changing nature of masculinity in American society.

180 Cheng, Roger. "Women in Tech: The Numbers Don't Add Up." *CNET.* May 6, 2015. http://www.cnet.com/news/women-in-tech-the-numbers-dont-add-up/

181 Sherman, Erik. "Report: Disturbing Drop in Women in Computing Field." *Fortune.* March 26, 2015. http://fortune.com/2015/03/26/report-the-number-of-women-entering-computing-took-a-nosedive/

182 For more stories and a timeline of sexual harassment in tech, check out http://geekfeminism.wikia.com/wiki/Timeline_of_incidents

183 Hewlett, Sylvia A., and Laura Sherbin. *Athena Factor 2.0: Accelerating Female Talent in Science, Engineering & Technology.* Center for Talent Innovation. n.d. http://www.talentinnovation.org/_private/assets/Athena-2-ExecSummFINAL-CTI.pdf

Snyder, Kieran. "Why Women Leave Tech: It's the Culture, Not Because 'Math Is Hard.'" *Fortune.* October 2, 2014. http://fortune.com/2014/10/02/women-leave-tech-culture/

184 Snyder, Kieran. "Why Women Leave Tech: It's the Culture, Not Because 'Math Is Hard.'" *Fortune.* October 2, 2014. http://fortune.com/2014/10/02/women-leave-tech-culture/

185 Bennett, Jessica. "Behind 'The Good Girls Revolt': The 'Newsweek' Lawsuit That Paved the Way for Women Writers." *The Daily Beast.* September 11, 2012. http://www.thedailybeast.com/articles/2012/09/11/behind-the-good-girls-revolt-the-newsweek-lawsuit-that-paved-the-way-for-women-writers.html

For a great overview of this lawsuit, read Lynn Povich's *The Good Girls Revolt: How the Women of Newsweek Sued Their Bosses and Changed the Workplace* (PublicAffairs, 2013).

186 Povich, Lynn. "40 Years Later, Newsweek Sex Discrimination Persists." Womenenews.org. September 7, 2012. http://womensenews.org/2012/09/40-years-later-newsweek-sex-discrimination-persists/

187 Bennett, Jessica, and Jesse Ellison. "Young Women, Newsweek, and Sexism." *Newsweek.* March 18, 2010. http://www.newsweek.com/young-women-newsweek-and-sexism-69339

188 "Who Narrates the World?" The OpEd Project. 2012.

189 Lazar, Wendi S., and Jennifer L. Liu. "Pay and Promotion Equity for Women on Wall Street: Does Litigation Help?" *New York Law Journal* 250, no. 74 (October 2013). http://www.outtengolden.com/sites/default/files/pay-and-promotion-equity.pdf

190 "Financial Services in the Gulf: Addressing Gender Diversity." eFinancialCareers. Last modified October 2014. http://finance.efinancialcareers.com/rs/dice/images/eFC_Whitepaper_Diversity_Gulf_OCT2014.pdf

ENDNOTES

191 Craig, Susanne. "Lessons on Being a Success on Wall St., and Being a Casualty." *The New York Times.* April 1, 2013. http://dealbook.nytimes.com/2013/04/01/lessons-on-being-a-success-on-wall-st-and-being-a-casualty/

192 Epprecht, Margo. "The Real Reason Why Women Are Leaving Wall Street." *The Atlantic.* September 5, 2013. http://www.theatlantic.com/business/archive/2013/09/the-real-reason-why-women-are-leaving-wall-street/279379/

193 Barber, Brad M., and Terrance Odean. "Boys Will Be Boys: Gender, Overconfidence, and Common Stock Investment." *The Quarterly Journal of Economics*, February 2001. doi:10.2139/ssrn.139415

For a great overview on the subject, read:

Belsky, Gary. "Why We Need More Female Traders on Wall Street." *Time.* May 15, 2012. http://business.time.com/2012/05/15/why-we-need-more-female-traders-on-wall-street/
Key point: "Men on average traded 45% more frequently than women, and that hyperactive trading reduced their net returns by 2.65 percentage points a year, compared to 1.72 percentage points for women."

194 "Mending the Gender Gap: Advancing Tomorrow's Women Leaders in Financial Services." PricewaterhouseCoopers. May 2013. https://www.pwc.com/us/en/financial-services/publications/assets/pwc-advancing-women-in-financial-services.pdf

195 "Women Matter: Gender Diversity, a Corporate Performance Driver." McKinsey & Company. 2007. http://www.raeng.org.uk/publications/other/women-matter-oct-2007

196 Hunt, Vivian, Dennis Layton, and Sara Prince. "Why Diversity Matters." McKinsey & Company. January 2015. http://www.mckinsey.com/business-functions/organization/our-insights/why-diversity-matters

197 Díaz-García, Cristina, Angela González-Moreno, and Francisco J. Sáez-Martínez. "Gender Diversity Within R&D Teams: Its Impact on Radicalness of Innovation." *Innovation: Management, Policy & Practice* 15, no. 2 (2013): 2236–2259. doi:10.5172/impp.2012.2236

198 Guilford, Gwynn. "The Economic Case for Paternity Leave." *Quartz.* September 24, 2014. http://qz.com/266841/economic-case-for-paternity-leave/

199 Matos, Kenneth, and Ellen Galinsky. "2014 National Study of Employers." Families and Work Institute. Last modified 2014. http://www.familiesandwork.org/2014-national-study-of-employers/

200 Zumbrun, Josh. "The U.S. Economy Will Soon See Its Best Years in a Decade, Forecasters Say—Real Time Economics." *WSJ.* February 2, 2015. http://blogs.wsj.com/economics/2015/02/02/the-u-s-economy-will-soon-see-its-best-years-in-a-decade-federal-forecasters-say/

201 Richards, Emily, and Dave Terkanian. "Occupational Employment Projections to 2022." *Monthly Labor Review.* U.S. Department of Labor Bureau of Labor Statistics. 2013. http://www.bls.gov/opub/mlr/2013/article/pdf/occupational-employment-projections-to-2022.pdf

202 Abel, Jaison R., Richard Deitz, and Yaqin Su. "Are Recent College Graduates Finding Good Jobs?" *Current Issues in Economics and Finance* 20, no. 1 (2014). https://www.newyorkfed.org/medialibrary/media/research/current_issues/ci20-1.pdf

203 Kessler, Glenn. "Do 10,000 Baby Boomers Retire Every Day?" *The Washington Post.* July 24, 2014. https://www.washingtonpost.com/news/fact-checker/wp/2014/07/24/do-10000-baby-boomers-retire-every-day/

204 Ortman, Jennifer M., Victoria A. Velkoff, and Howard Hogan. "An Aging Nation: The Older Population in the United States." U.S. Census Bureau. 2014. https://www.census.gov/prod/2014pubs/p25-1140.pdf

205 Foster, Carol. "Citi: Managing Maternity Leave Positively." Equal Opportunities Review. January 8, 2009. http://www.rubensteinpublishing.com/default.aspx?id=1116962

"Financial Services in the Gulf: Addressing Gender Diversity." eFinancialCareers. Last modified October 2014. http://finance.efinancialcareers.com/rs/dice/images/eFC_Whitepaper_Diversity_Gulf_OCT2014.pdf

206 Florentine, Sharon. "Lack of Parental Leave Drives Employee Turnover." *CIO*. October 29, 2014. http://www.cio.com/article/2840574/staff-management/lack-of-parental-leave-drives-employee-turnover.html

207 Houser, Linda. "Pay Matters: The Positive Economic Impacts of Paid Family Leave for Families, Businesses and the Public." Rutgers Center for Women and Work. January 2012. http://go.nationalpartnership.org/site/DocServer/Pay_Matters_-_Positive_Economic_Impacts_of_Paid_Family_L.pdf?docID=9681

Florentine, Sharon. "Lack of Parental Leave Drives Employee Turnover." *CIO*. October 29, 2014. http://www.cio.com/article/2840574/staff-management/lack-of-parental-leave-drives-employee-turnover.html

Appelbaum, Eileen, and Ruth Milkman. "Leaves That Pay: Employer and Worker Experiences with Paid Family Leave in California." Center for Economic and Policy Research. January 15, 2011. http://www.issuelab.org/permalink/resource/7423

208 Houser, Linda. "Pay Matters: The Positive Economic Impacts of Paid Family Leave for Families, Businesses and the Public." Rutgers Center for Women and Work. January 2012. http://go.nationalpartnership.org/site/DocServer/Pay_Matters_-_Positive_Economic_Impacts_of_Paid_Family_L.pdf?docID=9681

209 Gillett, Rachel. "'I Didn't Feel Appreciated'—Inside the 'Backwards' Reality of Taking Unpaid Maternity Leave in America." Business Insider. June 20, 2015. http://www.businessinsider.com/the-reality-of-unpaid-maternity-leave-in-america-2015-6

210 "Navy, Marine Corps Now Offer 18 Weeks of Maternity Leave." NPR.org. July 8, 2015. http://www.npr.org/2015/07/08/421083589/navy-marine-corps-now-offer-18-weeks-of-maternity-leave

211 Ibid.

212 Johansson, Elly-Ann. "The Effect of Own and Spousal Parental Leave on Earnings." Uppsala, Sweden: Institute for Labor Market Policy Evaluation (2010): 35.

213 Houser, Linda. "Pay Matters: The Positive Economic Impacts of Paid Family Leave for Families, Businesses and the Public." Rutgers Center for Women and Work. January 2012. http://go.nationalpartnership.org/site/DocServer/Pay_Matters_-_Positive_Economic_Impacts_of_Paid_Family_L.pdf?docID=9681

214 Guilford, Gwynn. "The Economic Case for Paternity Leave." *Quartz*. September 24, 2014. http://qz.com/266841/economic-case-for-paternity-leave/

215 "Paternity Leave: Why Parental Leave for Fathers Is So Important for Working Families." U.S. Department of Labor. n.d. https://www.dol.gov/asp/policy-development/PaternityBrief.pdf

216 Ibid.

217 Connelly, Rachel, Deborah S. DeGraff, and Rachel A. Willis. *Kids at Work: The Value of Employer-Sponsored On-Site Child Care Centers*. Kalamazoo, MI: W.E. Upjohn Institute for Employment Research, 2004.

218 "Investing in Child Care." Southwestern Community Services. Accessed July 25, 2016. http://www.scshelps.org/_childfirst/download/investinginchildcare.pdf

219 "Questions and Answers About Employer-Supported Child Care: A Sloan Work and Family Research Network Fact Sheet." The Sloan Work and Family Research Network. 2009. https://workfamily.sas.upenn.edu/sites/workfamily.sas.upenn.edu/files/imported/pdfs/ESCC.pdf

220 Dourado, Eli, and Christopher Koopman. "Evaluating the Growth of the 1099 Workforce." Mercatus Center at George Mason University. December 10, 2015. http://mercatus.org/publication/evaluating-growth-1099-workforce

221 Baumann, Greg. "Silicon Valley Age Discrimination: If You've Experienced It, Say Something." *Silicon Valley Business Journal*. January 5, 2015. http://www.bizjournals.com/sanjose/news/2015/01/05/silicon-valley-age-discrimination-if-youve.html

"Median Age of the Labor Force, by Gender, Race and Ethnicity." U.S. Department of Labor Bureau of Labor Statistics. Last modified December 8, 2015. http://www.bls.gov/emp/ep_table_306.htm

222 Livingston, Gretchen. "For Most Highly Educated Women, Motherhood Doesn't Start Until the 30s." Pew Research Center. January 15, 2015. http://www.pewresearch.org/fact-tank/2015/01/15/for-most-highly-educated-women-motherhood-doesnt-start-until-the-30s/

223 Armstrong, Traci. "Team Detroit Launches Returnship Program for Women Ready to Get Back to Work." LinkedIn.https://www.linkedin.com/pulse/team-detroit-launches-returnship-program-traci-armstrong

224 Thibodeau, Patrick. "IT Jobs Will Grow 22% Through 2020, Says U.S." *Computerworld*. March 29, 2012. http://www.computerworld.com/article/2502348/it-management/it-jobs-will-grow-22--through-2020--says-u-s-.html

225 Whitehouse, Kaja. "Intel Could Spend More Than $300M on Diversity: CEO." *USA Today*. January 13, 2015. http://www.usatoday.com/story/tech/2015/01/13/intel-diversity-hiring-silicvalley/21712183/

226 Giang, Vivian. "The Man Who Is Attempting to Repair GoDaddy's Sexist Reputation." *Fast Company*. January 29, 2015. http://www.fastcompany.com/3041434/strong-female-lead/why-godaddy-is-finally-trying-to-repairing-its-sexist-reputation

227 Schireson, Max. "Why I Am Leaving the Best Job I Ever Had." *Max Schireson's Blog*. August 5, 2014. http://maxschireson.com/2014/08/05/1137/

228 Monster Jobs. Monster.com. Accessed August 2, 2016. http://monster.com

Job Search. Indeed.com. Accessed August 2, 2016. http://indeed.com

229 Dot.com. Accessed August 2, 2016. http://dot.com

230 "Managing Unconscious Bias." Managing Bias. Facebook. Accessed July 25, 2016. https://managingbias.fb.com/

231 Wagner, Kurt. "Facebook Offers to Help You Fight Your Race and Gender Biases." Recode. July 28, 2015. http://www.recode.net/2015/7/28/11615132/youre-probably-biased-but-facebook-thinks-it-can-help

232 "Women by the Numbers." Infoplease. Accessed July 25, 2016. http://www.infoplease.com/spot/womencensus1.html

233 "The Future of Families to 2030: Projections, Policy Challenges and Policy Options." OECD. 2011. http://www.oecd.org/futures/49093502.pdf

234 "Millennials: Confident. Connected. Open to Change." Pew Research Center. February 2010. http://www.pewsocialtrends.org/files/2010/10/millennials-confident-connected-open-to-change.pdf

235 HubSpot has gotten much attention since the publication of Dan Lyons's book, *Disrupted: My Misadventure in the Start-Up Bubble* (Hachette Books, 2016). Is the company the horrid place Lyons describes or the oasis Fitton experiences? Hard to tell, but it is clear what works at work for one may not work for another.

236 Sandberg, Sheryl. *Lean In: Women, Work, and the Will to Lead*. 117. New York: Random House, 2013.

237 "Work-Life Challenges Across Generations: Global Study." Ernst & Young. Last modified 2015. http://www.ey.com/US/en/About-us/Our-people-and-culture/EY-study-highlights-dual-career-dynamics-in-the-us#.V5YuBbgrKM8

238 McGinn, Kathleen L., and Nicole Tempest. "Heidi Roizen." Harvard Business School Case 800-228, January 2000. (Revised April 2010.) For more on Heidi Roizen and networking, read this:

http://www.gsb.stanford.edu/insights/heidi-roizen-networking-more-collecting-lots-names

239 Bartz, Carol, and Lisa Lambert. "Why Women Should Do Less and Network More." *Fortune*. November 12, 2014. http://fortune.com/2014/11/12/why-women-should-do-less-and-network-more/

240 For the best overview of this, check out the LeanIn.org and McKinsey & Company study at http://www.mckinsey.com/business-functions/organization/our-insights/women-in-the-workplace

241 Raine-Fenning, Nick. "No, Women's Fertility Doesn't 'Drop Off a Cliff' at 35." *The Washington Post*. July 22, 2014. https://www.washingtonpost.com/posteverything/wp/2014/07/22/no-womens-fertility-doesnt-drop-off-a-cliff-at-35/

242 Greene, Barbara A., and Teresa K. DeBacker. "Gender and Orientations Toward the Future: Links to Motivation." *Educational Psychology Review* 16, no. 2 (2004): 91–120. doi:10.1023/b:edpr.0000026608.50611.b4

243 Let's acknowledge that only in the United States is anything more than six weeks considered "extended." As detailed in chapters 5 and 7, our national parental leave policies are pathetic in comparison to other countries across the world.

244 Kay, Katty, and Claire Shipman. *The Confidence Code: The Science and Art of Self-Assurance—What Women Should Know*. 21. New York: HarperCollins, 2014.

245 Wang, Wendy. "Mothers and Work: What's 'Ideal'?" Pew Research Center. August 19, 2013. http://www.pewresearch.org/fact-tank/2013/08/19/mothers-and-work-whats-ideal/

246 Stiglitz, Joseph E. *The Price of Inequality: How Today's Divided Society Endangers Our Future*. 131–132. New York: W. W. Norton & Co, 2012.

247 Monge-Naranjo, Alexander, and Faisal Sohail. "Age and Gender Differences in Long-Term Unemployment: Before and After the Great Recession." *Economic Synopses* (2015).

248 Cohen, Patricia. "Over 50, Female and Jobless Even as Others Return to Work." *The New York Times*. January 2, 2016. http://www.nytimes.com/2016/01/02/business/economy/over-50-female-and-jobless-even-as-others-return-to-work.html?emc=edit_th_20160102&nl=todaysheadlines&nlid=49311288&_r=0

249 Popova, Maria. "An Antidote to the Age of Anxiety: Alan Watts on Happiness and How to Live with Presence." *Brain Pickings*. January 6, 2014. https://www.brainpickings.org/2014/01/06/alan-watts-wisdom-of-insecurity-1/

250 Schulte, Brigid. *Overwhelmed: How to Work, Love, and Play When No One Has the Time*. 45. New York: Picador, 2014.

251 Popova, Maria. "How We Spend Our Days Is How We Spend Our Lives: Annie Dillard on Choosing Presence Over Productivity." *Brain Pickings*. 2013. https://www.brainpickings.org/2013/06/07/annie-dillard-the-writing-life-1/

252 Ross, Ruth K. *Coming Alive: The Journey to Reengage Your Life and Career*. Sacramento, CA: Authority Publishing, 2014.

253 Hersch, Joni, and Jennifer B. Shinall. "Something to Talk About: Information Exchange Under Employment Law." *Vanderbilt Law and Economics Research Paper Series* 16, no. 7 (2016). http://papers.ssrn.com/sol3/papers.cfm?abstract_id=2765455##

254 Wolf, Amy. "For Women Re-entering Workforce, Sharing Personal Information May Get You Hired." Vanderbilt University. May 19, 2016. http://news.vanderbilt.edu/2016/05/for-women-re-entering-workforce-sharing-personal-information-may-get-you-hired/

255 Cohen, Carol Fishman, and Vivian Steir Rabin. *Back on the Career Track: A Guide for Stay-at-Home Moms Who Want to Return to Work*. 41. New York: Business Plus, 2007.

ENDNOTES

256 Crittenden, Ann. *The Price of Motherhood: Why the Most Important Job in the World Is Still the Least Valued.* 112. New York: Henry Holt and Company, 2001.

257 Detjen, Jodi Ecker, Michelle A. Waters, and Kelly Watson. *The Orange Line: A Woman's Guide to Integrating Career, Family & Life.* 29–30. Newton, MA: JMK Publishing, 2013.

258 Kawasaki, Guy. "'Everything You Should Know About Me as an Entrepreneur You Could Learn from My OB/GYN.'" *Guy Kawasaki.* February 2, 2008. http://guykawasaki.com/everything-you-2/

259 For more information, check out the USDA Cost of Raising a Child report: http://www.usda.gov/wps/portal/usda/usdahome?contentid=2014/08/0179.xml&contentidonly=true

260 Ibid.

261 Check out this state-by-state child care calculator map to learn what the average cost is where you live: https://www.bostonglobe.com/2014/07/02/map-the-average-cost-for-child-care-state/LN65rSHXKNjr4eypyxT0WM/story.html

262 "Cost of Raising a Child Calculator." U.S. Department of Agriculture. 2013. http://www.cnpp.usda.gov/calculatorintro.htm

263 Zarya, Valentina. "Staying Home with Your Kids Will Cost Way More Than Childcare." *Fortune.* June 22, 2016. http://fortune.com/2016/06/22/stay-at-home-parent-cost/?utm_content=buffer5b09d&utm_medium=so-cial&utm_source=linkedin.com&utm_campaign=buffer

"The Hidden Cost of a Failing Child Care System." Center for American Progress. Accessed July 25, 2016. http://interactives.americanprogress.org/childcarecosts/

264 You can check out the 2016 index here: http://www.insure.com/life-insurance/the-mothers-day-index.html

265 Rose, Stephen, and Heidi Hartmann. "Still a Man's Labor Market: The Long-Term Earnings Gap." Institute for Women's Policy Research. Last modified February 2008. http://www.iwpr.org/publications/pubs/still-a-man2019s-labor-market-the-long-term-earnings-gap

266 "USA Life Expectancy All Races Female." World Life Expectancy. Last modified 2014. http://www.worldlifeexpectancy.com/usa/life-expectancy-female

267 Riffkin, Rebecca. "Average U.S. Retirement Age Rises to 62." Gallup. April 28, 2014. http://www.gallup.com/poll/168707/average-retirement-age-rises.aspx

268 Lam, Bourree. "Women Are Beating Men at Retirement Savings." *The Atlantic.* November 6, 2015. http://www.theatlantic.com/business/archive/2015/11/women-men-retirement-savings/414681/

269 Ibid.

270 Jordon, Steve. "Gender Gap: Fewer Women Than Men Have Life Insurance, Leaving Families Vulnerable." *Omaha World-Herald.* August 27, 2015. http://www.omaha.com/money/gender-gap-fewer-women-than-men-have-life-insurance-leaving/article_9c0276cf-2e6e-57c8-a45c-32af51c30c6f.html

271 Ibid.

272 The Hartford's Benefits for Tomorrow survey, 2014 and 2014 Millennial Leadership Survey.

273 Wang, Wendy. "The Link Between a College Education and a Lasting Marriage." Pew Research Center. December 4, 2015. http://www.pewresearch.org/fact-tank/2015/12/04/education-and-marriage/

274 Dew, Jeffrey, Sonya Britt, and Sandra Huston. "Examining the Relationship Between Financial Issues and Divorce." *Family Relations* 61, no. 4 (2012): 615–628. doi:10.1111/j.1741-3729.2012.00715.x

ENDNOTES

275 "Divorce Study: Financial Arguments Early in Relationship May Predict Divorce." *The Huffington Post*. Last modified July 16, 2013. http://www.huffingtonpost.com/2013/07/12/divorce-study_n_3587811.html

276 "The Economics of Paid and Unpaid Leave." The Council of Economic Advisers. June 2014. https://www.whitehouse.gov/sites/default/files/docs/leave_report_final.pdf

277 Ruiz, Rebecca. "No Family Left Behind: America's 12-week Maternity Policy Has Nothing to Do with Families." *Mashable*. January 25, 2015. http://mashable.com/2015/01/25/maternity-leave-policy-united-states/#hik029dKSkq6

278 "The Need for Paid Family Leave." A Better Balance. Accessed July 25, 2016. http://www.abetterbalance.org/web/ourissues/familyleave

279 "The Economics of Paid and Unpaid Leave." The Council of Economic Advisers. June 2014. https://www.whitehouse.gov/sites/default/files/docs/leave_report_final.pdf

280 Blades, Joan, and Kristin Rowe-Finkbeiner. "The Motherhood Manifesto." *The Nation*. May 22, 2006. http://www.thenation.com/article/motherhood-manifesto/

281 Westervelt, Amy. "Having It All Kinda Sucks." *The Huffington Post*. February 15, 2016. http://www.huffingtonpost.com/amy-westervelt/having-it-all-kinda-sucks_b_9237772.html

282 Davies, Anna. "I Want All the Perks of Maternity Leave—Without Having Any Kids." *New York Post*. April 28, 2016. http://nypost.com/2016/04/28/i-want-all-the-perks-of-maternity-leave-without-having-any-kids/

283 Jezer-Morton, Kathryn. "The 'Meternity' Backlash Isn't Really About Children at All." *Jezebel*. May 4, 2016. http://jezebel.com/the-meternity-backlash-isn-t-really-about-children-at-a-1774656880

284 "Mending the Gender Gap: Advancing Tomorrow's Women Leaders in Financial Services." PricewaterhouseCoopers. May 2013. https://www.pwc.com/us/en/financial-services/publications/assets/pwc-advancing-women-in-financial-services.pdf

285 Ibid.

286 Zarya, Valentina. "New Proof That More Female Bosses Equals Higher Profits." *Fortune*. February 8, 2016. http://fortune.com/2016/02/08/women-leadership-profits/?iid=sr-link1

Hunt, Vivian, Dennis Layton, and Sara Prince. "Why Diversity Matters." McKinsey & Company. January 2015. http://www.mckinsey.com/business-functions/organization/our-insights/why-diversity-matters

287 "Managing Unconscious Bias." Managing Bias. Facebook. Accessed July 25, 2016. https://managingbias.fb.com/

288 Norton, Ken. "Unconscious Bias at Work." Google Ventures. March 20, 2014. https://library.gv.com/unconscious-bias-at-work-22e698e9b2d#.nvi3ai5vf

289 "Project Implicit." Accessed July 25, 2016. https://implicit.harvard.edu/implicit/

290 Slaughter, Anne-Marie. *Unfinished Business: Women Men Work Family*. 59. New York: Random House, 2015.

291 For a great read on unconscious bias, check out this Google blog: googleblog.blogspot.com/2014/09/you-dont-know-what-you-dont-know-how.html

292 Forrest, Conner. "Diversity Stats: 10 Tech Companies That Have Come Clean." *TechRepublic*. August 28, 2014. http://www.techrepublic.com/article/diversity-stats-10-tech-companies-that-have-come-clean/

293 Garside, Juliette. "Amazon Employs 18 Women Among 120 Most Senior Managers." *The Guardian*. April 25, 2014. http://www.theguardian.com/technology/2014/apr/25/amazon-employs-18-women-among-120-senior-managers

294 Kantor, Jodi, and David Streitfeld. "Inside Amazon: Wrestling Big Ideas in a Bruising Workplace." *The New York Times*. August 15, 2015. http://www.nytimes.com/2015/08/16/technology/inside-amazon-wrestling-big-ideas-in-a-bruising-workplace.html

295 "Buffer Diversity Dashboard." Accessed July 25, 2016. http://diversity.buffer.com/

296 Coukos, Pamela. "Myth Busting the Pay Gap." *U.S. Department of Labor Blog*. June 7, 2012. https://blog.dol.gov/2012/06/07/myth-busting-the-pay-gap/

297 Puri, Ritika. "See What Happened When These Companies Made Their Employee Salaries Public." *LinkedIn Talent Blog*. March 30, 2015. https://business.linkedin.com/talent-solutions/blog/2015/03/what-happened-when-these-companies-made-their-employee-salaries-public

298 Ashcraft, Catherine, and Sarah Blithe. "Women in IT: The Facts." National Center for Women & Information Technology. Last modified April 2010. http://www.ncwit.org/sites/default/files/legacy/pdf/NCWIT_TheFacts_rev2010.pdf

299 Tanaka, Sakiko. "Parental Leave and Child Health Across OECD countries." *Economic Journal* 115, no. 501 (2005): F7–F28. doi:10.1111/j.0013-0133.2005.00970.x

300 Ruhm, Christopher J. "Parental Leave and Child Health." *Journal of Health Economics* 19, no. 6 (2000): 931–960. doi:10.1016/s0167-6296(00)00047-3

301 Read Sharon Lerner's 2012 article, "Is 40 Weeks the Ideal Maternity Leave Length?," in *Slate* magazine for a great review of the topic: http://www.slate.com/articles/double_x/doublex/2011/12/maternity_leave_how_much_time_off_is_healthiest_for_babies_and_mothers_.html

302 Nepomnyaschy, Lenna, and Jane Waldfogel. "Paternity Leave and Fathers' Involvement with Their Young Children." *Community, Work & Family* 10, no. 4 (2007): 427–453. doi:10.1080/13668800701575077

303 Covert, Bryce. "How Everyone Benefits When New Fathers Take Paid Leave." *ThinkProgress*. February 13, 2015. http://thinkprogress.org/economy/2015/02/13/3622428/benefits-paid-paternity-leave/

304 Harrington, Brad, Fred Van Deusen, Jennifer S. Fraone, and Samantha Eddy. *The New Dad: Take Your Leave. Perspectives on Paternity Leave from Fathers, Leading Organizations, and Global Policies*. Boston College Center for Work & Family. 2014. http://www.bc.edu/content/dam/files/centers/cwf/news/pdf/BCCWF%20The%20New%20Dad%202014%20FINAL.pdf

305 Covert, Bryce. "How Everyone Benefits When New Fathers Take Paid Leave." *ThinkProgress*. February 13, 2015. http://thinkprogress.org/economy/2015/02/13/3622428/benefits-paid-paternity-leave/

306 Harrington, Brad, Fred Van Deusen, Jennifer S. Fraone, and Samantha Eddy. *The New Dad: Take Your Leave. Perspectives on Paternity Leave from Fathers, Leading Organizations, and Global Policies*. Boston College Center for Work & Family. 2014. http://www.bc.edu/content/dam/files/centers/cwf/news/pdf/BCCWF%20The%20New%20Dad%202014%20FINAL.pdf

307 "How Dependent Care FSAs Work." Practical Money Skills. Accessed July 25, 2016. http://www.practicalmoneyskills.com/personalfinance/lifeevents/benefits/dependentFSAs.php

308 Gullekson, Nicole L., Rodger Griffeth, Jeffrey B. Vancouver, Christine T. Kovner, and Debra Cohen. "Vouching for Childcare Assistance with Two Quasi-Experimental Studies." *Journal of Managerial Psychology* 29, no. 8 (2014): 994–1008. doi:10.1108/jmp-06-2012-0182

309 "The Flexible Work and Well-Being Study." Flexible Work and Well-Being Center at the University of Minnesota. Accessed July 25, 2016. http://www.flexiblework.umn.edu/

ENDNOTES

310 Clennett, Ross. "Global Staffing Industry Sales Top $400 Billion." *Recruiting Blogs*. October 16, 2014. http://www.recruitingblogs.com/profiles/blogs/global-staffing-industry-sales-top-400-billion

311 Nahm, Sarah. "When It Comes to Diversity in Tech, Look to Small Companies for Leadership." *Lever*. September 22, 2015. http://www.lever.co/inside/when-it-comes-to-diversity-in-tech-look-to-small-companies-for-leadership

312 Levenson, Alec, Michael Fenlon, and George Benson. "Rethinking Retention Strategies: Work-Life Versus Deferred Compensation in a Total Rewards Strategy." Center for Effective Organizations, University of Southern California: June 2010. https://ceo.usc.edu/rethinking-retention-strategies-work-life-versus-deferred-compensation-in-a-total-rewards-strategy/

313 In her book, *Overwhelmed: How to Work, Love, and Play When No One Has the Time*, author Brigid Schulte highlights Menlo Innovations. She shows that great culture can include a work–life balance imperative.

314 This research would not have been possible without the indefatigable help of my intern, Aparajita Pande. "Thank you" cannot express my deep gratitude for her ongoing support and commitment to this work.

315 To recruit respondents, we used Facebook, LinkedIn, Twitter, Pinterest, college and graduate school alumni networks, women's professional networks, moms groups, and good old-fashioned word of mouth.

316 "Life & Leadership after HBS." Harvard Business School. May 2015. http://www.hbs.edu/women50/docs/L_and_L_Survey_2Findings_12final.pdf

317 Hewlett, Sylvia Ann, and Carolyn Buck Luce. "Off-Ramps and On-Ramps: Keeping Talented Women on the Road to Success." *Harvard Business Review*. March 2005. https://hbr.org/2005/03/off-ramps-and-on-ramps-keeping-talented-women-on-the-road-to-success

INDEX

INDEX

INDEX

INDEX

INDEX

INDEX

ABOUT THE AUTHOR

After a successful career in marketing and advertising, Lisen Stromberg left the business world frustrated by the lack of support for mothers in the workplace. She zigged and zagged professionally and eventually became an award-winning journalist whose work can be found in *The New York Times*, *Fortune*, *Salon*, *Newsweek*, and other high-profile media outlets.

Now, as CEO and founder of PrismWork, a culture innovation consultancy, Lisen is back to her business roots partnering with companies, leaders, and advocates to ensure the next generation isn't forced to choose between work and family.

Lisen has a BA from Dartmouth College, an MBA from the Haas School of Business at UC Berkeley, and an MFA from Mills College. Now that their children are launched, Lisen and her husband, Bill, live in San Francisco where they are making a new nest.